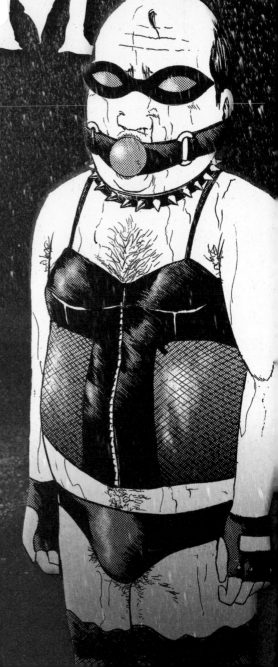

Detroit Metal City

DMC

8

KIMINORI
WAKASUGI

Detroit Metal City

DMC

WARNING!
THIS ALBUM CONTAINS NOTHING BUT THE MOST PROFANE OF PROFANITIES! LISTEN AT THE RISK OF YOUR IMMORTAL SOUL.

DETROIT METAL CITY IS
KRAUSER II (LEAD GUITAR, VOCALS) CAMUS (DRUMS) JAGI (VOCALS AND BASS)

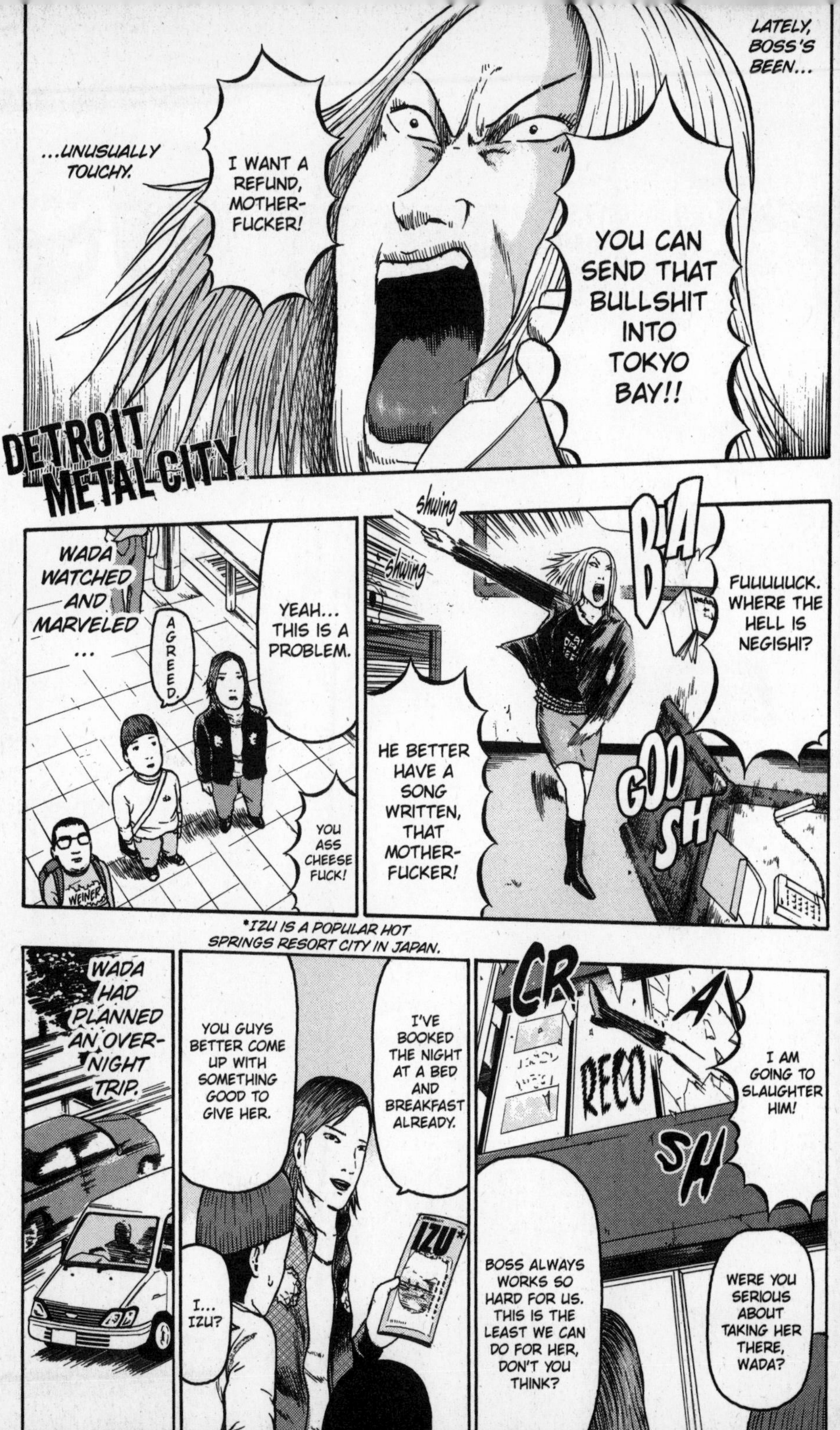
LATELY, BOSS'S BEEN...
YOU CAN SEND THAT BULLSHIT INTO TOKYO BAY!!
I WANT A REFUND, MOTHER-FUCKER!
...UNUSUALLY TOUCHY.
DETROIT METAL CITY
shwing
shwing
BA
FUUUUUCK. WHERE THE HELL IS NEGISHI?
GOOSH
HE BETTER HAVE A SONG WRITTEN, THAT MOTHER-FUCKER!
YEAH... THIS IS A PROBLEM.
AGREED.
WADA WATCHED AND MARVELED ...
YOU ASS CHEESE FUCK!
WEINER
CRASH
I AM GOING TO SLAUGHTER HIM!
RECO
WERE YOU SERIOUS ABOUT TAKING HER THERE, WADA?
BOSS ALWAYS WORKS SO HARD FOR US. THIS IS THE LEAST WE CAN DO FOR HER, DON'T YOU THINK?
I'VE BOOKED THE NIGHT AT A BED AND BREAKFAST ALREADY.
YOU GUYS BETTER COME UP WITH SOMETHING GOOD TO GIVE HER.
IZU*
I... IZU?
WADA HAD PLANNED AN OVER-NIGHT TRIP.

*IZU IS A POPULAR HOT SPRINGS RESORT CITY IN JAPAN.

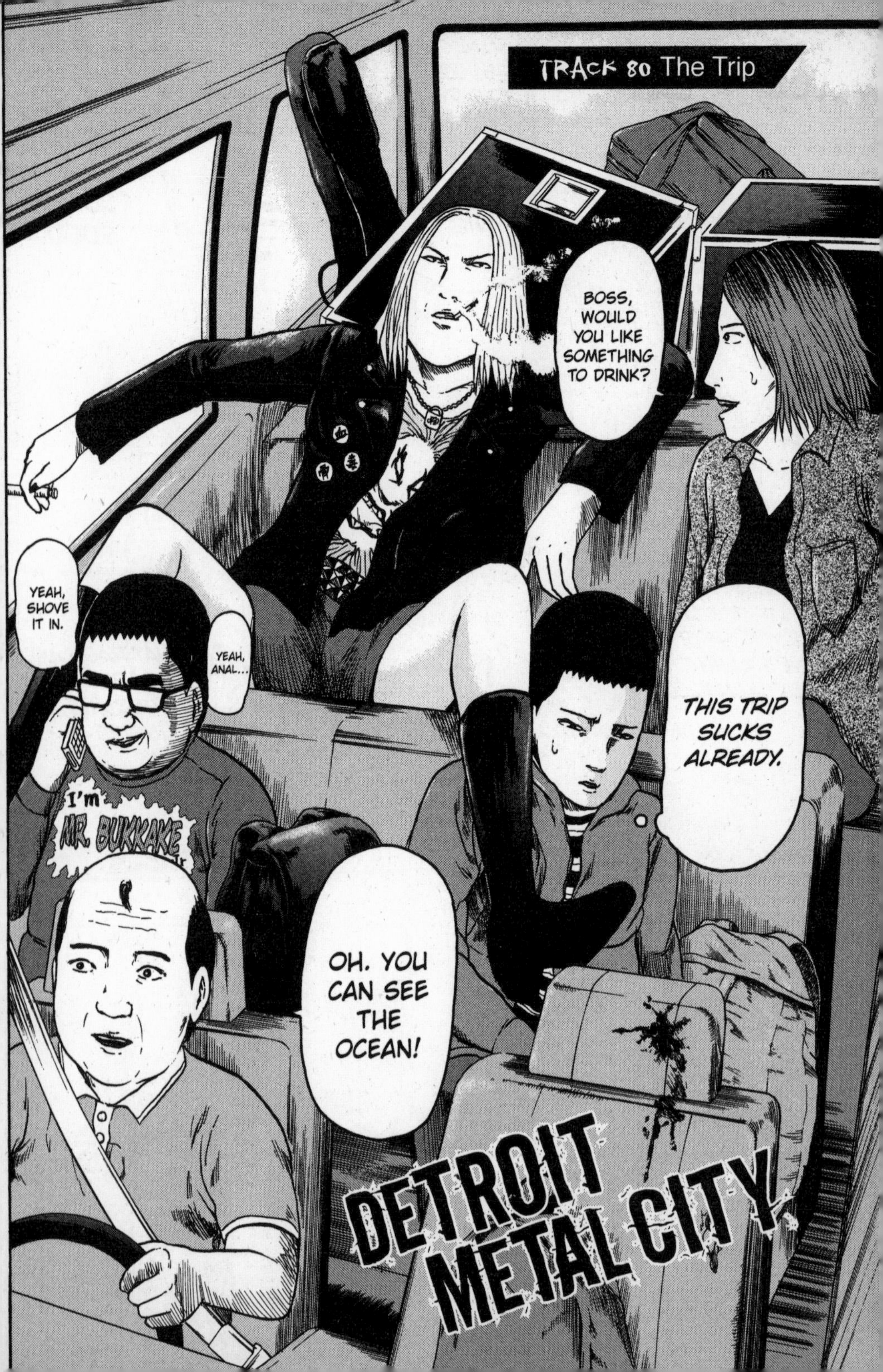
TRACK 80 The Trip
BOSS, WOULD YOU LIKE SOMETHING TO DRINK?
THIS TRIP SUCKS ALREADY.
YEAH, ANAL...
YEAH, SHOVE IT IN.
I'm MR. BUKKAKE
OH. YOU CAN SEE THE OCEAN!
DETROIT METAL CITY

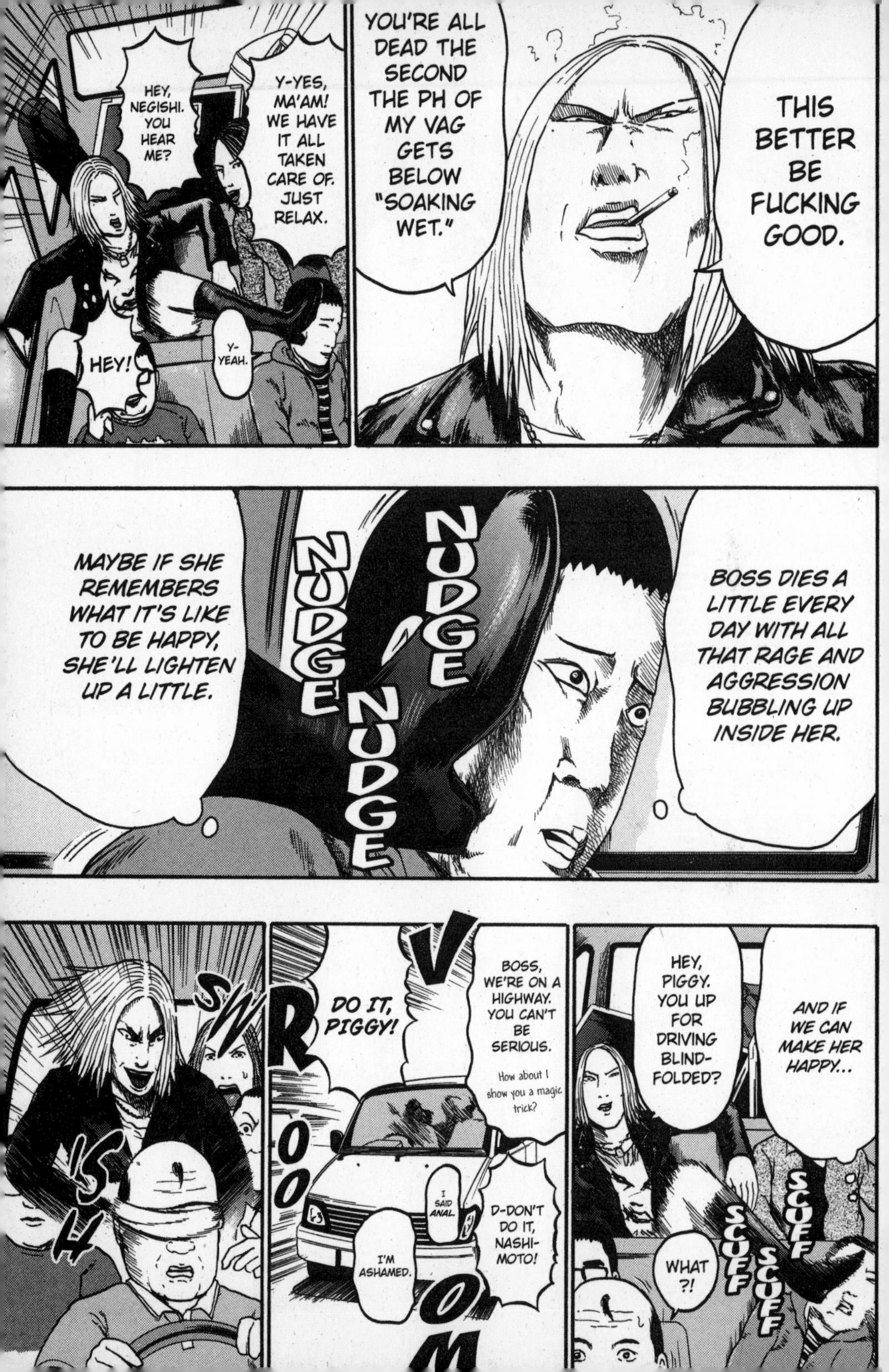
THIS BETTER BE FUCKING GOOD.
YOU'RE ALL DEAD THE SECOND THE PH OF MY VAG GETS BELOW "SOAKING WET."
Y-YES, MA'AM! WE HAVE IT ALL TAKEN CARE OF. JUST RELAX.
HEY, NEGISHI. YOU HEAR ME?
Y-YEAH.
HEY!
BOSS DIES A LITTLE EVERY DAY WITH ALL THAT RAGE AND AGGRESSION BUBBLING UP INSIDE HER.
NUDGE
NUDGE
NUDGE
MAYBE IF SHE REMEMBERS WHAT IT'S LIKE TO BE HAPPY, SHE'LL LIGHTEN UP A LITTLE.
AND IF WE CAN MAKE HER HAPPY...
HEY, PIGGY. YOU UP FOR DRIVING BLIND-FOLDED?
SCUFF
SCUFF
SCUFF
WHAT ?!
BOSS, WE'RE ON A HIGHWAY. YOU CAN'T BE SERIOUS.
How about I show you a magic trick?
DO IT, PIGGY!
VROOOOM
D-DON'T DO IT, NASHI-MOTO!
I SAID ANAL.
I'M ASHAMED.
SWISH

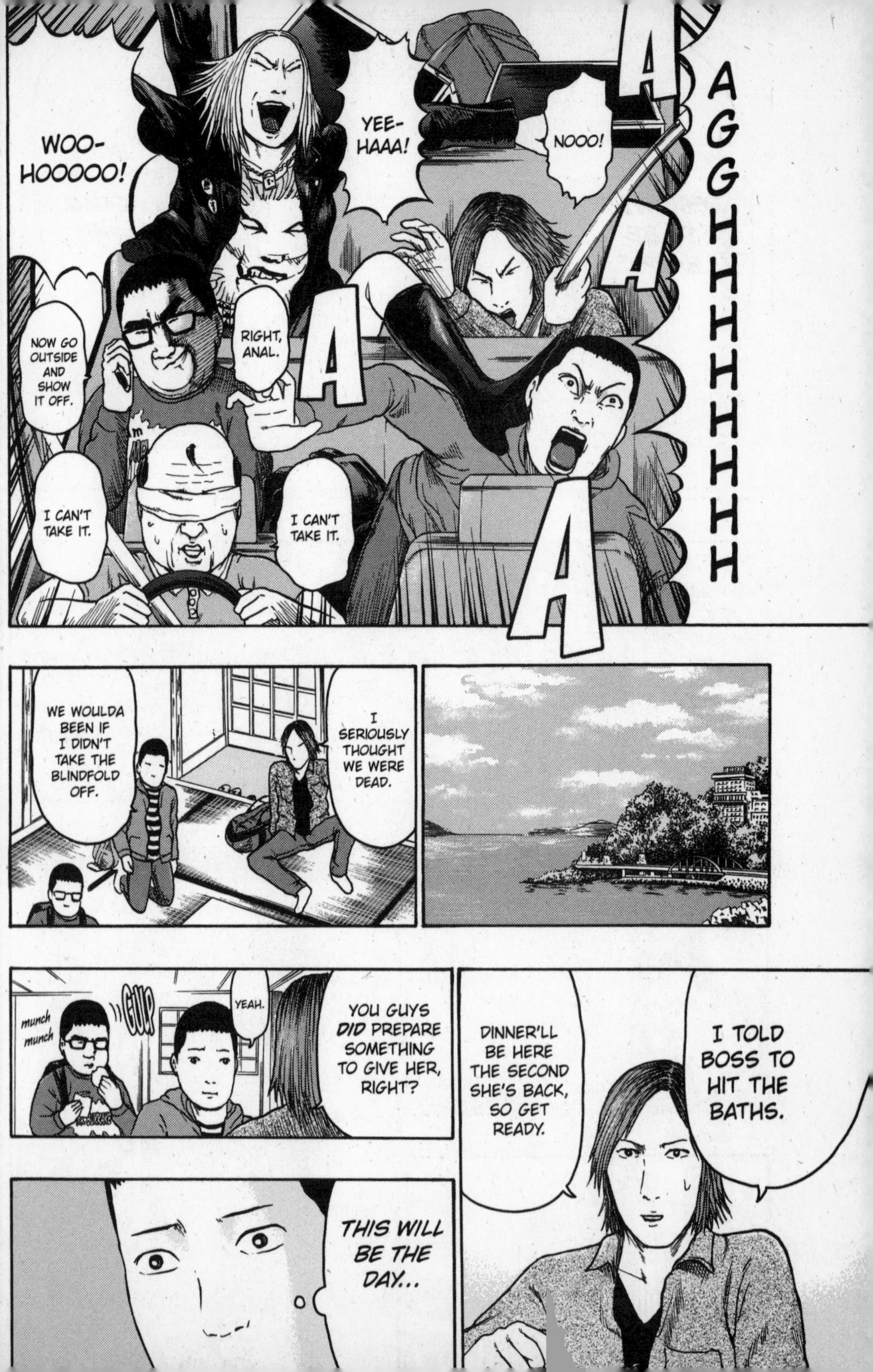
A
AGGHHHHHHHHHH
NOOO!
A
YEE-HAAA!
WOO-HOOOOO!
A
RIGHT, ANAL.
NOW GO OUTSIDE AND SHOW IT OFF.
A
I CAN'T TAKE IT.
I CAN'T TAKE IT.
I SERIOUSLY THOUGHT WE WERE DEAD.
WE WOULDA BEEN IF I DIDN'T TAKE THE BLINDFOLD OFF.
I TOLD BOSS TO HIT THE BATHS.
DINNER'LL BE HERE THE SECOND SHE'S BACK, SO GET READY.
YOU GUYS *DID* PREPARE SOMETHING TO GIVE HER, RIGHT?
YEAH.
GULP
munch munch
THIS WILL BE THE DAY...

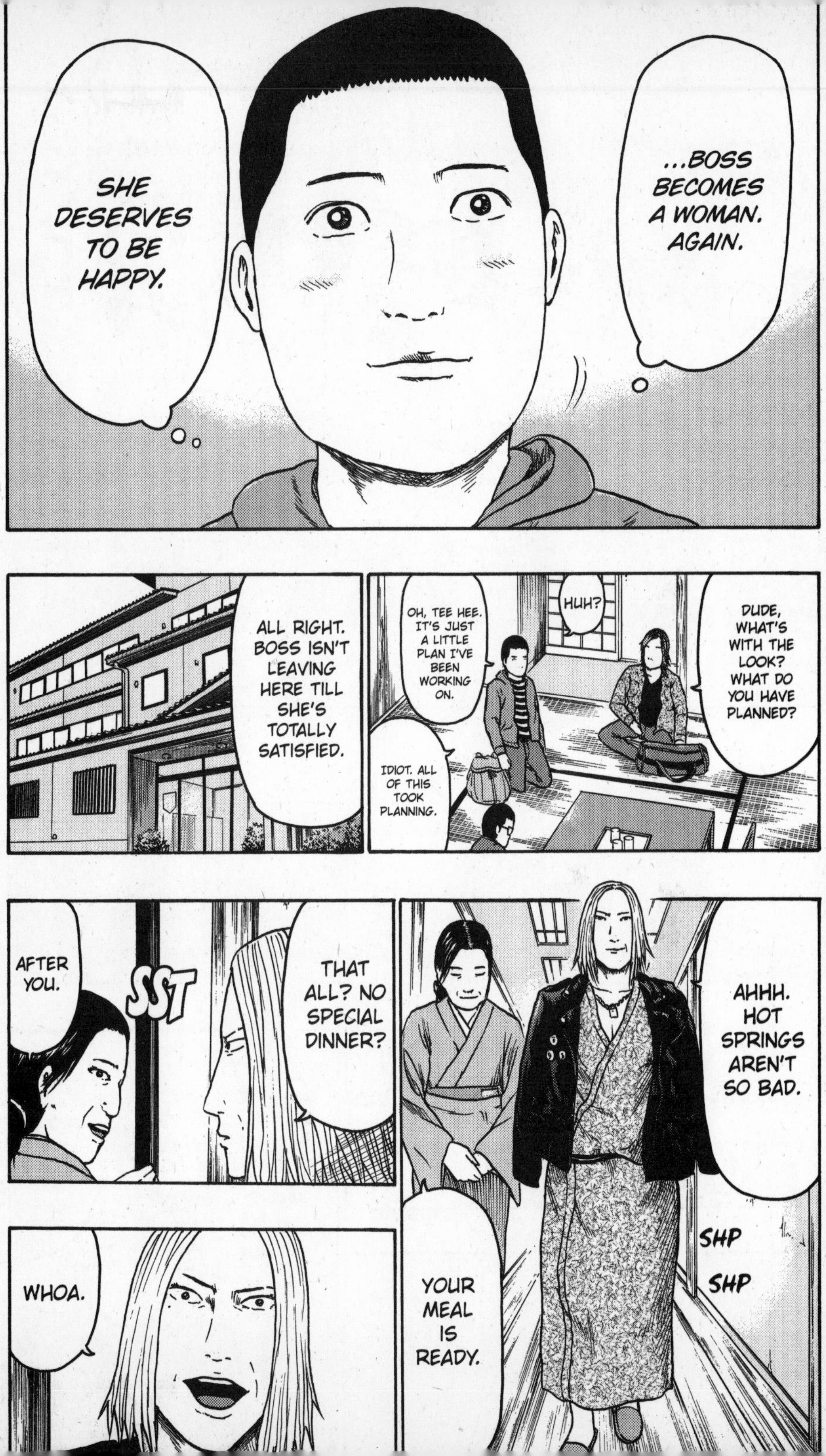
...BOSS BECOMES A WOMAN. AGAIN.
SHE DESERVES TO BE HAPPY.
DUDE, WHAT'S WITH THE LOOK? WHAT DO YOU HAVE PLANNED?
HUH?
OH, TEE HEE. IT'S JUST A LITTLE PLAN I'VE BEEN WORKING ON.
IDIOT. ALL OF THIS TOOK PLANNING.
ALL RIGHT. BOSS ISN'T LEAVING HERE TILL SHE'S TOTALLY SATISFIED.
AHHH. HOT SPRINGS AREN'T SO BAD.
SHP
SHP
YOUR MEAL IS READY.
THAT ALL? NO SPECIAL DINNER?
SST
AFTER YOU.
WHOA.

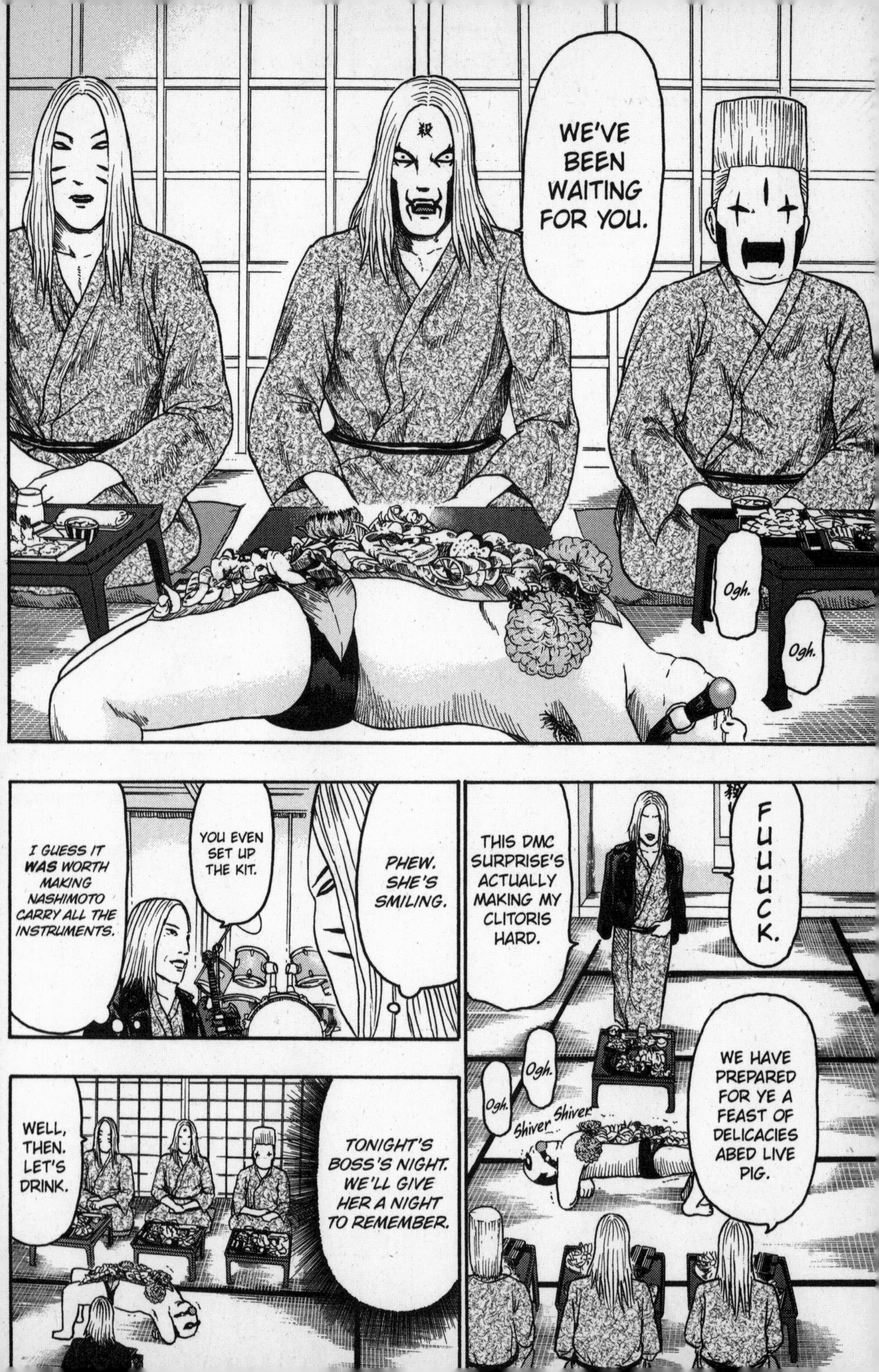
WE'VE BEEN WAITING FOR YOU.
Ogh.
Ogh.
FUUUCK.
THIS DMC SURPRISE'S ACTUALLY MAKING MY CLITORIS HARD.
WE HAVE PREPARED FOR YE A FEAST OF DELICACIES ABED LIVE PIG.
Ogh.
Ogh.
Shiver Shiver
PHEW. SHE'S SMILING.
YOU EVEN SET UP THE KIT.
I GUESS IT **WAS** WORTH MAKING NASHIMOTO CARRY ALL THE INSTRUMENTS.
TONIGHT'S BOSS'S NIGHT. WE'LL GIVE HER A NIGHT TO REMEMBER.
WELL, THEN. LET'S DRINK.

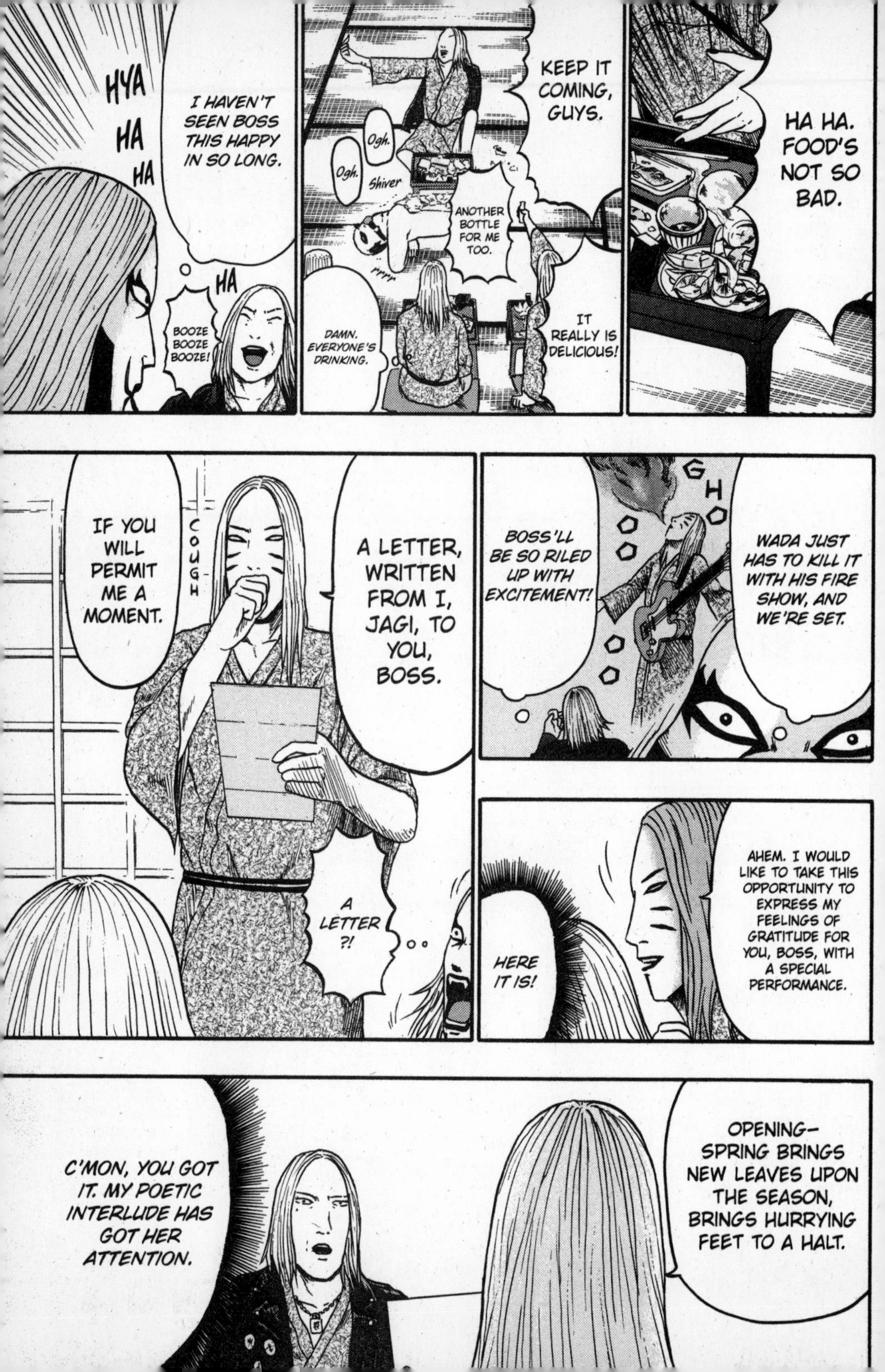
HA HA. FOOD'S NOT SO BAD.
KEEP IT COMING, GUYS.
Ogh.
Ogh.
Shiver
ANOTHER BOTTLE FOR ME TOO.
IT REALLY IS DELICIOUS!
DAMN. EVERYONE'S DRINKING.
I HAVEN'T SEEN BOSS THIS HAPPY IN SO LONG.
HYA HA HA
HA
BOOZE BOOZE BOOZE!
WADA JUST HAS TO KILL IT WITH HIS FIRE SHOW, AND WE'RE SET.
GHO
BOSS'LL BE SO RILED UP WITH EXCITEMENT!
AHEM. I WOULD LIKE TO TAKE THIS OPPORTUNITY TO EXPRESS MY FEELINGS OF GRATITUDE FOR YOU, BOSS, WITH A SPECIAL PERFORMANCE.
HERE IT IS!
A LETTER, WRITTEN FROM I, JAGI, TO YOU, BOSS.
COUGH
IF YOU WILL PERMIT ME A MOMENT.
A LETTER?!
OPENING— SPRING BRINGS NEW LEAVES UPON THE SEASON, BRINGS HURRYING FEET TO A HALT.
C'MON, YOU GOT IT. MY POETIC INTERLUDE HAS GOT HER ATTENTION.

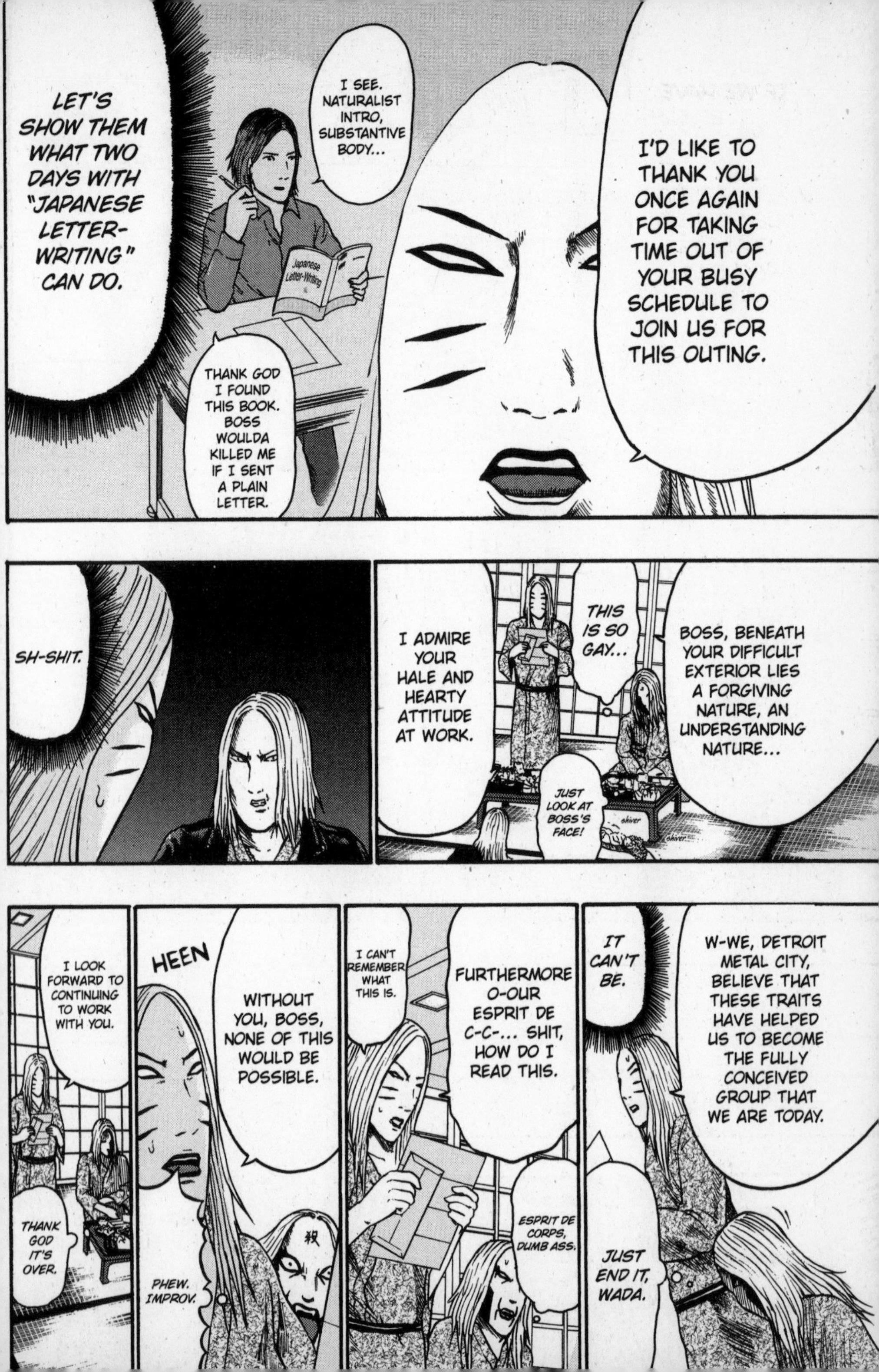
I'D LIKE TO THANK YOU ONCE AGAIN FOR TAKING TIME OUT OF YOUR BUSY SCHEDULE TO JOIN US FOR THIS OUTING.
I SEE. NATURALIST INTRO, SUBSTANTIVE BODY...
LET'S SHOW THEM WHAT TWO DAYS WITH "JAPANESE LETTER-WRITING" CAN DO.
Japanese Letter-Writing
THANK GOD I FOUND THIS BOOK. BOSS WOULDA KILLED ME IF I SENT A PLAIN LETTER.
BOSS, BENEATH YOUR DIFFICULT EXTERIOR LIES A FORGIVING NATURE, AN UNDERSTANDING NATURE...
THIS IS SO GAY...
I ADMIRE YOUR HALE AND HEARTY ATTITUDE AT WORK.
JUST LOOK AT BOSS'S FACE!
shiver
shiver
SH-SHIT.
W-WE, DETROIT METAL CITY, BELIEVE THAT THESE TRAITS HAVE HELPED US TO BECOME THE FULLY CONCEIVED GROUP THAT WE ARE TODAY.
IT CAN'T BE.
JUST END IT, WADA.
FURTHERMORE O-OUR ESPRIT DE C-C-... SHIT, HOW DO I READ THIS.
I CAN'T REMEMBER WHAT THIS IS.
ESPRIT DE CORPS, DUMB ASS.
HEEN
WITHOUT YOU, BOSS, NONE OF THIS WOULD BE POSSIBLE.
PHEW. IMPROV.
I LOOK FORWARD TO CONTINUING TO WORK WITH YOU.
THANK GOD IT'S OVER.

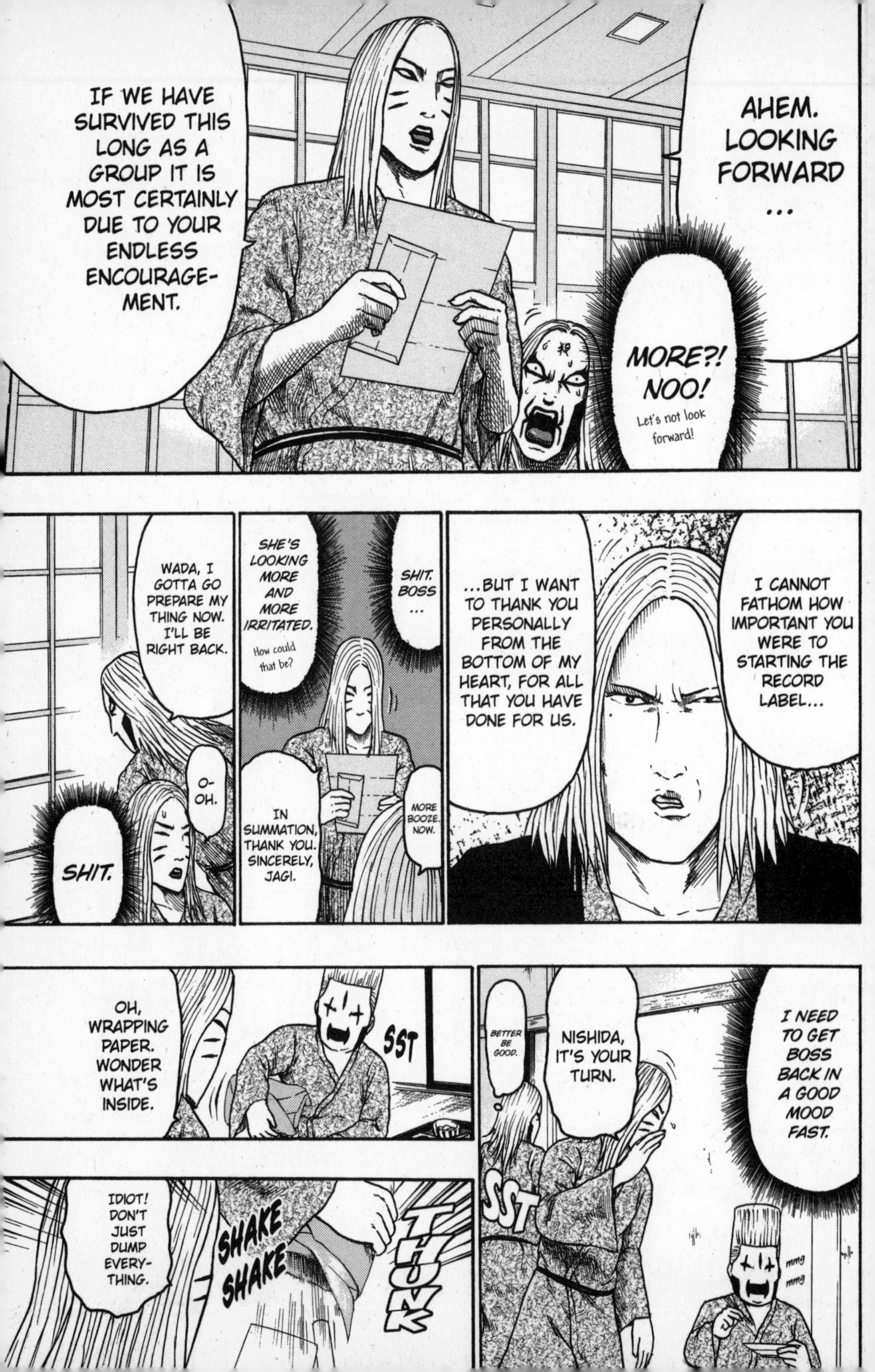
AHEM. LOOKING FORWARD ...
IF WE HAVE SURVIVED THIS LONG AS A GROUP IT IS MOST CERTAINLY DUE TO YOUR ENDLESS ENCOURAGE-MENT.
MORE?! NOO!
Let's not look forward!
I CANNOT FATHOM HOW IMPORTANT YOU WERE TO STARTING THE RECORD LABEL...
...BUT I WANT TO THANK YOU PERSONALLY FROM THE BOTTOM OF MY HEART, FOR ALL THAT YOU HAVE DONE FOR US.
SHIT. BOSS ...
SHE'S LOOKING MORE AND MORE IRRITATED.
How could that be?
MORE BOOZE. NOW.
IN SUMMATION, THANK YOU. SINCERELY, JAGI.
WADA, I GOTTA GO PREPARE MY THING NOW. I'LL BE RIGHT BACK.
O-OH.
SHIT.
I NEED TO GET BOSS BACK IN A GOOD MOOD FAST.
NISHIDA, IT'S YOUR TURN.
BETTER BE GOOD.
SST
mmg mmg
SST
OH, WRAPPING PAPER. WONDER WHAT'S INSIDE.
THUNK
SHAKE SHAKE
IDIOT! DON'T JUST DUMP EVERY-THING.

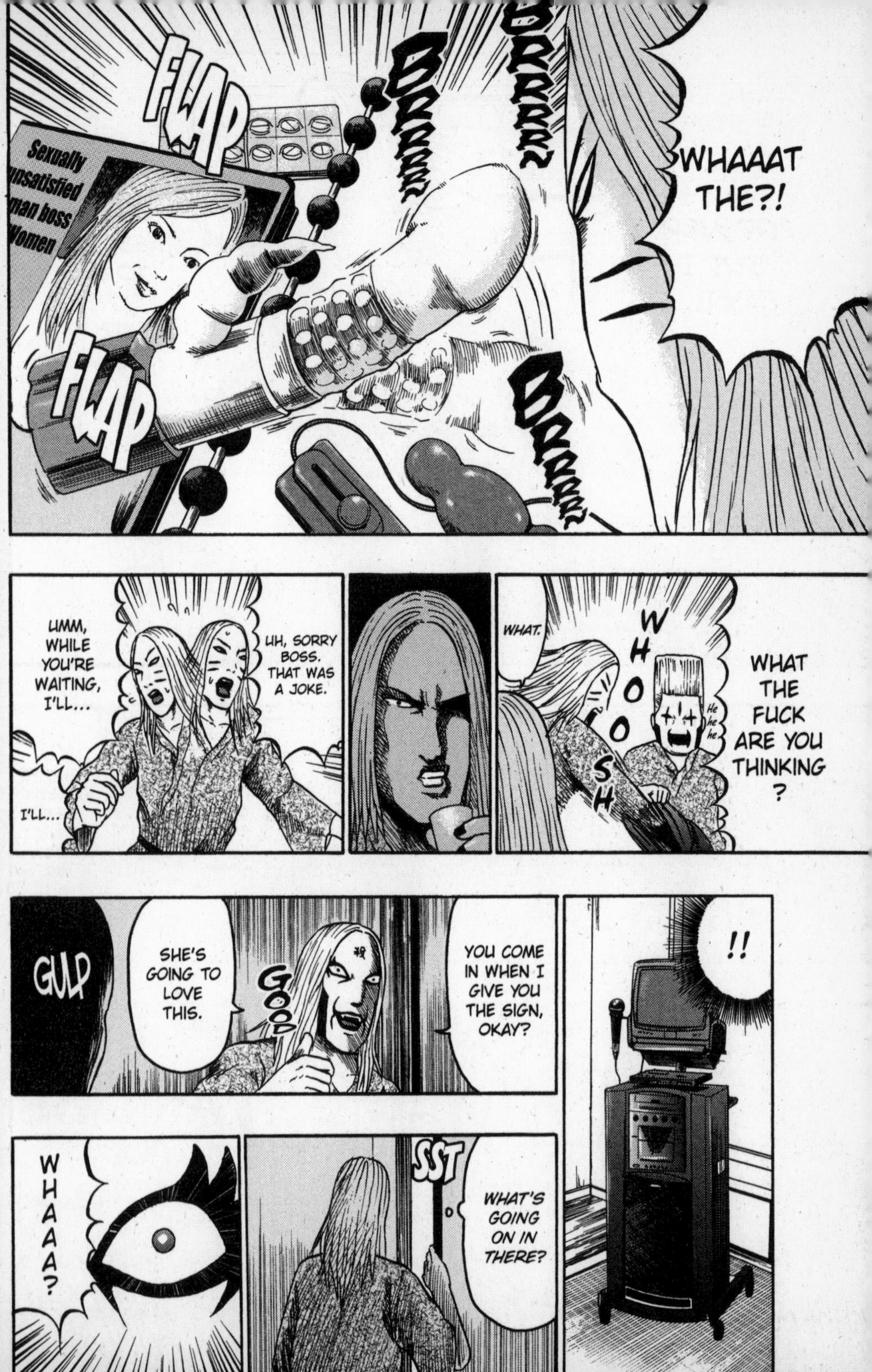
WHAAAT THE?!
BRRRRRN
BRRRRRN
FLAP
Sexually
unsatisfied
man boss
Women
FLAP
BRRRRRN
WHAT THE FUCK ARE YOU THINKING?
WHAT.
WHOOOSH
He he he
UH, SORRY BOSS. THAT WAS A JOKE.
UMM, WHILE YOU'RE WAITING, I'LL...
I'LL...
!!
YOU COME IN WHEN I GIVE YOU THE SIGN, OKAY?
GOOD
SHE'S GOING TO LOVE THIS.
GULP
WHAT'S GOING ON IN THERE?
SST
WHAAAA?

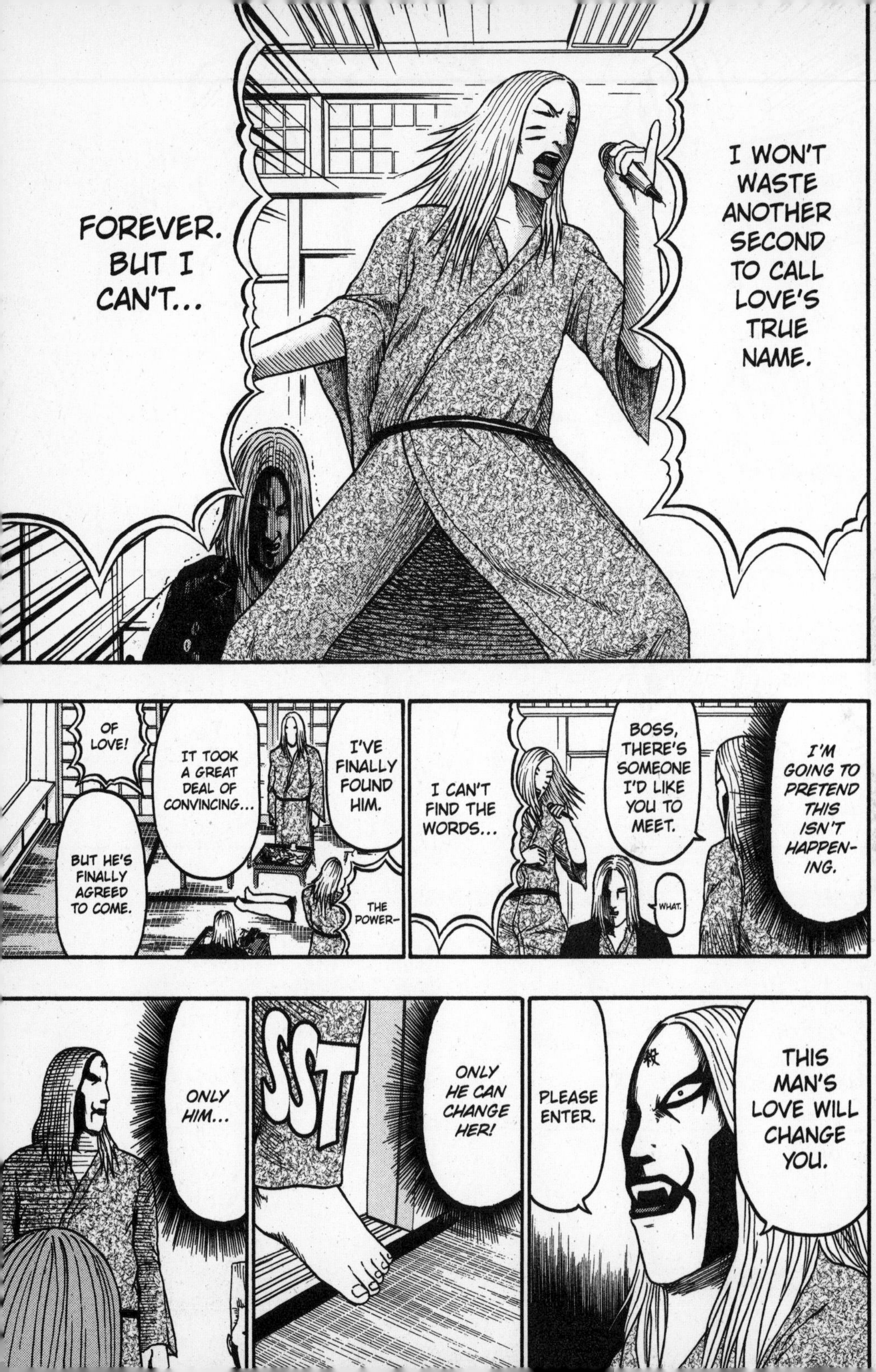
I WON'T WASTE ANOTHER SECOND TO CALL LOVE'S TRUE NAME.
FOREVER. BUT I CAN'T...
I'M GOING TO PRETEND THIS ISN'T HAPPEN-ING.
BOSS, THERE'S SOMEONE I'D LIKE YOU TO MEET.
WHAT.
I CAN'T FIND THE WORDS...
I'VE FINALLY FOUND HIM.
IT TOOK A GREAT DEAL OF CONVINCING...
OF LOVE!
BUT HE'S FINALLY AGREED TO COME.
THE POWER-
THIS MAN'S LOVE WILL CHANGE YOU.
PLEASE ENTER.
ONLY HE CAN CHANGE HER!
SST
ONLY HIM...

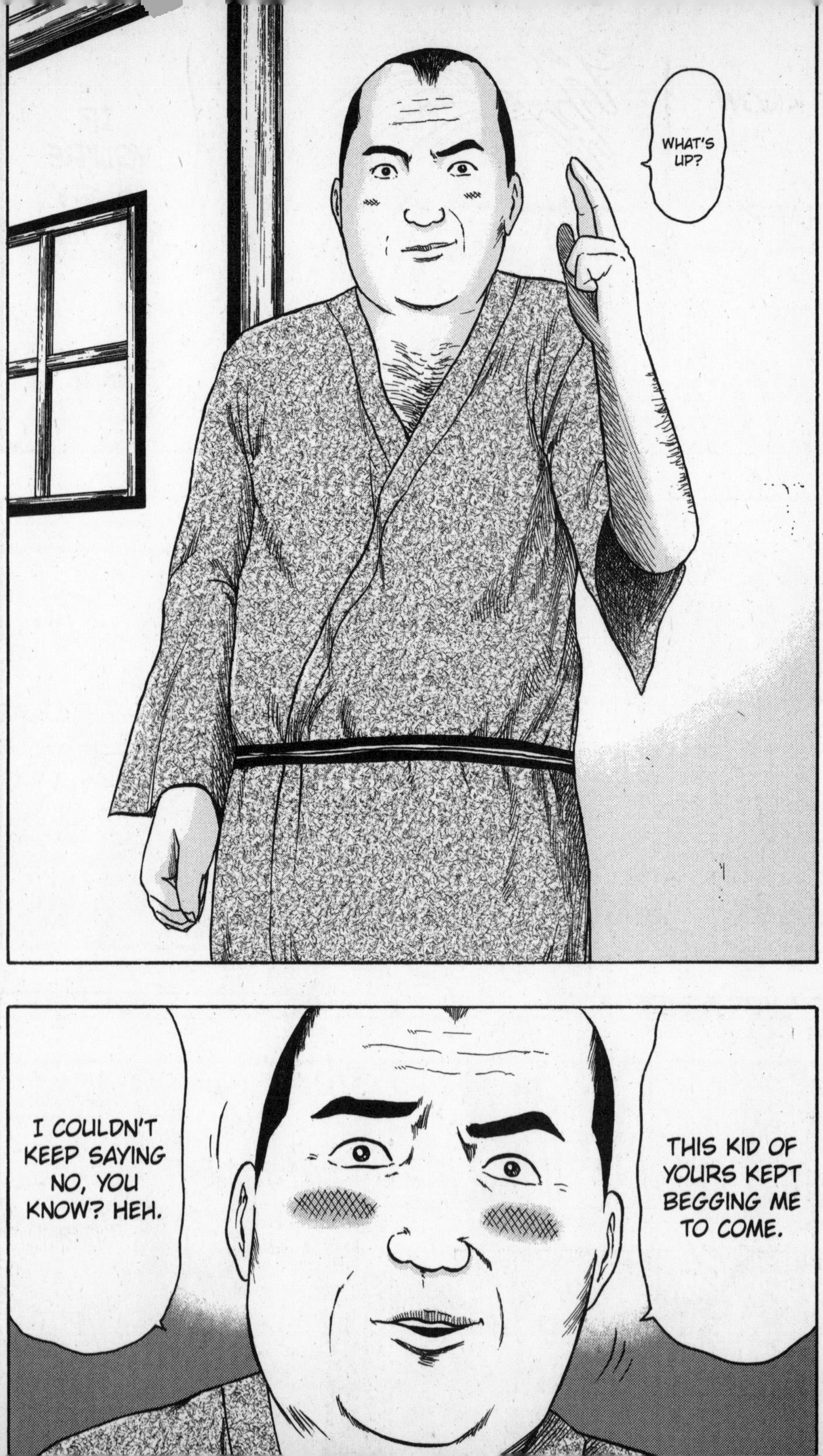
WHAT'S UP?
THIS KID OF YOURS KEPT BEGGING ME TO COME.
I COULDN'T KEEP SAYING NO, YOU KNOW? HEH.

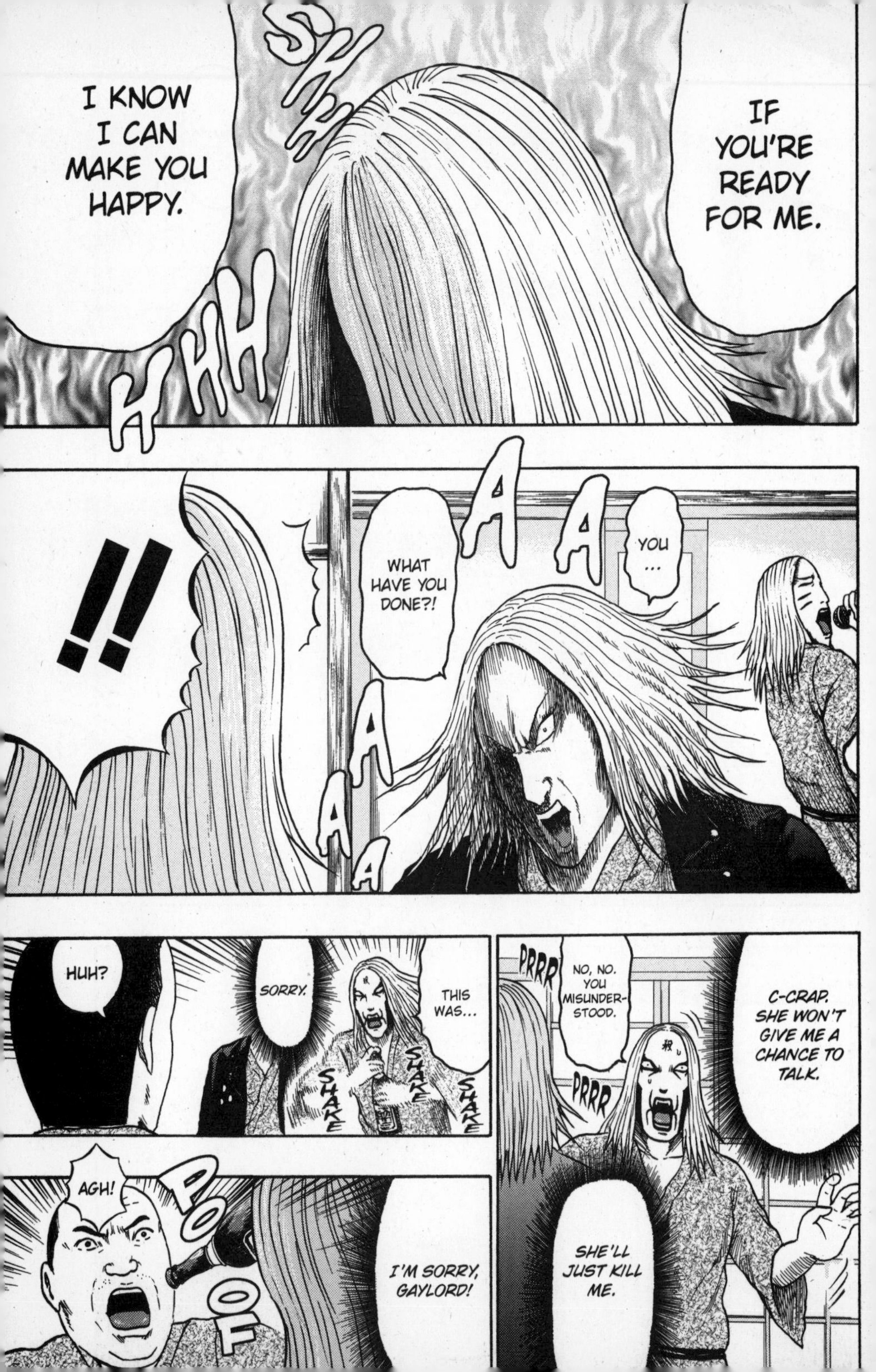
IF YOU'RE READY FOR ME.
SHHHH
I KNOW I CAN MAKE YOU HAPPY.
AAAA
YOU...
AAAA
WHAT HAVE YOU DONE?!
!!
C-CRAP. SHE WON'T GIVE ME A CHANCE TO TALK.
NO, NO. YOU MISUNDERSTOOD.
PRRR
PRRR
SHE'LL JUST KILL ME.
THIS WAS...
SORRY.
SHAKE
SHAKE
SHAKE
HUH?
I'M SORRY, GAYLORD!
POOF
AGH!

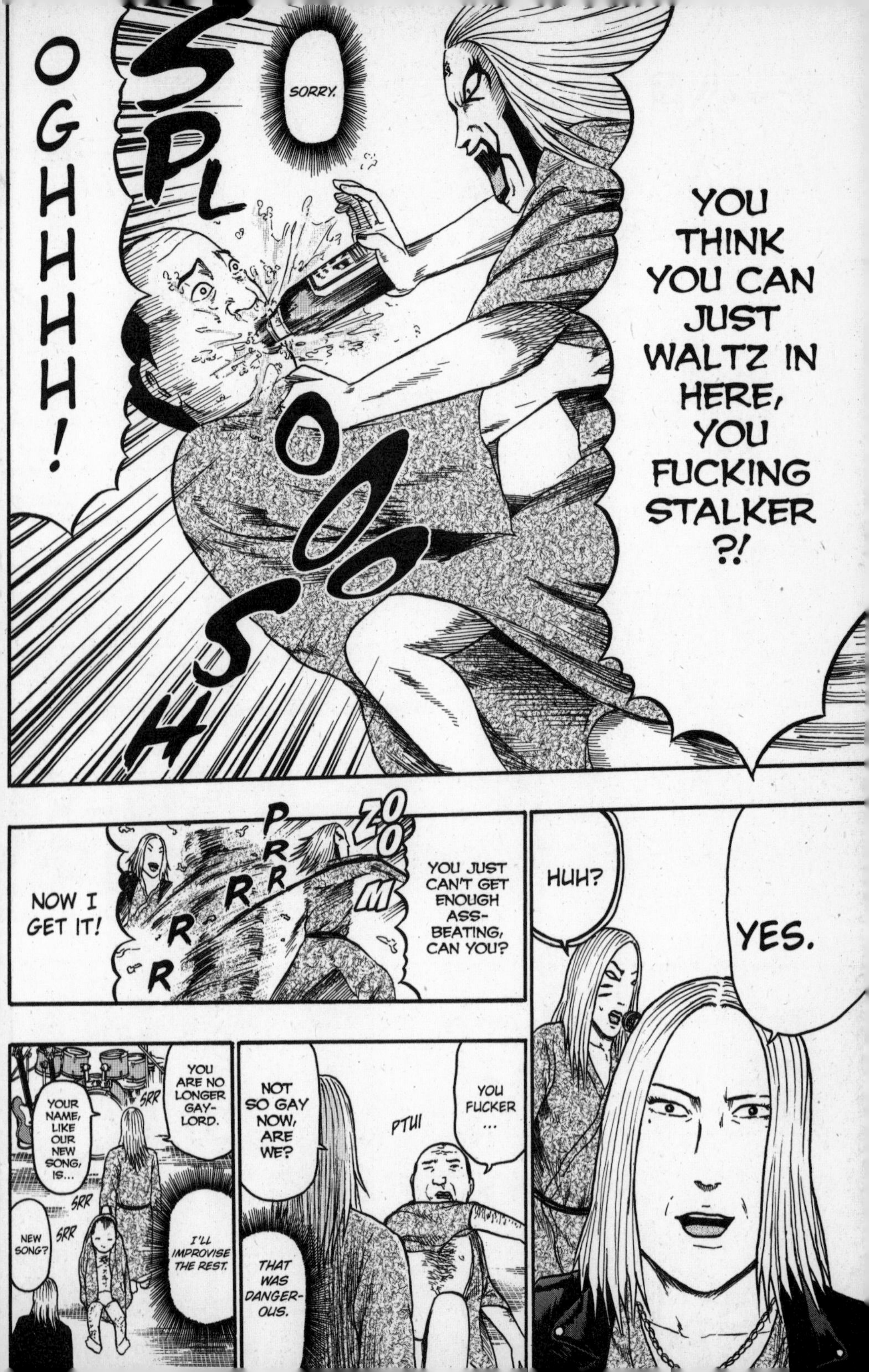
YOU THINK YOU CAN JUST WALTZ IN HERE, YOU FUCKING STALKER?!
SORRY.
SPLOOOSH
OGHHHH!
HUH?
YES.
YOU JUST CAN'T GET ENOUGH ASS-BEATING, CAN YOU?
ZOOM
PRRRRR
NOW I GET IT!
YOU FUCKER ...
PTUI
NOT SO GAY NOW, ARE WE?
THAT WAS DANGER-OUS.
YOU ARE NO LONGER GAY-LORD.
SRR
YOUR NAME, LIKE OUR NEW SONG, IS...
I'LL IMPROVISE THE REST.
SRR
SRR
NEW SONG?

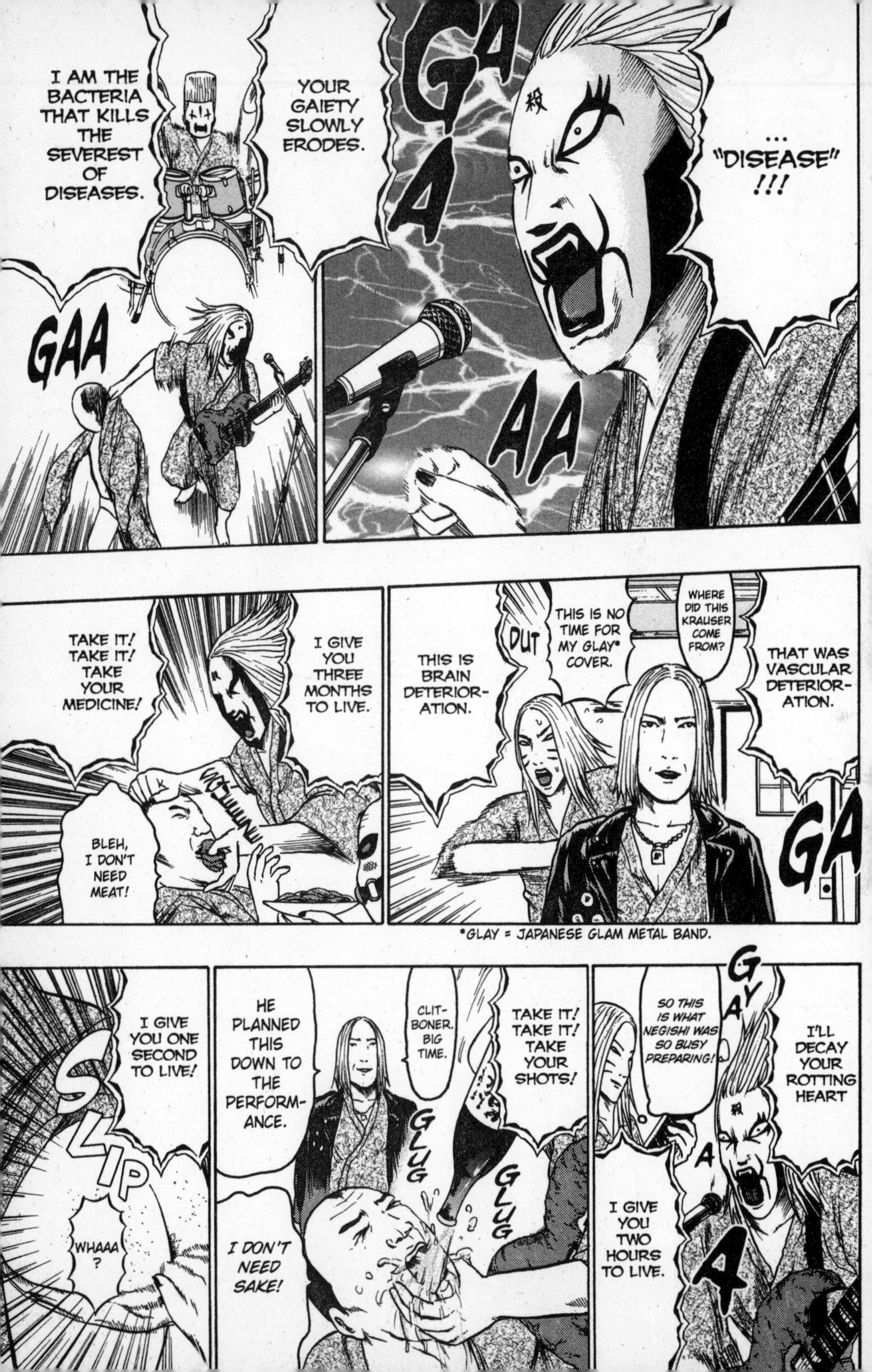
... "DISEASE" !!!
GA A
AA
YOUR GAIETY SLOWLY ERODES.
I AM THE BACTERIA THAT KILLS THE SEVEREST OF DISEASES.
GAA
THAT WAS VASCULAR DETERIOR-ATION.
WHERE DID THIS KRAUSER COME FROM?
THIS IS NO TIME FOR MY GLAY* COVER.
DUT
THIS IS BRAIN DETERIOR-ATION.
GA
I GIVE YOU THREE MONTHS TO LIVE.
TAKE IT! TAKE IT! TAKE YOUR MEDICINE!
BLEH, I DON'T NEED MEAT!
*GLAY = JAPANESE GLAM METAL BAND.
I'LL DECAY YOUR ROTTING HEART
GAY
SO THIS IS WHAT NEGISHI WAS SO BUSY PREPARING!
I GIVE YOU TWO HOURS TO LIVE.
A A
TAKE IT! TAKE IT! TAKE YOUR SHOTS!
CLIT-BONER. BIG TIME.
HE PLANNED THIS DOWN TO THE PERFORM-ANCE.
GLUG
GLUG
I DON'T NEED SAKE!
I GIVE YOU ONE SECOND TO LIVE!
SLIP
WHAAA ?

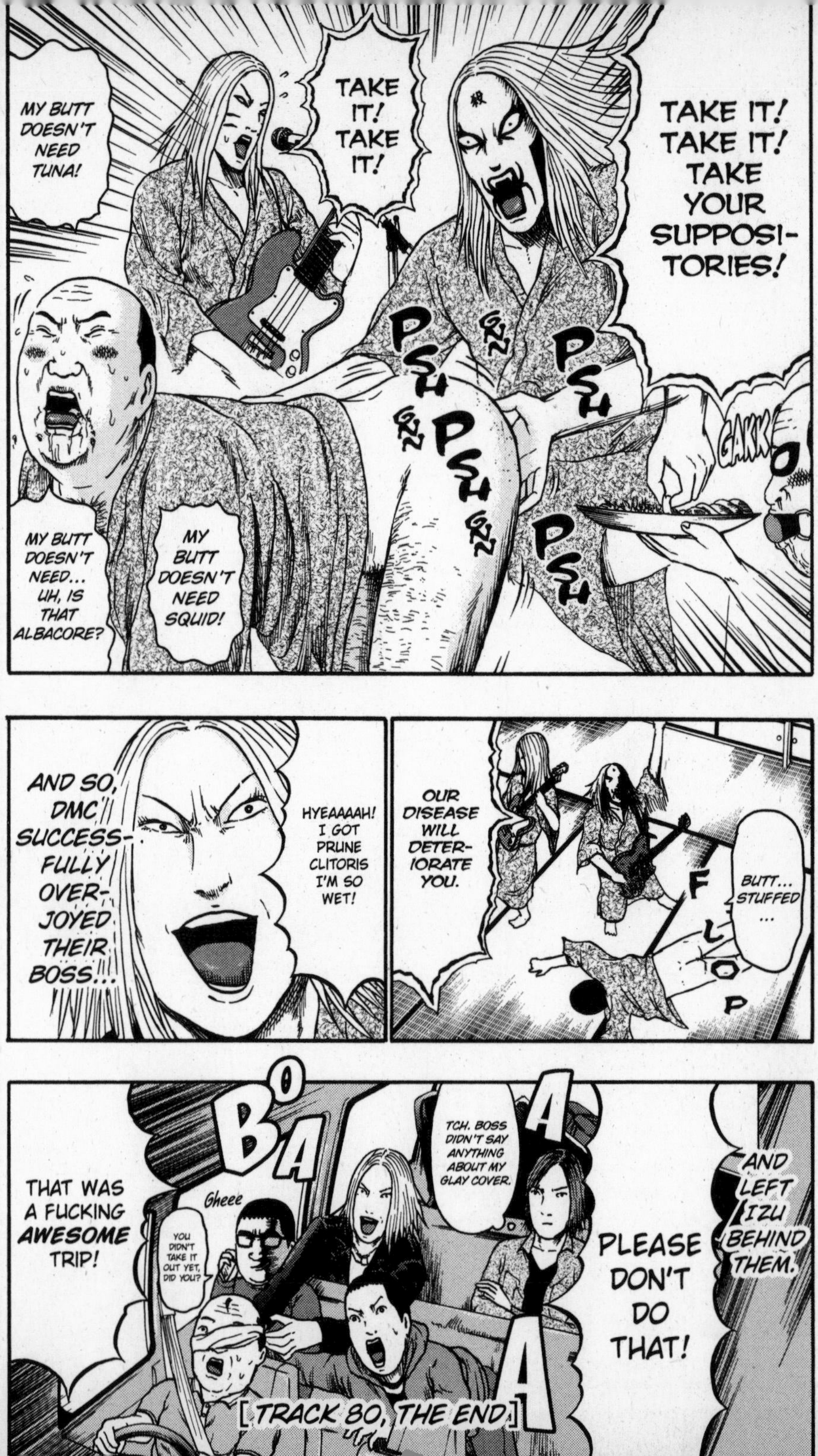
TAKE IT! TAKE IT! TAKE YOUR SUPPOSI-TORIES!
TAKE IT! TAKE IT!
MY BUTT DOESN'T NEED TUNA!
GAKK
O
PSH
GNN
PSH
GNN
PSH
GNN
PSH
PSH
MY BUTT DOESN'T NEED SQUID!
MY BUTT DOESN'T NEED... UH, IS THAT ALBACORE?
BUTT... STUFFED ...
FLOP
OUR DISEASE WILL DETER-IORATE YOU.
HYEAAAAH! I GOT PRUNE CLITORIS I'M SO WET!
AND SO, DMC SUCCESS-FULLY OVER-JOYED THEIR BOSS...
AND LEFT IZU BEHIND THEM.
PLEASE DON'T DO THAT!
A
TCH. BOSS DIDN'T SAY ANYTHING ABOUT MY GLAY COVER.
BOA
A
YOU DIDN'T TAKE IT OUT YET, DID YOU?
Gheee
THAT WAS A FUCKING **AWESOME** TRIP!
[TRACK 80, THE END]

DMC LEXICON

❤ SUPPOSITORIES

━━━━━━━━━━━━━━━━━━━━━━━━

A form of medical treatment used in only the most metal of illness. The medication absorbs more directly into the mucus membrane of the rectum by means of humiliation. There are many benefits to rectal administration of medication, not the least of which is shutting up a talkative M.

━━━━━━━━━━━━━━━━━━━━━━━━

Usage: Dear Customer, we appreciate your business but our nurses cannot be "hired" to administer "suppositories."

デトロイト・メタル・シティ

Detroit Metal City

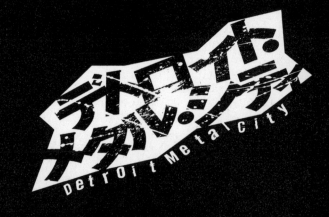

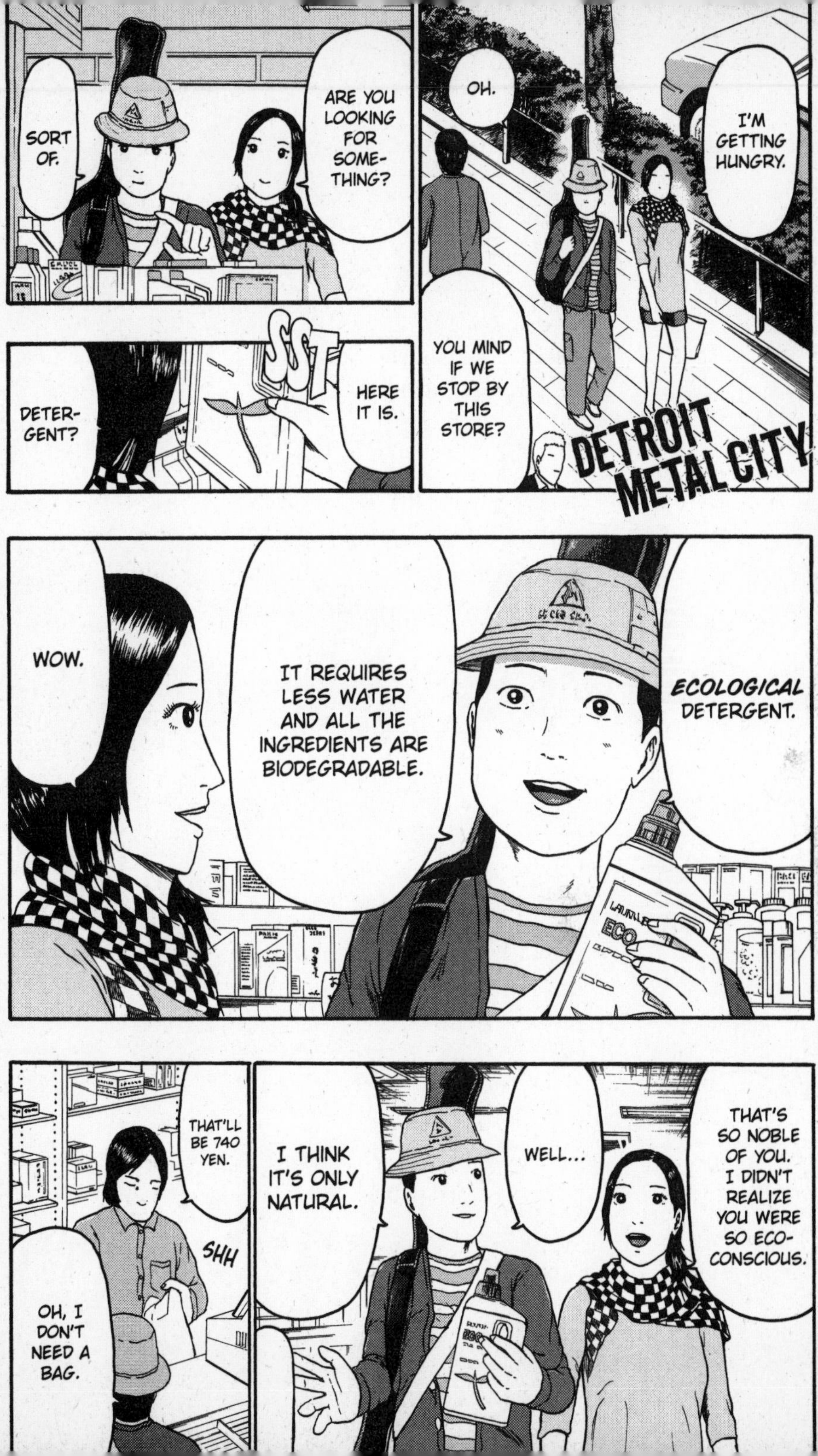
I'M GETTING HUNGRY.
OH.
YOU MIND IF WE STOP BY THIS STORE?
DETROIT METAL CITY
ARE YOU LOOKING FOR SOME-THING?
SORT OF.
SST
HERE IT IS.
DETER-GENT?
ECOLOGICAL DETERGENT.
IT REQUIRES LESS WATER AND ALL THE INGREDIENTS ARE BIODEGRADABLE.
WOW.
THAT'S SO NOBLE OF YOU. I DIDN'T REALIZE YOU WERE SO ECO-CONSCIOUS.
WELL...
I THINK IT'S ONLY NATURAL.
THAT'LL BE 740 YEN.
SHH
OH, I DON'T NEED A BAG.

TRACK 81 Ecology

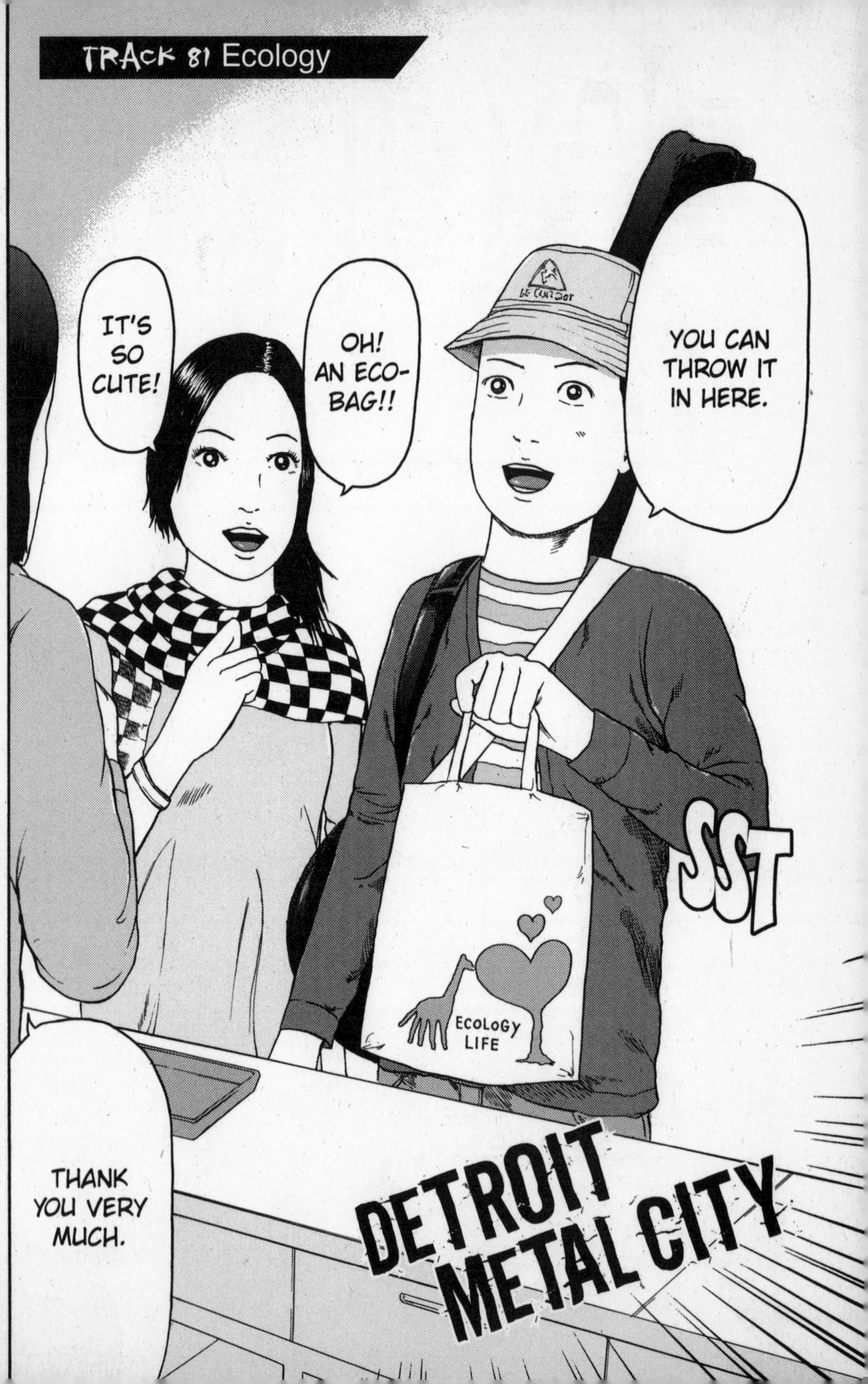
YOU CAN THROW IT IN HERE.
OH! AN ECO-BAG!!
IT'S SO CUTE!
SST
ECOLOGY LIFE
DETROIT METAL CITY
THANK YOU VERY MUCH.

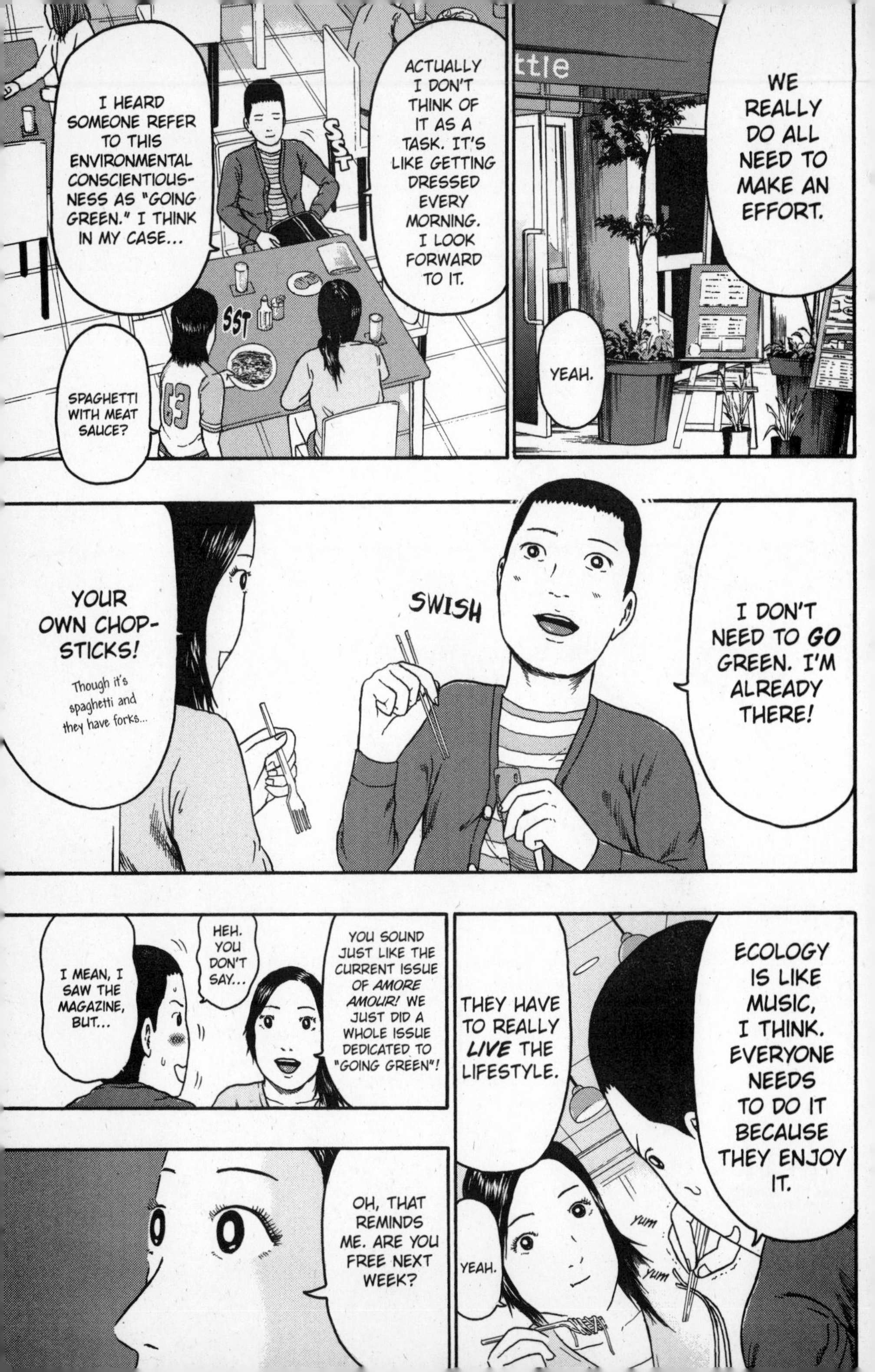
ttle
WE REALLY DO ALL NEED TO MAKE AN EFFORT.
YEAH.
ACTUALLY I DON'T THINK OF IT AS A TASK. IT'S LIKE GETTING DRESSED EVERY MORNING. I LOOK FORWARD TO IT.
SST
I HEARD SOMEONE REFER TO THIS ENVIRONMENTAL CONSCIENTIOUS-NESS AS "GOING GREEN." I THINK IN MY CASE...
SST
SPAGHETTI WITH MEAT SAUCE?
I DON'T NEED TO *GO* GREEN. I'M ALREADY THERE!
SWISH
YOUR OWN CHOP-STICKS!
Though it's spaghetti and they have forks...
ECOLOGY IS LIKE MUSIC, I THINK. EVERYONE NEEDS TO DO IT BECAUSE THEY ENJOY IT.
THEY HAVE TO REALLY *LIVE* THE LIFESTYLE.
yum
yum
YEAH.
YOU SOUND JUST LIKE THE CURRENT ISSUE OF *AMORE AMOUR!* WE JUST DID A WHOLE ISSUE DEDICATED TO "GOING GREEN"!
HEH. YOU DON'T SAY...
I MEAN, I SAW THE MAGAZINE, BUT...
OH, THAT REMINDS ME. ARE YOU FREE NEXT WEEK?

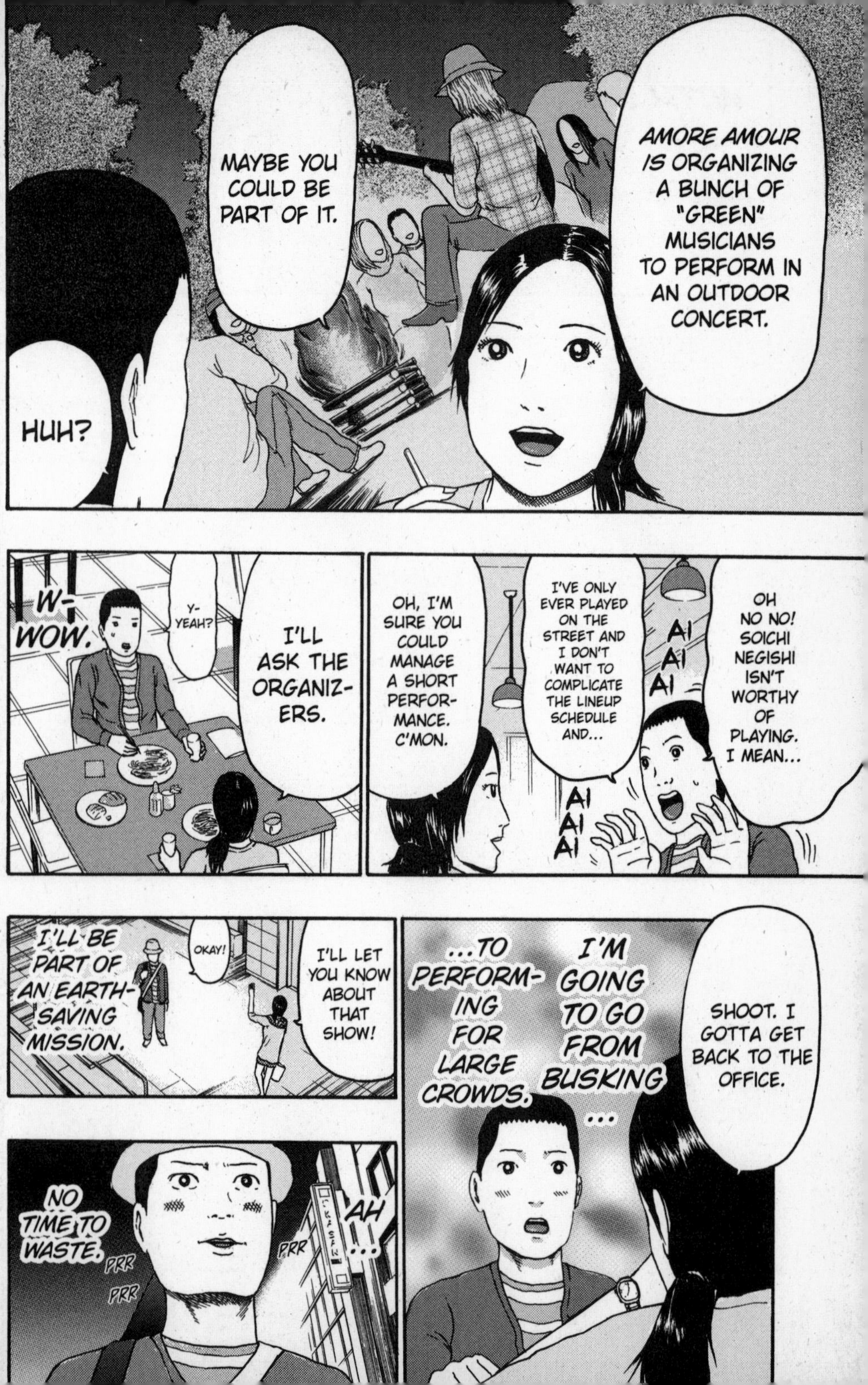
AMORE AMOUR IS ORGANIZING A BUNCH OF "GREEN" MUSICIANS TO PERFORM IN AN OUTDOOR CONCERT.
MAYBE YOU COULD BE PART OF IT.
HUH?
OH NO NO! SOICHI NEGISHI ISN'T WORTHY OF PLAYING. I MEAN...
AI AI AI
I'VE ONLY EVER PLAYED ON THE STREET AND I DON'T WANT TO COMPLICATE THE LINEUP SCHEDULE AND...
AI AI AI
OH, I'M SURE YOU COULD MANAGE A SHORT PERFOR-MANCE. C'MON.
I'LL ASK THE ORGANIZ-ERS.
Y-YEAH?
W-WOW.
SHOOT. I GOTTA GET BACK TO THE OFFICE.
I'M GOING TO GO FROM BUSKING...
...TO PERFORM-ING FOR LARGE CROWDS.
I'LL LET YOU KNOW ABOUT THAT SHOW!
OKAY!
I'LL BE PART OF AN EARTH-SAVING MISSION.
AH...
PRR
NO TIME TO WASTE.
PRR
PRR

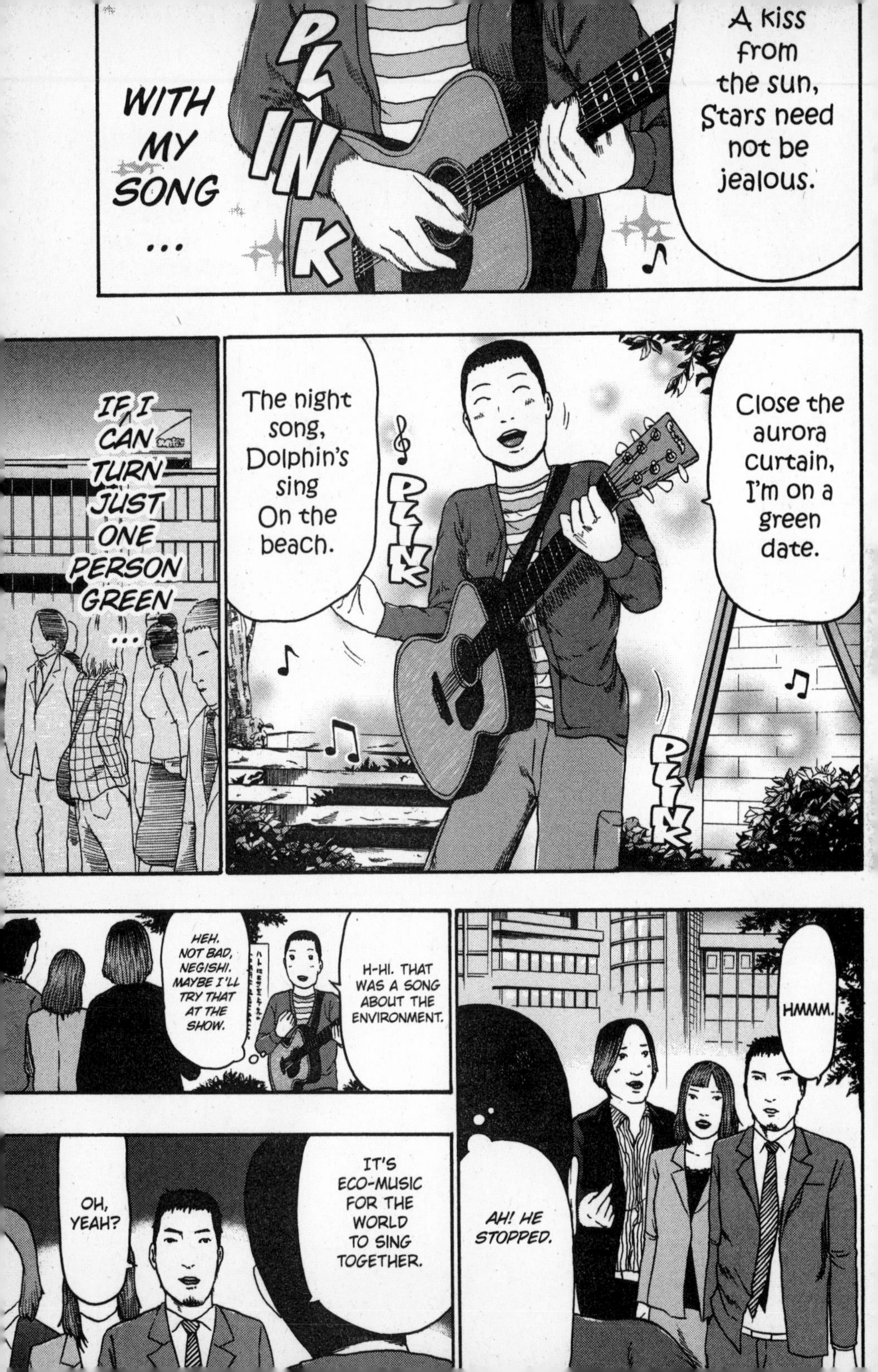
A kiss from the sun, Stars need not be jealous.
PLINK
WITH MY SONG ...
Close the aurora curtain, I'm on a green date.
PLINK
The night song, Dolphin's sing On the beach.
PLINK
IF I CAN TURN JUST ONE PERSON GREEN...
HMMM.
AH! HE STOPPED.
H-HI. THAT WAS A SONG ABOUT THE ENVIRONMENT.
HEH. NOT BAD, NEGISHI. MAYBE I'LL TRY THAT AT THE SHOW.
IT'S ECO-MUSIC FOR THE WORLD TO SING TOGETHER.
OH, YEAH?

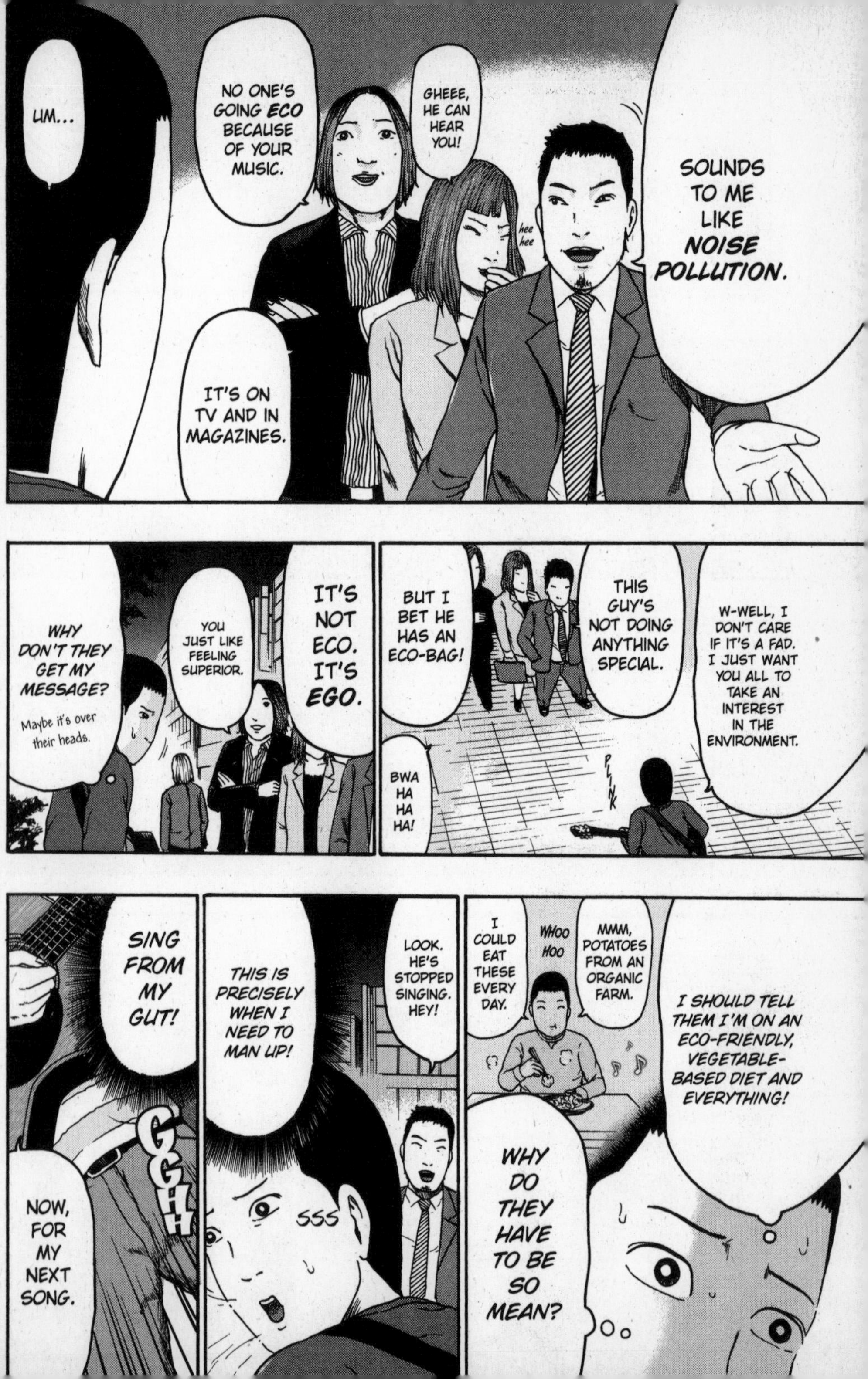
SOUNDS TO ME LIKE NOISE POLLUTION.
hee hee
GHEEE, HE CAN HEAR YOU!
NO ONE'S GOING ECO BECAUSE OF YOUR MUSIC.
IT'S ON TV AND IN MAGAZINES.
UM...
W-WELL, I DON'T CARE IF IT'S A FAD. I JUST WANT YOU ALL TO TAKE AN INTEREST IN THE ENVIRONMENT.
THIS GUY'S NOT DOING ANYTHING SPECIAL.
PLINK
BUT I BET HE HAS AN ECO-BAG!
BWA HA HA HA!
IT'S NOT ECO. IT'S EGO.
YOU JUST LIKE FEELING SUPERIOR.
WHY DON'T THEY GET MY MESSAGE?
Maybe it's over their heads.
MMM, POTATOES FROM AN ORGANIC FARM.
WHOO HOO
I COULD EAT THESE EVERY DAY.
I SHOULD TELL THEM I'M ON AN ECO-FRIENDLY, VEGETABLE-BASED DIET AND EVERYTHING!
WHY DO THEY HAVE TO BE SO MEAN?
LOOK. HE'S STOPPED SINGING. HEY!
THIS IS PRECISELY WHEN I NEED TO MAN UP!
SSS
SING FROM MY GUT!
GGH
NOW, FOR MY NEXT SONG.

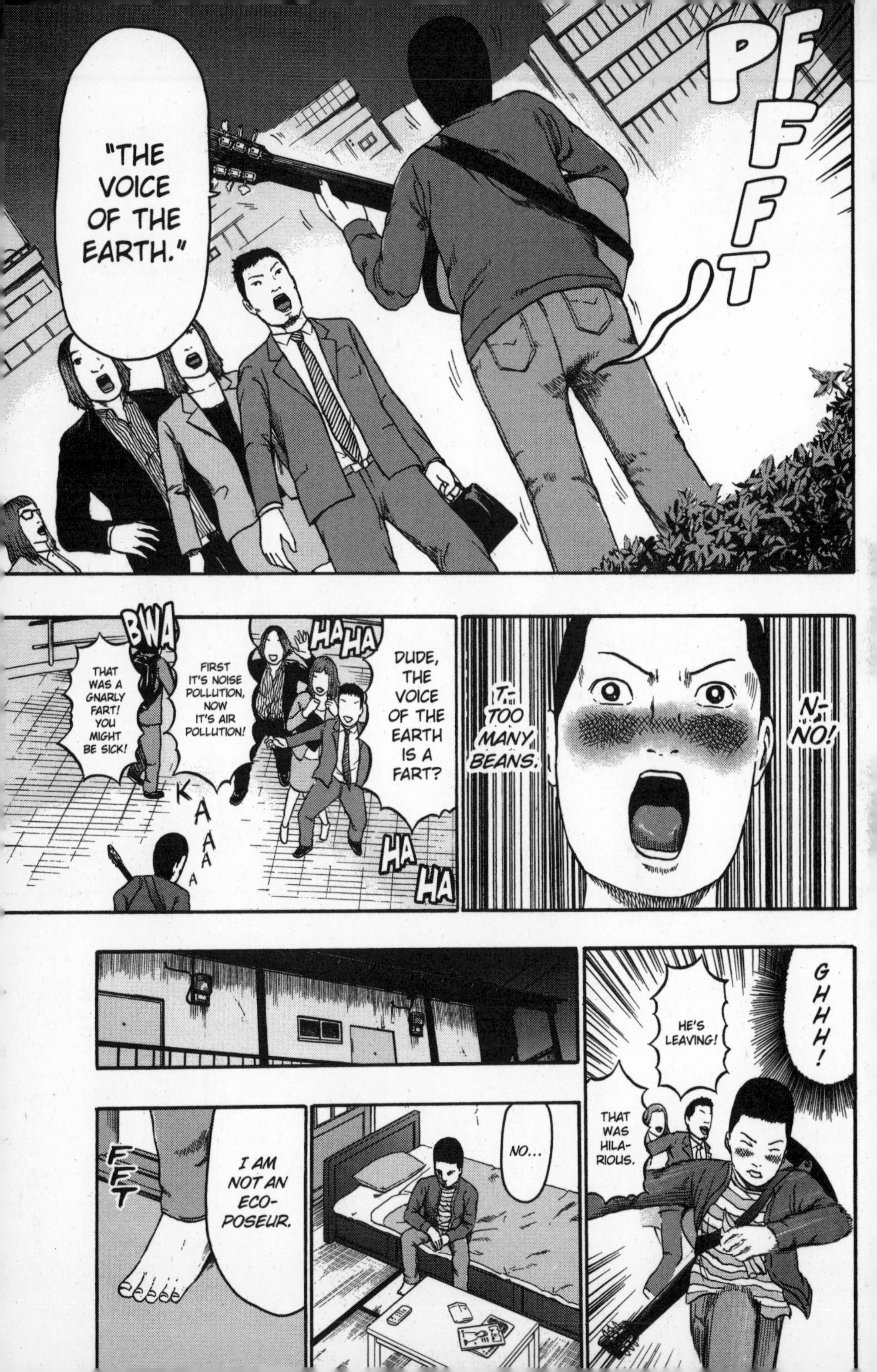
PFFFT
"THE VOICE OF THE EARTH."
N-NO!
T-TOO MANY BEANS.
DUDE, THE VOICE OF THE EARTH IS A FART?
HAHA
FIRST IT'S NOISE POLLUTION, NOW IT'S AIR POLLUTION!
BWA
THAT WAS A GNARLY FART! YOU MIGHT BE SICK!
KAAAA
HAHA
GHHH!
HE'S LEAVING!
THAT WAS HILA-RIOUS.
NO...
I AM NOT AN ECO-POSEUR.
FFT

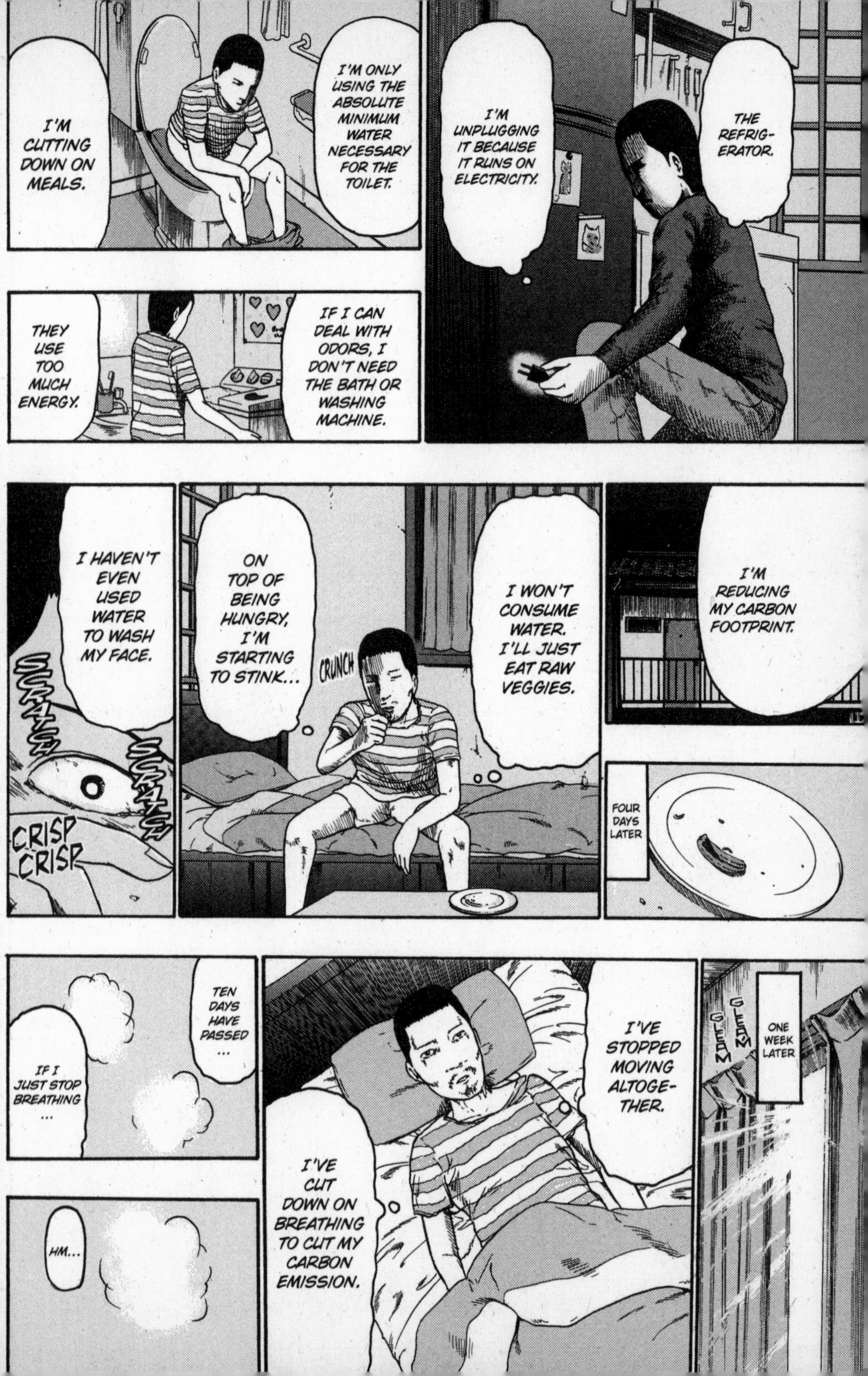
THE REFRIGERATOR.
I'M UNPLUGGING IT BECAUSE IT RUNS ON ELECTRICITY.
I'M ONLY USING THE ABSOLUTE MINIMUM WATER NECESSARY FOR THE TOILET.
I'M CUTTING DOWN ON MEALS.
IF I CAN DEAL WITH ODORS, I DON'T NEED THE BATH OR WASHING MACHINE.
THEY USE TOO MUCH ENERGY.
I'M REDUCING MY CARBON FOOTPRINT.
FOUR DAYS LATER
I WON'T CONSUME WATER. I'LL JUST EAT RAW VEGGIES.
CRUNCH
ON TOP OF BEING HUNGRY, I'M STARTING TO STINK...
I HAVEN'T EVEN USED WATER TO WASH MY FACE.
SCRATCH
SCRATCH
CRISP CRISP
ONE WEEK LATER
GLEAM
GLEAM
I'VE STOPPED MOVING ALTOGETHER.
I'VE CUT DOWN ON BREATHING TO CUT MY CARBON EMISSION.
TEN DAYS HAVE PASSED...
IF I JUST STOP BREATHING...
HM...

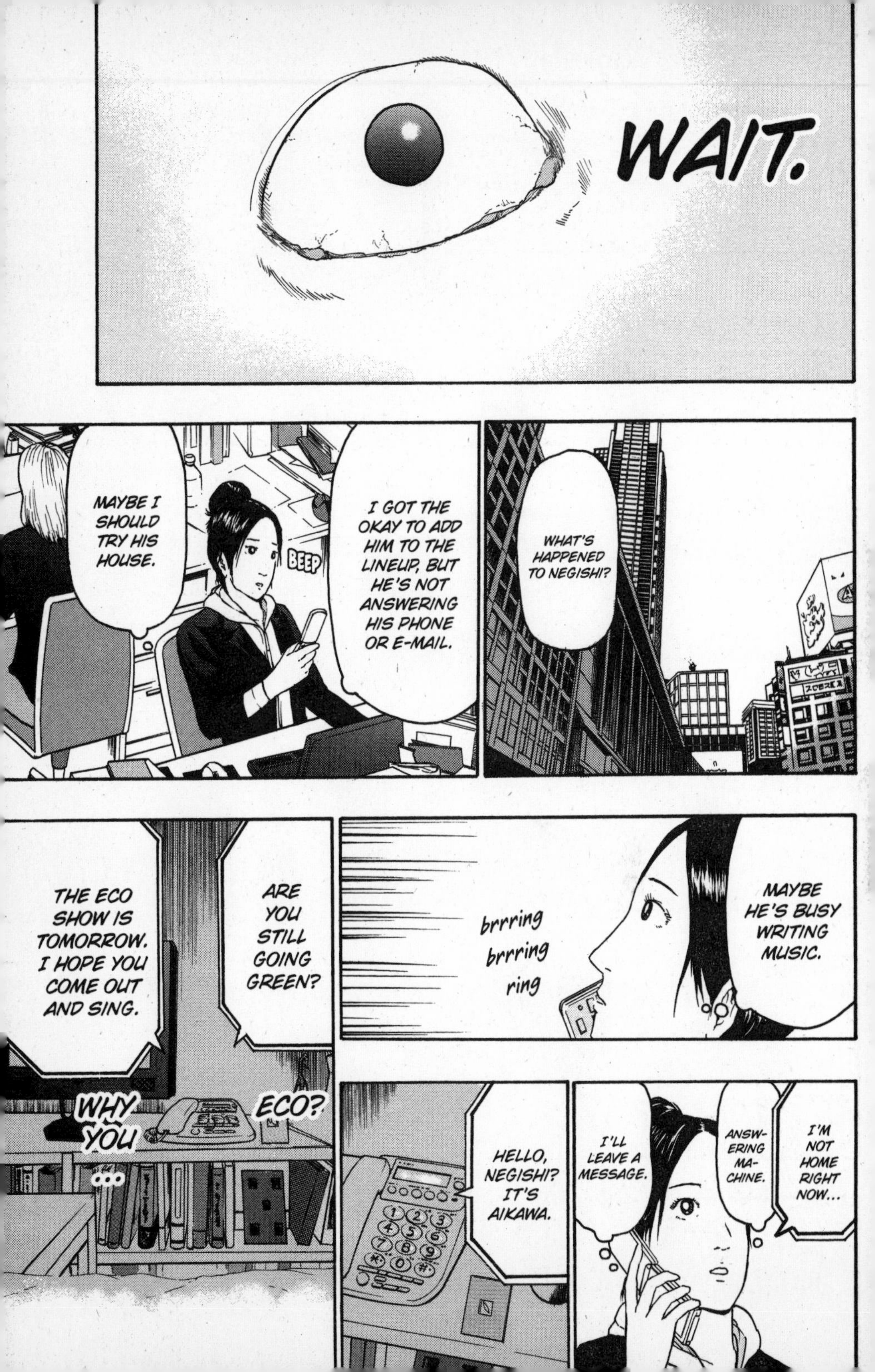
WAIT.
WHAT'S HAPPENED TO NEGISHI?
I GOT THE OKAY TO ADD HIM TO THE LINEUP, BUT HE'S NOT ANSWERING HIS PHONE OR E-MAIL.
BEEP
MAYBE I SHOULD TRY HIS HOUSE.
MAYBE HE'S BUSY WRITING MUSIC.
brrring brrring ring
I'M NOT HOME RIGHT NOW...
ANSWERING MACHINE.
I'LL LEAVE A MESSAGE.
HELLO, NEGISHI? IT'S AIKAWA.
ARE YOU STILL GOING GREEN?
THE ECO SHOW IS TOMORROW. I HOPE YOU COME OUT AND SING.
ECO?
WHY YOU ...

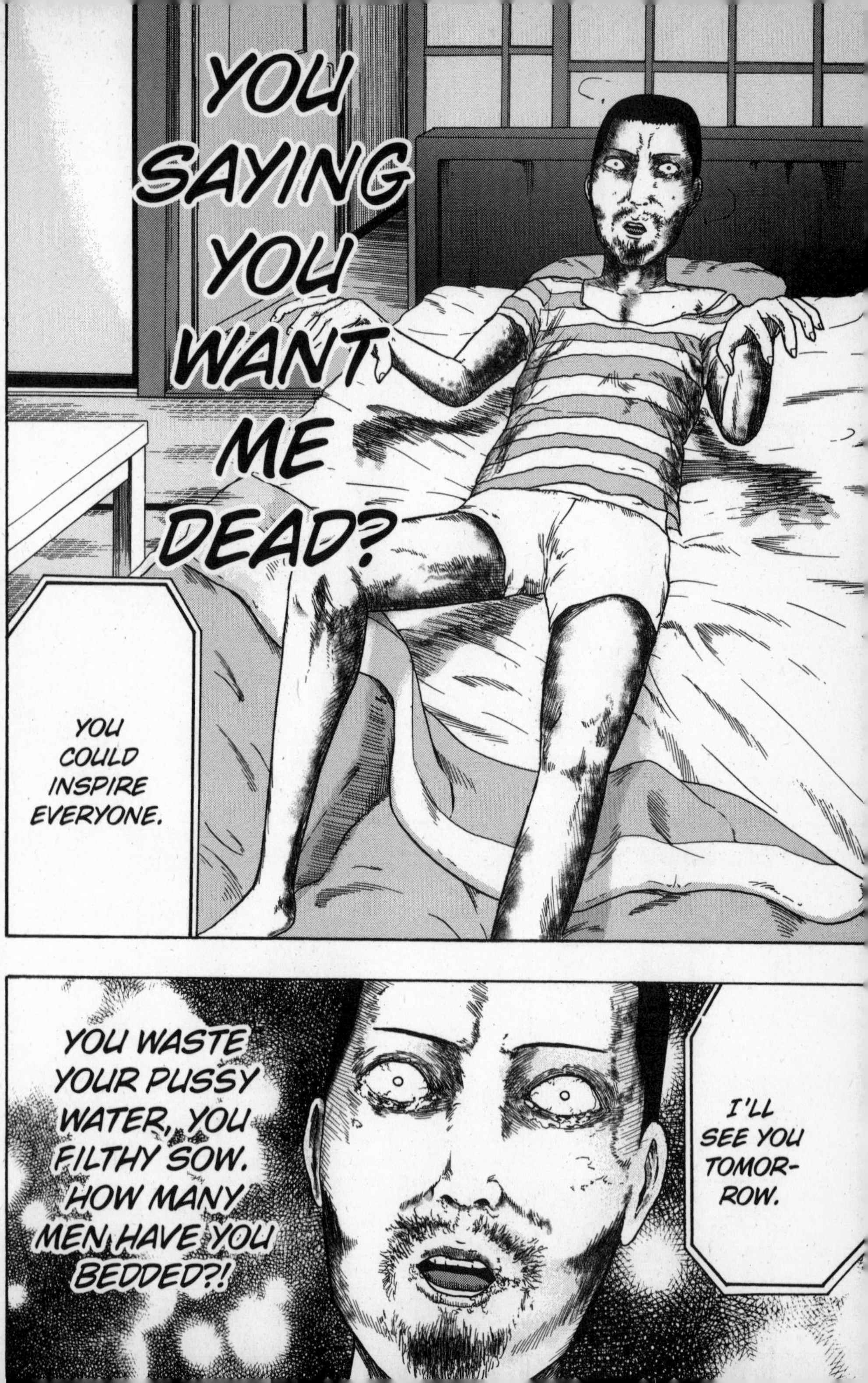
YOU SAYING YOU WANT ME DEAD?
YOU COULD INSPIRE EVERYONE.
I'LL SEE YOU TOMOR-ROW.
YOU WASTE YOUR PUSSY WATER, YOU FILTHY SOW. HOW MANY MEN HAVE YOU BEDDED?!

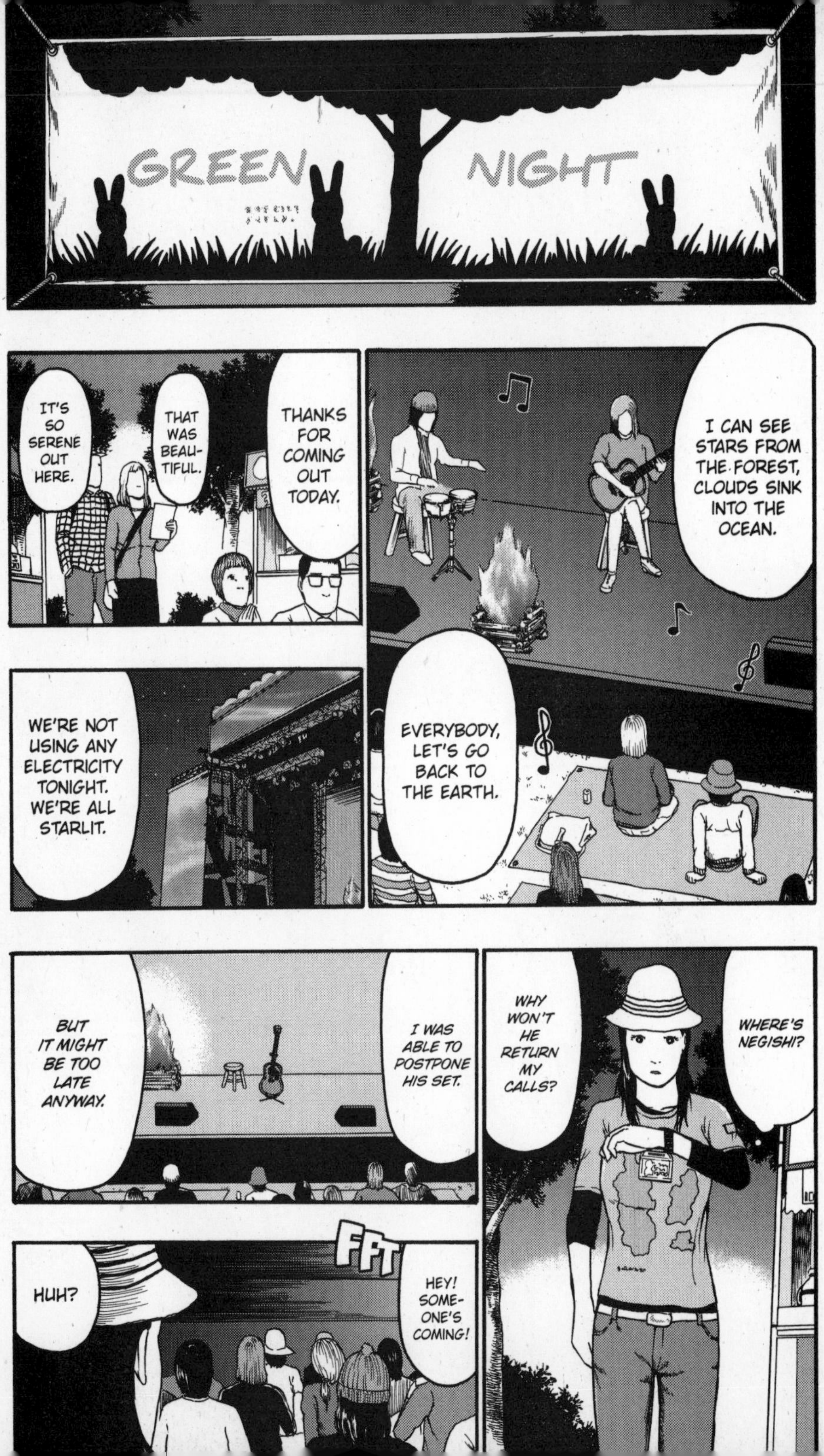
GREEN NIGHT
I CAN SEE STARS FROM THE FOREST, CLOUDS SINK INTO THE OCEAN.
EVERYBODY, LET'S GO BACK TO THE EARTH.
THANKS FOR COMING OUT TODAY.
THAT WAS BEAU-TIFUL.
IT'S SO SERENE OUT HERE.
WE'RE NOT USING ANY ELECTRICITY TONIGHT. WE'RE ALL STARLIT.
WHERE'S NEGISHI?
WHY WON'T HE RETURN MY CALLS?
I WAS ABLE TO POSTPONE HIS SET.
BUT IT MIGHT BE TOO LATE ANYWAY.
FFT
HEY! SOME-ONE'S COMING!
HUH?

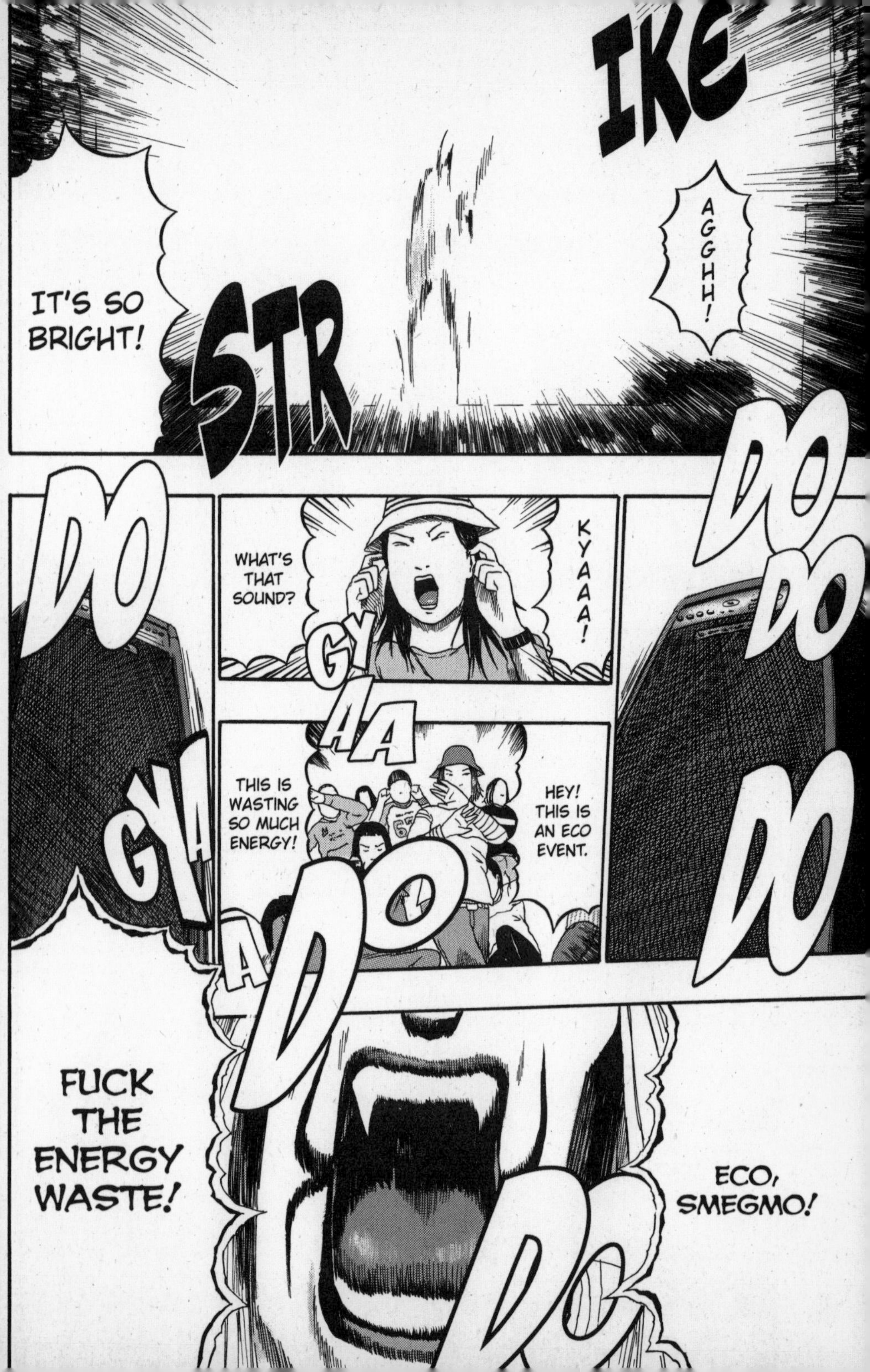
AGGHH!
IT'S SO BRIGHT!
STR
IKE
DO DO DO DO DO
KYAAAA!
WHAT'S THAT SOUND?
HEY! THIS IS AN ECO EVENT.
THIS IS WASTING SO MUCH ENERGY!
GYAA
GYAA
DO
ECO, SMEGMO!
FUCK THE ENERGY WASTE!
DO
DO

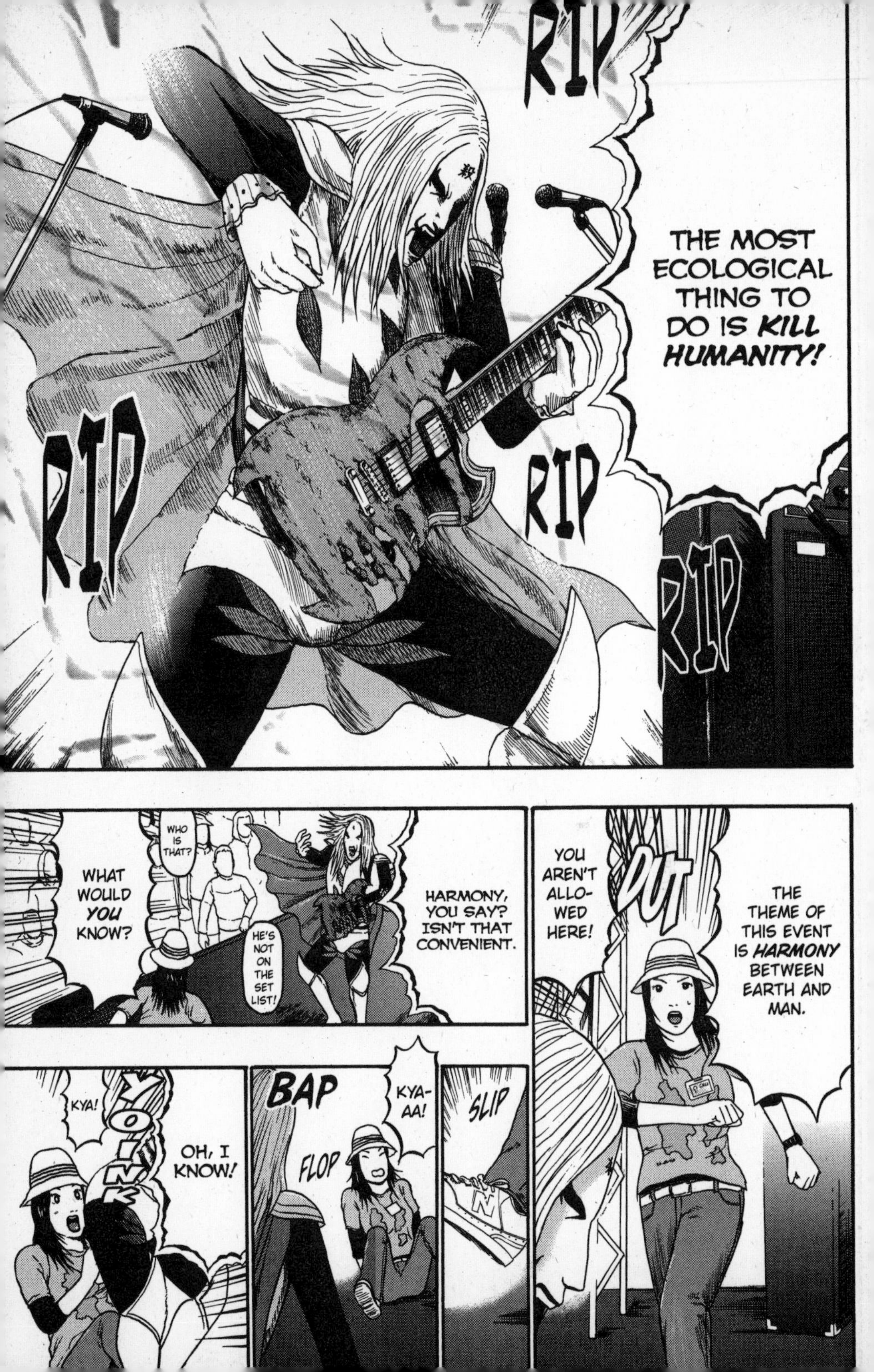
RIP
THE MOST ECOLOGICAL THING TO DO IS *KILL HUMANITY!*
RIP
RIP
RIP
THE THEME OF THIS EVENT IS *HARMONY* BETWEEN EARTH AND MAN.
OUT
YOU AREN'T ALLO-WED HERE!
HARMONY, YOU SAY? ISN'T THAT CONVENIENT.
WHO IS THAT?
HE'S NOT ON THE SET LIST!
WHAT WOULD *YOU* KNOW?
SLIP
KYA-AA!
BAP
FLOP
YOINK
KYA!
OH, I KNOW!

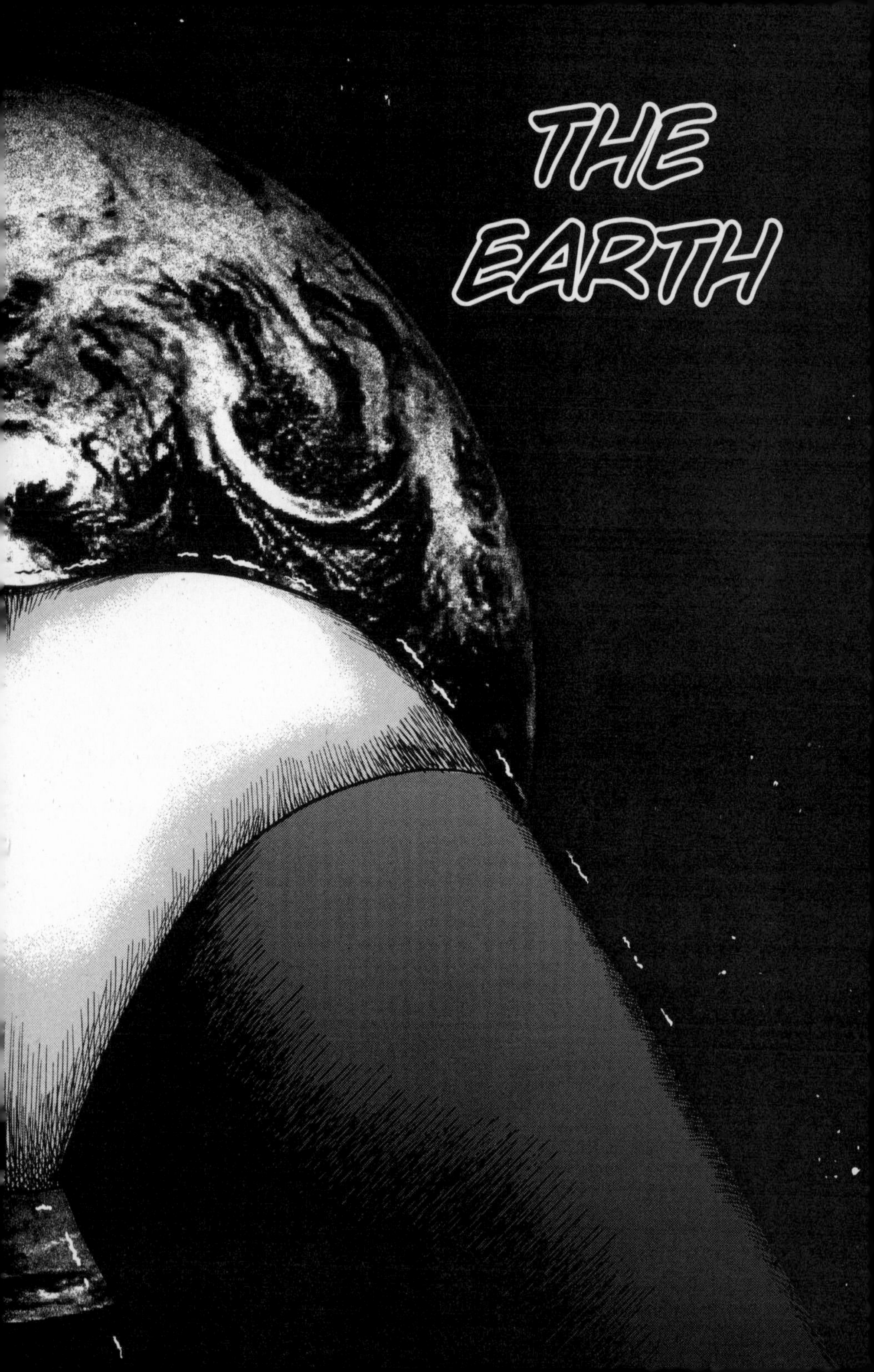
THE EARTH

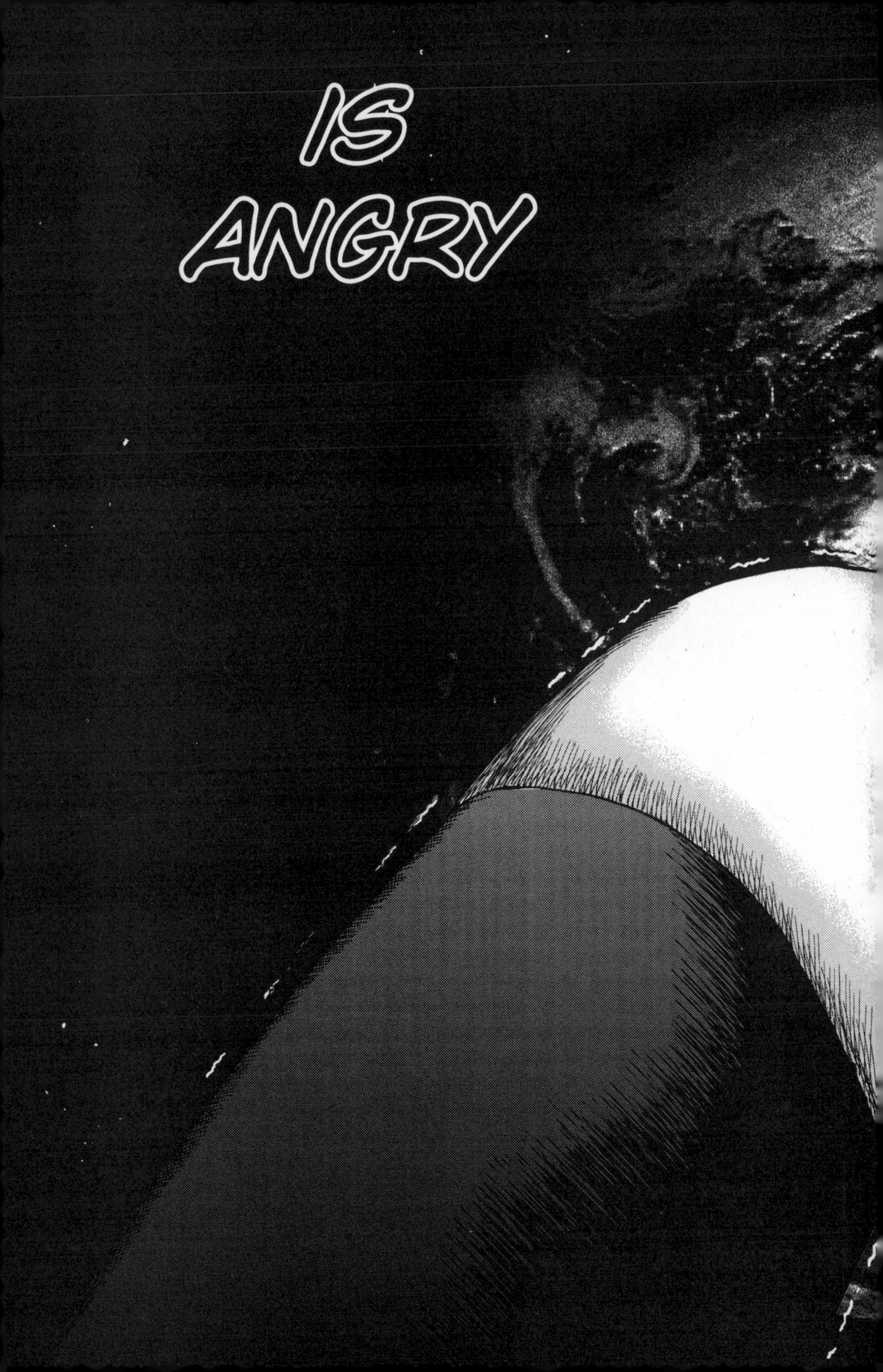
IS
ANGRY

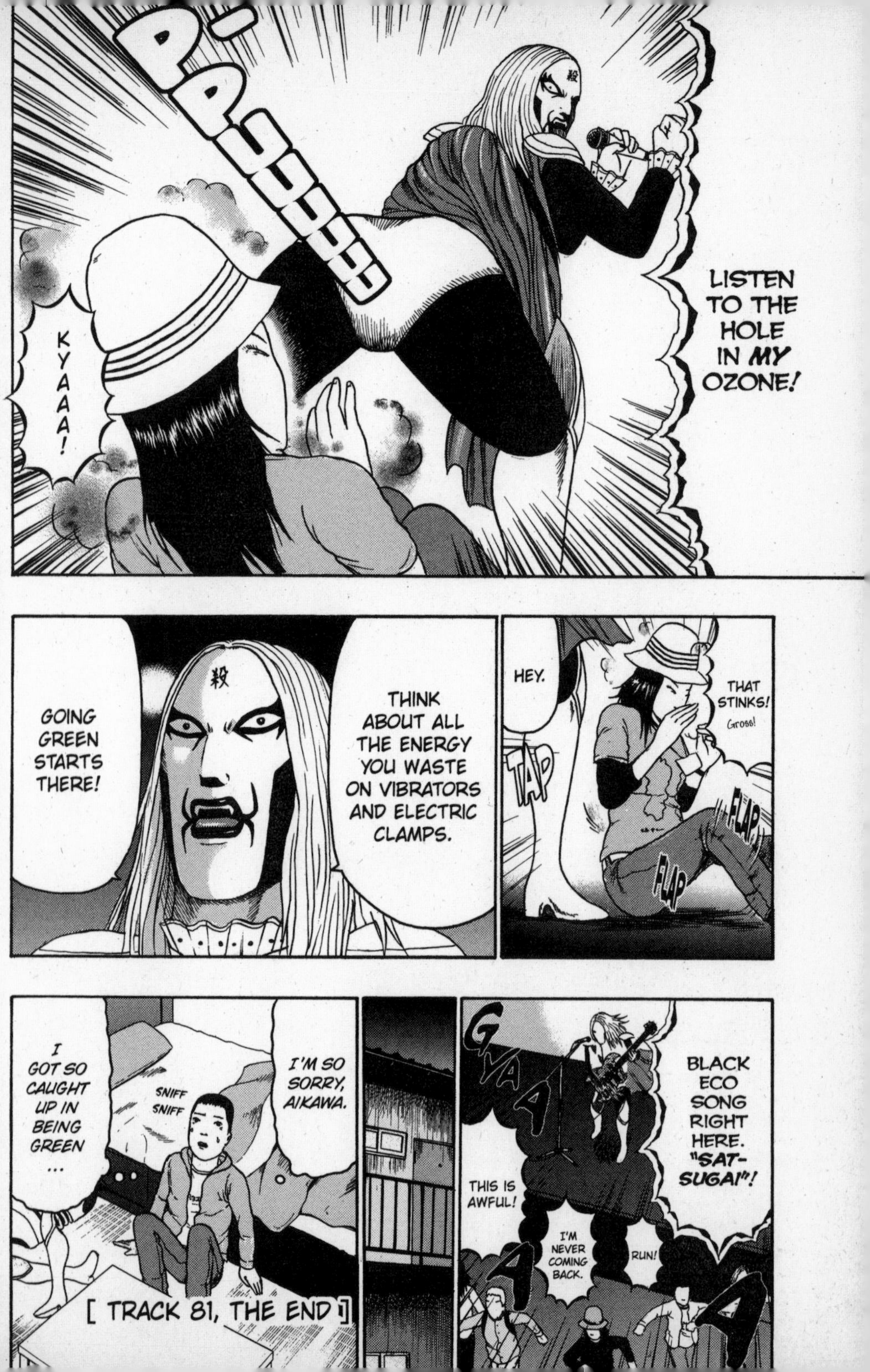
P-PUUUUUU
LISTEN TO THE HOLE IN *MY* OZONE!
KYAAAA!
HEY.
THAT STINKS!
Gross!
TAP
FLAP
FLAP
THINK ABOUT ALL THE ENERGY YOU WASTE ON VIBRATORS AND ELECTRIC CLAMPS.
GOING GREEN STARTS THERE!
GYAAA
BLACK ECO SONG RIGHT HERE. **"SAT-SUGAI"!**
THIS IS AWFUL!
I'M NEVER COMING BACK.
RUN!
I'M SO SORRY, AIKAWA.
SNIFF SNIFF
I GOT SO CAUGHT UP IN BEING GREEN...
[TRACK 81, THE END]

DMC LEXICON

ECO-BAG

A personal shopping bag used in the place of register-side plastic bags, in order to protect the Earth's natural resources. Speaking of natural resources, this book is made of paper, which is made of wood. In other words, a tremendous amount of natural resource is wasted every time a copy of the book is not purchased. You should prevent such waste by buying two copies of every volume.

Usage: When you meet chicks, show them your eco-bag. I guarantee you'll get eco-laid.

デトロイト・メタル・シティ
Detroit Metal City

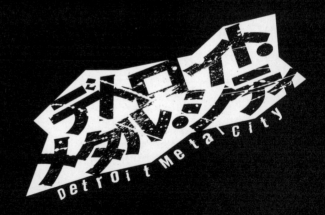

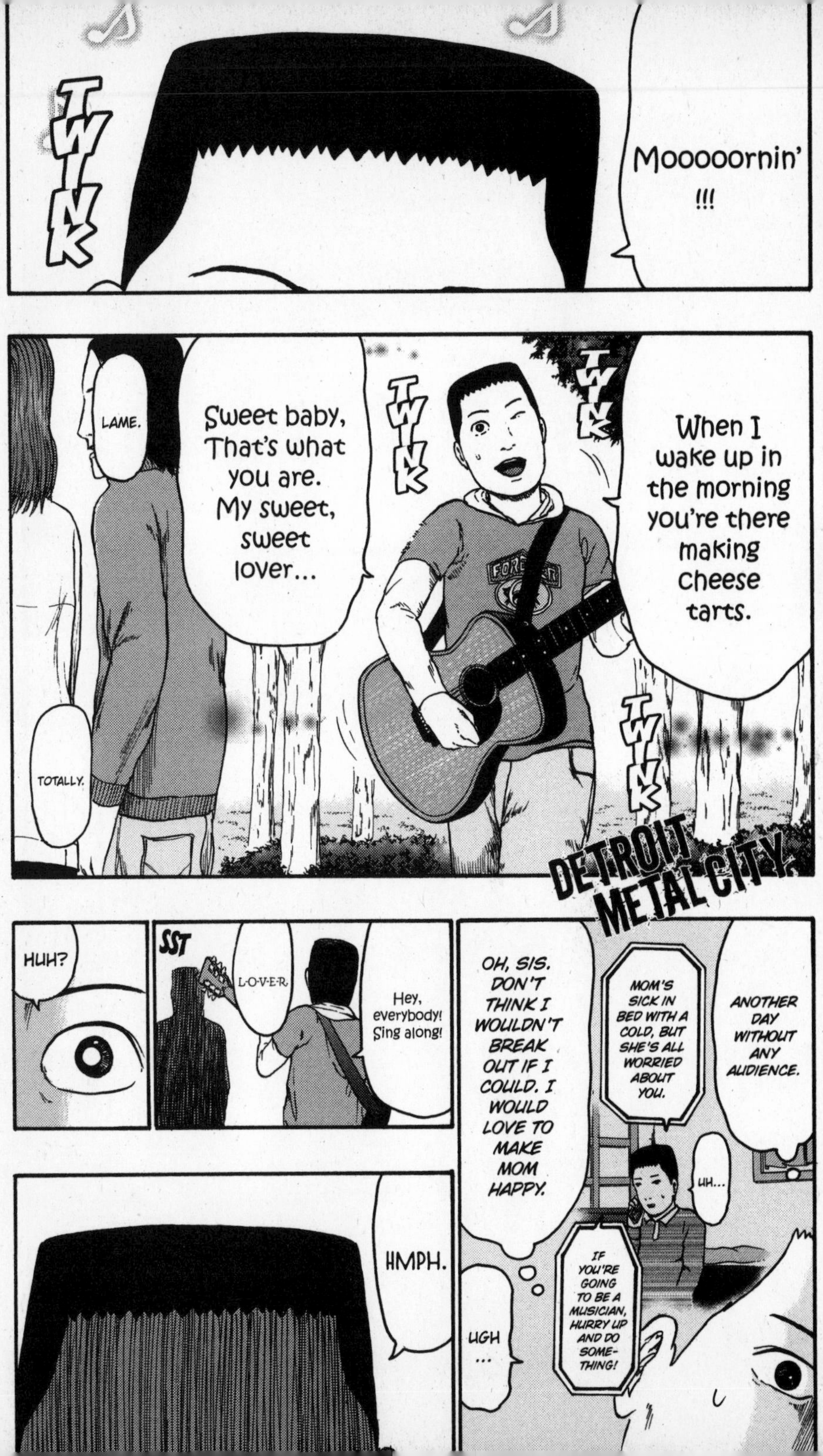
TWINK
Moooooornin' !!!
When I wake up in the morning you're there making cheese tarts.
TWINK
TWINK
TWINK
Sweet baby, That's what you are. My sweet, sweet lover...
LAME.
TOTALLY.
DETROIT METAL CITY
ANOTHER DAY WITHOUT ANY AUDIENCE.
MOM'S SICK IN BED WITH A COLD, BUT SHE'S ALL WORRIED ABOUT YOU.
UH...
OH, SIS. DON'T THINK I WOULDN'T BREAK OUT IF I COULD. I WOULD LOVE TO MAKE MOM HAPPY.
IF YOU'RE GOING TO BE A MUSICIAN, HURRY UP AND DO SOMETHING!
UGH...
Hey, everybody! Sing along!
L·O·V·E·R
SST
HUH?
HMPH.

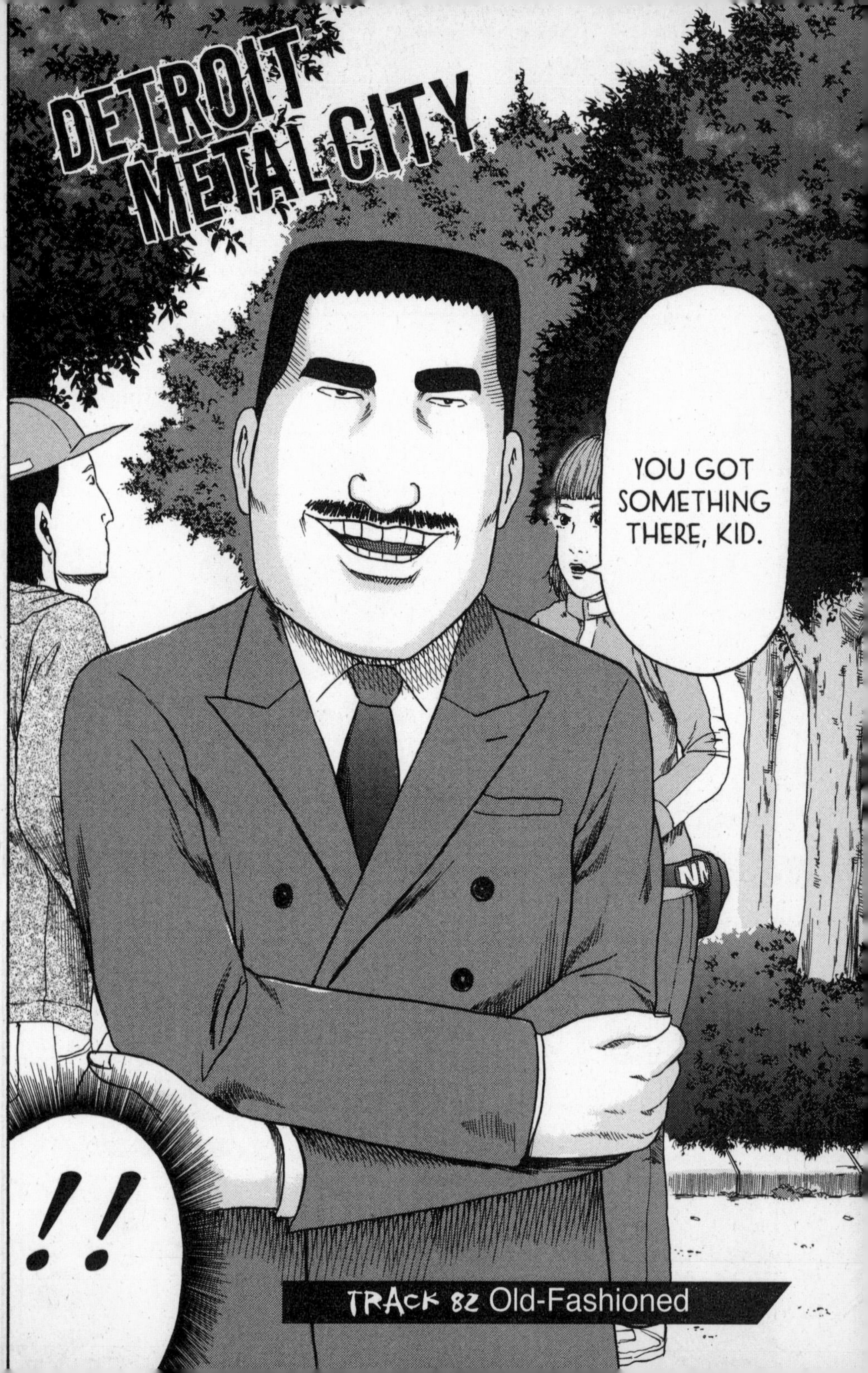
DETROIT METAL CITY
YOU GOT SOMETHING THERE, KID.
!!
TRACK 82 Old-Fashioned

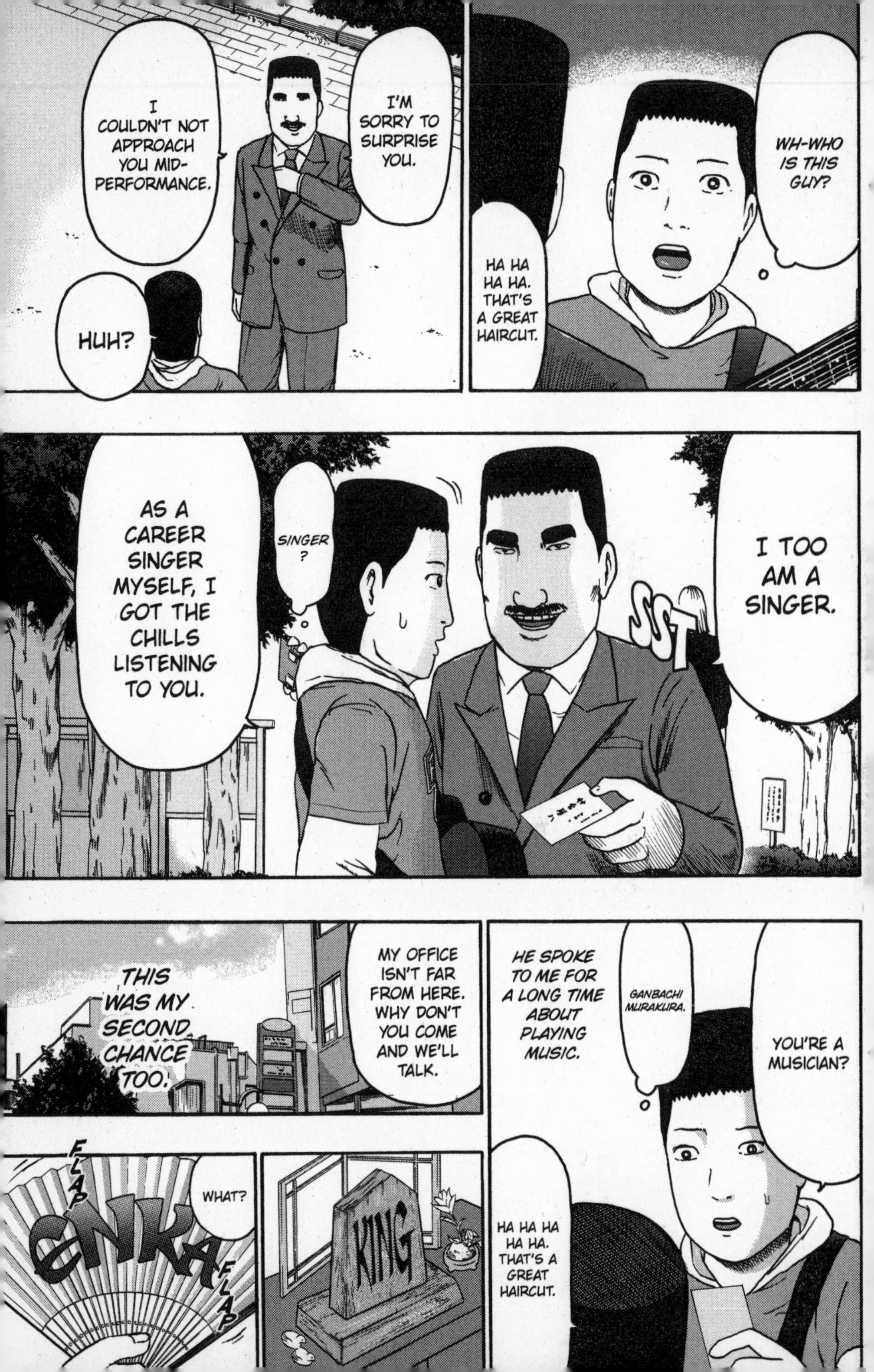
WH-WHO IS THIS GUY?
HA HA HA HA. THAT'S A GREAT HAIRCUT.
I'M SORRY TO SURPRISE YOU.
I COULDN'T NOT APPROACH YOU MID-PERFORMANCE.
HUH?
I TOO AM A SINGER.
SST
SINGER?
AS A CAREER SINGER MYSELF, I GOT THE CHILLS LISTENING TO YOU.
YOU'RE A MUSICIAN?
GANBACHI MURAKURA.
HE SPOKE TO ME FOR A LONG TIME ABOUT PLAYING MUSIC.
HA HA HA HA HA. THAT'S A GREAT HAIRCUT.
MY OFFICE ISN'T FAR FROM HERE. WHY DON'T YOU COME AND WE'LL TALK.
THIS WAS MY SECOND CHANCE TOO.
KING
WHAT?
FLAP
ENKA
FLAP

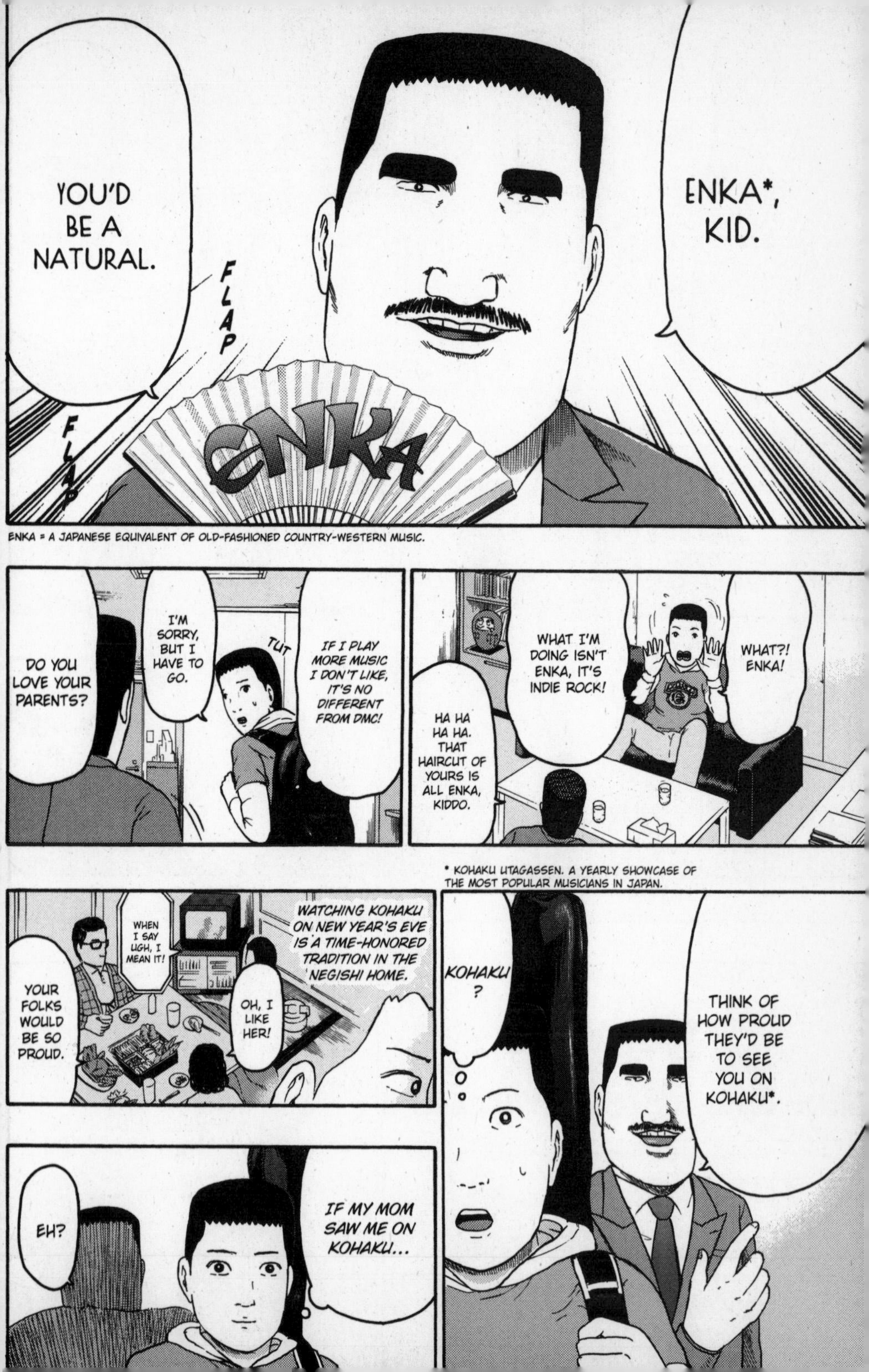
ENKA*, KID.
YOU'D BE A NATURAL.
FLAP
FLAP
ENKA
WHAT?! ENKA!
WHAT I'M DOING ISN'T ENKA, IT'S INDIE ROCK!
HA HA HA HA. THAT HAIRCUT OF YOURS IS ALL ENKA, KIDDO.
IF I PLAY MORE MUSIC I DON'T LIKE, IT'S NO DIFFERENT FROM DMC!
TUT
I'M SORRY, BUT I HAVE TO GO.
DO YOU LOVE YOUR PARENTS?
THINK OF HOW PROUD THEY'D BE TO SEE YOU ON KOHAKU*.
KOHAKU?
WATCHING KOHAKU ON NEW YEAR'S EVE IS A TIME-HONORED TRADITION IN THE NEGISHI HOME.
OH, I LIKE HER!
WHEN I SAY UGH, I MEAN IT!
YOUR FOLKS WOULD BE SO PROUD.
IF MY MOM SAW ME ON KOHAKU...
EH?

ENKA = A JAPANESE EQUIVALENT OF OLD-FASHIONED COUNTRY-WESTERN MUSIC.

* KOHAKU UTAGASSEN. A YEARLY SHOWCASE OF THE MOST POPULAR MUSICIANS IN JAPAN.

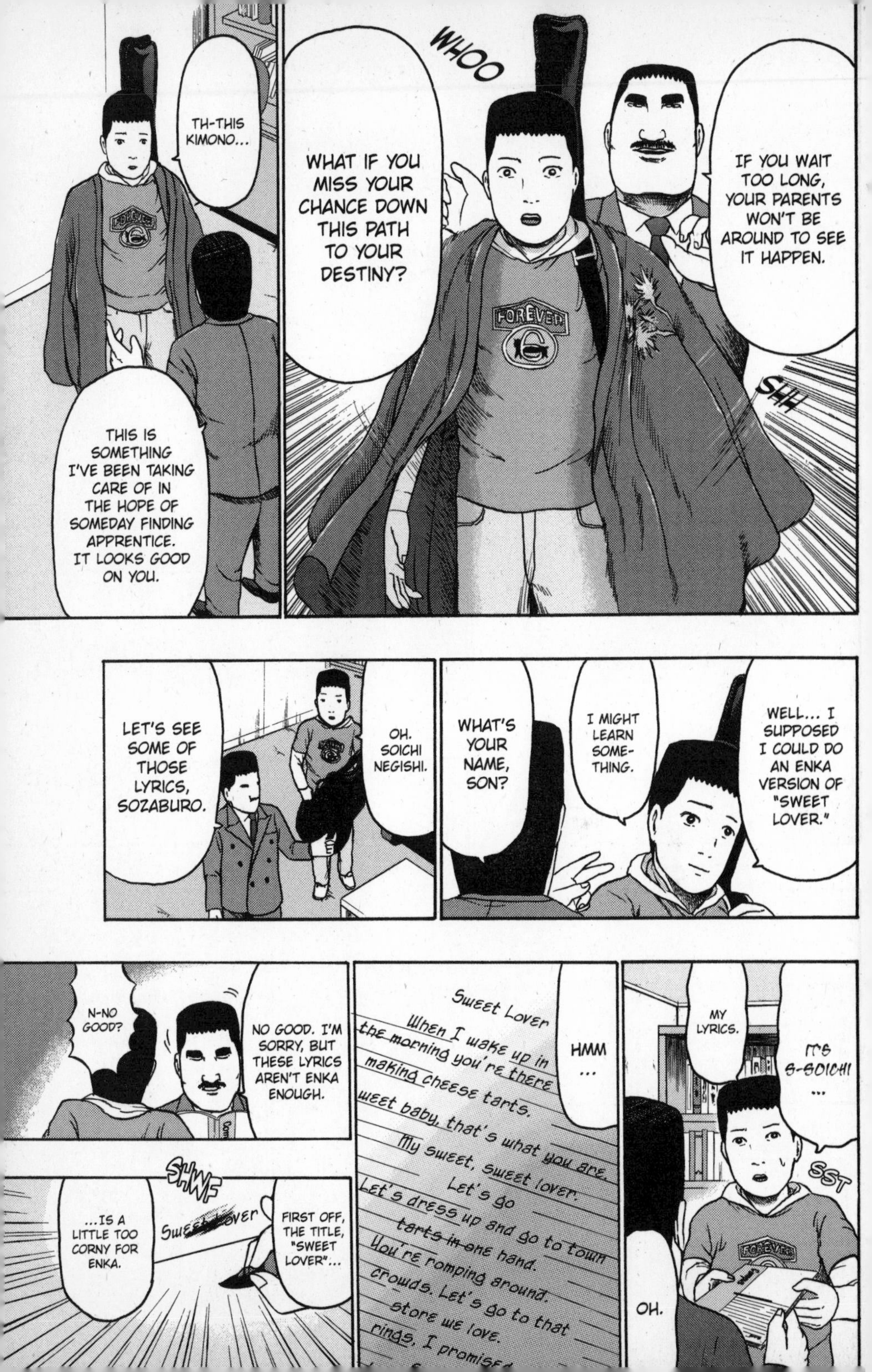
WHOO
IF YOU WAIT TOO LONG, YOUR PARENTS WON'T BE AROUND TO SEE IT HAPPEN.
WHAT IF YOU MISS YOUR CHANCE DOWN THIS PATH TO YOUR DESTINY?
SHH
TH-THIS KIMONO...
THIS IS SOMETHING I'VE BEEN TAKING CARE OF IN THE HOPE OF SOMEDAY FINDING APPRENTICE. IT LOOKS GOOD ON YOU.
WELL... I SUPPOSED I COULD DO AN ENKA VERSION OF "SWEET LOVER."
I MIGHT LEARN SOME-THING.
WHAT'S YOUR NAME, SON?
OH. SOICHI NEGISHI.
LET'S SEE SOME OF THOSE LYRICS, SOZABURO.
MY LYRICS.
IT'S S-SOICHI...
SST
OH.
HMM...
Sweet Lover
When I wake up in
the morning you're there
making cheese tarts.
weet baby, that's what you are.
My sweet, sweet lover.
Let's go
Let's dress up and go to town
tarts in one hand.
You're romping around
crowds. Let's go to that
store we love.
rings, I promis
NO GOOD. I'M SORRY, BUT THESE LYRICS AREN'T ENKA ENOUGH.
N-NO GOOD?
FIRST OFF, THE TITLE, "SWEET LOVER"...
SHWF
Sweet Lover
...IS A LITTLE TOO CORNY FOR ENKA.

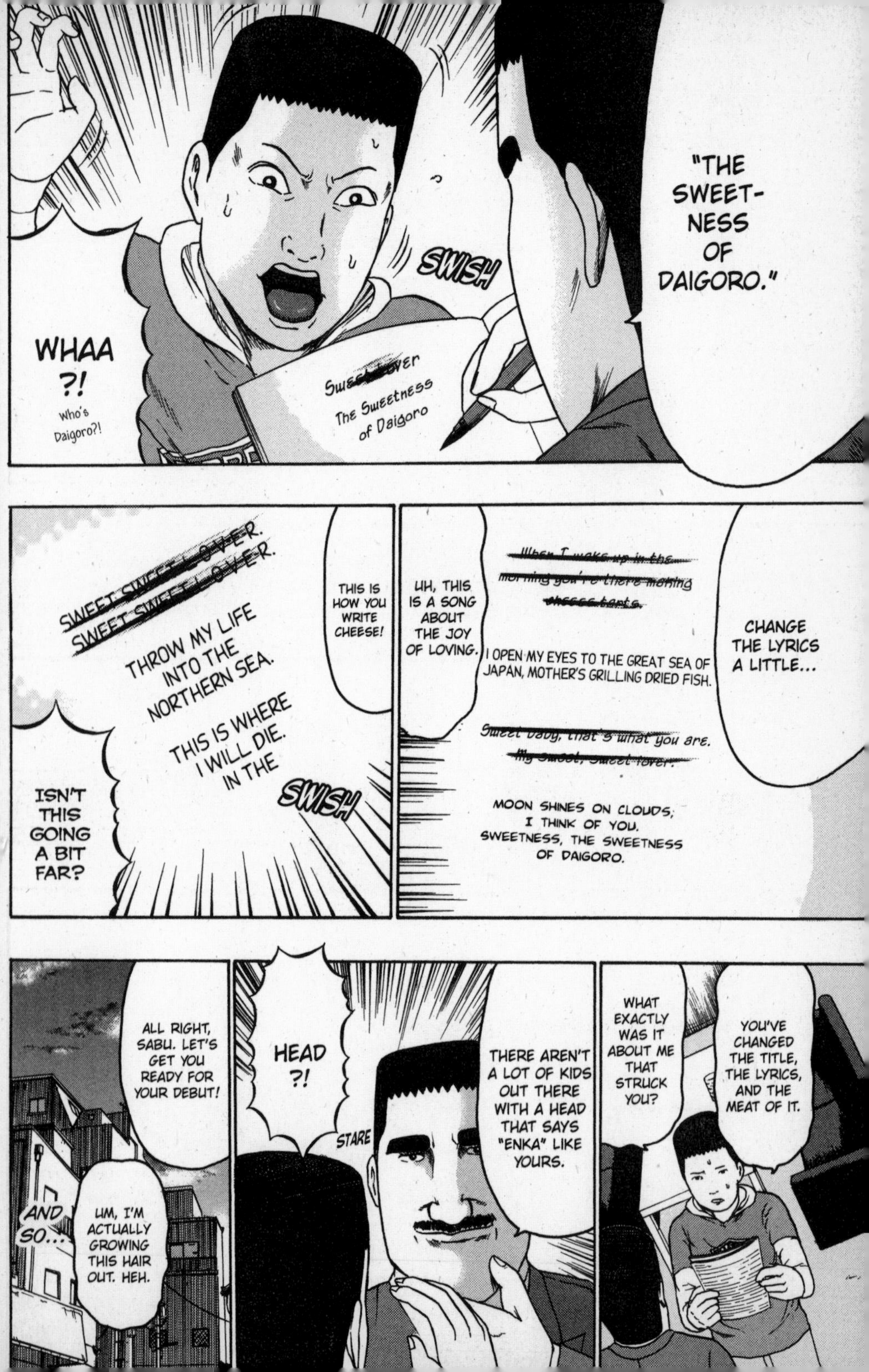
"THE SWEETNESS OF DAIGORO."
SWISH
WHAA?!
Who's Daigoro?!
The Sweetness of Daigoro
CHANGE THE LYRICS A LITTLE...
When I wake up in the morning you're there making cheese tarts.
I OPEN MY EYES TO THE GREAT SEA OF JAPAN, MOTHER'S GRILLING DRIED FISH.
Sweet baby, that's what you are. My Sweet, Sweet lover.
MOON SHINES ON CLOUDS, I THINK OF YOU. SWEETNESS, THE SWEETNESS OF DAIGORO.
UH, THIS IS A SONG ABOUT THE JOY OF LOVING.
THIS IS HOW YOU WRITE CHEESE!
SWEET SWEET LOVER. SWEET SWEET LOVER.
THROW MY LIFE INTO THE NORTHERN SEA.
THIS IS WHERE I WILL DIE. IN THE
SWISH
ISN'T THIS GOING A BIT FAR?
YOU'VE CHANGED THE TITLE, THE LYRICS, AND THE MEAT OF IT.
WHAT EXACTLY WAS IT ABOUT ME THAT STRUCK YOU?
THERE AREN'T A LOT OF KIDS OUT THERE WITH A HEAD THAT SAYS "ENKA" LIKE YOURS.
HEAD?!
STARE
ALL RIGHT, SABU. LET'S GET YOU READY FOR YOUR DEBUT!
UM, I'M ACTUALLY GROWING THIS HAIR OUT. HEH.
AND SO...

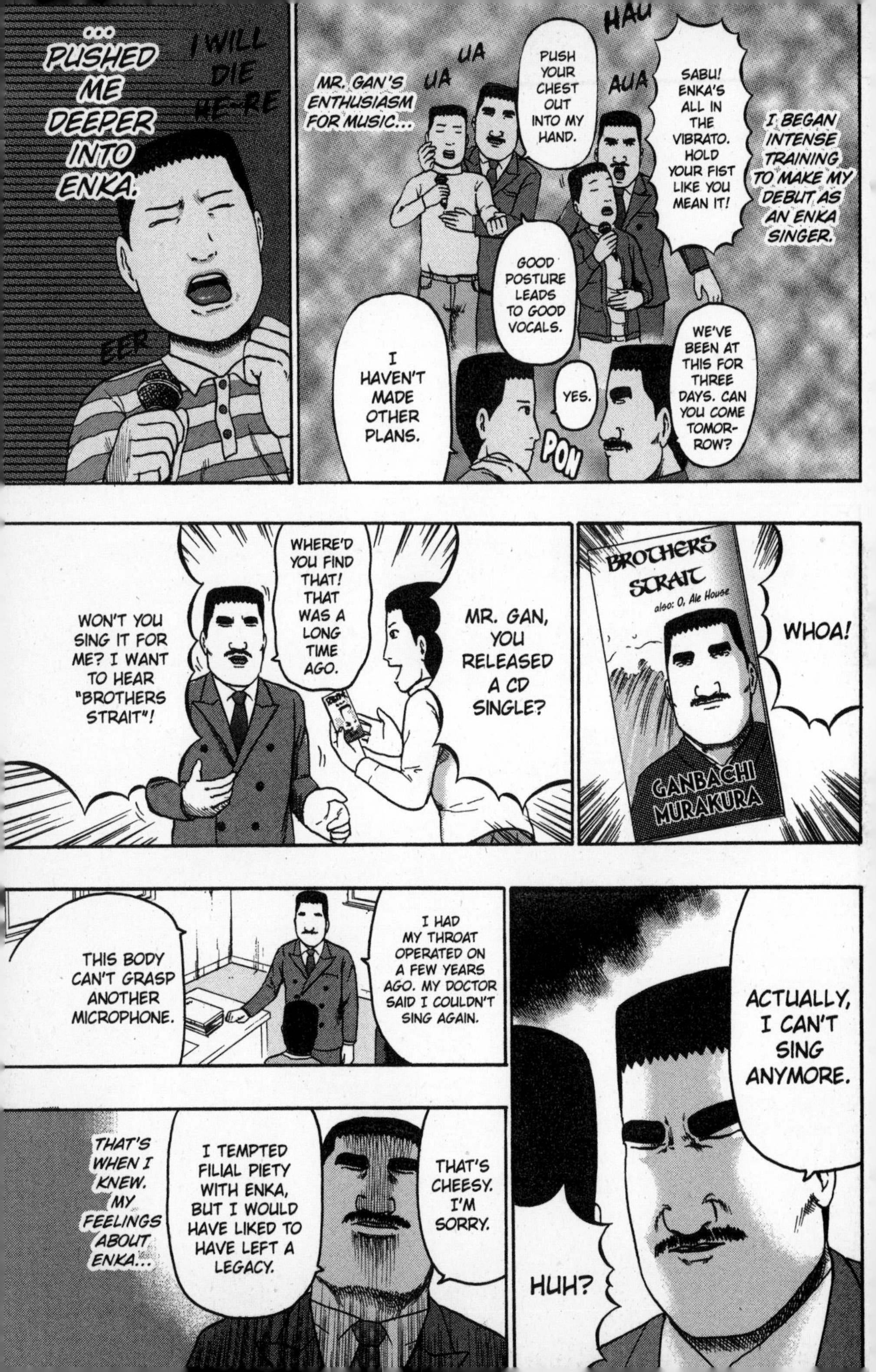
I BEGAN INTENSE TRAINING TO MAKE MY DEBUT AS AN ENKA SINGER.
SABU! ENKA'S ALL IN THE VIBRATO. HOLD YOUR FIST LIKE YOU MEAN IT!
HAU
AUA
PUSH YOUR CHEST OUT INTO MY HAND.
UA
UA
MR. GAN'S ENTHUSIASM FOR MUSIC...
GOOD POSTURE LEADS TO GOOD VOCALS.
WE'VE BEEN AT THIS FOR THREE DAYS. CAN YOU COME TOMORROW?
YES.
PON
I HAVEN'T MADE OTHER PLANS.
I WILL DIE HE-RE
...PUSHED ME DEEPER INTO ENKA.
EER
WHOA!
BROTHERS STRAIT
also: O, Ale House
GANBACHI MURAKURA
MR. GAN, YOU RELEASED A CD SINGLE?
WHERE'D YOU FIND THAT! THAT WAS A LONG TIME AGO.
WON'T YOU SING IT FOR ME? I WANT TO HEAR "BROTHERS STRAIT"!
ACTUALLY, I CAN'T SING ANYMORE.
HUH?
I HAD MY THROAT OPERATED ON A FEW YEARS AGO. MY DOCTOR SAID I COULDN'T SING AGAIN.
THIS BODY CAN'T GRASP ANOTHER MICROPHONE.
THAT'S CHEESY. I'M SORRY.
I TEMPTED FILIAL PIETY WITH ENKA, BUT I WOULD HAVE LIKED TO HAVE LEFT A LEGACY.
THAT'S WHEN I KNEW. MY FEELINGS ABOUT ENKA...

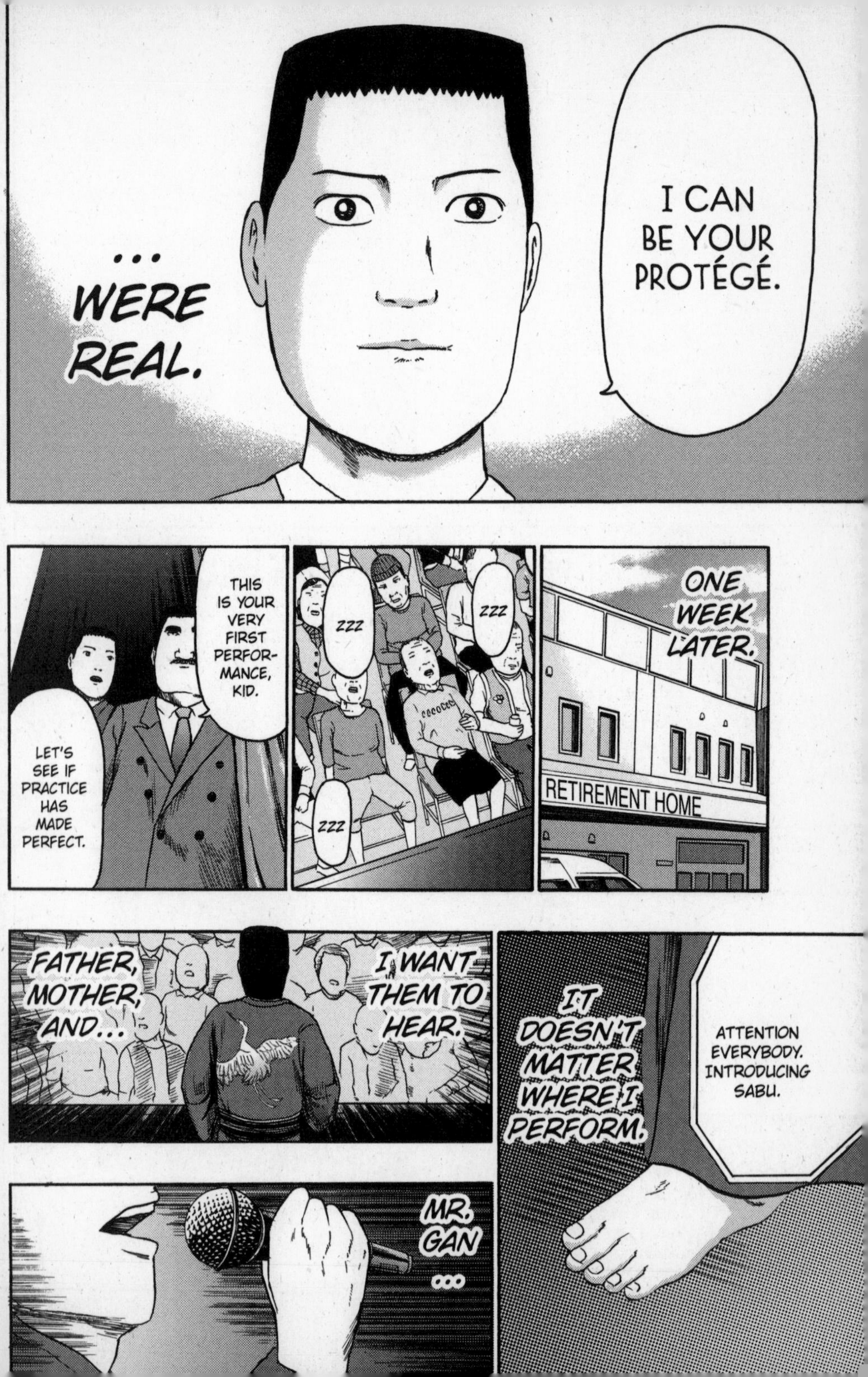
I CAN BE YOUR PROTÉGÉ.
... WERE REAL.
ONE WEEK LATER.
RETIREMENT HOME
ZZZ
ZZZ
ZZZ
THIS IS YOUR VERY FIRST PERFORMANCE, KID.
LET'S SEE IF PRACTICE HAS MADE PERFECT.
ATTENTION EVERYBODY. INTRODUCING SABU.
IT DOESN'T MATTER WHERE I PERFORM.
I WANT THEM TO HEAR.
FATHER, MOTHER, AND...
MR. GAN ...

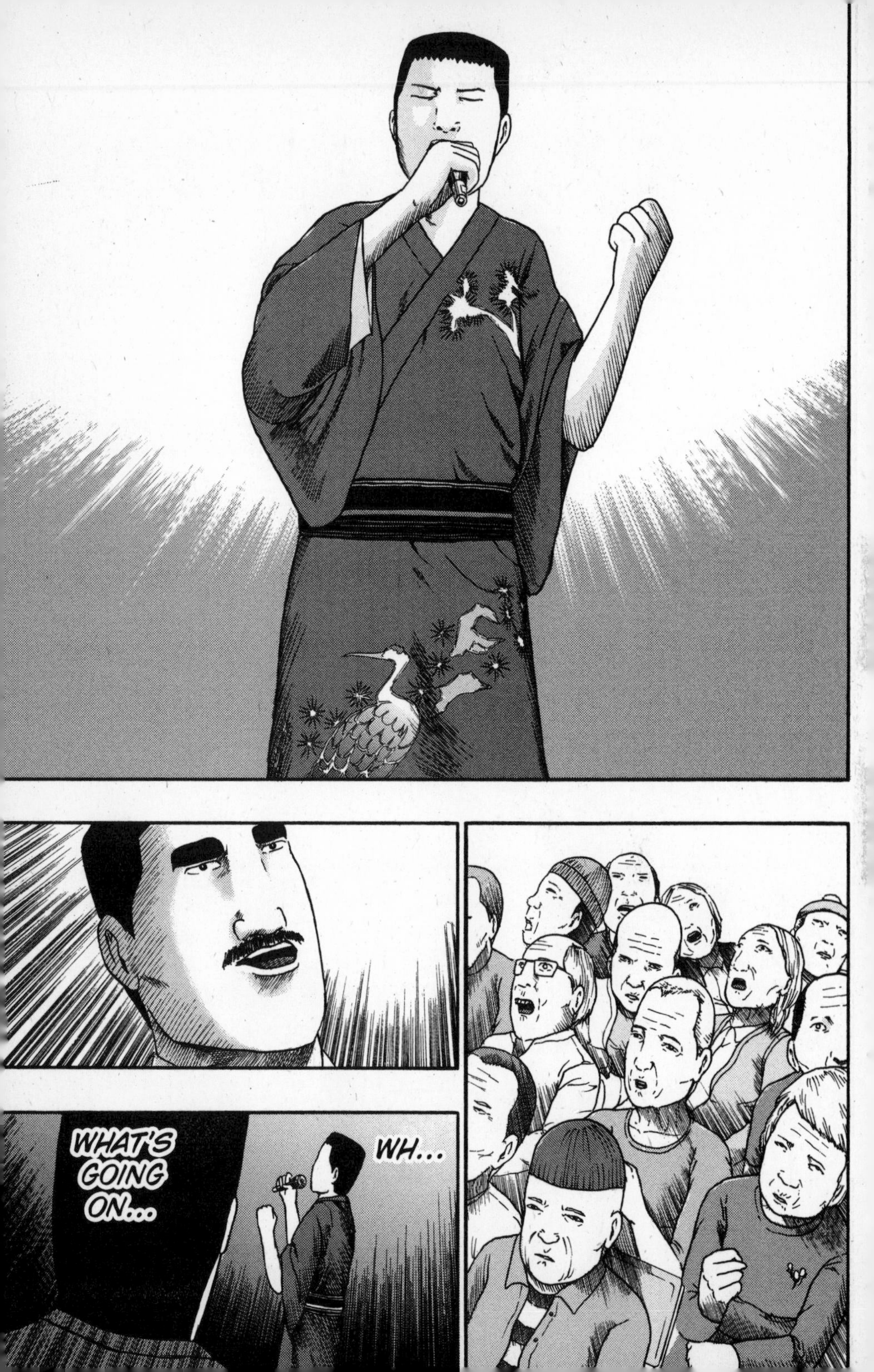
WH...
WHAT'S GOING ON...

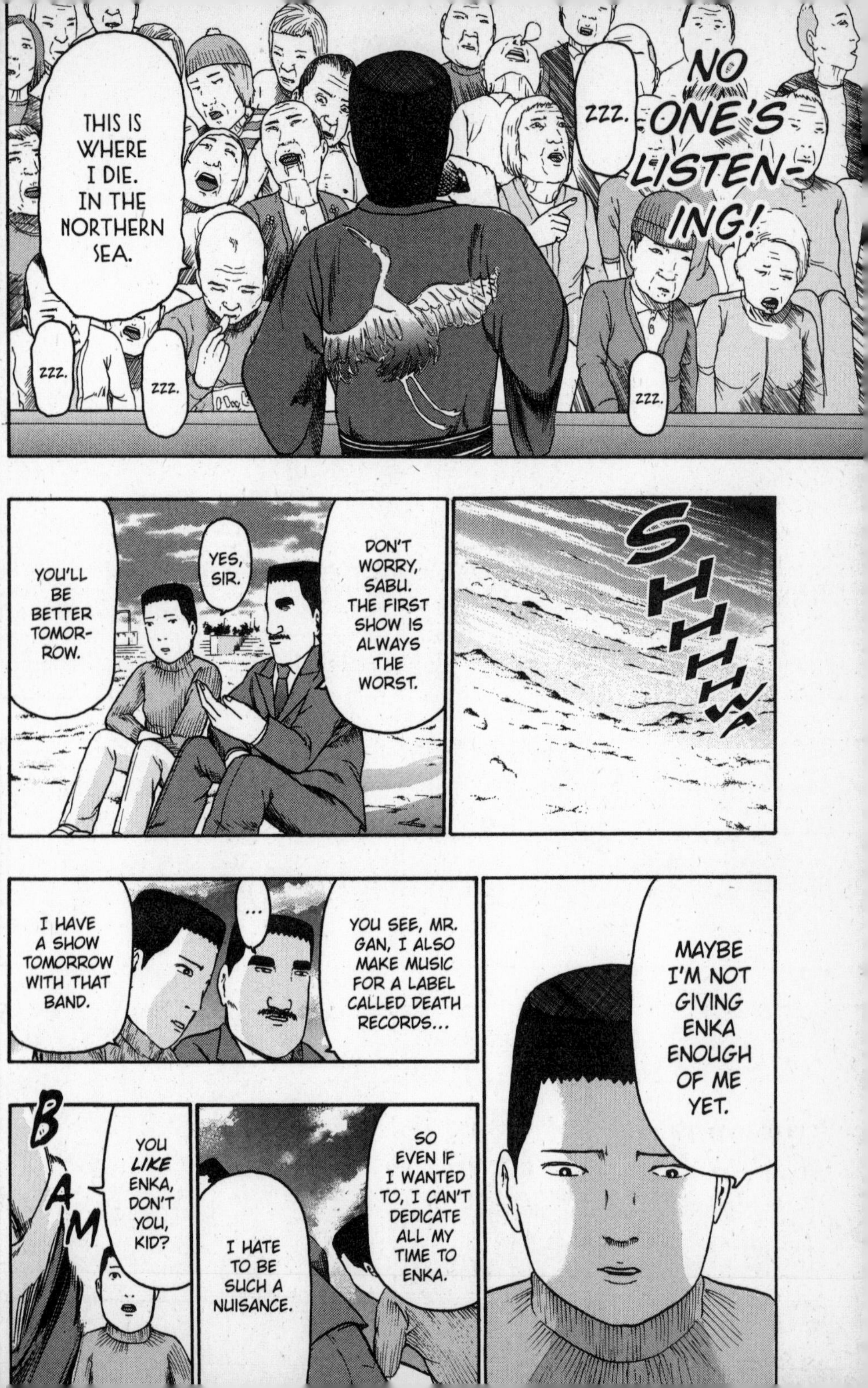
NO ONE'S LISTEN-ING!
ZZZ.
ZZZ.
THIS IS WHERE I DIE. IN THE NORTHERN SEA.
ZZZ.
ZZZ.
SHHHWA
DON'T WORRY, SABU. THE FIRST SHOW IS ALWAYS THE WORST.
YES, SIR.
YOU'LL BE BETTER TOMOR-ROW.
MAYBE I'M NOT GIVING ENKA ENOUGH OF ME YET.
YOU SEE, MR. GAN, I ALSO MAKE MUSIC FOR A LABEL CALLED DEATH RECORDS...
...
I HAVE A SHOW TOMORROW WITH THAT BAND.
SO EVEN IF I WANTED TO, I CAN'T DEDICATE ALL MY TIME TO ENKA.
I HATE TO BE SUCH A NUISANCE.
BAM
YOU *LIKE* ENKA, DON'T YOU, KID?

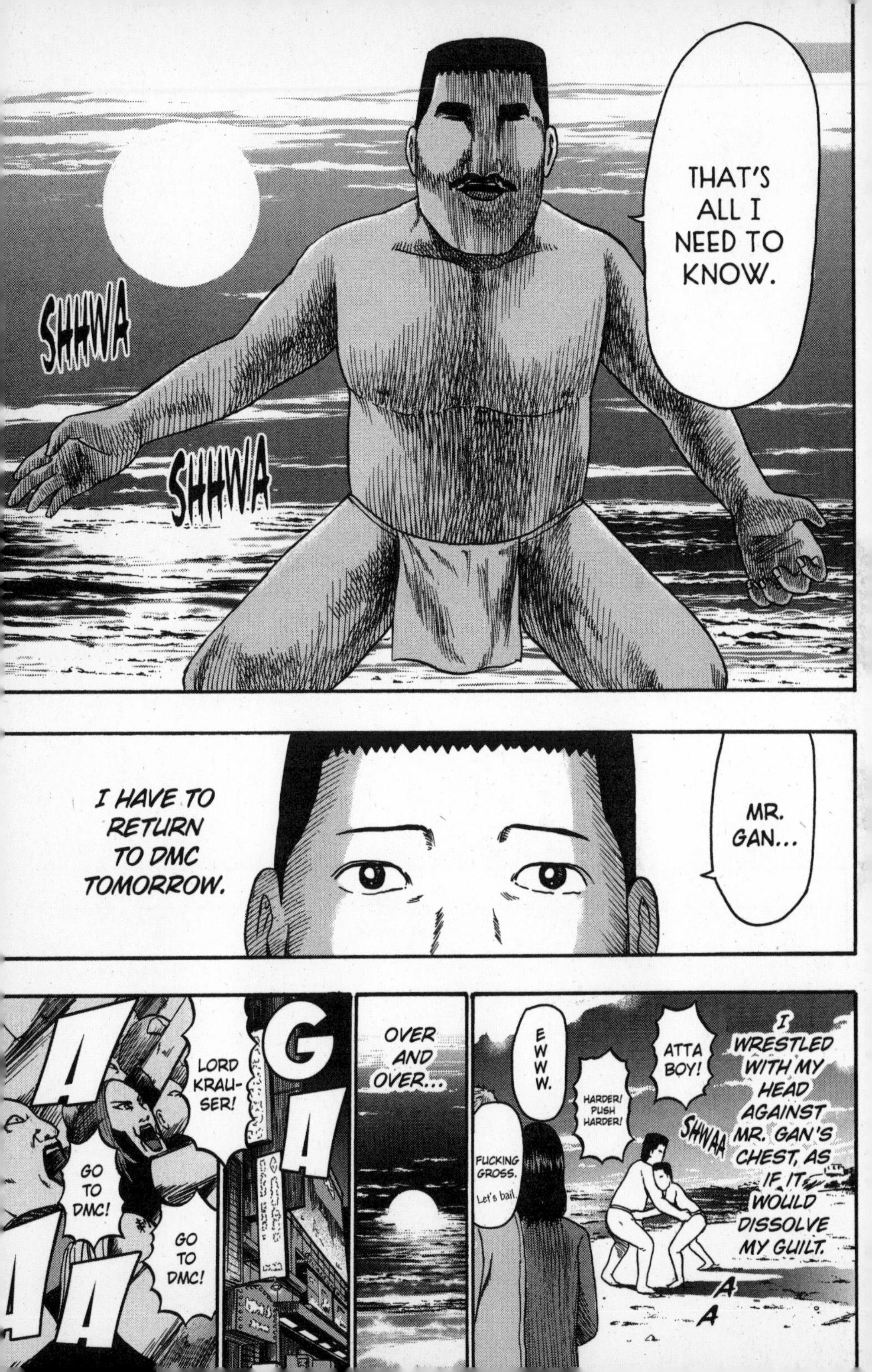
THAT'S ALL I NEED TO KNOW.
SHHWA
SHHWA
MR. GAN...
I HAVE TO RETURN TO DMC TOMORROW.
I WRESTLED WITH MY HEAD AGAINST MR. GAN'S CHEST, AS IF IT WOULD DISSOLVE MY GUILT.
ATTA BOY!
EWWW.
HARDER! PUSH HARDER!
SHWAA
FUCKING GROSS.
Let's bail.
A
A
OVER AND OVER...
G
A
LORD KRAUSER!
A
GO TO DMC!
GO TO DMC!
A
A

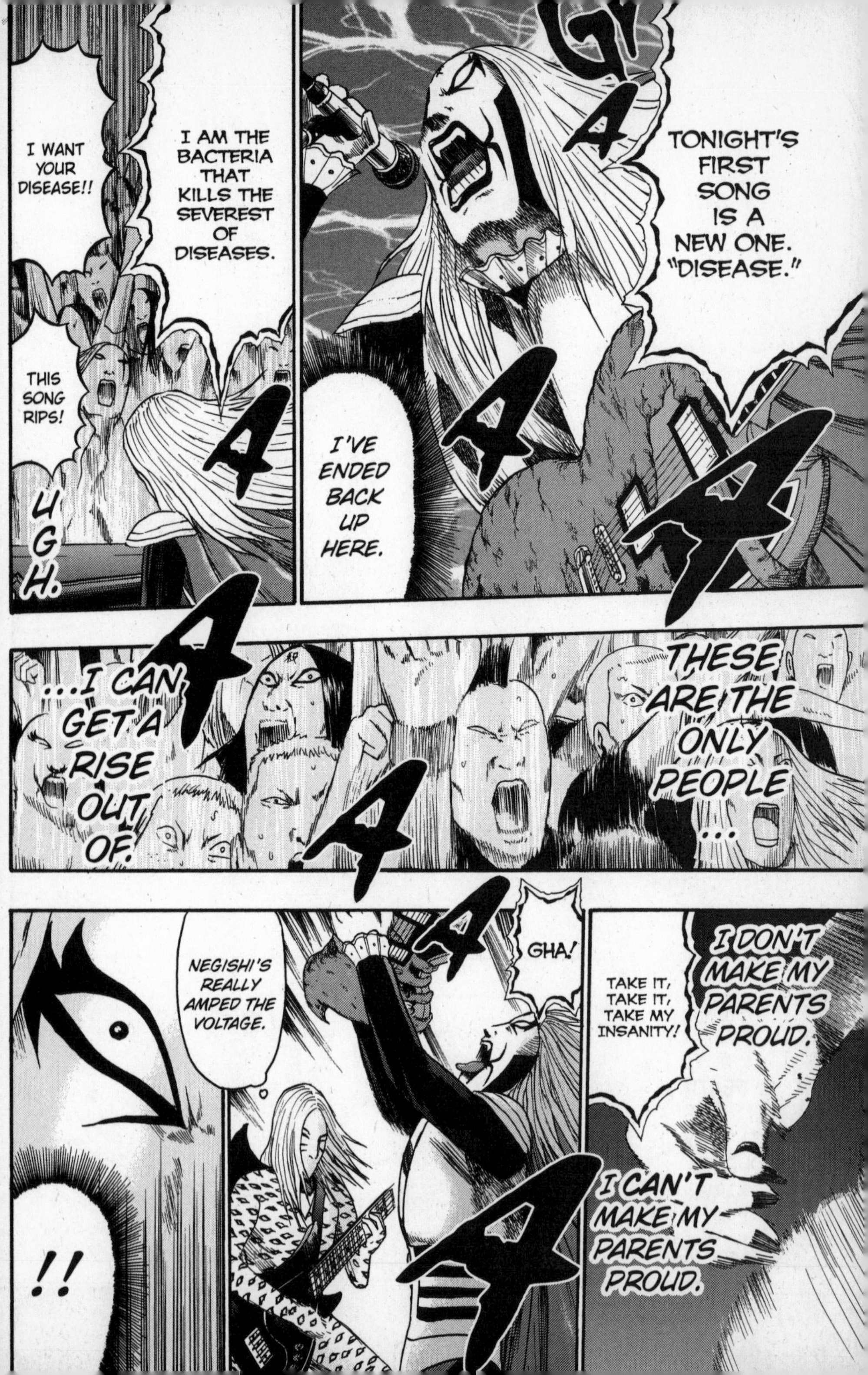
GYAAAA
TONIGHT'S FIRST SONG IS A NEW ONE. "DISEASE."
I'VE ENDED BACK UP HERE.
I AM THE BACTERIA THAT KILLS THE SEVEREST OF DISEASES.
I WANT YOUR DISEASE!!
THIS SONG RIPS!
UGH.
A
THESE ARE THE ONLY PEOPLE...
...I CAN GET A RISE OUT OF.
A
I DON'T MAKE MY PARENTS PROUD.
TAKE IT, TAKE IT, TAKE MY INSANITY!
I CAN'T MAKE MY PARENTS PROUD.
GHA!
A
NEGISHI'S REALLY AMPED THE VOLTAGE.
!!

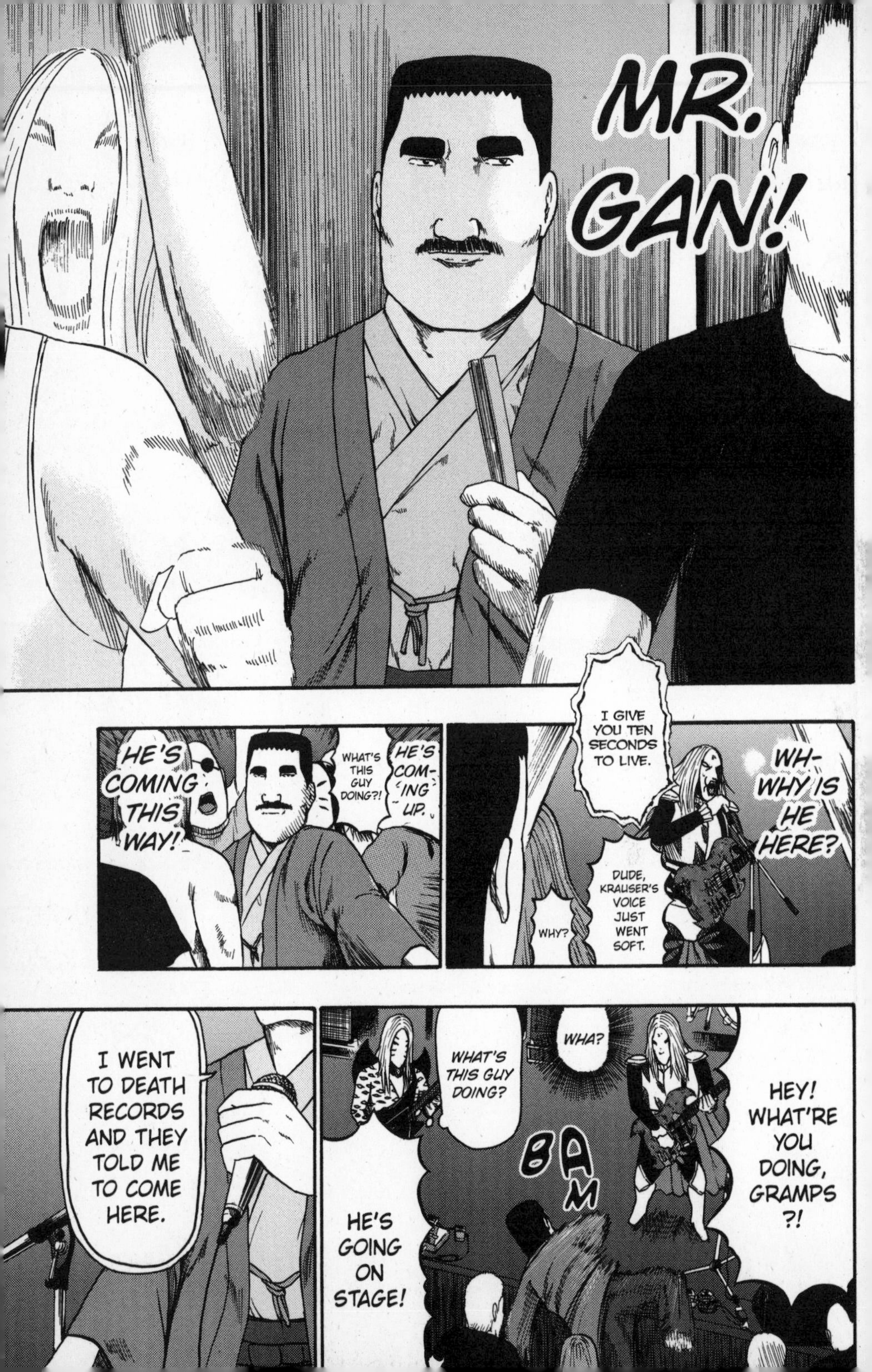
MR. GAN!
I GIVE YOU TEN SECONDS TO LIVE.
WH- WHY IS HE HERE?
DUDE, KRAUSER'S VOICE JUST WENT SOFT.
WHY?
HE'S COM-ING UP.
WHAT'S THIS GUY DOING?!
HE'S COMING THIS WAY!
WHA?
HEY! WHAT'RE YOU DOING, GRAMPS?!
WHAT'S THIS GUY DOING?
BAM
HE'S GOING ON STAGE!
I WENT TO DEATH RECORDS AND THEY TOLD ME TO COME HERE.

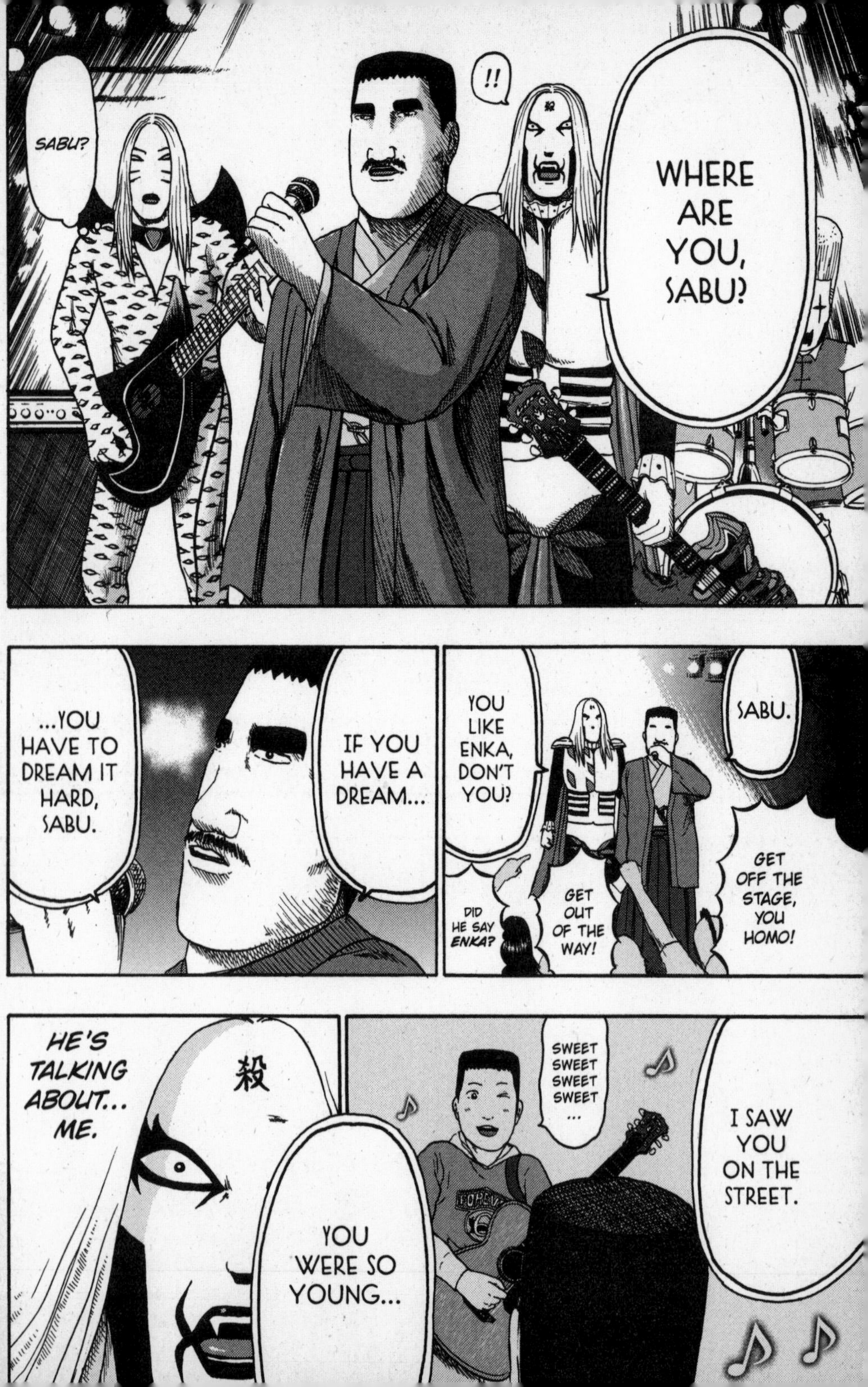
WHERE ARE YOU, SABU?
!!
SABU?
SABU.
YOU LIKE ENKA, DON'T YOU?
GET OFF THE STAGE, YOU HOMO!
GET OUT OF THE WAY!
DID HE SAY *ENKA*?
IF YOU HAVE A DREAM...
...YOU HAVE TO DREAM IT HARD, SABU.
I SAW YOU ON THE STREET.
SWEET SWEET SWEET SWEET ...
YOU WERE SO YOUNG...
HE'S TALKING ABOUT... ME.
殺

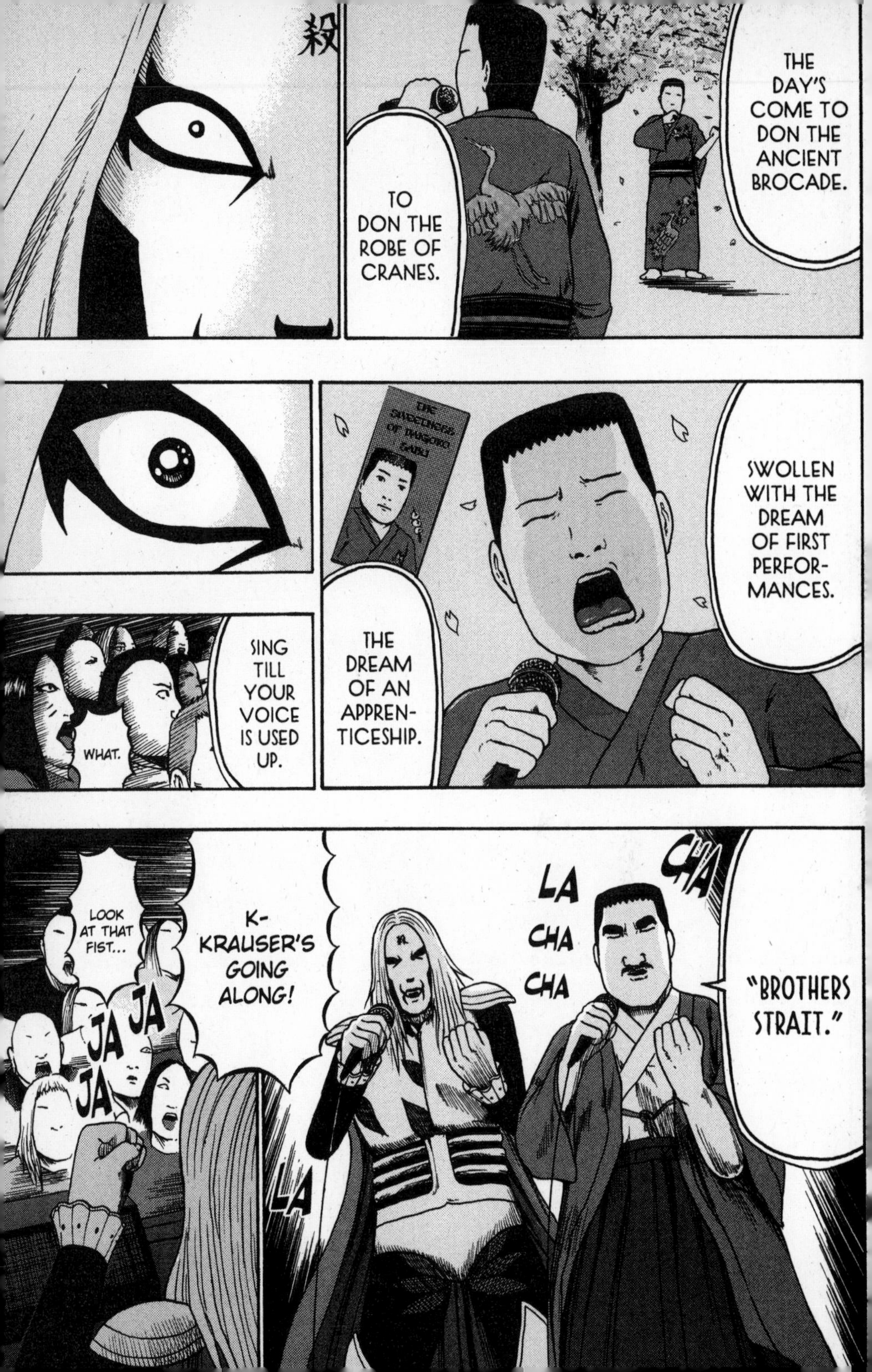
THE DAY'S COME TO DON THE ANCIENT BROCADE.
TO DON THE ROBE OF CRANES.
殺
SWOLLEN WITH THE DREAM OF FIRST PERFORMANCES.
THE DREAM OF AN APPRENTICESHIP.
SING TILL YOUR VOICE IS USED UP.
WHAT.
"BROTHERS STRAIT."
CHA
LA CHA CHA
K-KRAUSER'S GOING ALONG!
LOOK AT THAT FIST...
JA JA JA JA
LA

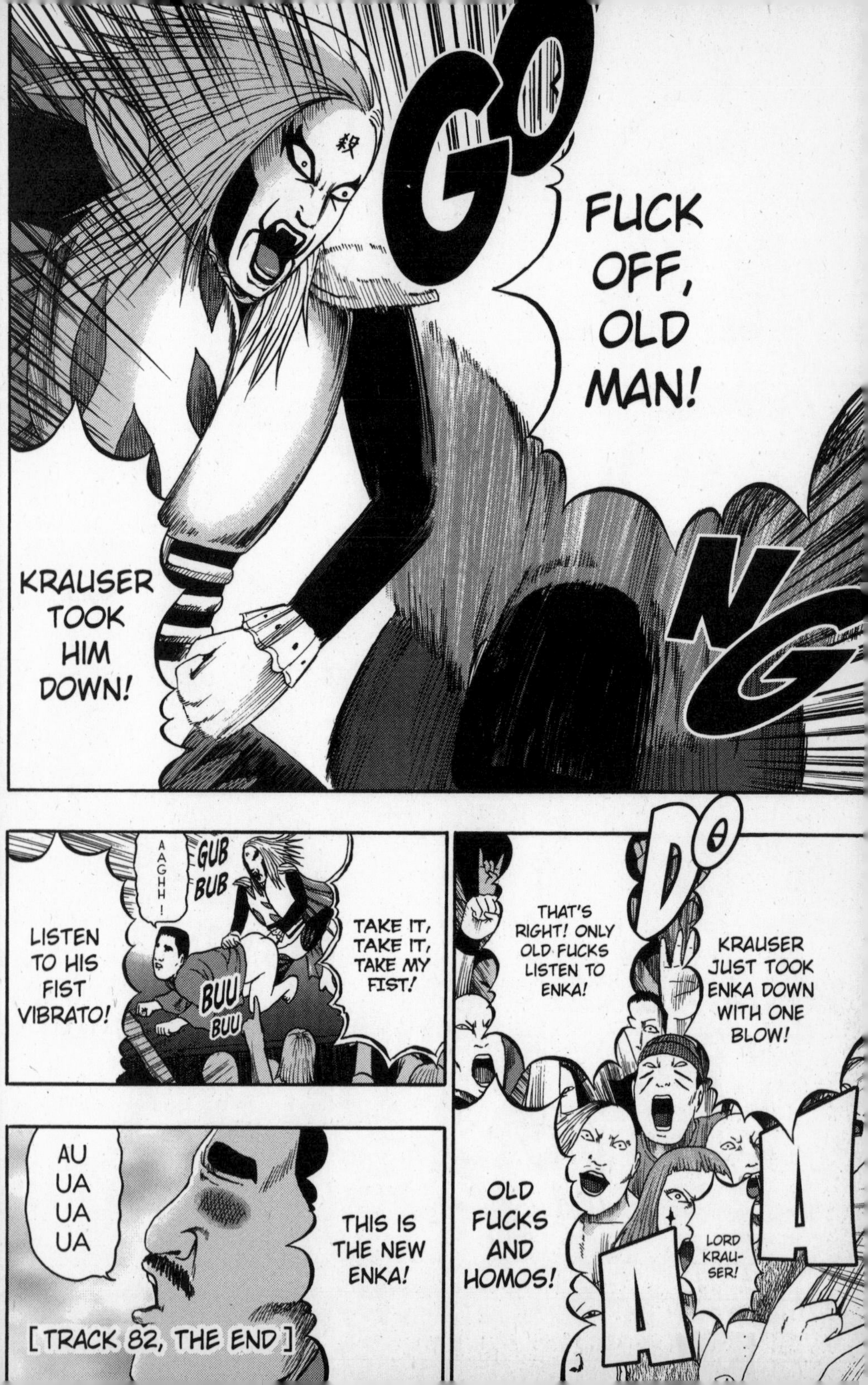
GO
FUCK OFF, OLD MAN!
NG
KRAUSER TOOK HIM DOWN!
D
KRAUSER JUST TOOK ENKA DOWN WITH ONE BLOW!
THAT'S RIGHT! ONLY OLD FUCKS LISTEN TO ENKA!
AAA
LORD KRAUSER!
OLD FUCKS AND HOMOS!
TAKE IT, TAKE IT, TAKE MY FIST!
GUB BUB
AAGHH!
BUU BUU
LISTEN TO HIS FIST VIBRATO!
THIS IS THE NEW ENKA!
AU UA UA UA
[TRACK 82, THE END]

DMC LEXICON
FIST VIBRATO

A singing maneuver unique to enka, used in order to embellish melodies that are not written in the song. Enka singers are notorious for raising a fist when singing, but while fisting and vibrating help enhance feeling, the two actions are totally unrelated.

Usage: You don't know the difference between Fisting and Fisting Vibrato? Tch. Kids these days

デトロイト・メタル・シティ

Detroit Metal city

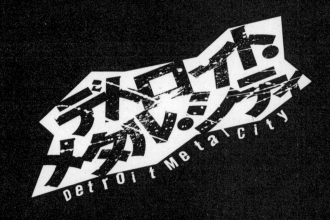

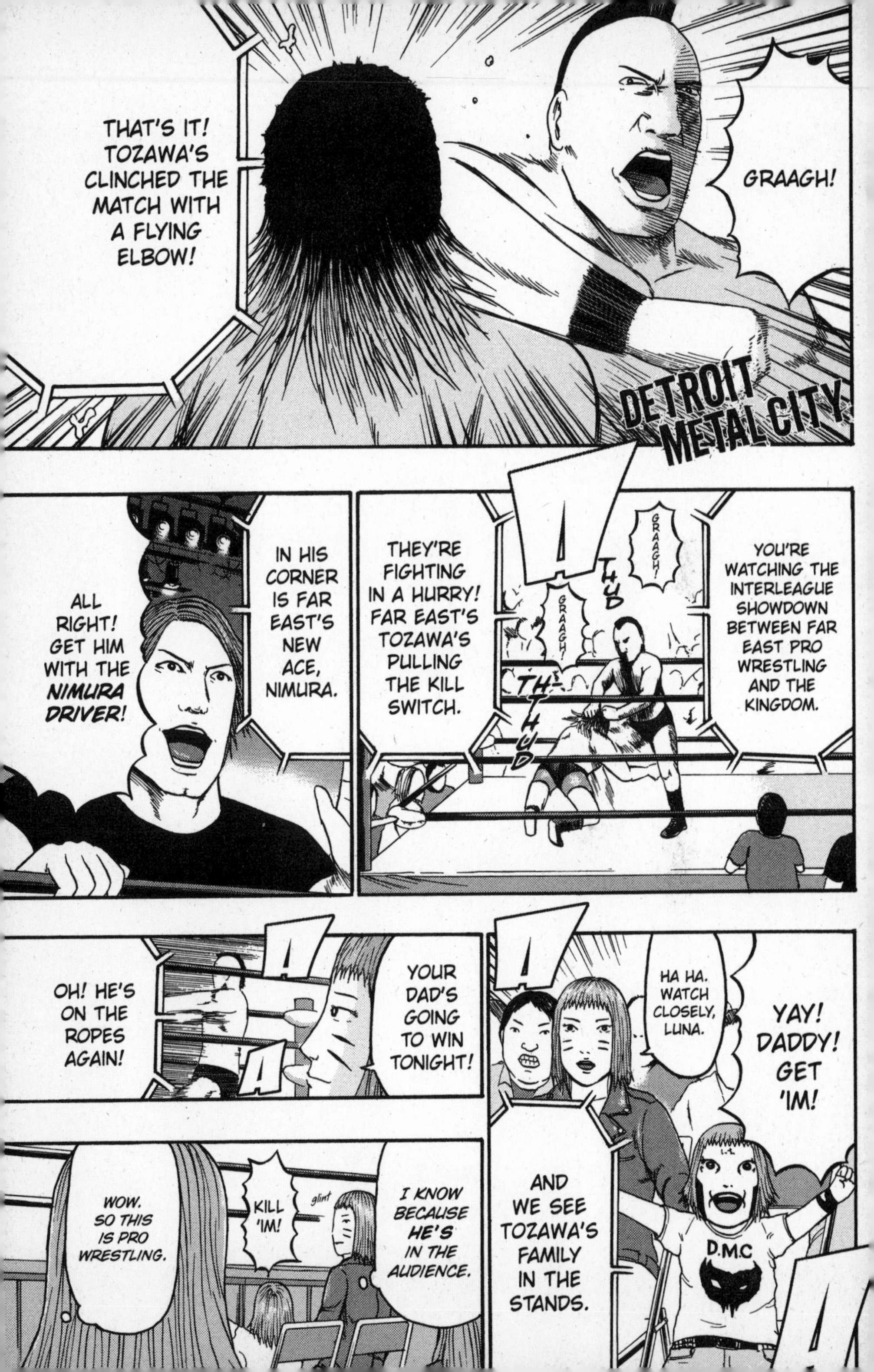

GRAAGH!
THAT'S IT! TOZAWA'S CLINCHED THE MATCH WITH A FLYING ELBOW!
DETROIT METAL CITY
YOU'RE WATCHING THE INTERLEAGUE SHOWDOWN BETWEEN FAR EAST PRO WRESTLING AND THE KINGDOM.
GRAAGH!
GRAAGH!
THUD
TH-THUD
THEY'RE FIGHTING IN A HURRY! FAR EAST'S TOZAWA'S PULLING THE KILL SWITCH.
IN HIS CORNER IS FAR EAST'S NEW ACE, NIMURA.
ALL RIGHT! GET HIM WITH THE *NIMURA DRIVER*!
YAY! DADDY! GET 'IM!
HA HA. WATCH CLOSELY, LUNA.
YOUR DAD'S GOING TO WIN TONIGHT!
OH! HE'S ON THE ROPES AGAIN!
D.M.C
AND WE SEE TOZAWA'S FAMILY IN THE STANDS.
*I KNOW BECAUSE **HE'S** IN THE AUDIENCE.*
glint
KILL 'IM!
WOW. SO THIS IS PRO WRESTLING.

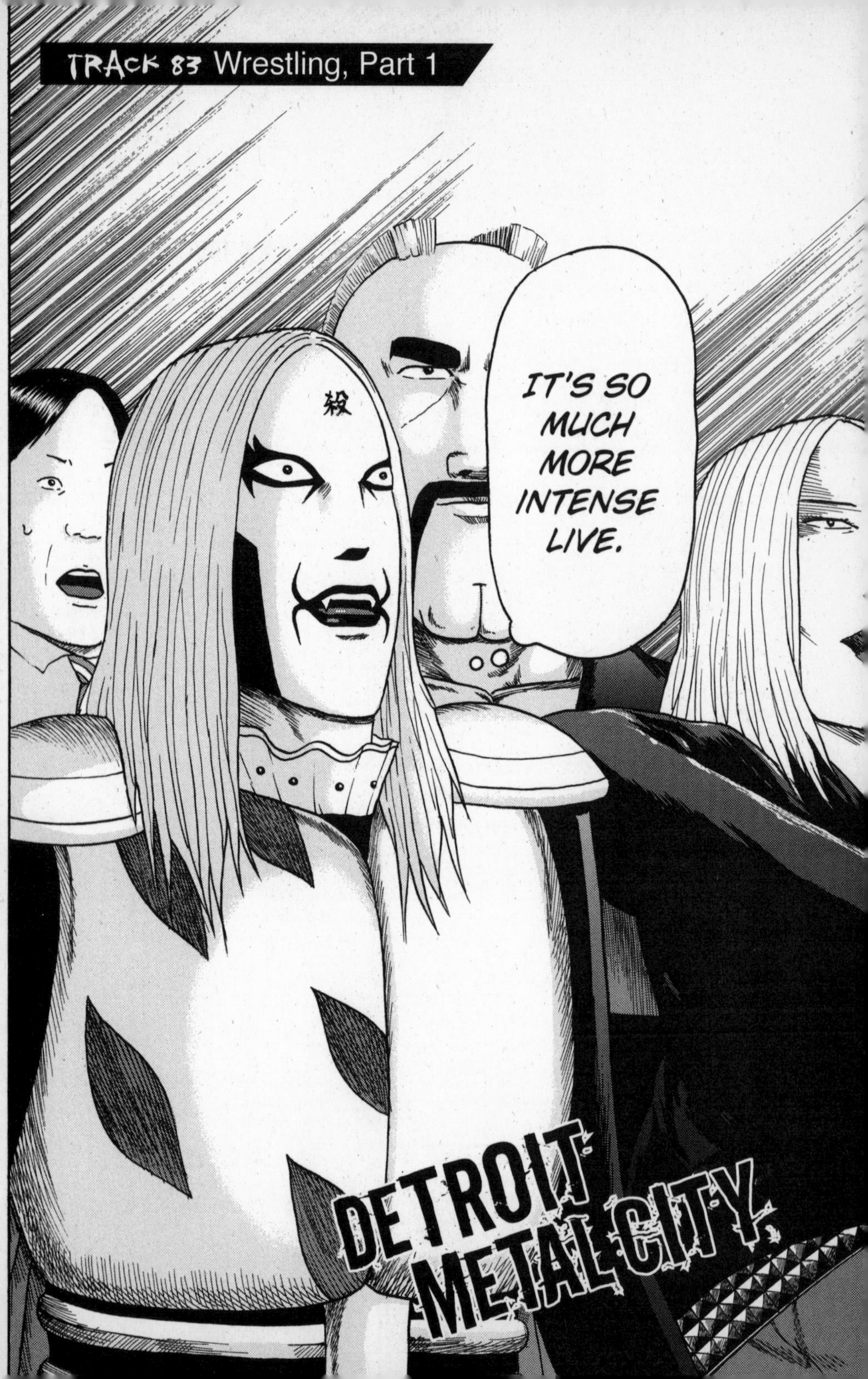
TRACK 83 Wrestling, Part 1
IT'S SO MUCH MORE INTENSE LIVE.
殺
DETROIT METAL CITY

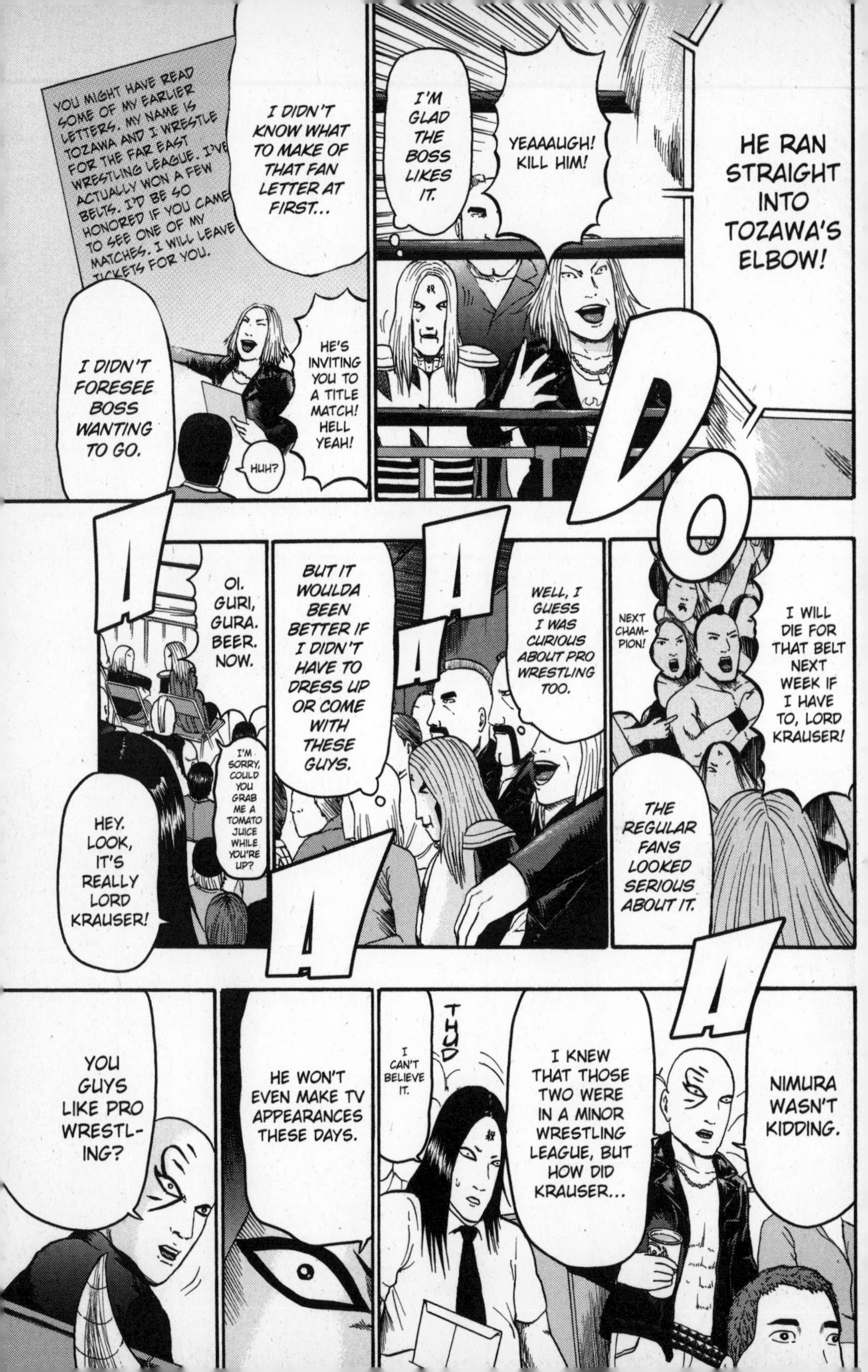
HE RAN STRAIGHT INTO TOZAWA'S ELBOW!
YEAAAUGH! KILL HIM!
I'M GLAD THE BOSS LIKES IT.
YOU MIGHT HAVE READ SOME OF MY EARLIER LETTERS. MY NAME IS TOZAWA AND I WRESTLE FOR THE FAR EAST WRESTLING LEAGUE. I'VE ACTUALLY WON A FEW BELTS. I'D BE SO HONORED IF YOU CAME TO SEE ONE OF MY MATCHES. I WILL LEAVE TICKETS FOR YOU.
I DIDN'T KNOW WHAT TO MAKE OF THAT FAN LETTER AT FIRST...
HE'S INVITING YOU TO A TITLE MATCH! HELL YEAH!
HUH?
I DIDN'T FORESEE BOSS WANTING TO GO.
DO
I WILL DIE FOR THAT BELT NEXT WEEK IF I HAVE TO, LORD KRAUSER!
NEXT CHAMPION!
THE REGULAR FANS LOOKED SERIOUS ABOUT IT.
WELL, I GUESS I WAS CURIOUS ABOUT PRO WRESTLING TOO.
BUT IT WOULDA BEEN BETTER IF I DIDN'T HAVE TO DRESS UP OR COME WITH THESE GUYS.
A
A
OI. GURI, GURA. BEER. NOW.
I'M SORRY, COULD YOU GRAB ME A TOMATO JUICE WHILE YOU'RE UP?
HEY. LOOK, IT'S REALLY LORD KRAUSER!
A
A
A
NIMURA WASN'T KIDDING.
I KNEW THAT THOSE TWO WERE IN A MINOR WRESTLING LEAGUE, BUT HOW DID KRAUSER...
THUD
I CAN'T BELIEVE IT.
HE WON'T EVEN MAKE TV APPEARANCES THESE DAYS.
YOU GUYS LIKE PRO WRESTLING?

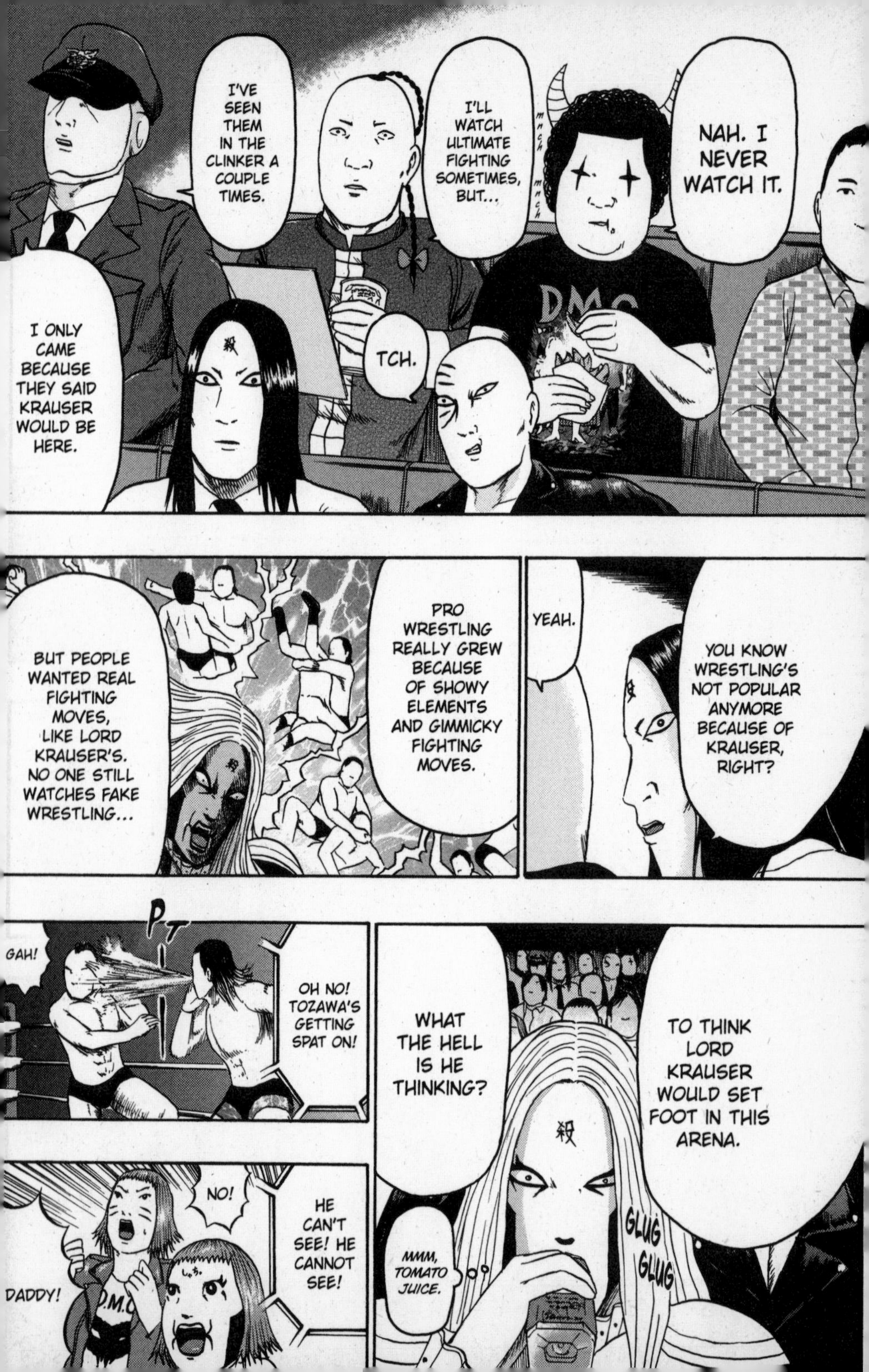
NAH. I NEVER WATCH IT.
mnch mnch
I'LL WATCH ULTIMATE FIGHTING SOMETIMES, BUT...
I'VE SEEN THEM IN THE CLINKER A COUPLE TIMES.
TCH.
I ONLY CAME BECAUSE THEY SAID KRAUSER WOULD BE HERE.
YOU KNOW WRESTLING'S NOT POPULAR ANYMORE BECAUSE OF KRAUSER, RIGHT?
YEAH.
PRO WRESTLING REALLY GREW BECAUSE OF SHOWY ELEMENTS AND GIMMICKY FIGHTING MOVES.
BUT PEOPLE WANTED REAL FIGHTING MOVES, LIKE LORD KRAUSER'S. NO ONE STILL WATCHES FAKE WRESTLING...
TO THINK LORD KRAUSER WOULD SET FOOT IN THIS ARENA.
WHAT THE HELL IS HE THINKING?
GLUG GLUG
MMM, TOMATO JUICE.
PT
OH NO! TOZAWA'S GETTING SPAT ON!
GAH!
HE CAN'T SEE! HE CANNOT SEE!
NO!
DADDY!

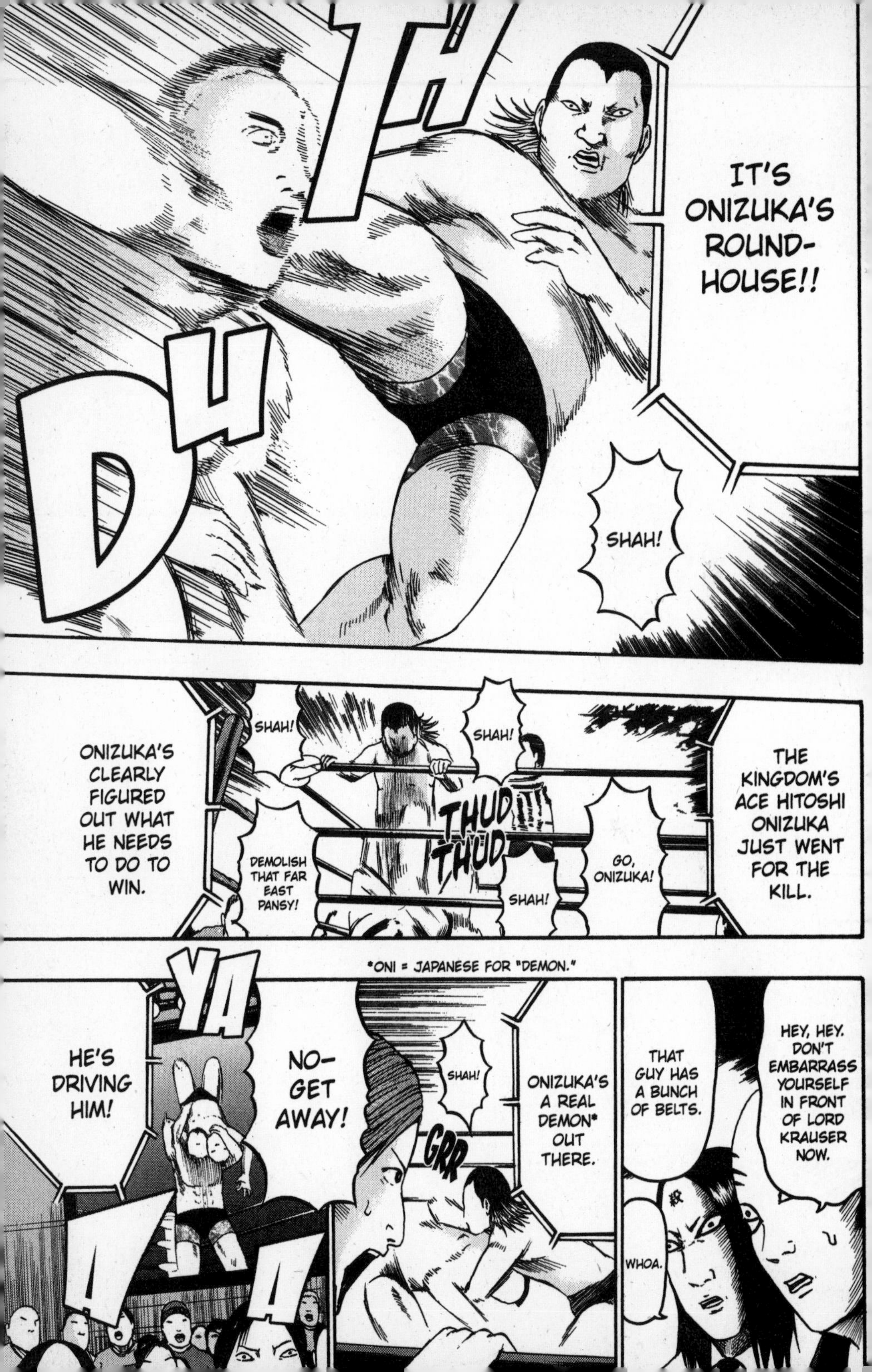
IT'S ONIZUKA'S ROUND-HOUSE!!
TH
UD
SHAH!
THE KINGDOM'S ACE HITOSHI ONIZUKA JUST WENT FOR THE KILL.
GO, ONIZUKA!
SHAH!
SHAH!
THUD THUD
SHAH!
DEMOLISH THAT FAR EAST PANSY!
ONIZUKA'S CLEARLY FIGURED OUT WHAT HE NEEDS TO DO TO WIN.
*ONI = JAPANESE FOR "DEMON."
HEY, HEY. DON'T EMBARRASS YOURSELF IN FRONT OF LORD KRAUSER NOW.
THAT GUY HAS A BUNCH OF BELTS.
WHOA.
ONIZUKA'S A REAL DEMON* OUT THERE.
SHAH!
GRR
NO– GET AWAY!
HE'S DRIVING HIM!
YA
A
A

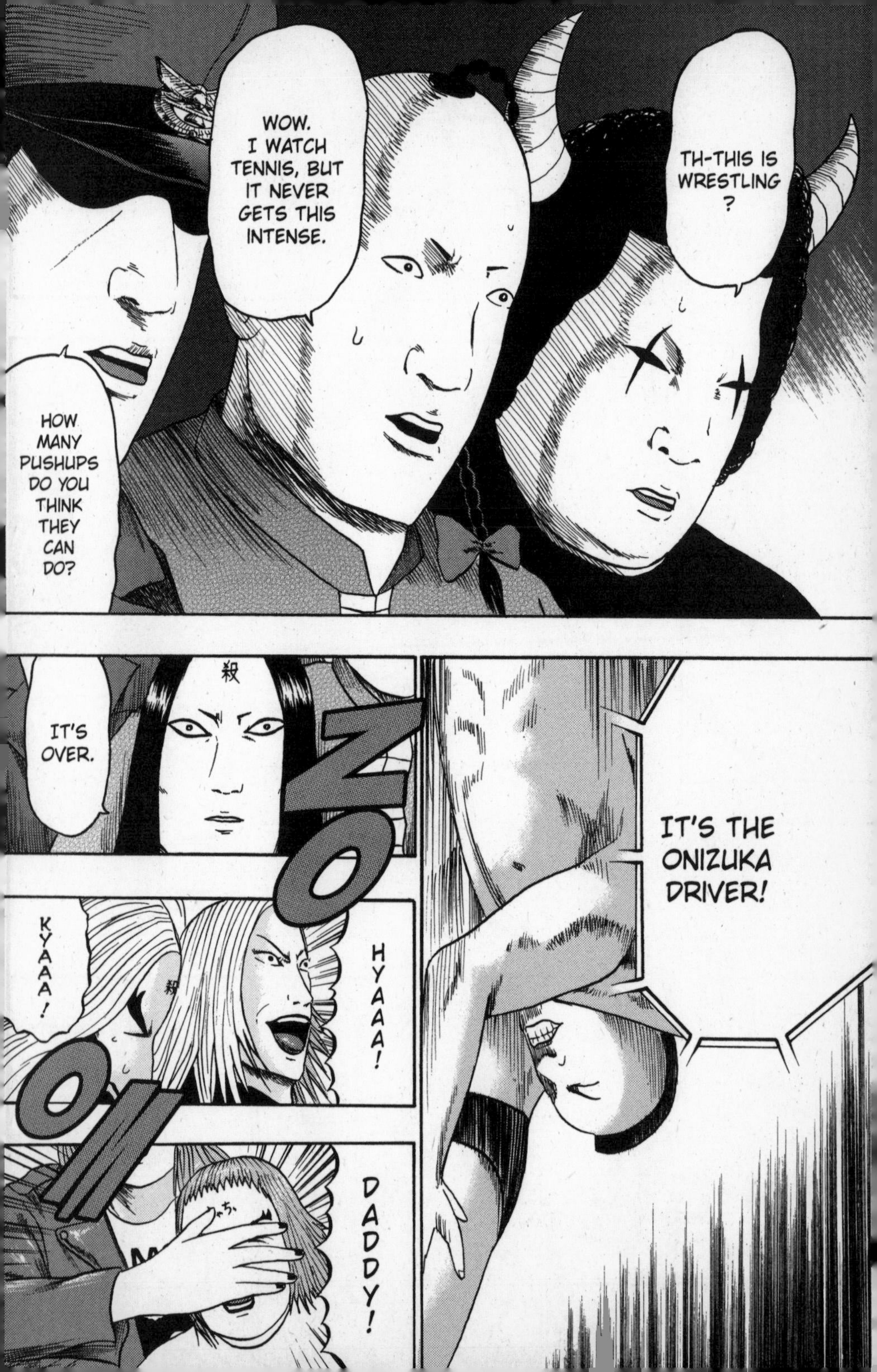
TH-THIS IS WRESTLING ?
WOW. I WATCH TENNIS, BUT IT NEVER GETS THIS INTENSE.
HOW MANY PUSHUPS DO YOU THINK THEY CAN DO?
IT'S THE ONIZUKA DRIVER!
IT'S OVER.
HYAAAA!
KYAAA!
DADDY!

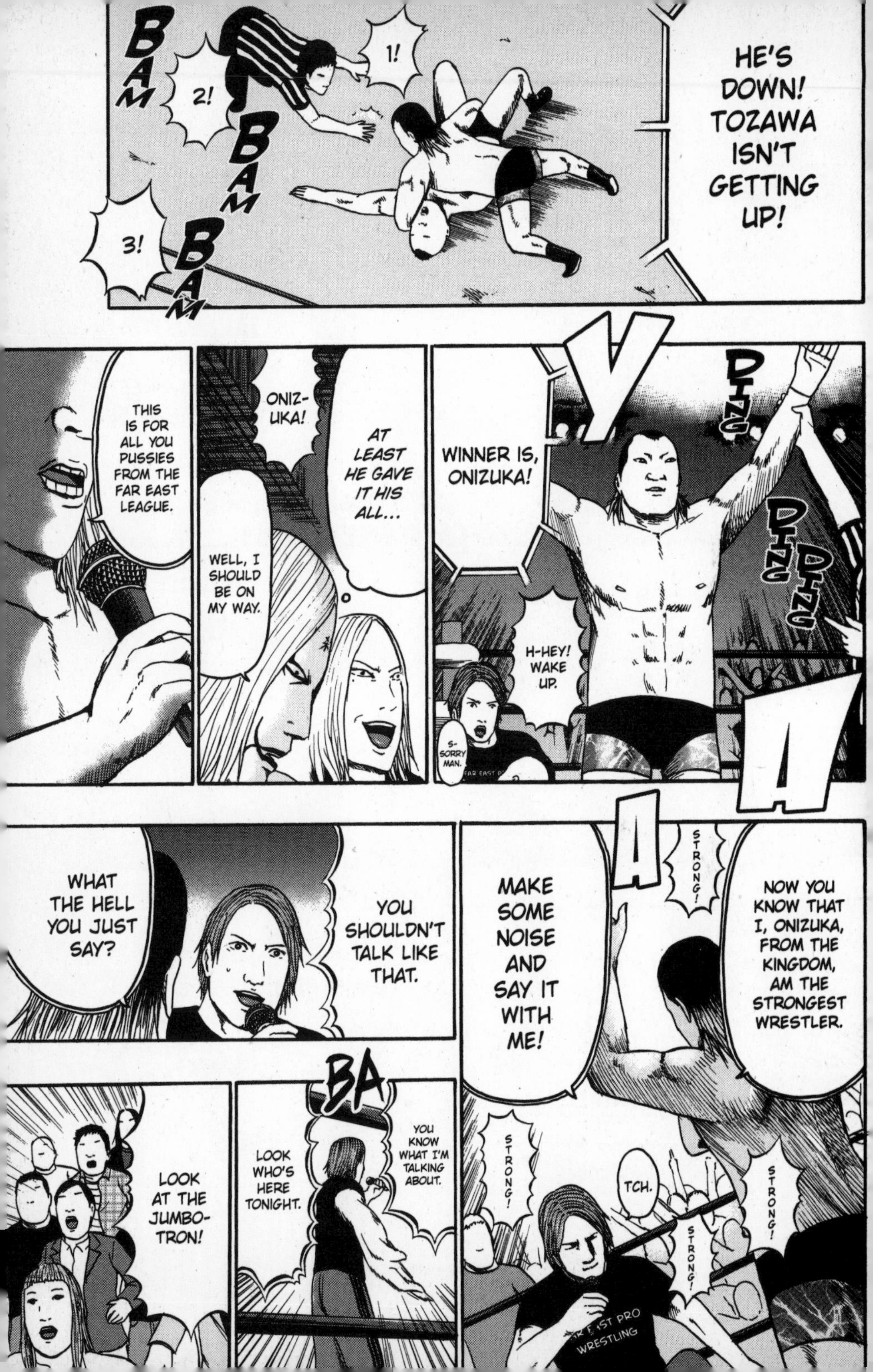
HE'S DOWN! TOZAWA ISN'T GETTING UP!
1!
BAM
2!
BAM
3!
BAM
DING
DING
DING
Y
WINNER IS, ONIZUKA!
H-HEY! WAKE UP.
S-SORRY MAN.
A
ONIZ-UKA!
AT LEAST HE GAVE IT HIS ALL...
WELL, I SHOULD BE ON MY WAY.
THIS IS FOR ALL YOU PUSSIES FROM THE FAR EAST LEAGUE.
A
NOW YOU KNOW THAT I, ONIZUKA, FROM THE KINGDOM, AM THE STRONGEST WRESTLER.
STRONG!
MAKE SOME NOISE AND SAY IT WITH ME!
STRONG!
STRONG!
TCH.
STRONG!
YOU SHOULDN'T TALK LIKE THAT.
WHAT THE HELL YOU JUST SAY?
BA
YOU KNOW WHAT I'M TALKING ABOUT.
LOOK WHO'S HERE TONIGHT.
LOOK AT THE JUMBO-TRON!

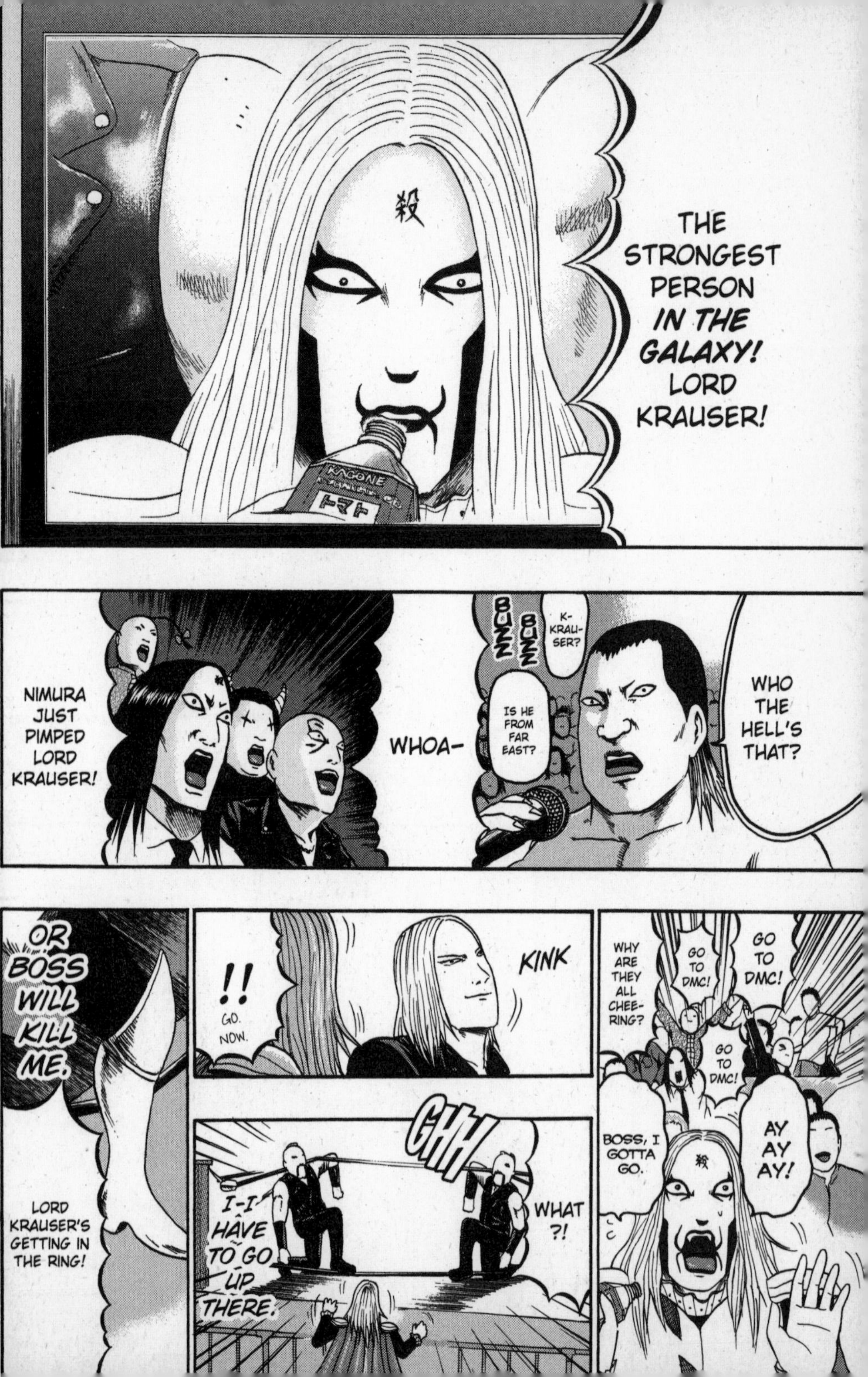
THE STRONGEST PERSON IN THE GALAXY! LORD KRAUSER!
KAGOME
トマト
WHO THE HELL'S THAT?
K-KRAUSER?
BUZZ BUZZ
IS HE FROM FAR EAST?
WHOA-
NIMURA JUST PIMPED LORD KRAUSER!
GO TO DMC!
GO TO DMC!
WHY ARE THEY ALL CHEERING?
GO TO DMC!
AY AY AY!
BOSS, I GOTTA GO.
KINK
!!
GO. NOW.
GHH
WHAT ?!
I-I HAVE TO GO UP THERE.
OR BOSS WILL KILL ME.
LORD KRAUSER'S GETTING IN THE RING!

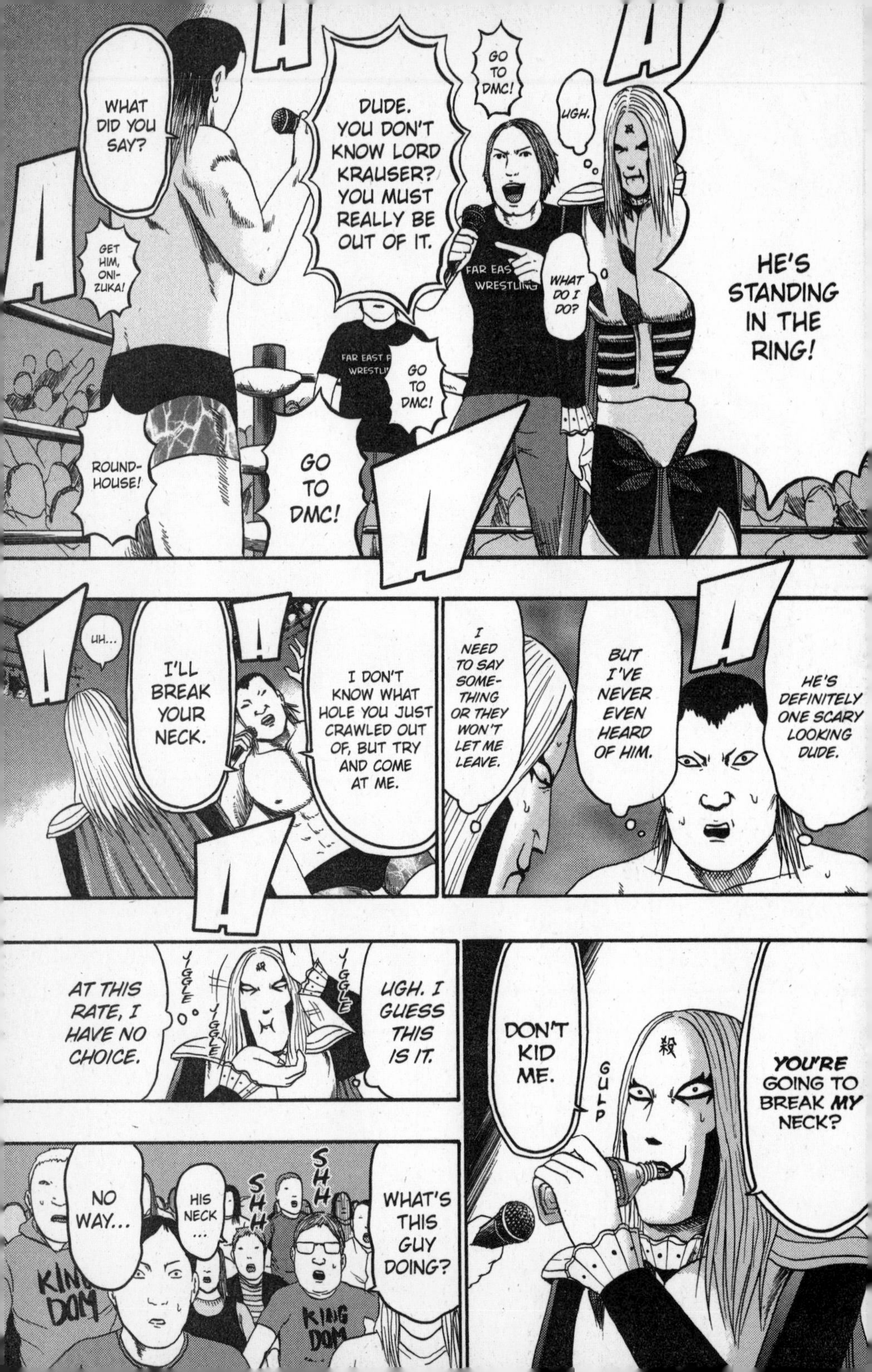
A
UGH.
GO TO DMC!
DUDE. YOU DON'T KNOW LORD KRAUSER? YOU MUST REALLY BE OUT OF IT.
WHAT DID YOU SAY?
HE'S STANDING IN THE RING!
WHAT DO I DO?
FAR EAST WRESTLING
GO TO DMC!
GET HIM, ONI-ZUKA!
GO TO DMC!
ROUNDHOUSE!
HE'S DEFINITELY ONE SCARY LOOKING DUDE.
BUT I'VE NEVER EVEN HEARD OF HIM.
I NEED TO SAY SOME-THING OR THEY WON'T LET ME LEAVE.
I DON'T KNOW WHAT HOLE YOU JUST CRAWLED OUT OF, BUT TRY AND COME AT ME.
I'LL BREAK YOUR NECK.
UH...
YOU'RE GOING TO BREAK *MY* NECK?
GULP
DON'T KID ME.
UGH. I GUESS THIS IS IT.
JIGGLE JIGGLE JIGGLE
AT THIS RATE, I HAVE NO CHOICE.
WHAT'S THIS GUY DOING?
SHH SHH
HIS NECK...
NO WAY...
KINGDOM

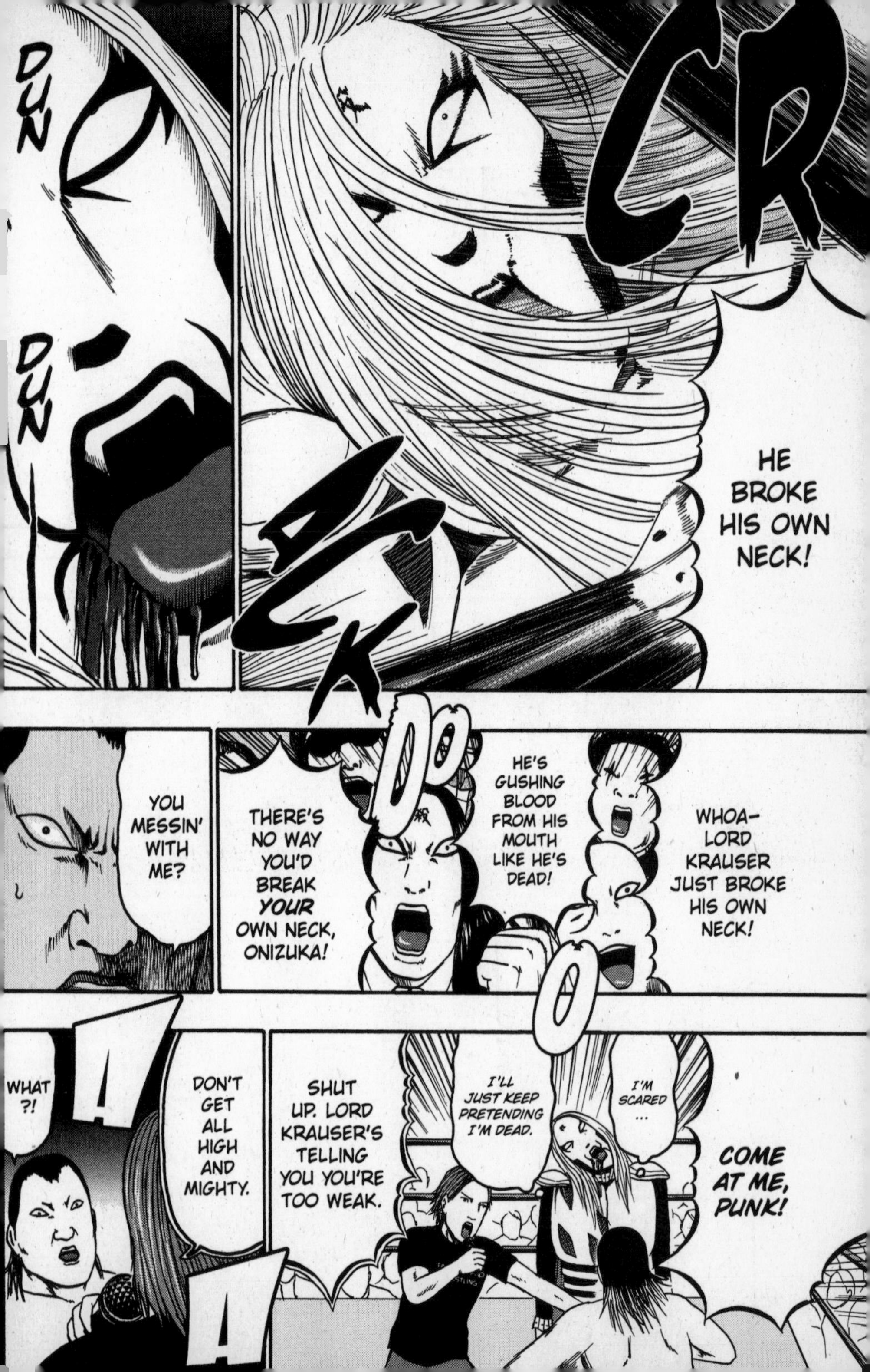
CR
ACK
HE BROKE HIS OWN NECK!
DUN DUN
WHOA- LORD KRAUSER JUST BROKE HIS OWN NECK!
HE'S GUSHING BLOOD FROM HIS MOUTH LIKE HE'S DEAD!
DOO
THERE'S NO WAY YOU'D BREAK ***YOUR*** OWN NECK, ONIZUKA!
YOU MESSIN' WITH ME?
COME AT ME, PUNK!
I'M SCARED ...
I'LL JUST KEEP PRETENDING I'M DEAD.
SHUT UP. LORD KRAUSER'S TELLING YOU YOU'RE TOO WEAK.
DON'T GET ALL HIGH AND MIGHTY.
A
WHAT ?!
A

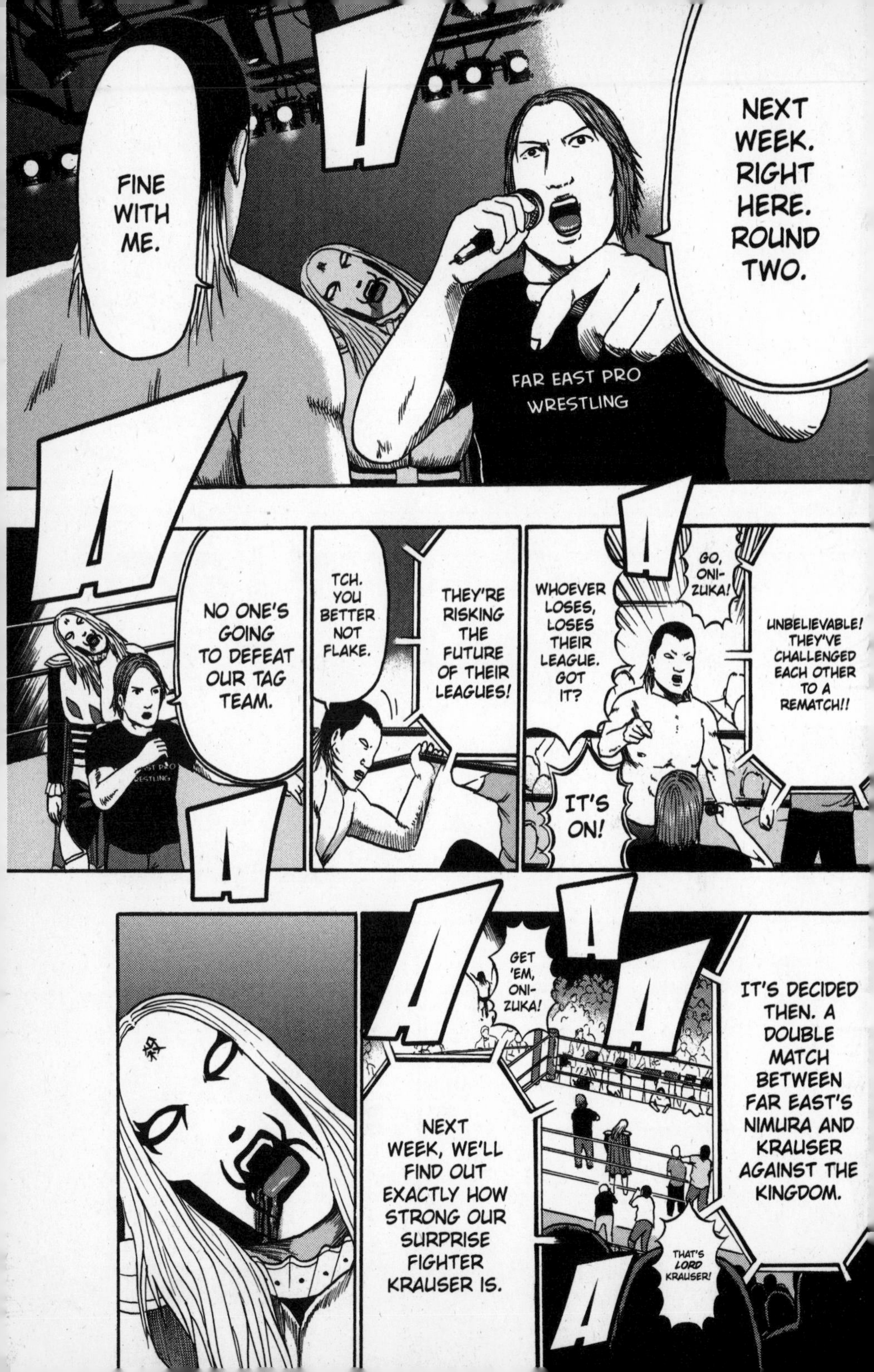
NEXT WEEK. RIGHT HERE. ROUND TWO.
FAR EAST PRO WRESTLING
FINE WITH ME.
UNBELIEVABLE! THEY'VE CHALLENGED EACH OTHER TO A REMATCH!!
GO, ONI-ZUKA!
WHOEVER LOSES, LOSES THEIR LEAGUE. GOT IT?
IT'S ON!
THEY'RE RISKING THE FUTURE OF THEIR LEAGUES!
TCH. YOU BETTER NOT FLAKE.
NO ONE'S GOING TO DEFEAT OUR TAG TEAM.
IT'S DECIDED THEN. A DOUBLE MATCH BETWEEN FAR EAST'S NIMURA AND KRAUSER AGAINST THE KINGDOM.
GET 'EM, ONI-ZUKA!
NEXT WEEK, WE'LL FIND OUT EXACTLY HOW STRONG OUR SURPRISE FIGHTER KRAUSER IS.
THAT'S *LORD* KRAUSER!

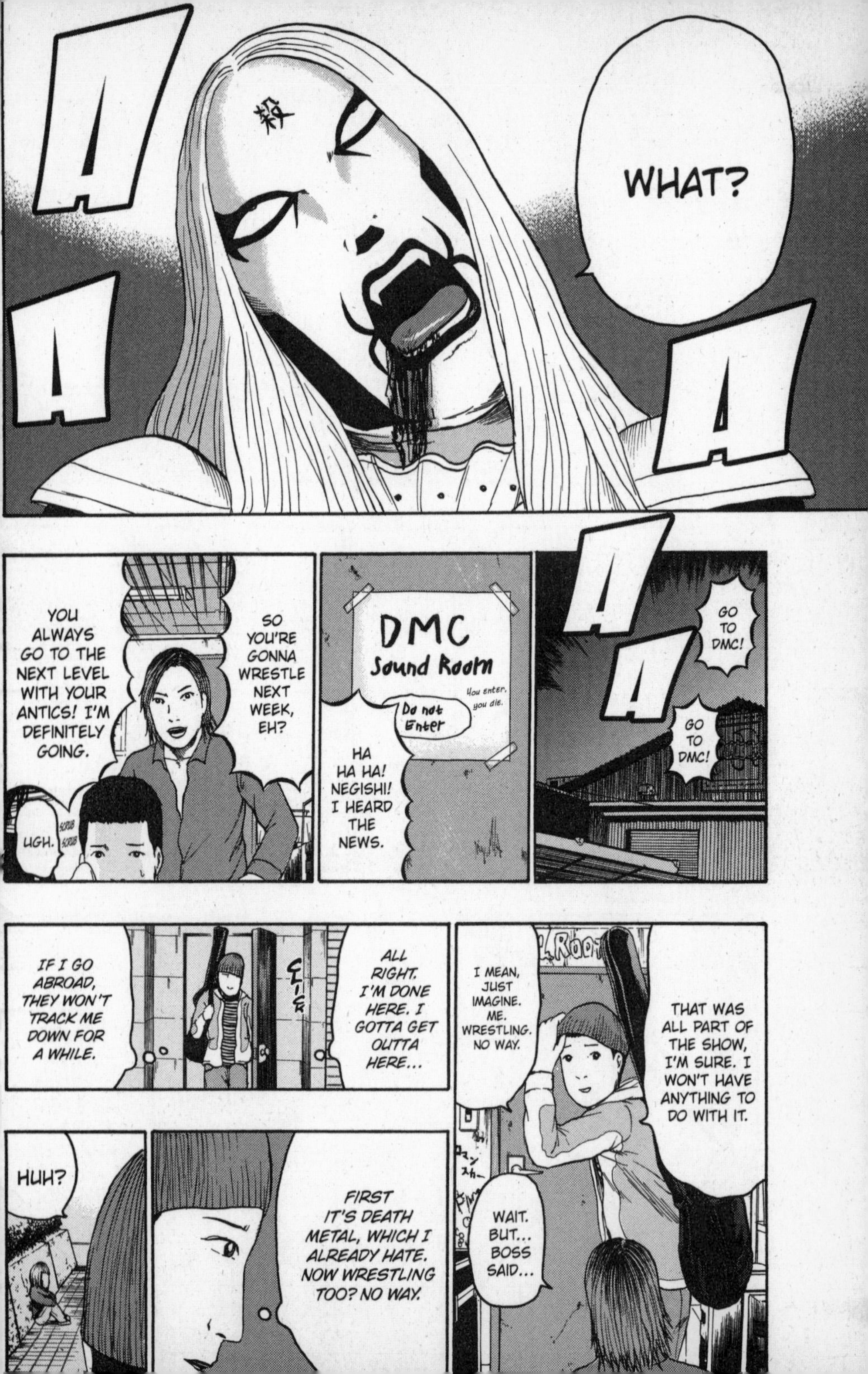
WHAT?
A
A
A
A
GO TO DMC!
A
A
GO TO DMC!
DMC
Sound Room
You enter, you die.
Do not Enter
HA HA HA! NEGISHI! I HEARD THE NEWS.
SO YOU'RE GONNA WRESTLE NEXT WEEK, EH?
YOU ALWAYS GO TO THE NEXT LEVEL WITH YOUR ANTICS! I'M DEFINITELY GOING.
SCRUB SCRUB
UGH.
THAT WAS ALL PART OF THE SHOW, I'M SURE. I WON'T HAVE ANYTHING TO DO WITH IT.
I MEAN, JUST IMAGINE. ME. WRESTLING. NO WAY.
WAIT. BUT... BOSS SAID...
ALL RIGHT. I'M DONE HERE. I GOTTA GET OUTTA HERE...
CLICK
IF I GO ABROAD, THEY WON'T TRACK ME DOWN FOR A WHILE.
FIRST IT'S DEATH METAL, WHICH I ALREADY HATE. NOW WRESTLING TOO? NO WAY.
HUH?

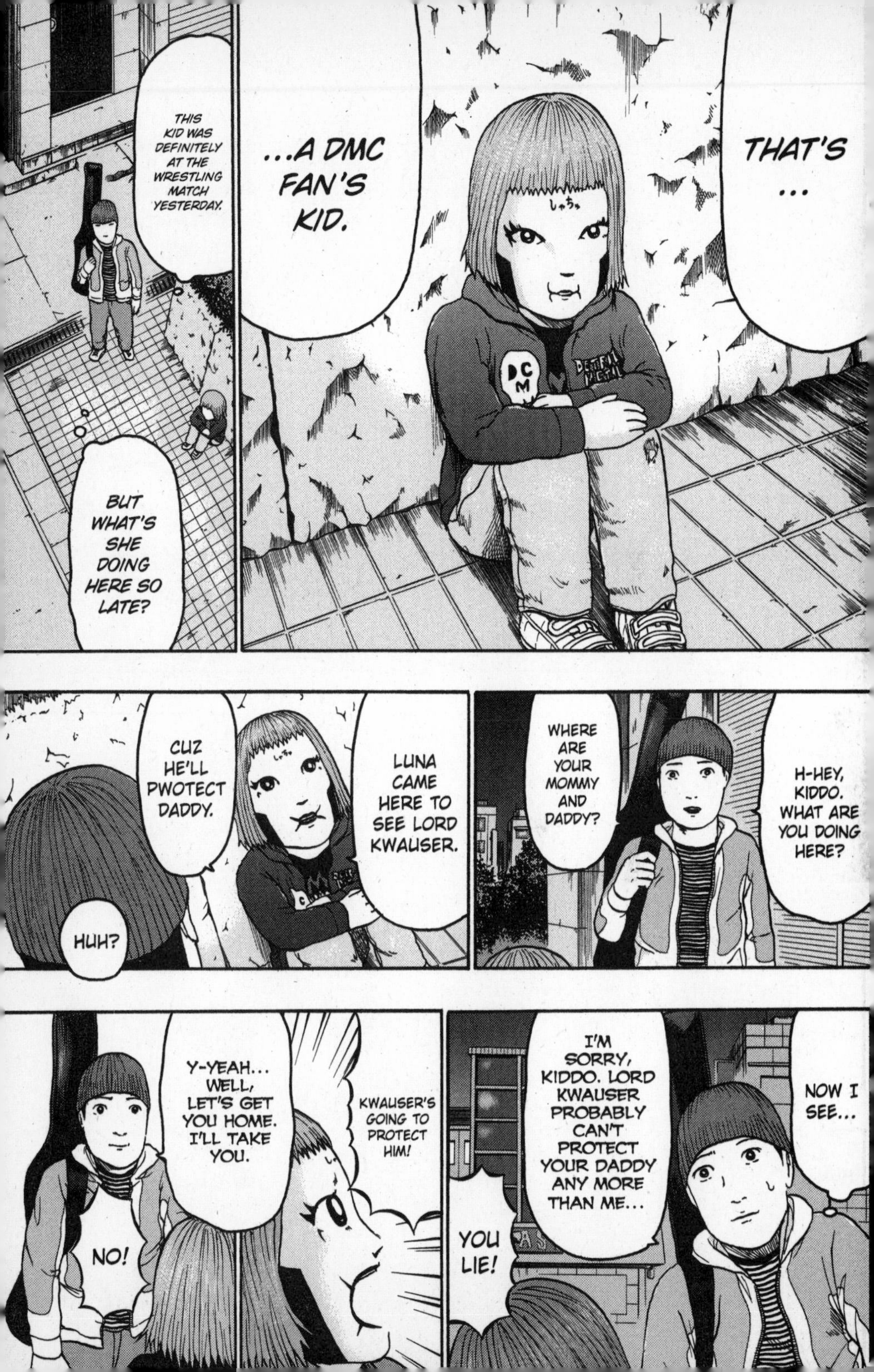
THAT'S ...
...A DMC FAN'S KID.
THIS KID WAS DEFINITELY AT THE WRESTLING MATCH YESTERDAY.
BUT WHAT'S SHE DOING HERE SO LATE?
H-HEY, KIDDO. WHAT ARE YOU DOING HERE?
WHERE ARE YOUR MOMMY AND DADDY?
LUNA CAME HERE TO SEE LORD KWAUSER.
CUZ HE'LL PWOTECT DADDY.
HUH?
NOW I SEE...
I'M SORRY, KIDDO. LORD KWAUSER PROBABLY CAN'T PROTECT YOUR DADDY ANY MORE THAN ME...
YOU LIE!
KWAUSER'S GOING TO PROTECT HIM!
Y-YEAH... WELL, LET'S GET YOU HOME. I'LL TAKE YOU.
NO!

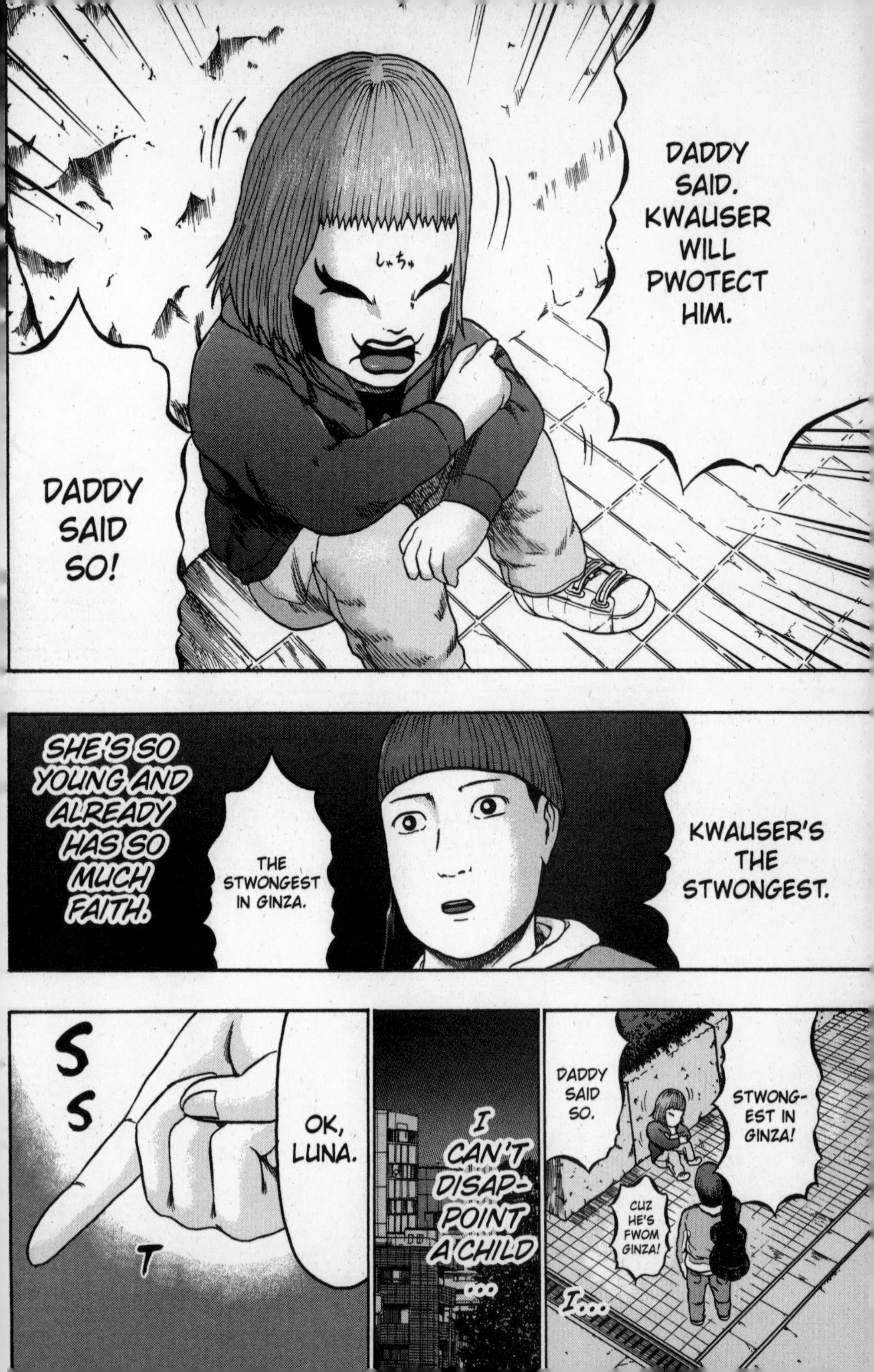
DADDY SAID. KWAUSER WILL PWOTECT HIM.
DADDY SAID SO!
KWAUSER'S THE STWONGEST.
THE STWONGEST IN GINZA.
SHE'S SO YOUNG AND ALREADY HAS SO MUCH FAITH.
STWONG-EST IN GINZA!
DADDY SAID SO.
CUZ HE'S FWOM GINZA!
I...
I CAN'T DISAP-POINT A CHILD...
OK, LUNA.
SS
T

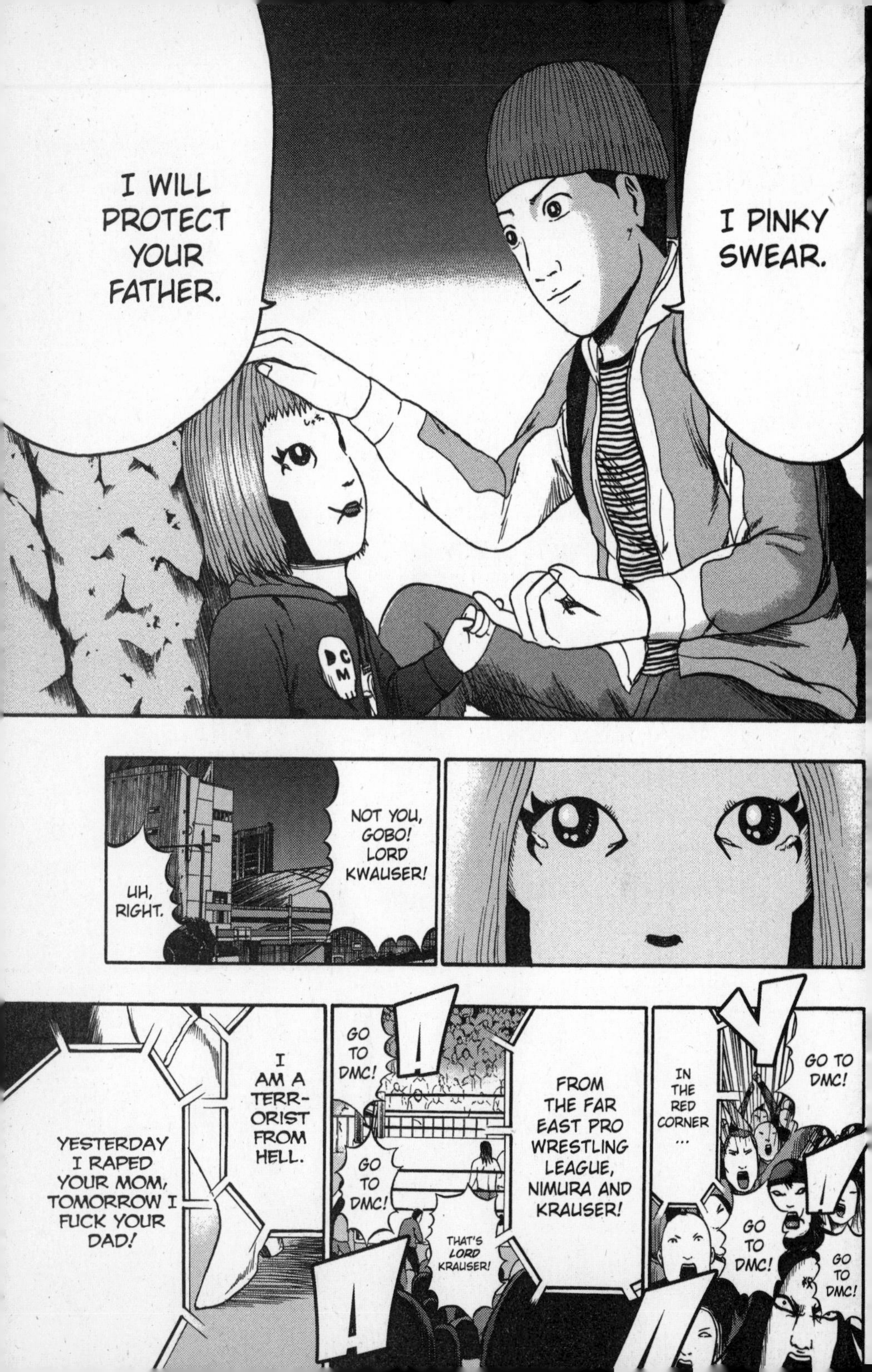

I PINKY SWEAR.
I WILL PROTECT YOUR FATHER.
NOT YOU, GOBO! LORD KWAUSER!
UH, RIGHT.
GO TO DMC!
IN THE RED CORNER ...
GO TO DMC!
GO TO DMC!
FROM THE FAR EAST PRO WRESTLING LEAGUE, NIMURA AND KRAUSER!
GO TO DMC!
GO TO DMC!
THAT'S *LORD* KRAUSER!
I AM A TERRORIST FROM HELL.
YESTERDAY I RAPED YOUR MOM, TOMORROW I FUCK YOUR DAD!

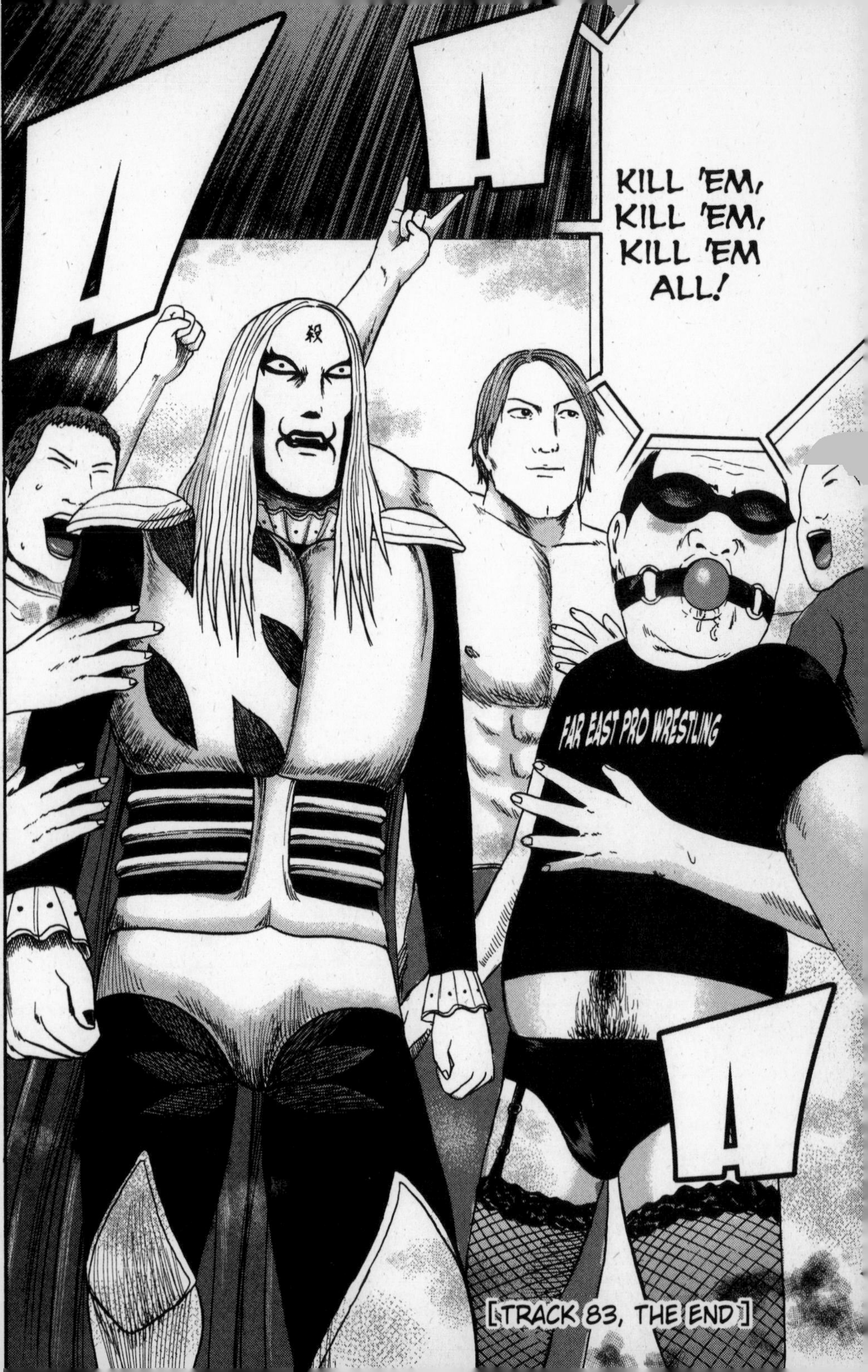
A
KILL 'EM, KILL 'EM, KILL 'EM ALL!
A
殺
FAR EAST PRO WRESTLING
A
[TRACK 83, THE END]

DMC LEXICON

🎭 GINZA

Generally designates the Ginza quarter of central Tokyo, from First Avenue to Eighth Avenue. There are many famous restaurants and bars lined up in this part of the city. To be the strongest in Ginza essentially means that you're strongest in a berth as long as seven blocks.

Usage: I saw Lord Krauser in Ginza. At least I'm pretty sure it was Ginza. And I'm pretty sure it was Krauser. He was all white.

デトロイト・メタル・シティ
Detroit Metal City

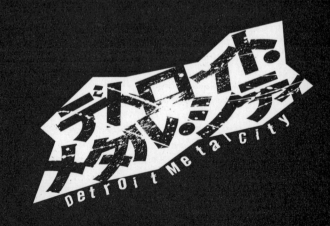

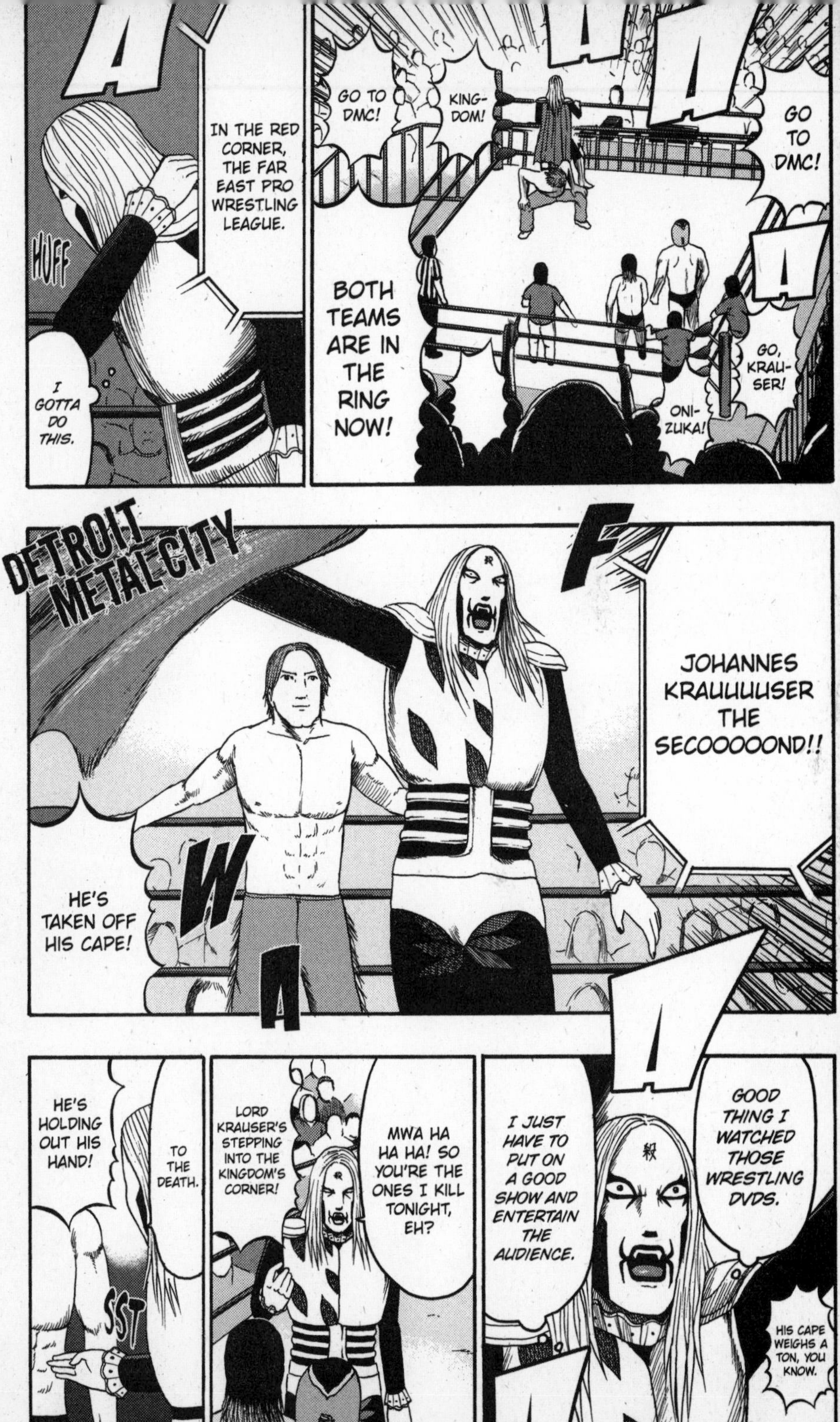
A
A
GO TO DMC!
KING-DOM!
GO TO DMC!
A
GO, KRAU-SER!
ONI-ZUKA!
BOTH TEAMS ARE IN THE RING NOW!
A
IN THE RED CORNER, THE FAR EAST PRO WRESTLING LEAGUE.
HUFF
I GOTTA DO THIS.
F
JOHANNES KRAUUUUSER THE SECOOOOOND!!
DETROIT METAL CITY
W
HE'S TAKEN OFF HIS CAPE!
A
A
GOOD THING I WATCHED THOSE WRESTLING DVDS.
I JUST HAVE TO PUT ON A GOOD SHOW AND ENTERTAIN THE AUDIENCE.
HIS CAPE WEIGHS A TON, YOU KNOW.
MWA HA HA HA! SO YOU'RE THE ONES I KILL TONIGHT, EH?
LORD KRAUSER'S STEPPING INTO THE KINGDOM'S CORNER!
TO THE DEATH.
HE'S HOLDING OUT HIS HAND!
SST

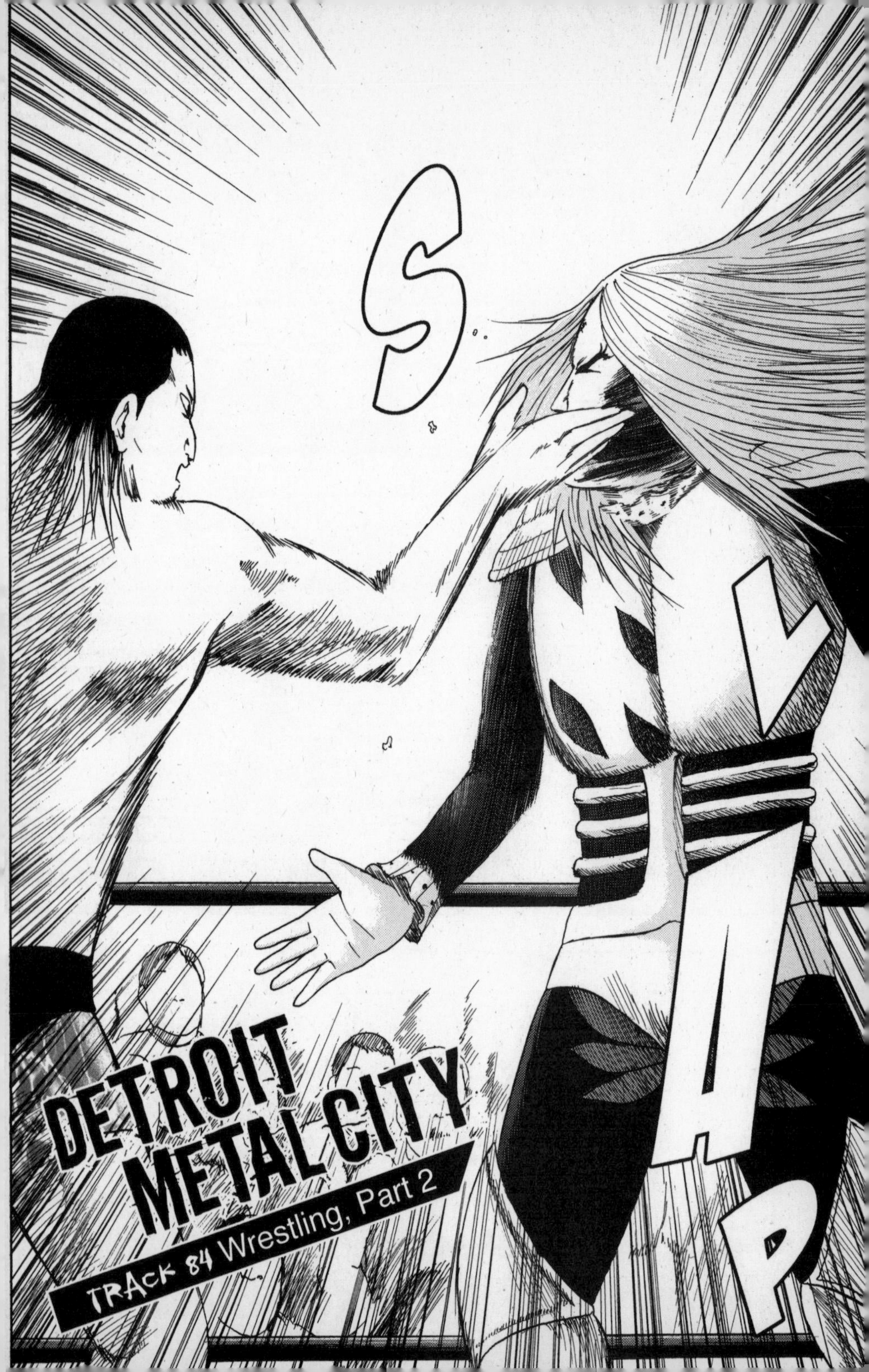

SLAP
DETROIT METAL CITY
TRACK 84 Wrestling, Part 2

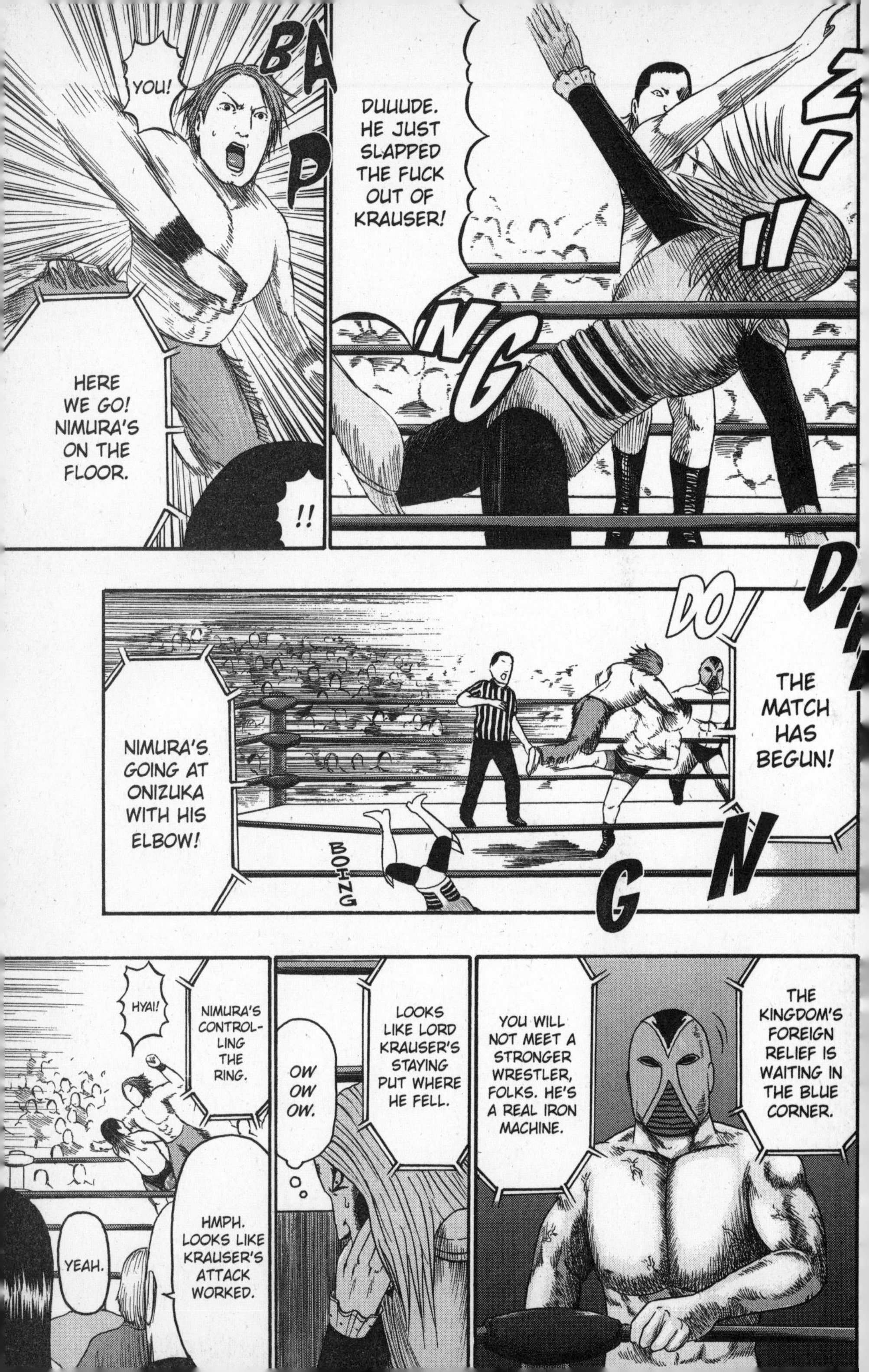
DUUUDE. HE JUST SLAPPED THE FUCK OUT OF KRAUSER!
NG
BA
P
YOU!
HERE WE GO! NIMURA'S ON THE FLOOR.
!!
DO
THE MATCH HAS BEGUN!
N
G
NIMURA'S GOING AT ONIZUKA WITH HIS ELBOW!
BOING
THE KINGDOM'S FOREIGN RELIEF IS WAITING IN THE BLUE CORNER.
YOU WILL NOT MEET A STRONGER WRESTLER, FOLKS. HE'S A REAL IRON MACHINE.
LOOKS LIKE LORD KRAUSER'S STAYING PUT WHERE HE FELL.
OW OW OW.
HYAI!
NIMURA'S CONTROL-LING THE RING.
HMPH. LOOKS LIKE KRAUSER'S ATTACK WORKED.
YEAH.

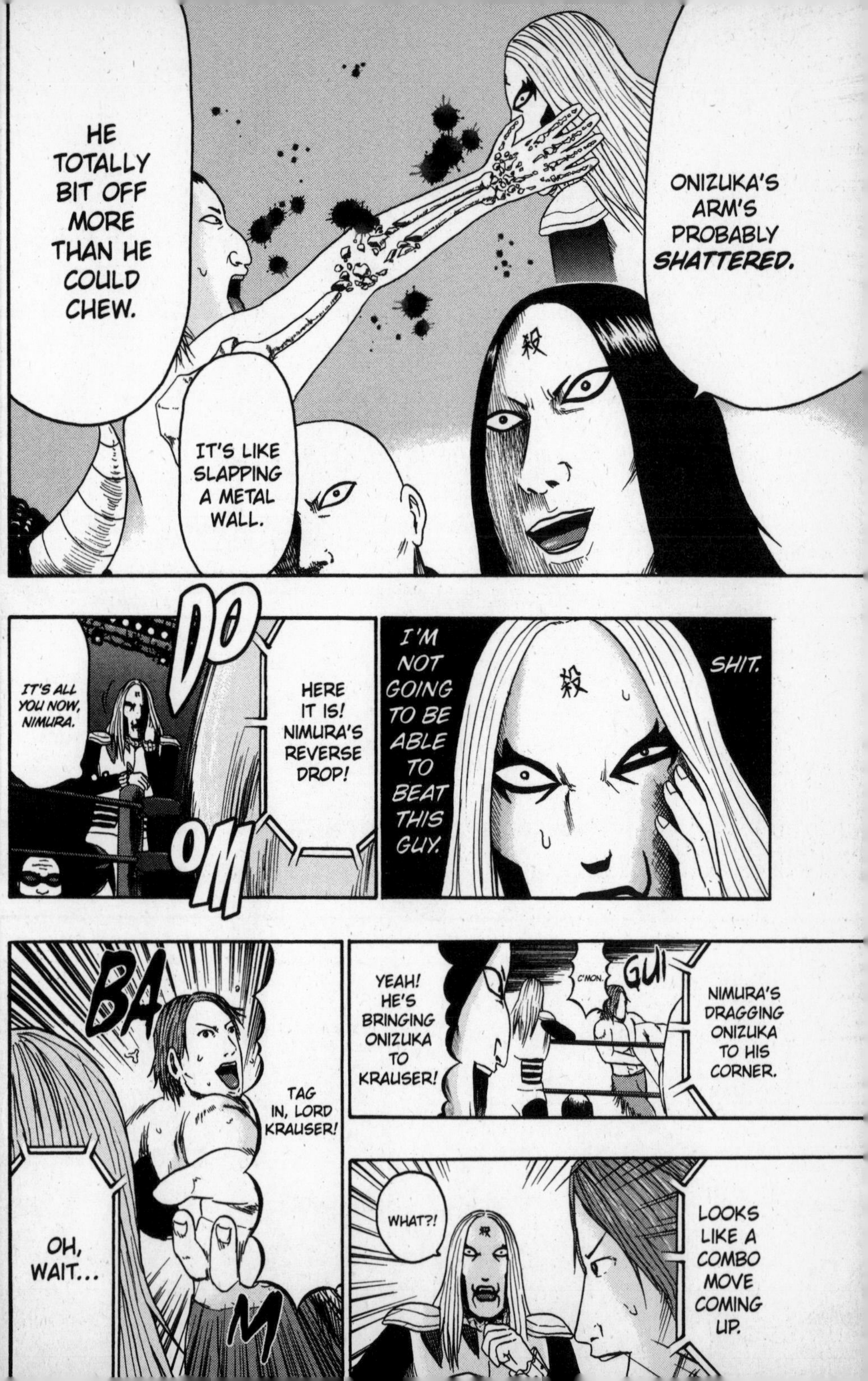

ONIZUKA'S ARM'S PROBABLY SHATTERED.
HE TOTALLY BIT OFF MORE THAN HE COULD CHEW.
IT'S LIKE SLAPPING A METAL WALL.
SHIT.
I'M NOT GOING TO BE ABLE TO BEAT THIS GUY.
DO
HERE IT IS! NIMURA'S REVERSE DROP!
IT'S ALL YOU NOW, NIMURA.
OM
NIMURA'S DRAGGING ONIZUKA TO HIS CORNER.
GUI
C'MON.
YEAH! HE'S BRINGING ONIZUKA TO KRAUSER!
LOOKS LIKE A COMBO MOVE COMING UP.
WHAT?!
BA
TAG IN, LORD KRAUSER!
OH, WAIT...
M

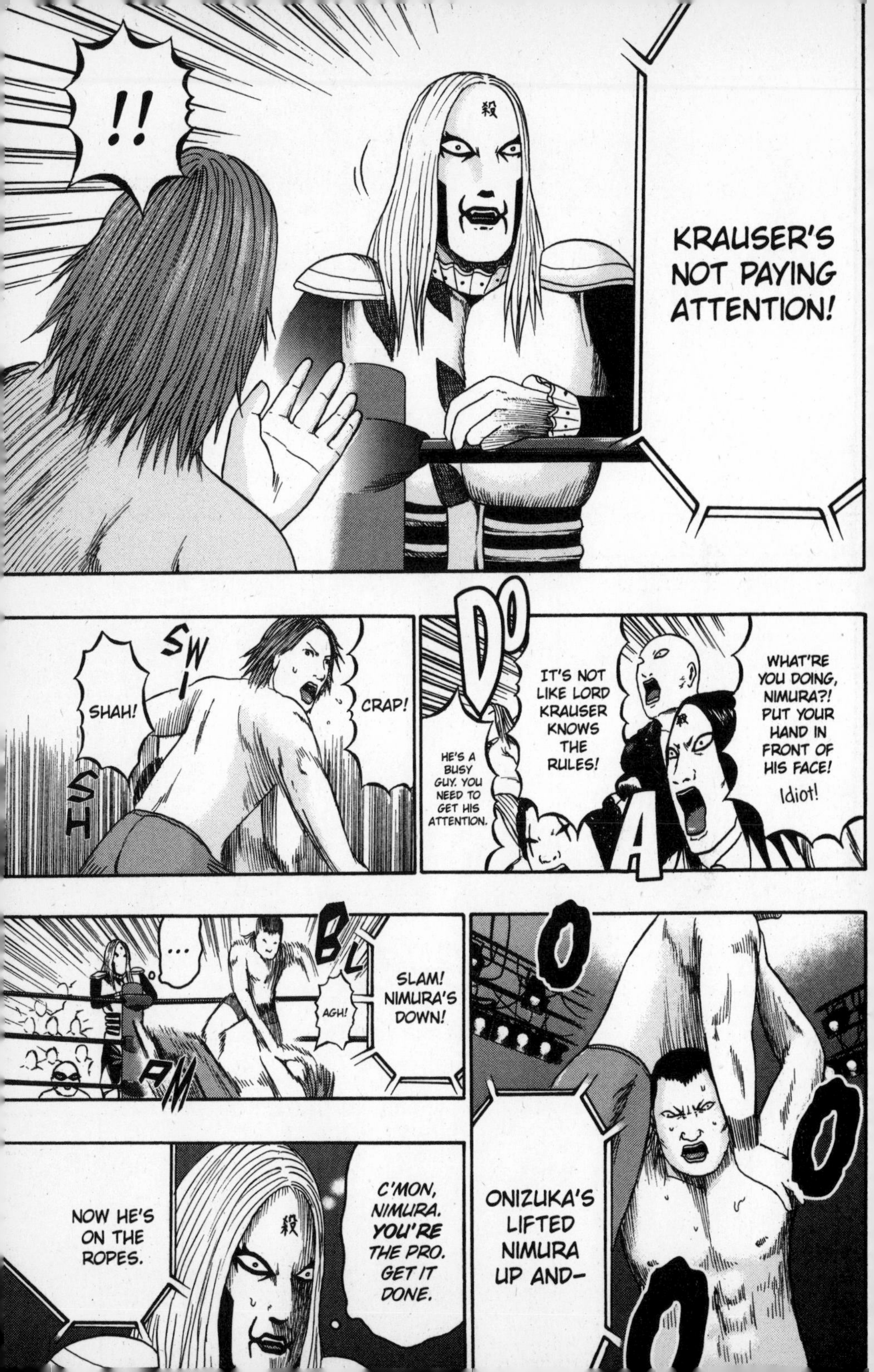

KRAUSER'S NOT PAYING ATTENTION!
!!
DO
WHAT'RE YOU DOING, NIMURA?! PUT YOUR HAND IN FRONT OF HIS FACE!
Idiot!
IT'S NOT LIKE LORD KRAUSER KNOWS THE RULES!
HE'S A BUSY GUY. YOU NEED TO GET HIS ATTENTION.
A
CRAP!
SWISH
SHAH!
ONIZUKA'S LIFTED NIMURA UP AND-
SLAM! NIMURA'S DOWN!
BLAM
AGH!
...
C'MON, NIMURA. YOU'RE THE PRO. GET IT DONE.
NOW HE'S ON THE ROPES.

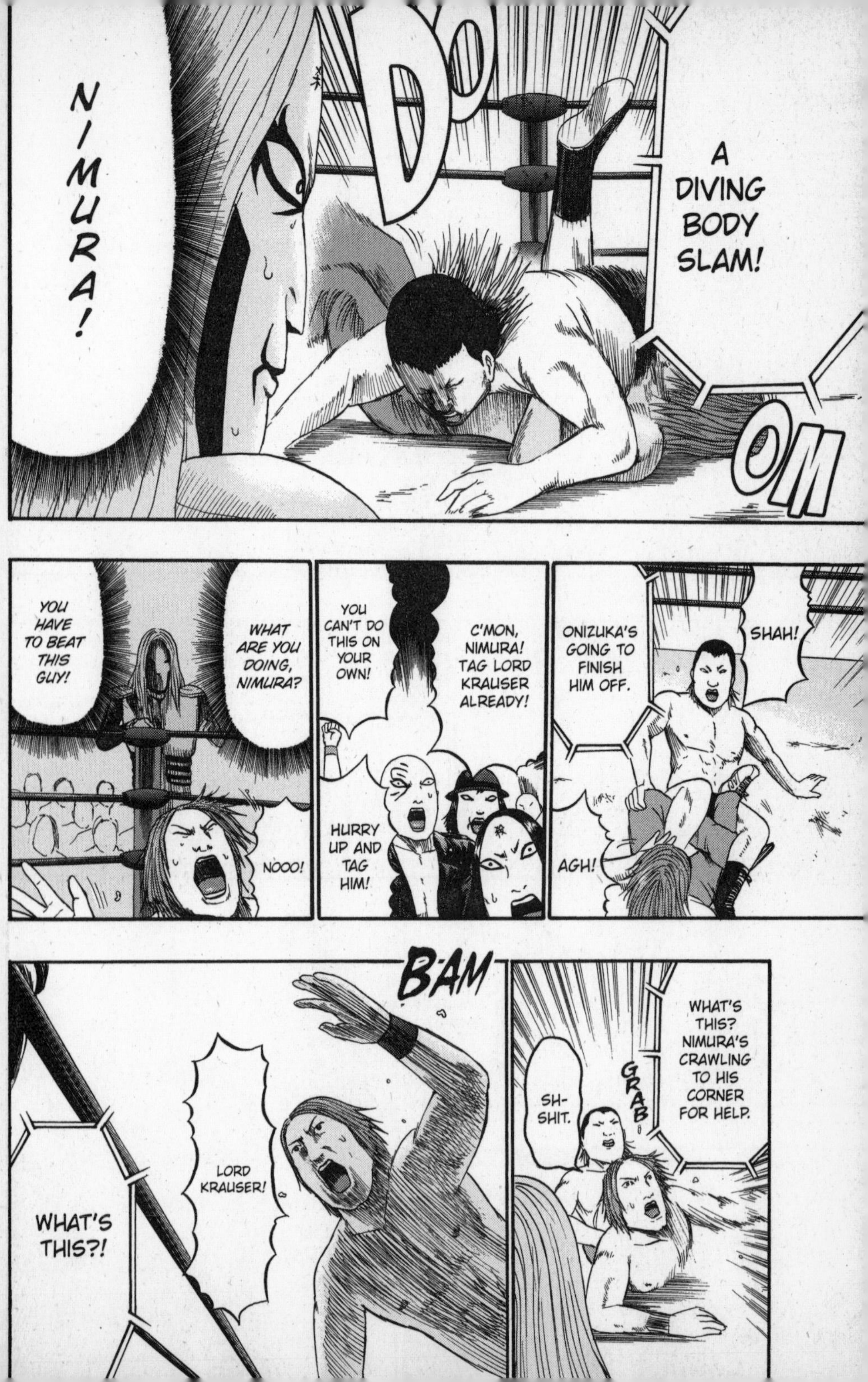
A DIVING BODY SLAM!
DO
OM
NIMURA!
SHAH!
ONIZUKA'S GOING TO FINISH HIM OFF.
AGH!
C'MON, NIMURA! TAG LORD KRAUSER ALREADY!
YOU CAN'T DO THIS ON YOUR OWN!
HURRY UP AND TAG HIM!
WHAT ARE YOU DOING, NIMURA?
YOU HAVE TO BEAT THIS GUY!
NOOO!
WHAT'S THIS? NIMURA'S CRAWLING TO HIS CORNER FOR HELP.
GRAB
SH-SHIT.
BAM
LORD KRAUSER!
WHAT'S THIS?!

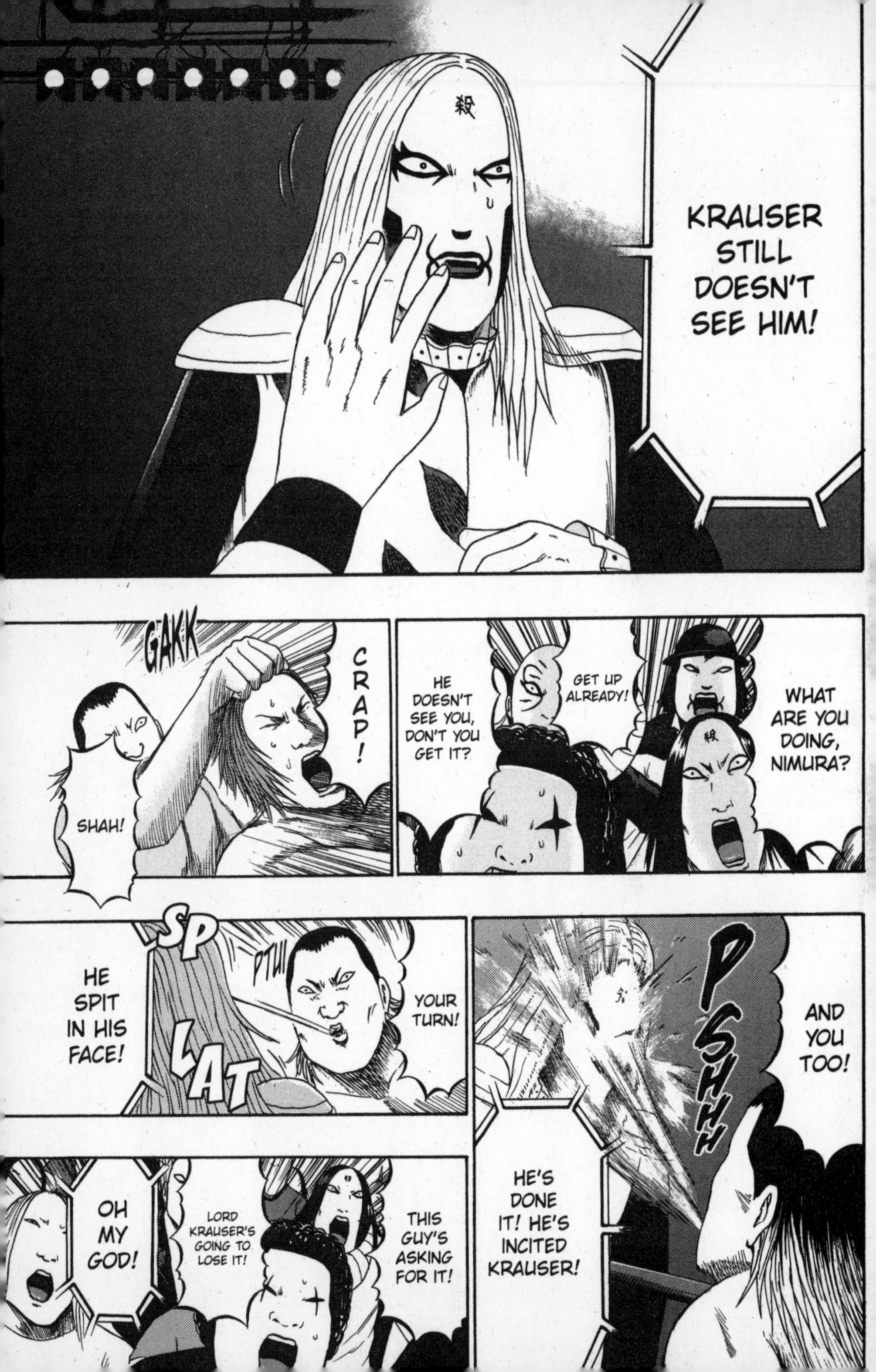
KRAUSER STILL DOESN'T SEE HIM!
WHAT ARE YOU DOING, NIMURA?
GET UP ALREADY!
HE DOESN'T SEE YOU, DON'T YOU GET IT?
CRAP!
GAKK
SHAH!
AND YOU TOO!
PSHHH
YOUR TURN!
PTUI
SPLAT
HE SPIT IN HIS FACE!
HE'S DONE IT! HE'S INCITED KRAUSER!
THIS GUY'S ASKING FOR IT!
LORD KRAUSER'S GOING TO LOSE IT!
OH MY GOD!

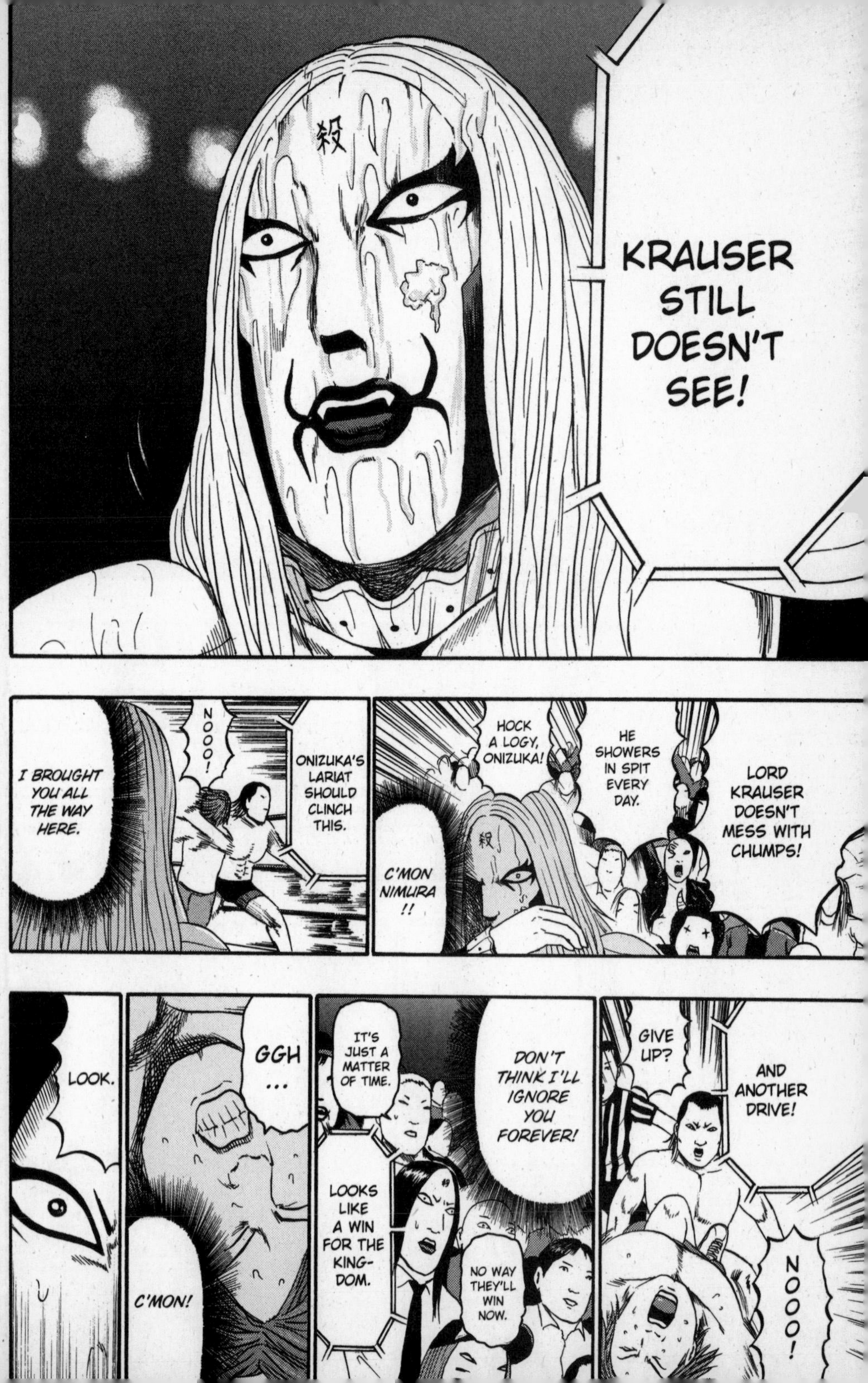
KRAUSER STILL DOESN'T SEE!
LORD KRAUSER DOESN'T MESS WITH CHUMPS!
HE SHOWERS IN SPIT EVERY DAY.
HOCK A LOGY, ONIZUKA!
C'MON NIMURA!!
ONIZUKA'S LARIAT SHOULD CLINCH THIS.
NOOO!
I BROUGHT YOU ALL THE WAY HERE.
AND ANOTHER DRIVE!
GIVE UP?
NOOO!
DON'T THINK I'LL IGNORE YOU FOREVER!
IT'S JUST A MATTER OF TIME.
LOOKS LIKE A WIN FOR THE KINGDOM.
NO WAY THEY'LL WIN NOW.
GGH ...
C'MON!
LOOK.

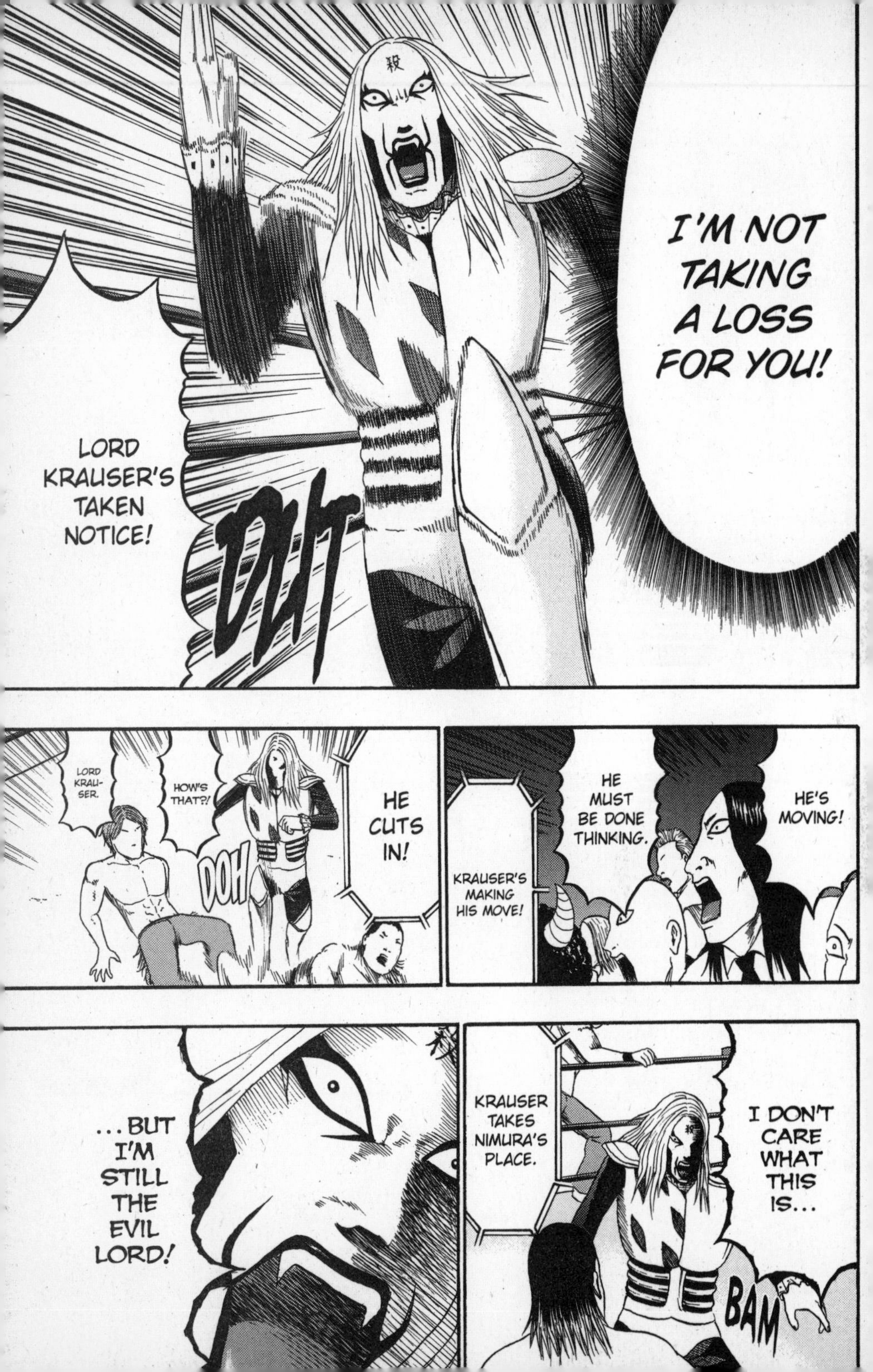

I'M NOT TAKING A LOSS FOR YOU!
LORD KRAUSER'S TAKEN NOTICE!
HE'S MOVING!
HE MUST BE DONE THINKING.
KRAUSER'S MAKING HIS MOVE!
HE CUTS IN!
HOW'S THAT?!
LORD KRAUSER.
DOH
I DON'T CARE WHAT THIS IS...
KRAUSER TAKES NIMURA'S PLACE.
BAM
...BUT I'M STILL THE EVIL LORD!

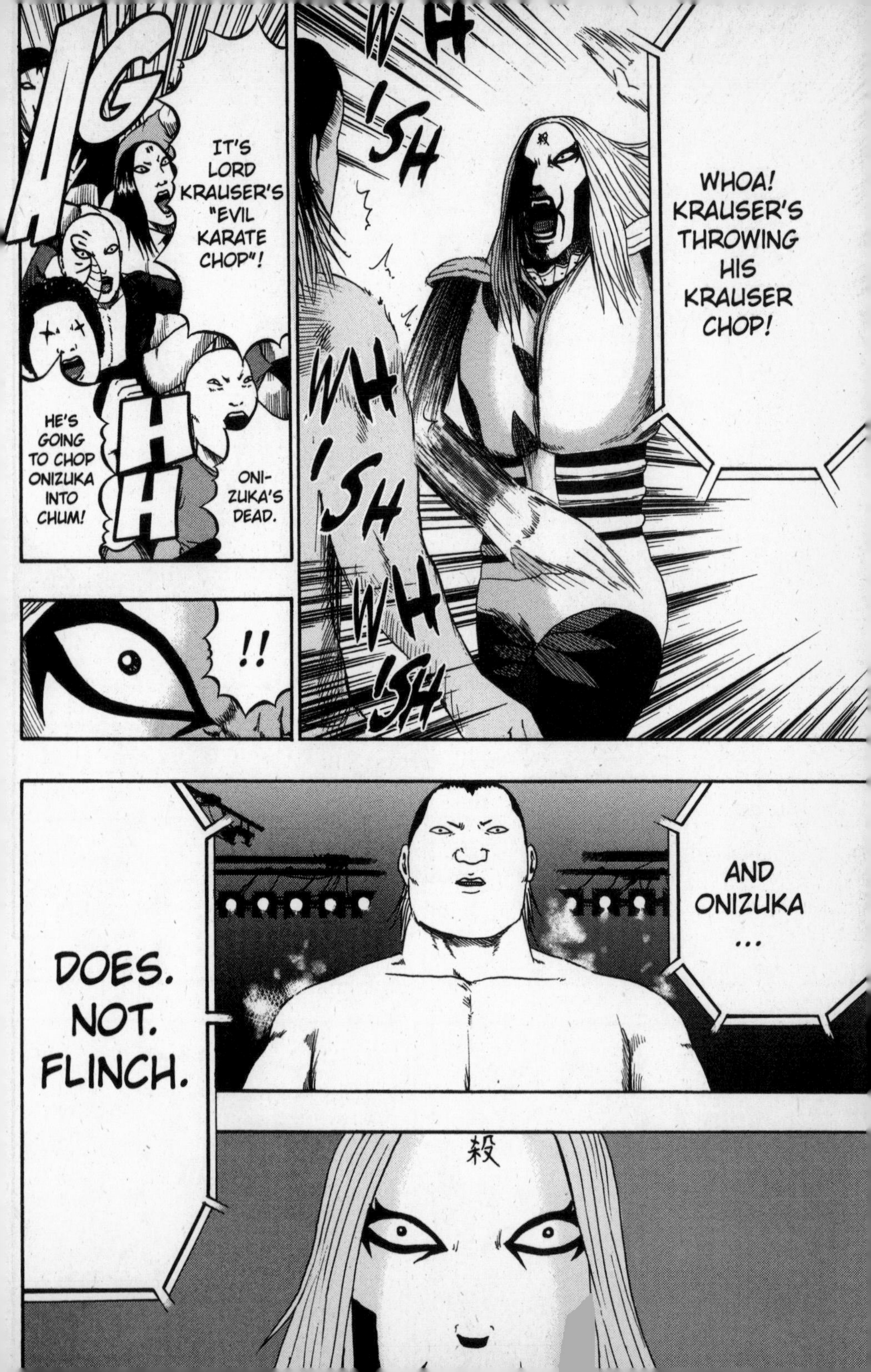
WHOA! KRAUSER'S THROWING HIS KRAUSER CHOP!
WHISH
WHISH WHISH
IT'S LORD KRAUSER'S "EVIL KARATE CHOP"!
AG
HHH
ONI-ZUKA'S DEAD.
HE'S GOING TO CHOP ONIZUKA INTO CHUM!
!!
AND ONIZUKA ...
DOES. NOT. FLINCH.
殺

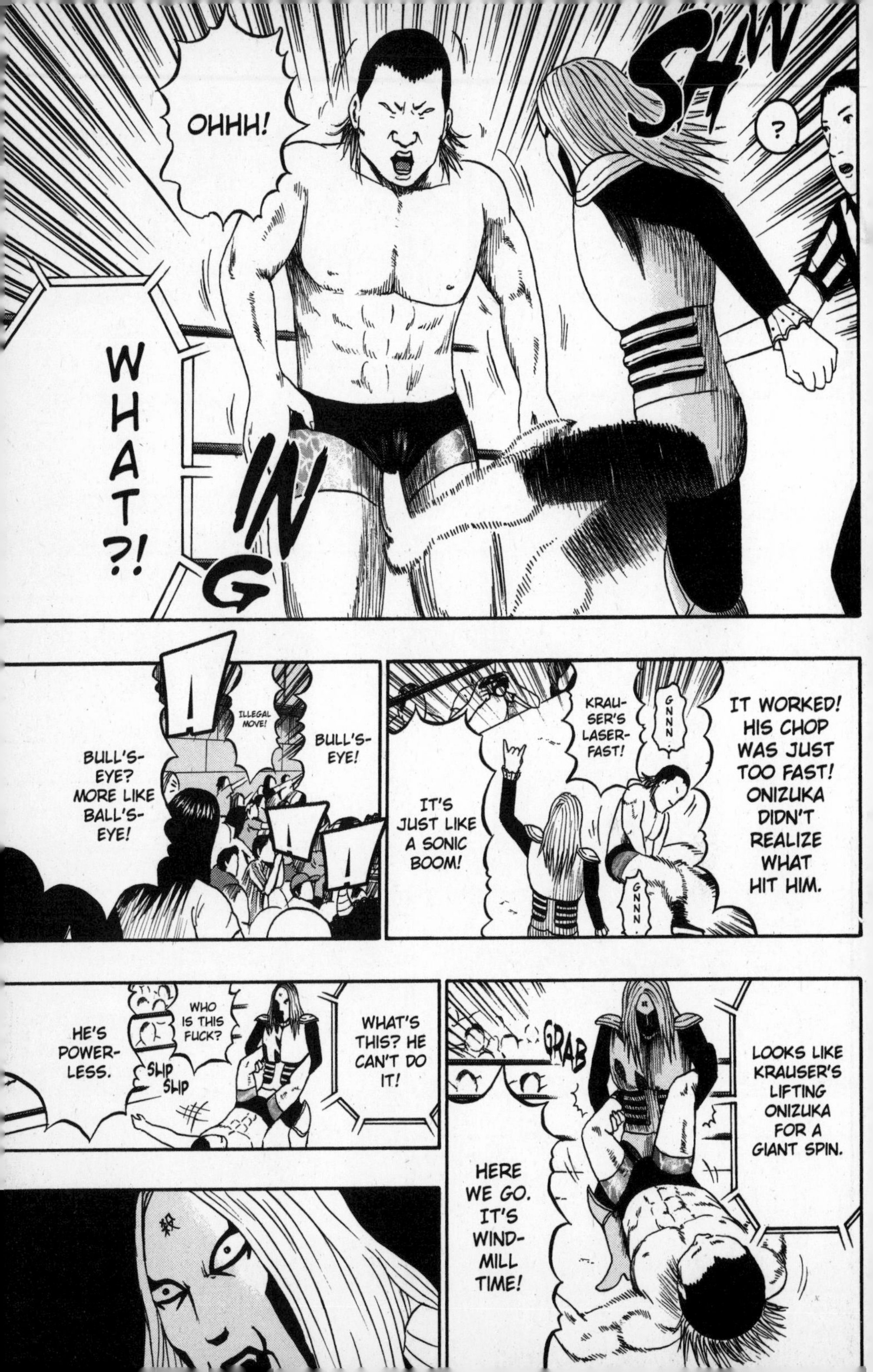
SHW
?
OHHH!
WHAT?!
ING
IT WORKED! HIS CHOP WAS JUST TOO FAST! ONIZUKA DIDN'T REALIZE WHAT HIT HIM.
GNNN...
KRAUSER'S LASER-FAST!
IT'S JUST LIKE A SONIC BOOM!
GNNN...
BULL'S-EYE!
ILLEGAL MOVE!
BULL'S-EYE? MORE LIKE BALL'S-EYE!
LOOKS LIKE KRAUSER'S LIFTING ONIZUKA FOR A GIANT SPIN.
GRAB
HERE WE GO. IT'S WINDMILL TIME!
WHAT'S THIS? HE CAN'T DO IT!
WHO IS THIS FUCK?
HE'S POWERLESS.
SLIP SLIP

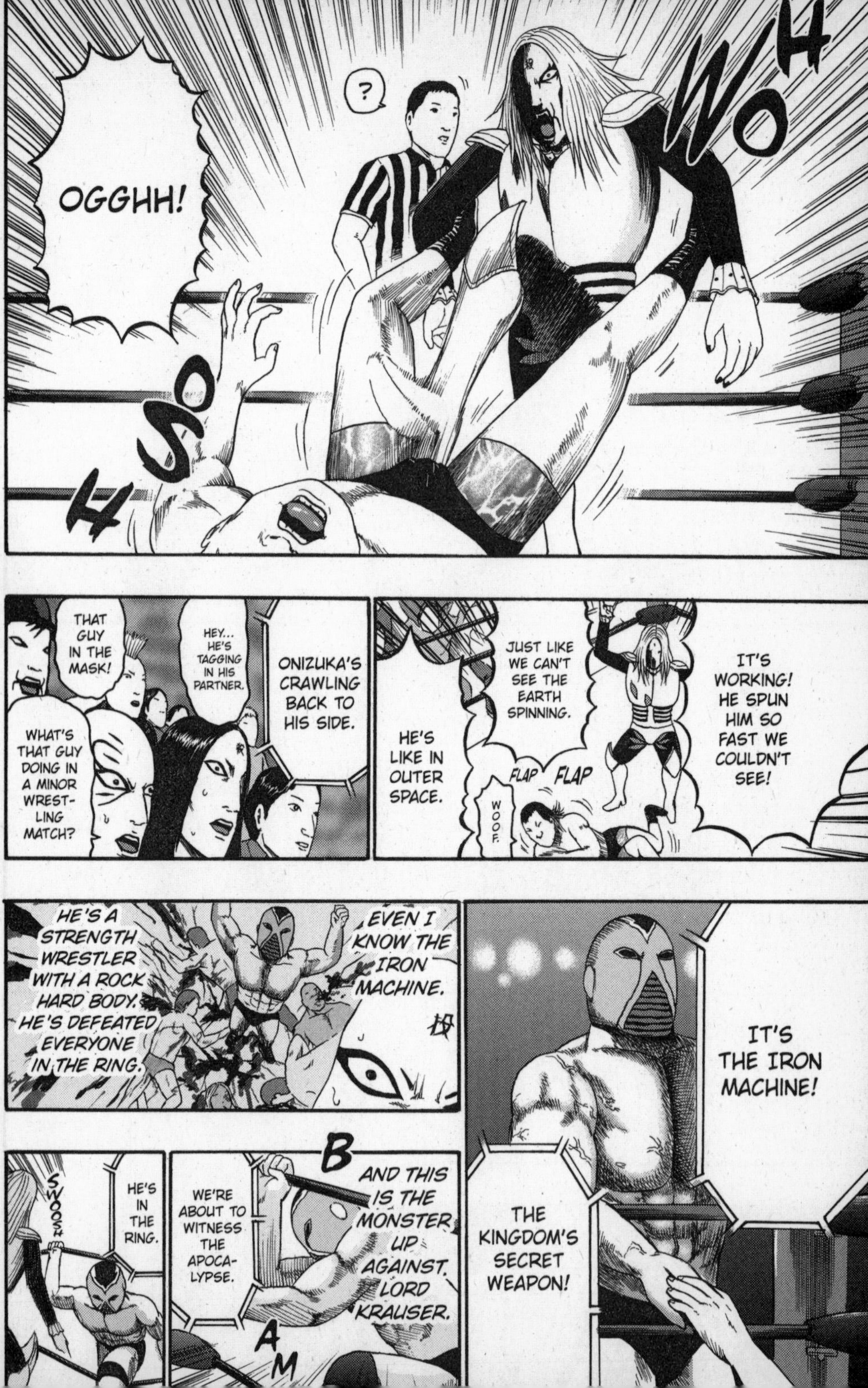
WOH
?
OGGHH!
OSH
IT'S WORKING! HE SPUN HIM SO FAST WE COULDN'T SEE!
JUST LIKE WE CAN'T SEE THE EARTH SPINNING.
HE'S LIKE IN OUTER SPACE.
FLAP
FLAP
WOOF.
ONIZUKA'S CRAWLING BACK TO HIS SIDE.
HEY... HE'S TAGGING IN HIS PARTNER.
THAT GUY IN THE MASK!
WHAT'S THAT GUY DOING IN A MINOR WRESTLING MATCH?
IT'S THE IRON MACHINE!
THE KINGDOM'S SECRET WEAPON!
EVEN I KNOW THE IRON MACHINE.
HE'S A STRENGTH WRESTLER WITH A ROCK HARD BODY. HE'S DEFEATED EVERYONE IN THE RING.
BAM
AND THIS IS THE MONSTER UP AGAINST LORD KRAUSER.
WE'RE ABOUT TO WITNESS THE APOCALYPSE.
HE'S IN THE RING.
SWOOSH

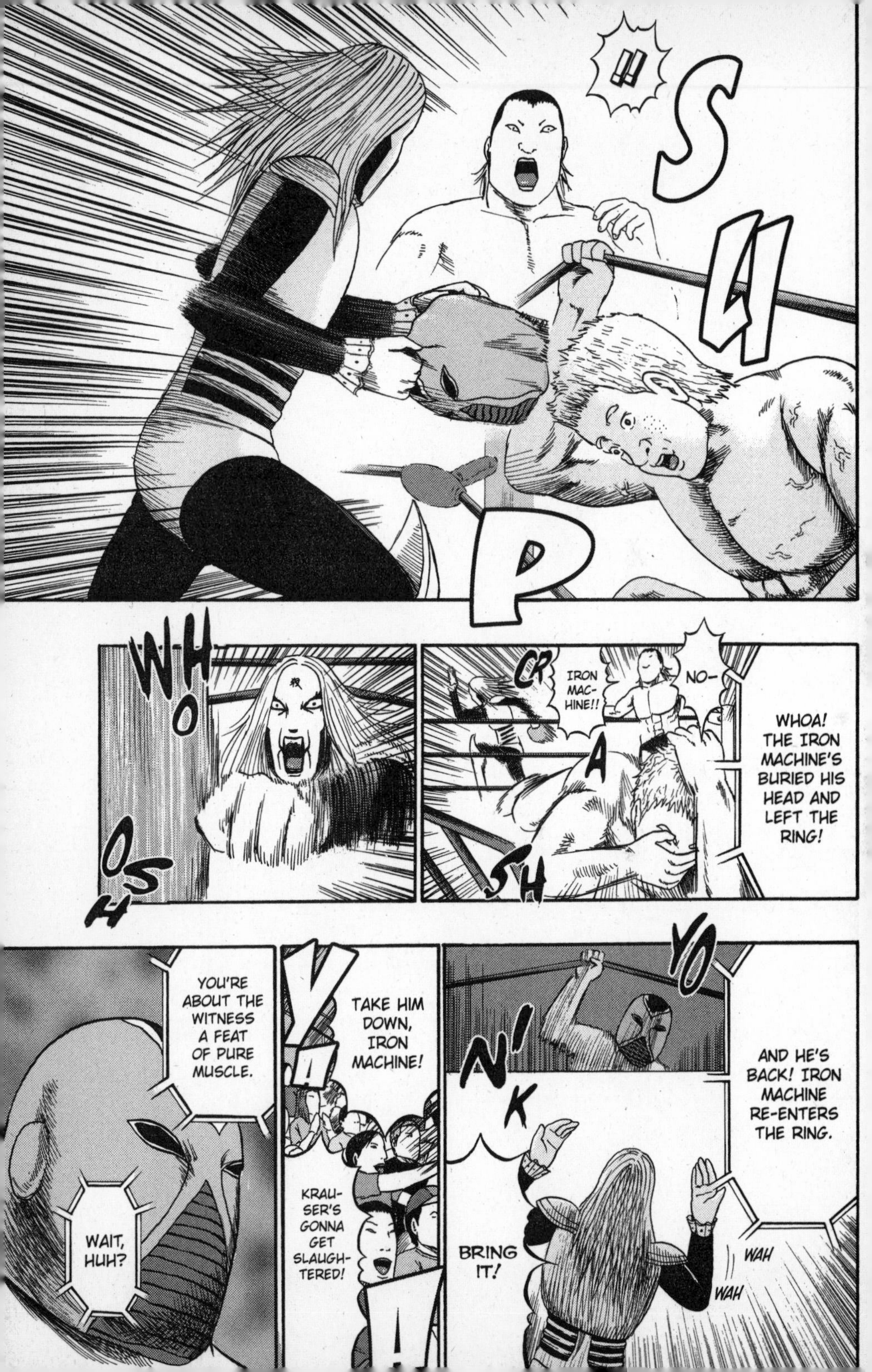
!!
NO—
IRON MACHINE!!
WHOA! THE IRON MACHINE'S BURIED HIS HEAD AND LEFT THE RING!
CRASH
WHOOSH
YOINK
AND HE'S BACK! IRON MACHINE RE-ENTERS THE RING.
BRING IT!
WAH
WAH
TAKE HIM DOWN, IRON MACHINE!
KRAUSER'S GONNA GET SLAUGHTERED!
YOU'RE ABOUT THE WITNESS A FEAT OF PURE MUSCLE.
WAIT, HUH?

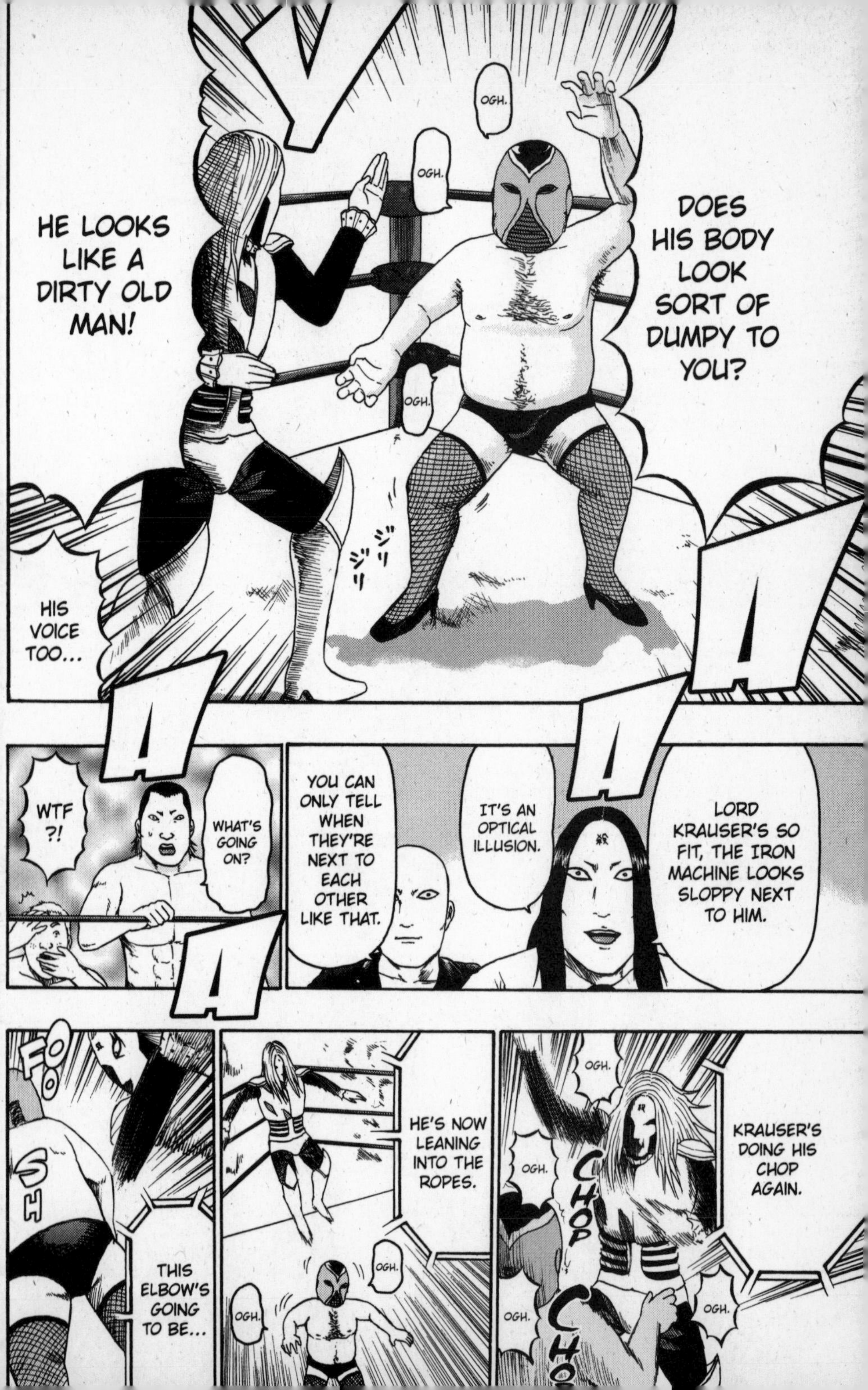
OGH.
OGH.
DOES HIS BODY LOOK SORT OF DUMPY TO YOU?
HE LOOKS LIKE A DIRTY OLD MAN!
OGH.
ジリジリ
HIS VOICE TOO...
AAAA
LORD KRAUSER'S SO FIT, THE IRON MACHINE LOOKS SLOPPY NEXT TO HIM.
IT'S AN OPTICAL ILLUSION.
YOU CAN ONLY TELL WHEN THEY'RE NEXT TO EACH OTHER LIKE THAT.
WHAT'S GOING ON?
WTF ?!
OGH.
KRAUSER'S DOING HIS CHOP AGAIN.
OGH.
CHOP
OGH.
OGH.
CHOP
HE'S NOW LEANING INTO THE ROPES.
OGH.
OGH.
FOO
SH
THIS ELBOW'S GOING TO BE...

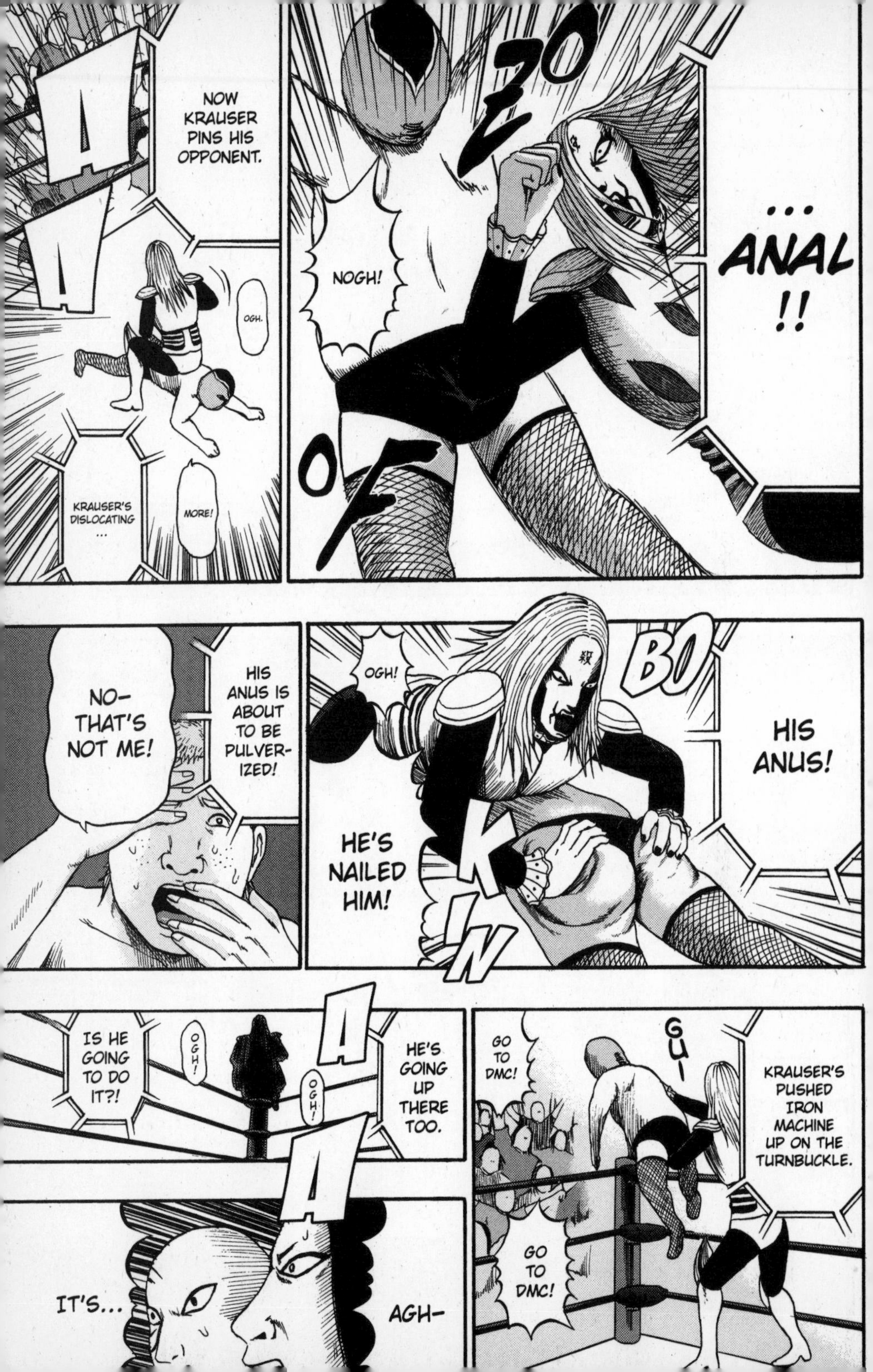
ZO
...ANAL!!
NOGH!
OF
NOW KRAUSER PINS HIS OPPONENT.
A
A
OGH.
MORE!
KRAUSER'S DISLOCATING ...
BO
OGH!
HIS ANUS!
HE'S NAILED HIM!
K
IN
HIS ANUS IS ABOUT TO BE PULVER-IZED!
NO—THAT'S NOT ME!
GUI
GO TO DMC!
KRAUSER'S PUSHED IRON MACHINE UP ON THE TURNBUCKLE.
GO TO DMC!
A
HE'S GOING UP THERE TOO.
OGH!
OGH!
IS HE GOING TO DO IT?!
A
AGH-
IT'S...

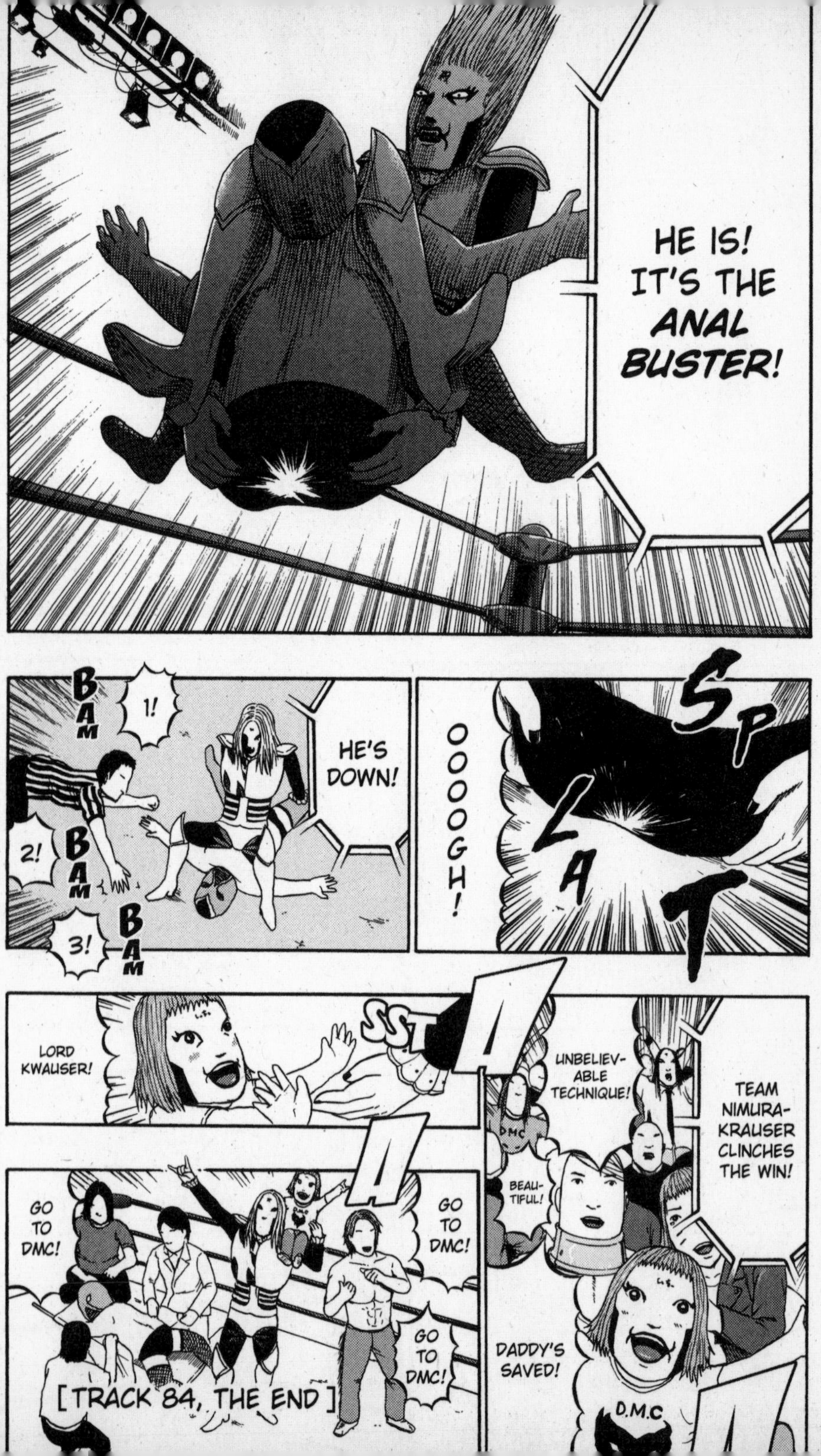
HE IS! IT'S THE ANAL BUSTER!
SPLAT
OOOOGH!
HE'S DOWN!
1!
BAM
2!
BAM
3!
BAM
TEAM NIMURA-KRAUSER CLINCHES THE WIN!
UNBELIEV-ABLE TECHNIQUE!
DMC
BEAU-TIFUL!
DADDY'S SAVED!
D.M.C
SSTAA
LORD KWAUSER!
GO TO DMC!
GO TO DMC!
GO TO DMC!
[TRACK 84, THE END]

DMC LEXICON

🎭 PRO WRESTLING

The ultimate in grappling. The author of this manga, Kiminori Wakasugi, would like to ask everyone to first read his favorite wrestling manga from when he was growing up: Ultimate Muscle. If you mistakenly get the amateur wrestling comic book Amateur Wrestler Ken-chan, well, go ahead and read that too.

Usage: Your girlfriend looks like a pro wrestler, dude.

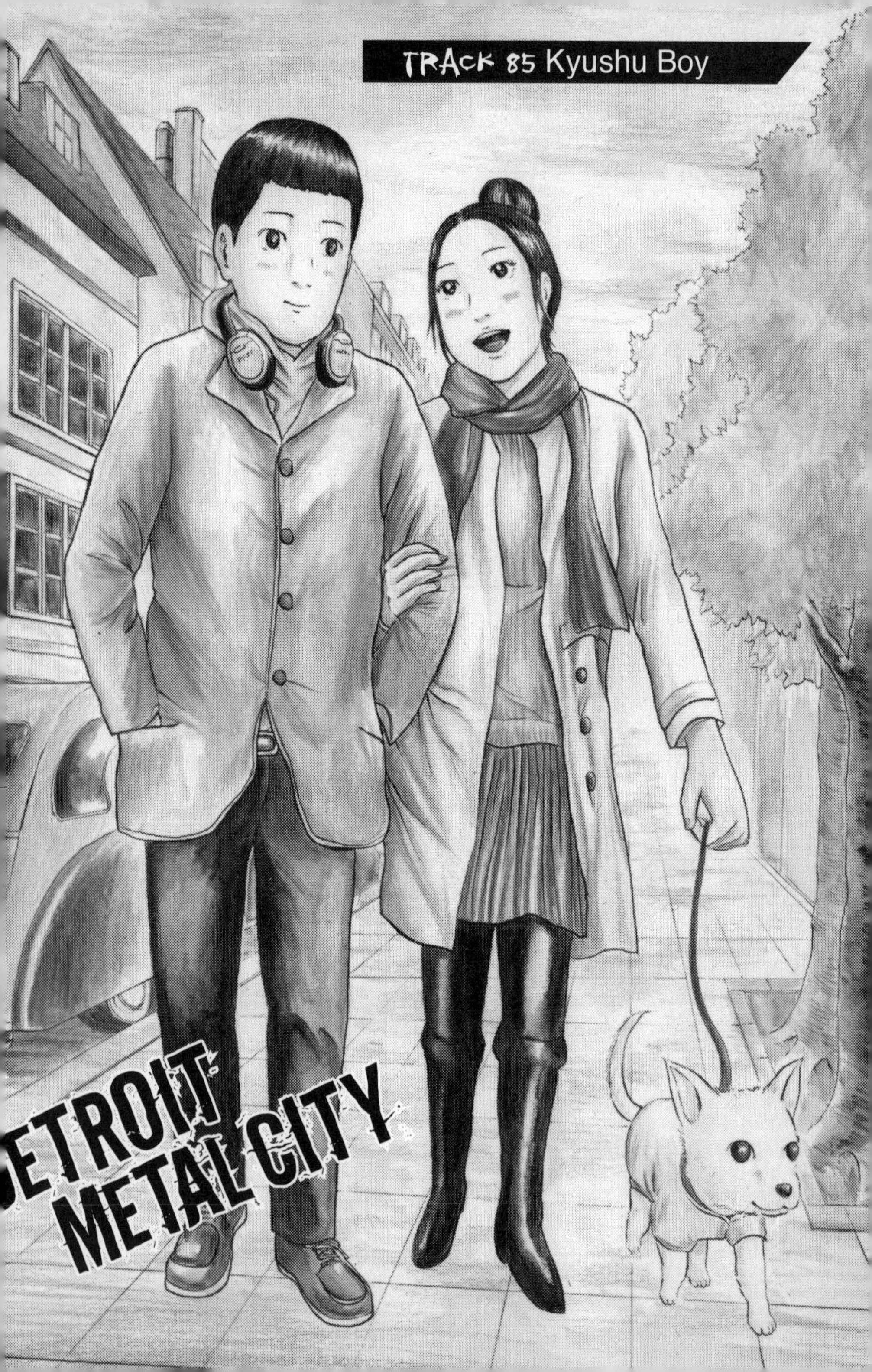
TRACK 85 Kyushu Boy
DETROIT METAL CITY

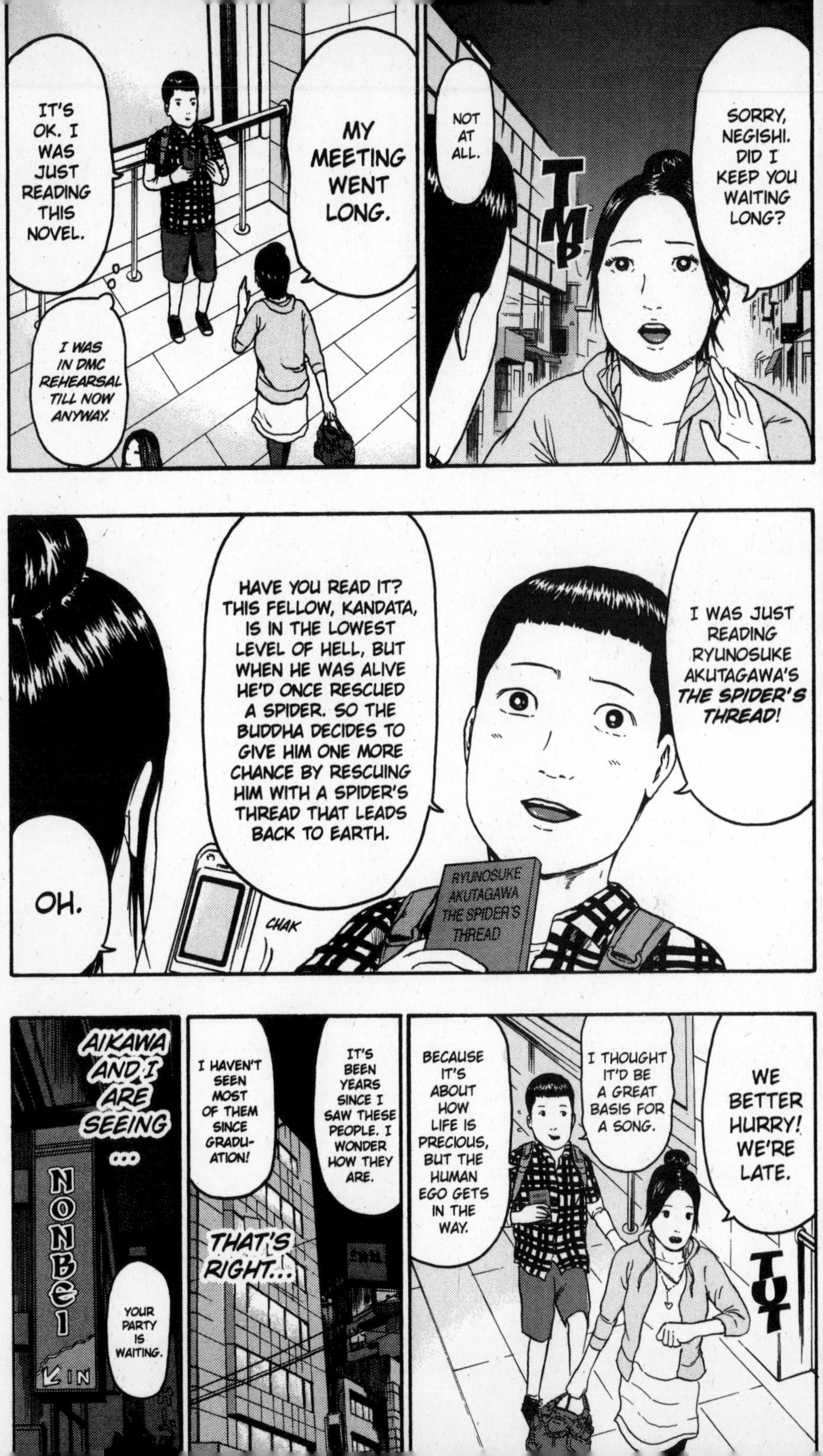
SORRY, NEGISHI. DID I KEEP YOU WAITING LONG?
TMP
NOT AT ALL.
MY MEETING WENT LONG.
IT'S OK. I WAS JUST READING THIS NOVEL.
I WAS IN DMC REHEARSAL TILL NOW ANYWAY.
I WAS JUST READING RYUNOSUKE AKUTAGAWA'S THE SPIDER'S THREAD!
HAVE YOU READ IT? THIS FELLOW, KANDATA, IS IN THE LOWEST LEVEL OF HELL, BUT WHEN HE WAS ALIVE HE'D ONCE RESCUED A SPIDER. SO THE BUDDHA DECIDES TO GIVE HIM ONE MORE CHANCE BY RESCUING HIM WITH A SPIDER'S THREAD THAT LEADS BACK TO EARTH.
RYUNOSUKE AKUTAGAWA THE SPIDER'S THREAD
CHAK
OH.
WE BETTER HURRY! WE'RE LATE.
TUT
I THOUGHT IT'D BE A GREAT BASIS FOR A SONG.
BECAUSE IT'S ABOUT HOW LIFE IS PRECIOUS, BUT THE HUMAN EGO GETS IN THE WAY.
IT'S BEEN YEARS SINCE I SAW THESE PEOPLE. I WONDER HOW THEY ARE.
I HAVEN'T SEEN MOST OF THEM SINCE GRADUATION!
THAT'S RIGHT...
AIKAWA AND I ARE SEEING ...
NONBEI
IN
YOUR PARTY IS WAITING.

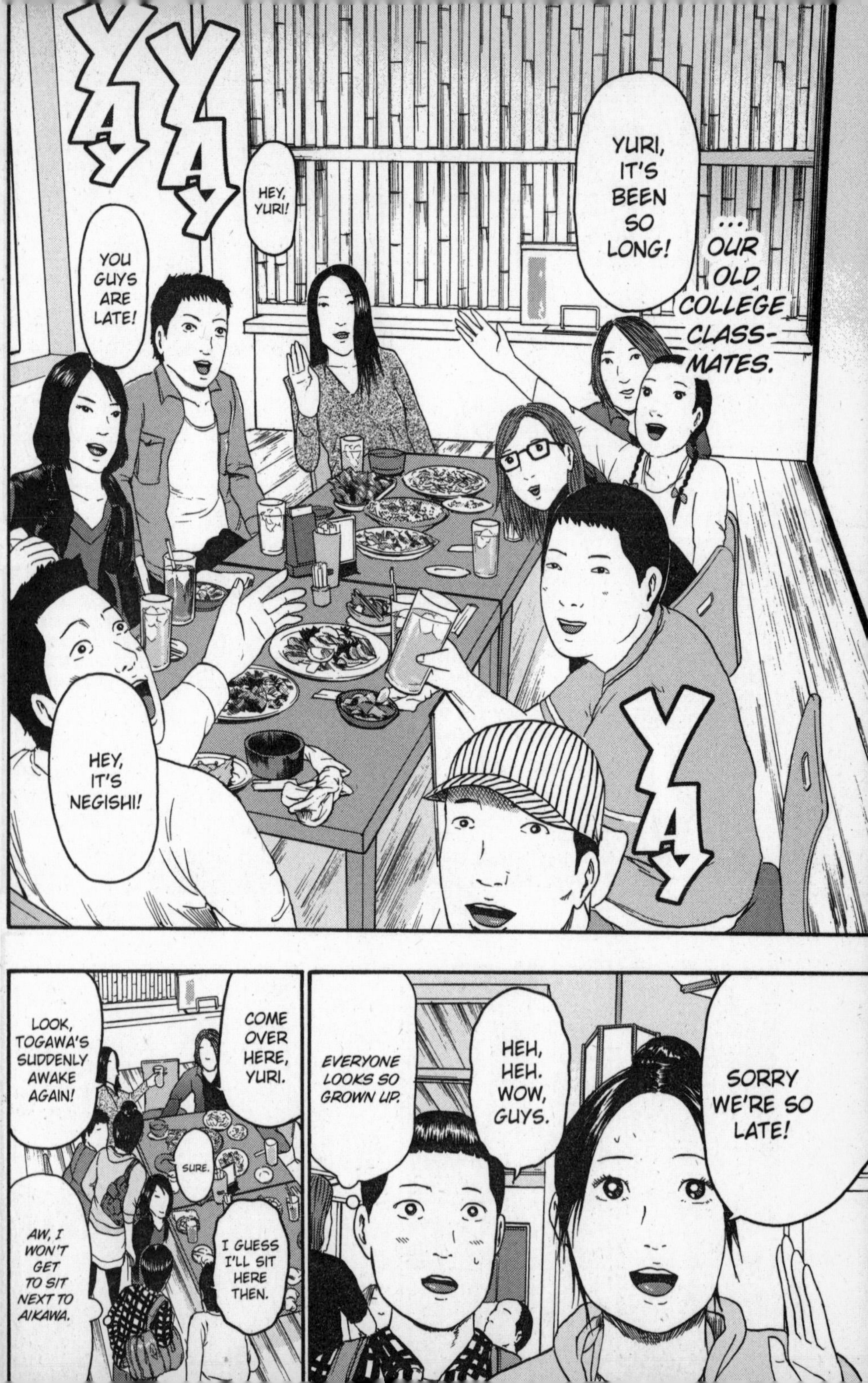
YURI, IT'S BEEN SO LONG!
...OUR OLD COLLEGE CLASS-MATES.
HEY, YURI!
YAY YAY
YOU GUYS ARE LATE!
YAY
HEY, IT'S NEGISHI!
SORRY WE'RE SO LATE!
HEH, HEH. WOW, GUYS.
EVERYONE LOOKS SO GROWN UP.
COME OVER HERE, YURI.
LOOK, TOGAWA'S SUDDENLY AWAKE AGAIN!
SURE.
I GUESS I'LL SIT HERE THEN.
AW, I WON'T GET TO SIT NEXT TO AIKAWA.

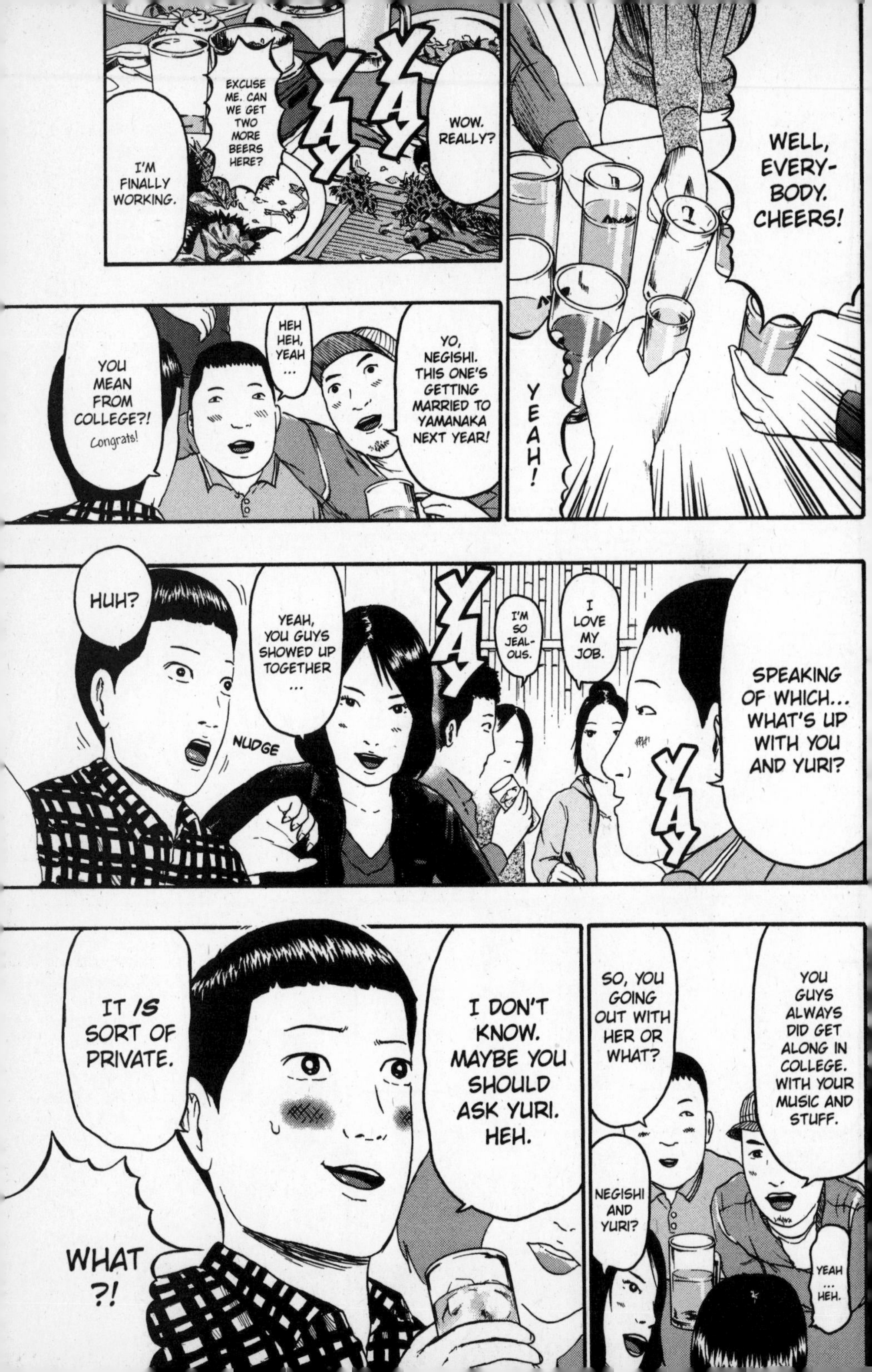
WELL, EVERY-BODY. CHEERS!
YEAH!
WOW. REALLY?
YAY
YAY
EXCUSE ME. CAN WE GET TWO MORE BEERS HERE?
I'M FINALLY WORKING.
YO, NEGISHI. THIS ONE'S GETTING MARRIED TO YAMANAKA NEXT YEAR!
HEH HEH, YEAH ...
YOU MEAN FROM COLLEGE?!
Congrats!
SPEAKING OF WHICH... WHAT'S UP WITH YOU AND YURI?
YAY
I LOVE MY JOB.
I'M SO JEAL-OUS.
YAY
YEAH, YOU GUYS SHOWED UP TOGETHER ...
NUDGE
HUH?
YOU GUYS ALWAYS DID GET ALONG IN COLLEGE. WITH YOUR MUSIC AND STUFF.
SO, YOU GOING OUT WITH HER OR WHAT?
NEGISHI AND YURI?
YEAH ... HEH.
I DON'T KNOW. MAYBE YOU SHOULD ASK YURI. HEH.
IT *IS* SORT OF PRIVATE.
WHAT?!

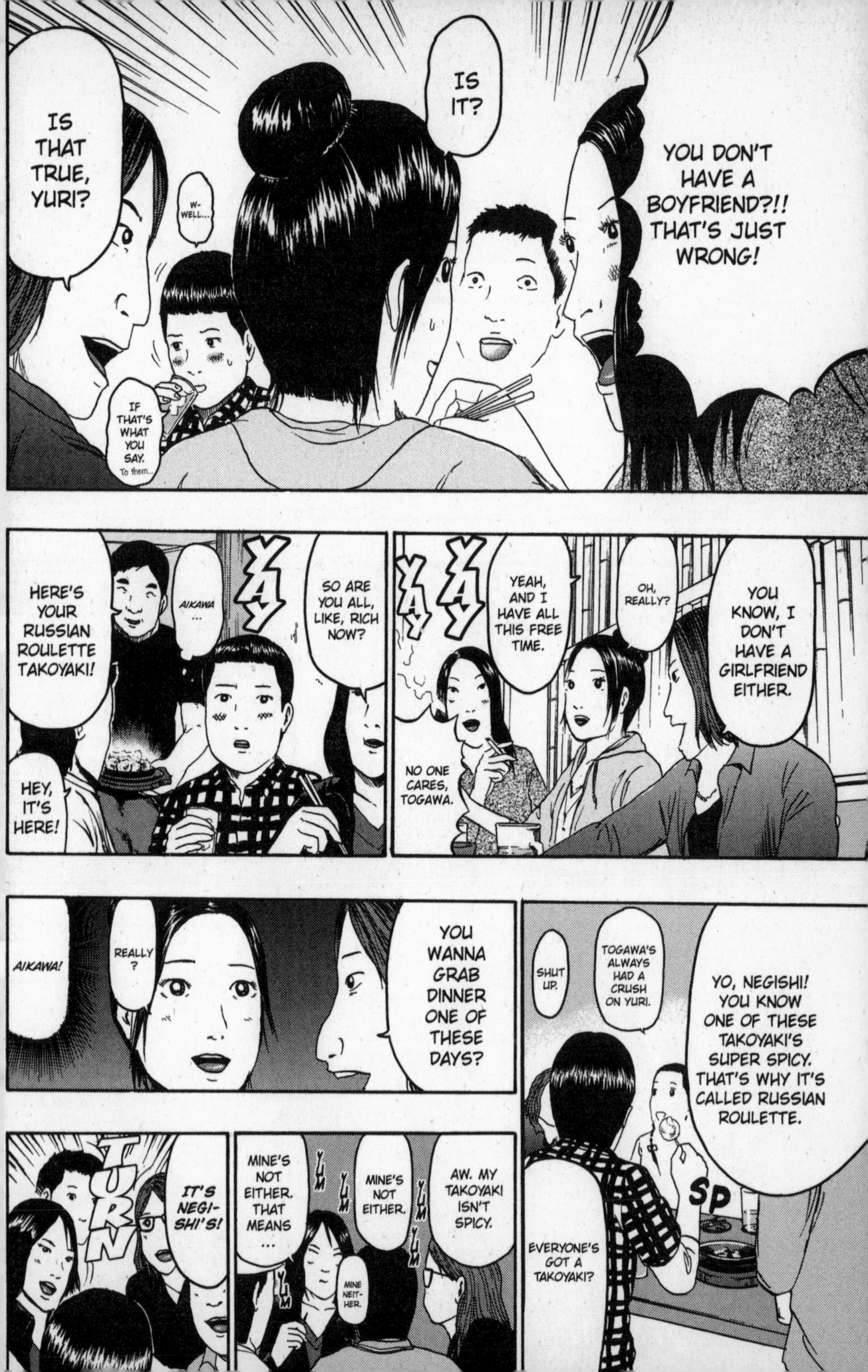
YOU DON'T HAVE A BOYFRIEND?!! THAT'S JUST WRONG!
IS IT?
W-WELL...
IS THAT TRUE, YURI?
IF THAT'S WHAT YOU SAY. To them...
YOU KNOW, I DON'T HAVE A GIRLFRIEND EITHER.
OH, REALLY?
YEAH, AND I HAVE ALL THIS FREE TIME.
YAY
YAY
NO ONE CARES, TOGAWA.
YAY
SO ARE YOU ALL, LIKE, RICH NOW?
AIKAWA ...
HERE'S YOUR RUSSIAN ROULETTE TAKOYAKI!
HEY, IT'S HERE!
YO, NEGISHI! YOU KNOW ONE OF THESE TAKOYAKI'S SUPER SPICY. THAT'S WHY IT'S CALLED RUSSIAN ROULETTE.
TOGAWA'S ALWAYS HAD A CRUSH ON YURI.
SHUT UP.
SP
EVERYONE'S GOT A TAKOYAKI?
YOU WANNA GRAB DINNER ONE OF THESE DAYS?
REALLY?
AIKAWA!
AW. MY TAKOYAKI ISN'T SPICY.
YUM
MINE'S NOT EITHER.
YUM
MINE'S NOT EITHER. THAT MEANS ...
MINE NEITHER.
TURN
IT'S NEGISHI'S!

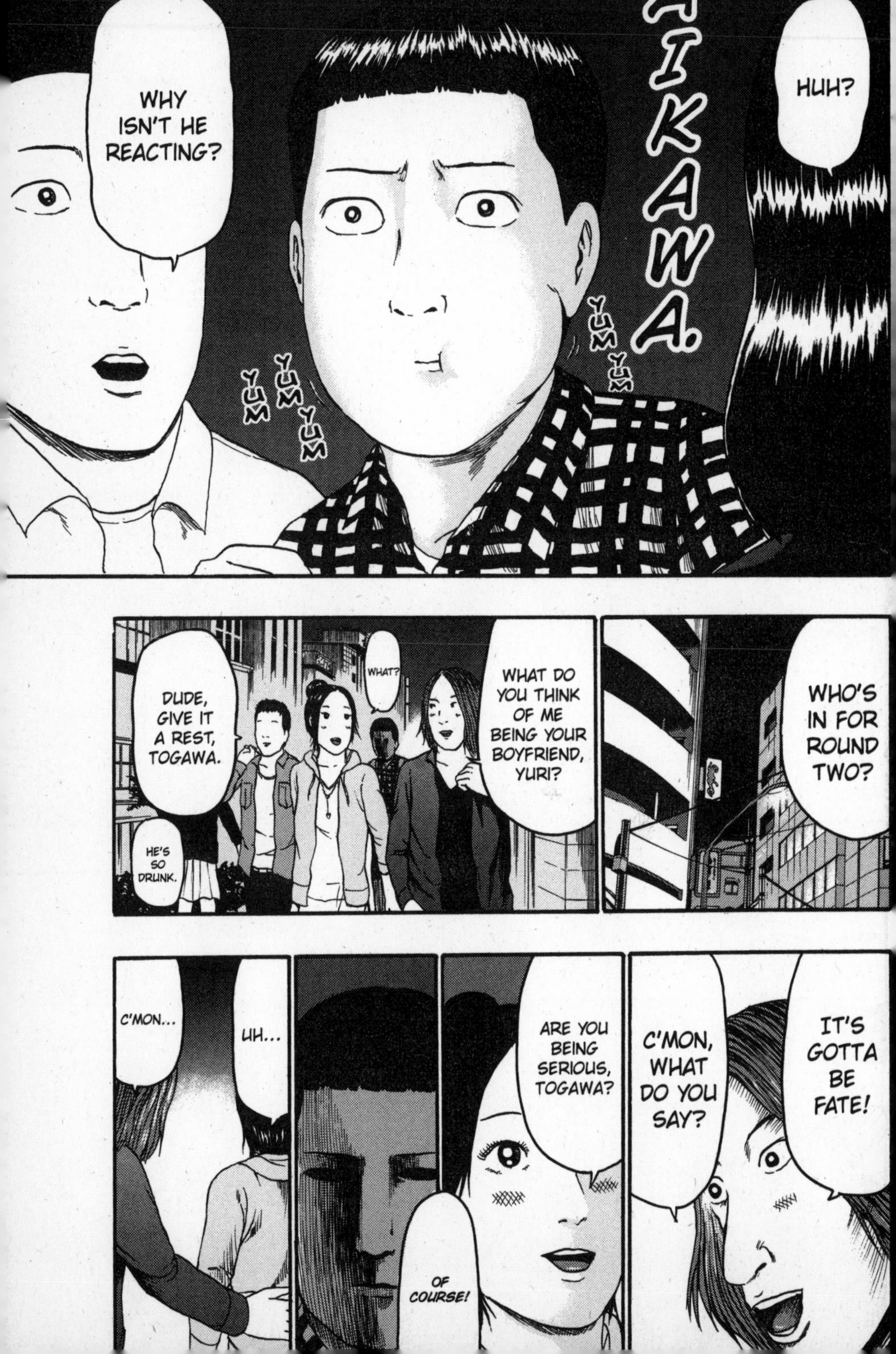
HUH?
AIKAWA.
YUM YUM
YUM YUM YUM
WHY ISN'T HE REACTING?
WHO'S IN FOR ROUND TWO?
WHAT DO YOU THINK OF ME BEING YOUR BOYFRIEND, YURI?
WHAT?
DUDE, GIVE IT A REST, TOGAWA.
HE'S SO DRUNK.
IT'S GOTTA BE FATE!
C'MON, WHAT DO YOU SAY?
ARE YOU BEING SERIOUS, TOGAWA?
OF COURSE!
UH...
C'MON...

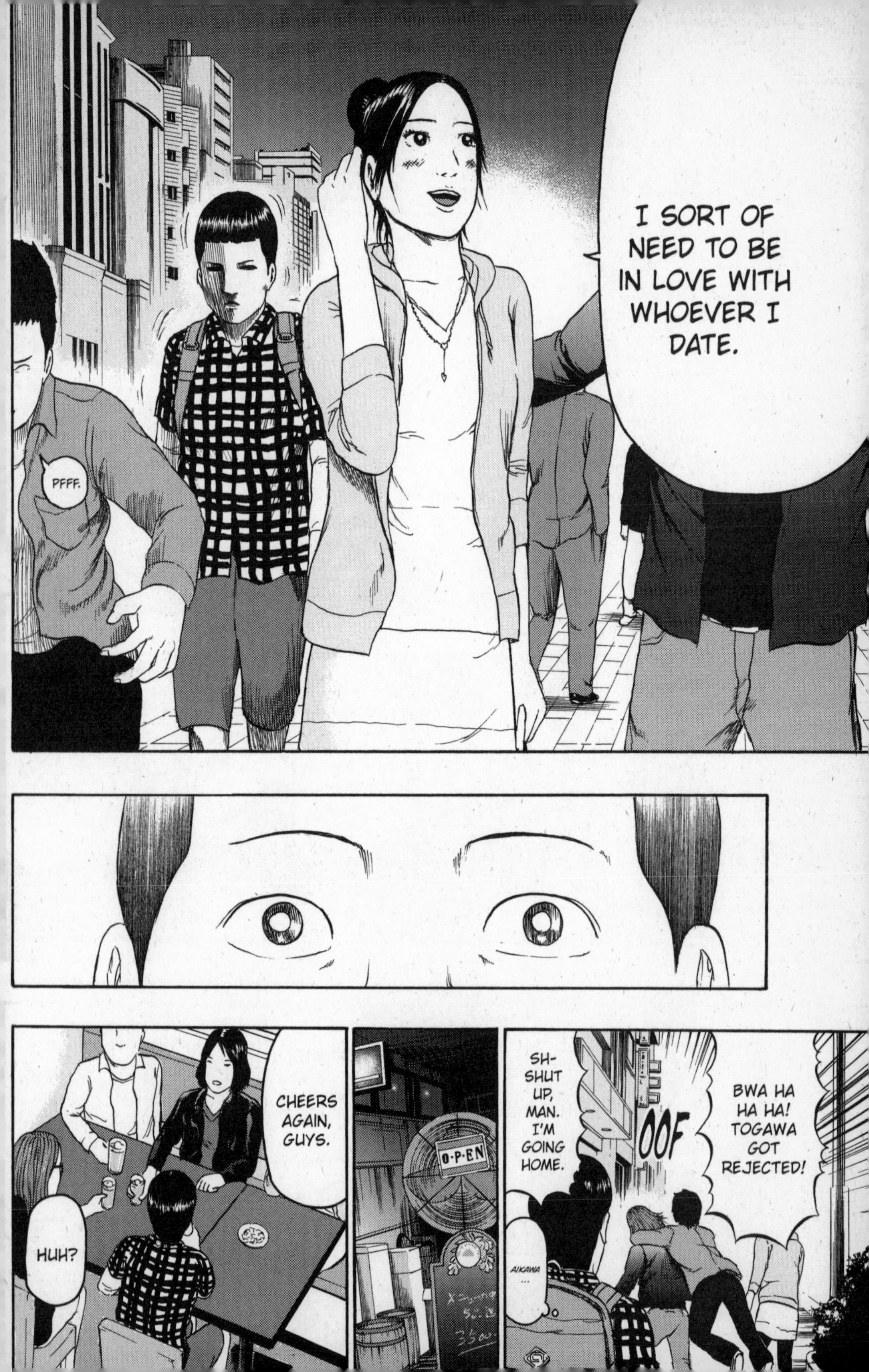
I SORT OF NEED TO BE IN LOVE WITH WHOEVER I DATE.
PFFF.
BWA HA HA HA! TOGAWA GOT REJECTED!
OOF
SH-SHUT UP, MAN. I'M GOING HOME.
AIKAWA ...
O·P·EN
CHEERS AGAIN, GUYS.
HUH?

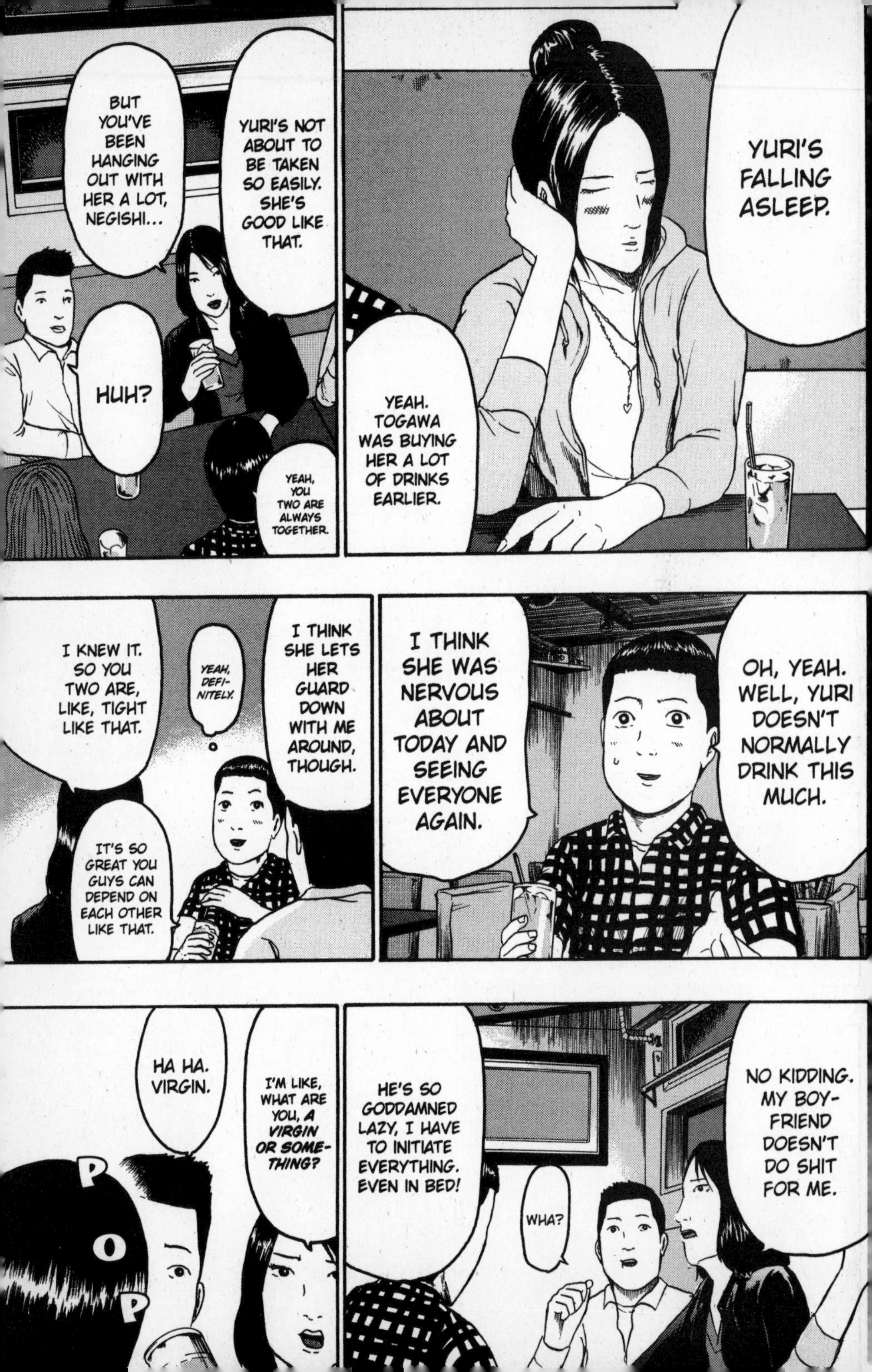
YURI'S FALLING ASLEEP.
YEAH. TOGAWA WAS BUYING HER A LOT OF DRINKS EARLIER.
YURI'S NOT ABOUT TO BE TAKEN SO EASILY. SHE'S GOOD LIKE THAT.
BUT YOU'VE BEEN HANGING OUT WITH HER A LOT, NEGISHI...
HUH?
YEAH, YOU TWO ARE ALWAYS TOGETHER.
OH, YEAH. WELL, YURI DOESN'T NORMALLY DRINK THIS MUCH.
I THINK SHE WAS NERVOUS ABOUT TODAY AND SEEING EVERYONE AGAIN.
I THINK SHE LETS HER GUARD DOWN WITH ME AROUND, THOUGH.
YEAH, DEFINITELY.
I KNEW IT. SO YOU TWO ARE, LIKE, TIGHT LIKE THAT.
IT'S SO GREAT YOU GUYS CAN DEPEND ON EACH OTHER LIKE THAT.
NO KIDDING. MY BOYFRIEND DOESN'T DO SHIT FOR ME.
HE'S SO GODDAMNED LAZY, I HAVE TO INITIATE EVERYTHING. EVEN IN BED!
WHA?
I'M LIKE, WHAT ARE YOU, *A VIRGIN OR SOMETHING?*
HA HA. VIRGIN.
POP

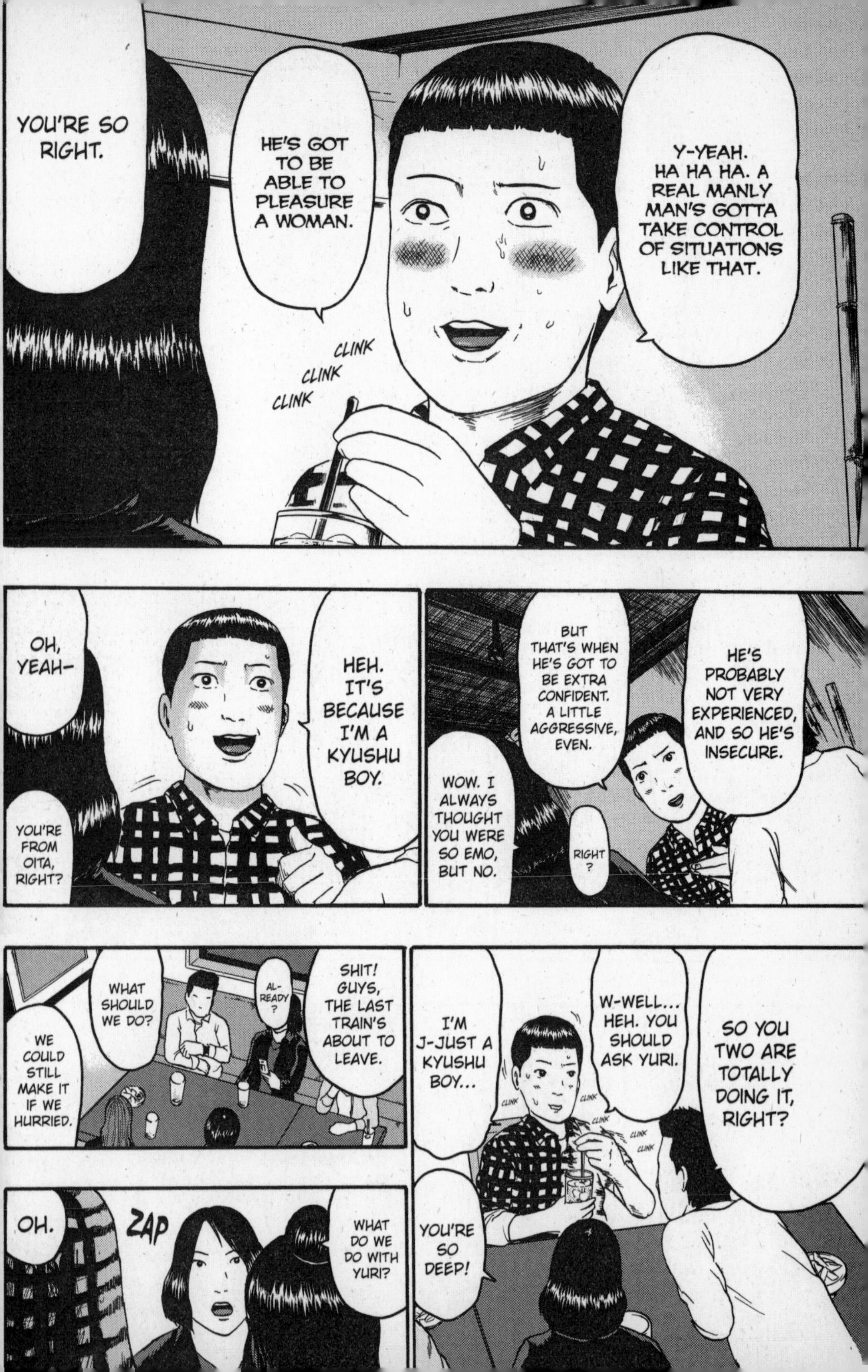
Y-YEAH. HA HA HA. A REAL MANLY MAN'S GOTTA TAKE CONTROL OF SITUATIONS LIKE THAT.
HE'S GOT TO BE ABLE TO PLEASURE A WOMAN.
YOU'RE SO RIGHT.
CLINK
CLINK
CLINK
HE'S PROBABLY NOT VERY EXPERIENCED, AND SO HE'S INSECURE.
BUT THAT'S WHEN HE'S GOT TO BE EXTRA CONFIDENT. A LITTLE AGGRESSIVE, EVEN.
RIGHT?
WOW. I ALWAYS THOUGHT YOU WERE SO EMO, BUT NO.
HEH. IT'S BECAUSE I'M A KYUSHU BOY.
OH, YEAH-
YOU'RE FROM OITA, RIGHT?
SO YOU TWO ARE TOTALLY DOING IT, RIGHT?
W-WELL... HEH. YOU SHOULD ASK YURI.
I'M J-JUST A KYUSHU BOY...
CLINK
CLINK
CLINK
CLINK
CLINK
YOU'RE SO DEEP!
SHIT! GUYS, THE LAST TRAIN'S ABOUT TO LEAVE.
AL-READY?
WHAT SHOULD WE DO?
WE COULD STILL MAKE IT IF WE HURRIED.
WHAT DO WE DO WITH YURI?
ZAP
OH.

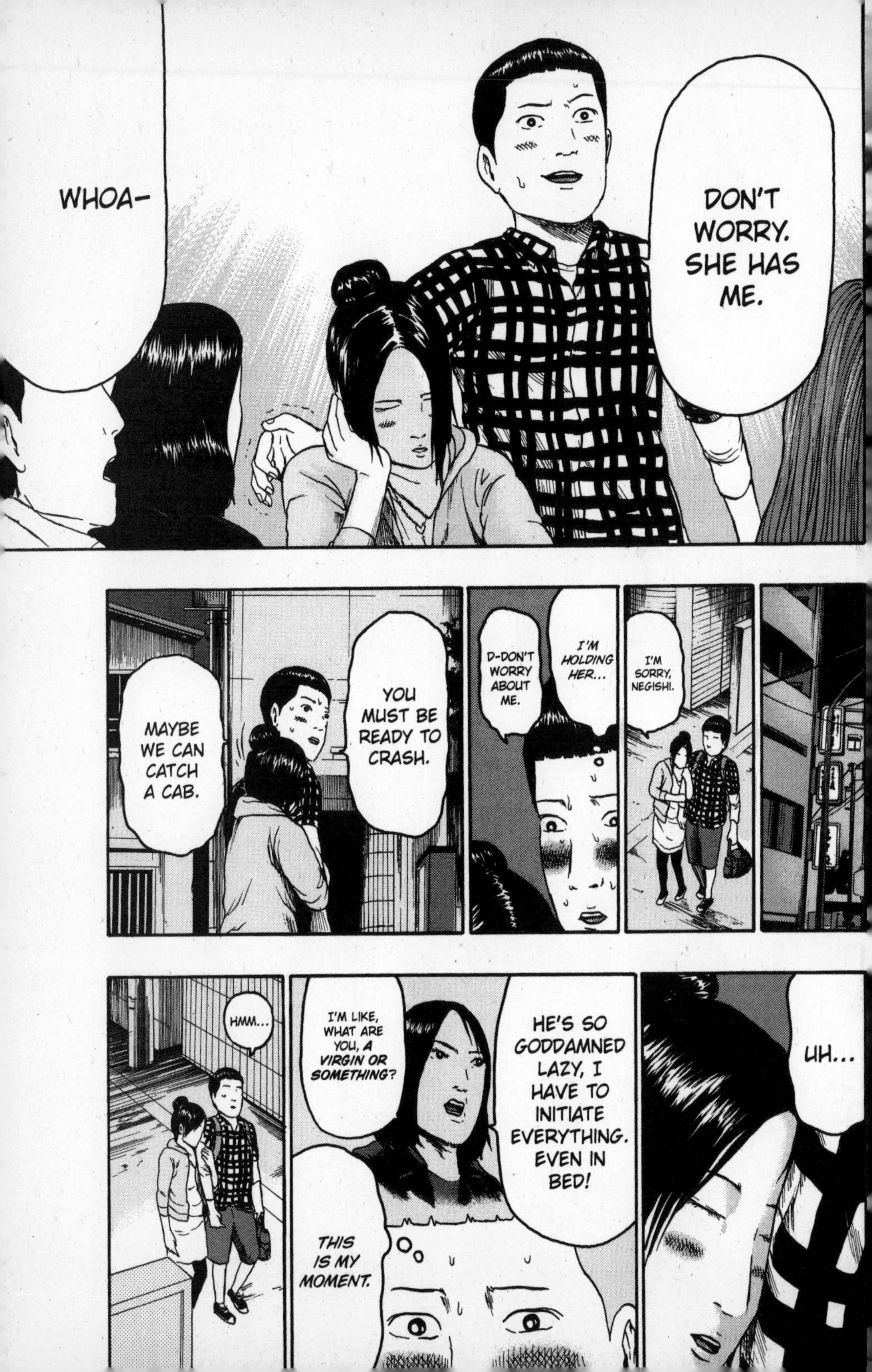
DON'T WORRY. SHE HAS ME.
WHOA-
I'M SORRY, NEGISHI.
I'M HOLDING HER...
D-DON'T WORRY ABOUT ME.
YOU MUST BE READY TO CRASH.
MAYBE WE CAN CATCH A CAB.
UH...
HE'S SO GODDAMNED LAZY, I HAVE TO INITIATE EVERYTHING. EVEN IN BED!
I'M LIKE, WHAT ARE YOU, A *VIRGIN OR SOMETHING*?
THIS IS MY MOMENT.
HMM...

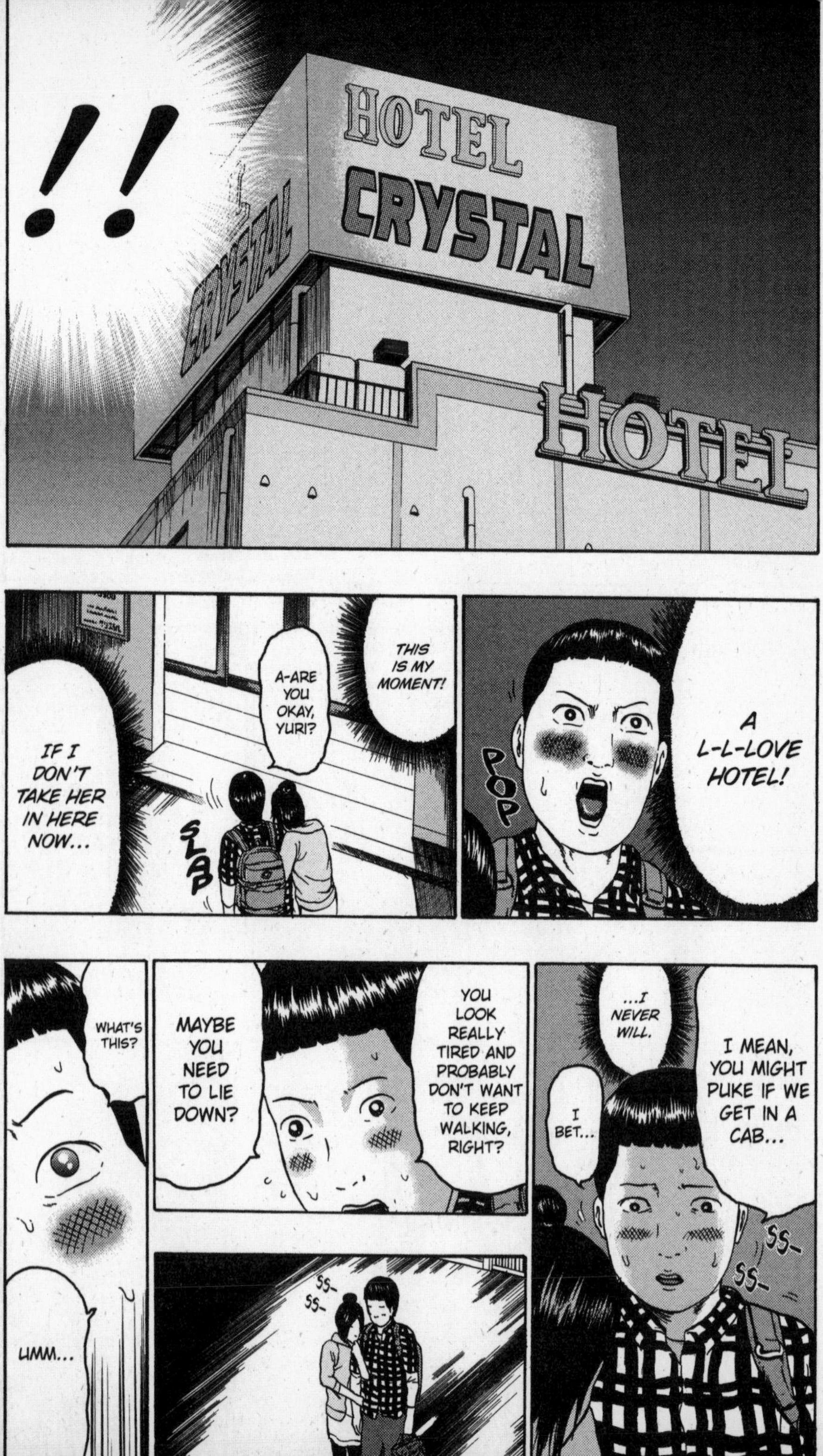
!!
HOTEL
CRYSTAL
CRYSTAL
HOTEL
POP
POP
A L-L-LOVE HOTEL!
THIS IS MY MOMENT!
A-ARE YOU OKAY, YURI?
IF I DON'T TAKE HER IN HERE NOW...
SLAP
...I NEVER WILL.
I MEAN, YOU MIGHT PUKE IF WE GET IN A CAB...
I BET...
SS-
SS-
YOU LOOK REALLY TIRED AND PROBABLY DON'T WANT TO KEEP WALKING, RIGHT?
MAYBE YOU NEED TO LIE DOWN?
SS-
SS-
WHAT'S THIS?
UMM...

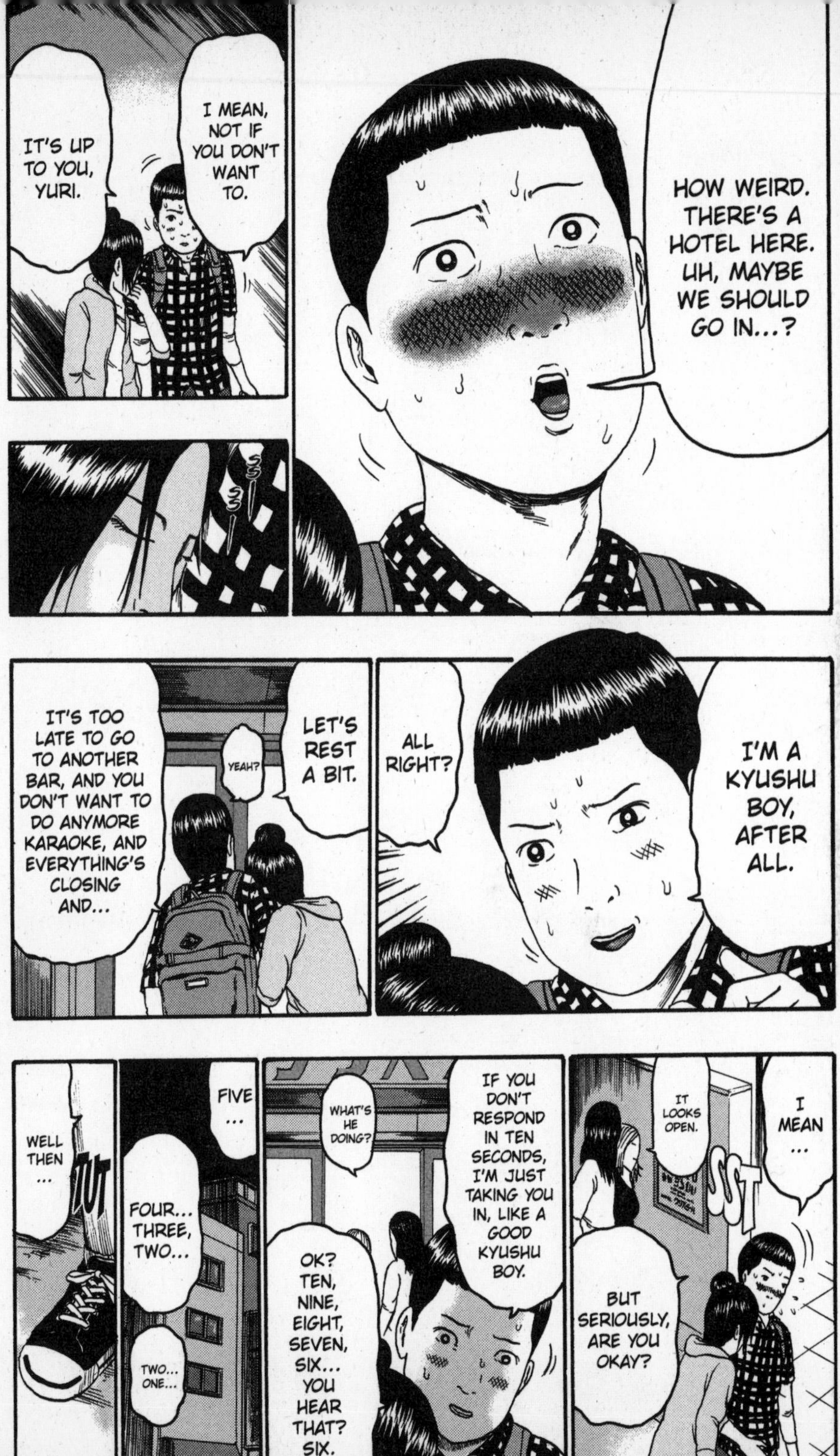
HOW WEIRD. THERE'S A HOTEL HERE. UH, MAYBE WE SHOULD GO IN...?
I MEAN, NOT IF YOU DON'T WANT TO.
IT'S UP TO YOU, YURI.
I'M A KYUSHU BOY, AFTER ALL.
ALL RIGHT?
LET'S REST A BIT.
YEAH?
IT'S TOO LATE TO GO TO ANOTHER BAR, AND YOU DON'T WANT TO DO ANYMORE KARAOKE, AND EVERYTHING'S CLOSING AND...
I MEAN...
IT LOOKS OPEN.
SST
BUT SERIOUSLY, ARE YOU OKAY?
IF YOU DON'T RESPOND IN TEN SECONDS, I'M JUST TAKING YOU IN, LIKE A GOOD KYUSHU BOY.
WHAT'S HE DOING?
OK? TEN, NINE, EIGHT, SEVEN, SIX... YOU HEAR THAT? SIX.
FIVE...
FOUR... THREE, TWO...
TWO... ONE...
WELL THEN...
TUT

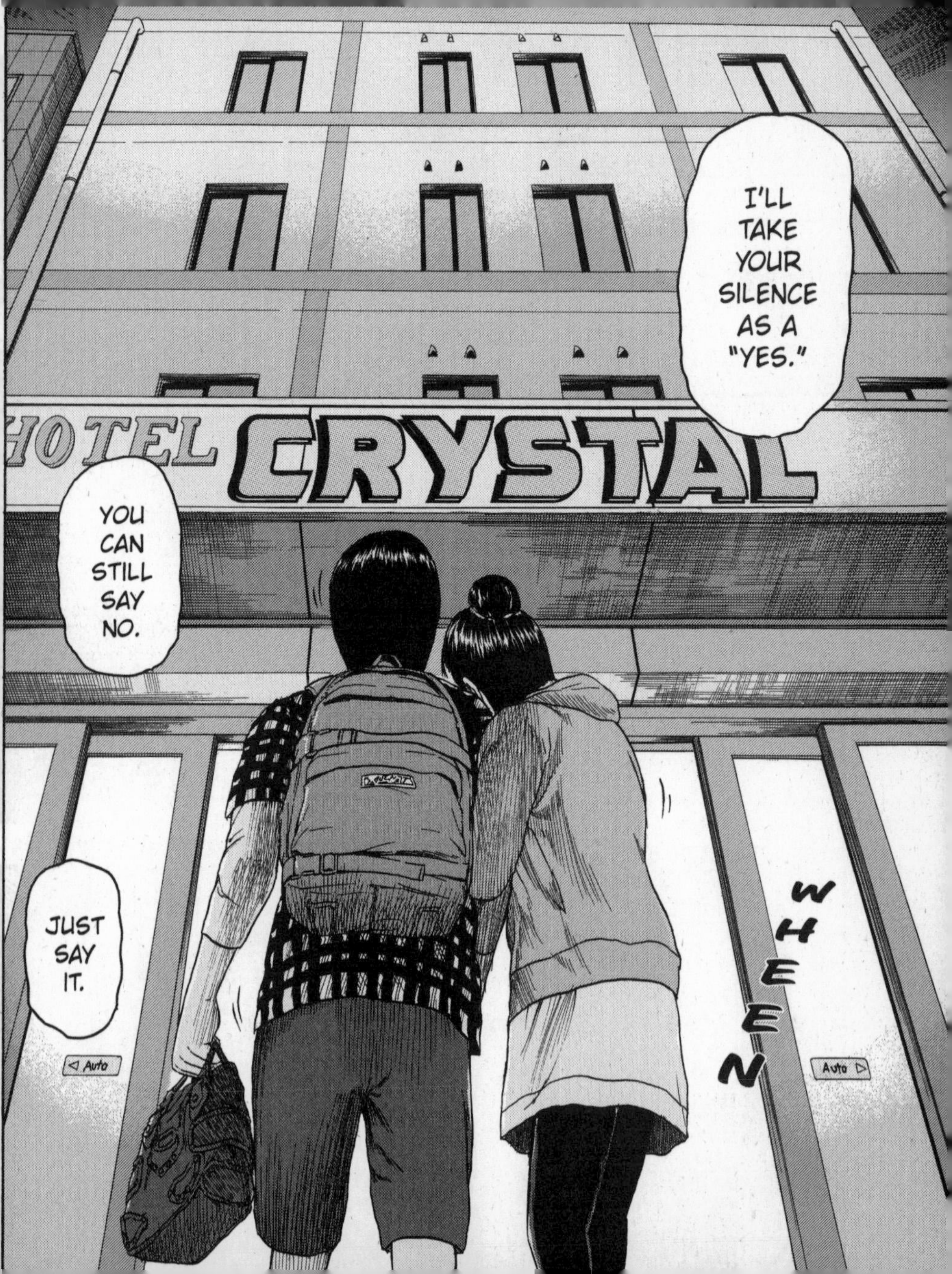
I'LL TAKE YOUR SILENCE AS A "YES."
HOTEL CRYSTAL
YOU CAN STILL SAY NO.
WHEEEN
JUST SAY IT.
Auto
Auto

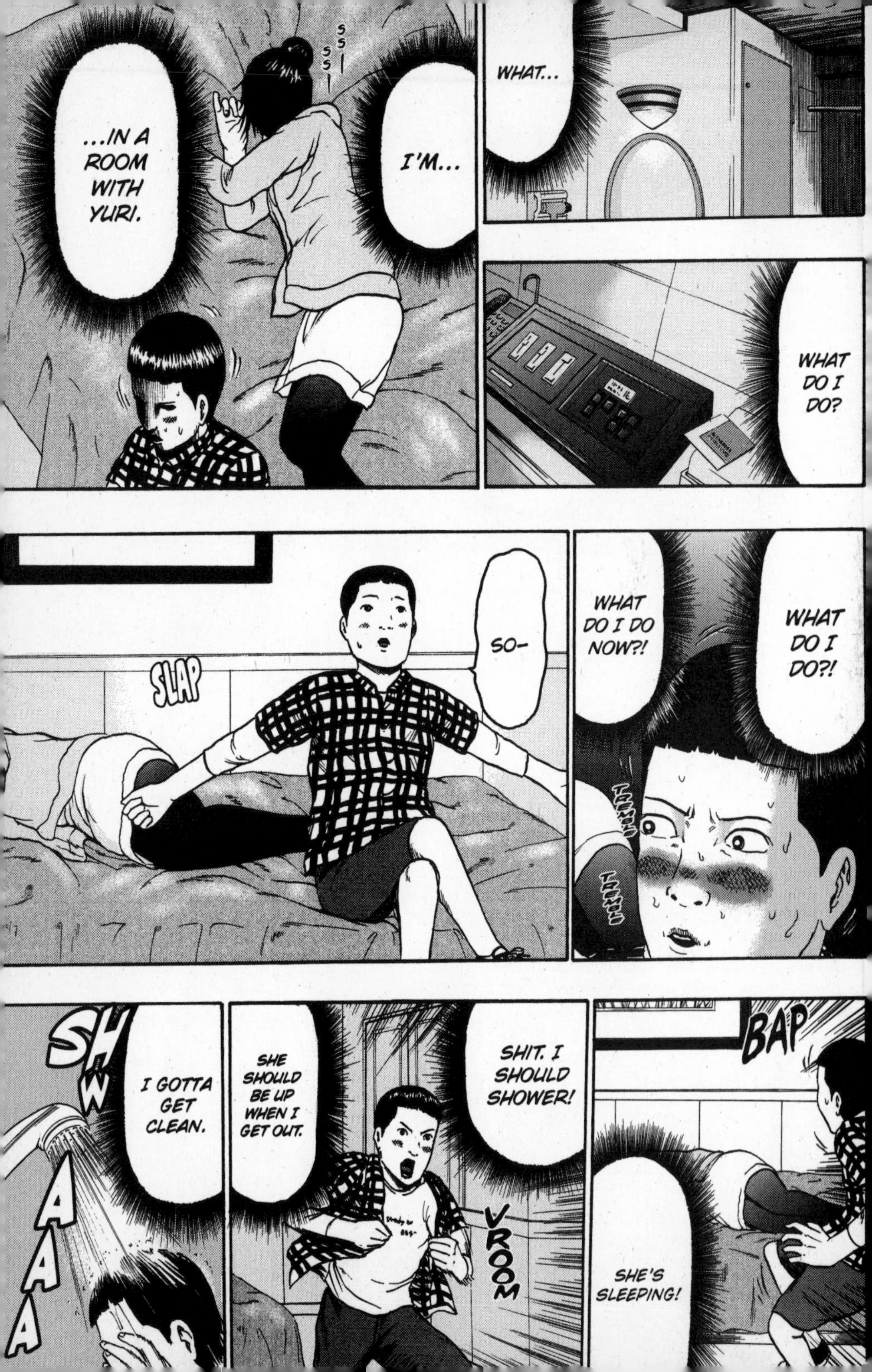
WHAT...
WHAT DO I DO?
I'M...
...IN A ROOM WITH YURI.
WHAT DO I DO?!
WHAT DO I DO NOW?!
SO-
SLAP
BAP
SHE'S SLEEPING!
SHIT. I SHOULD SHOWER!
SHE SHOULD BE UP WHEN I GET OUT.
VROOM
I GOTTA GET CLEAN.
SHWAAAAA

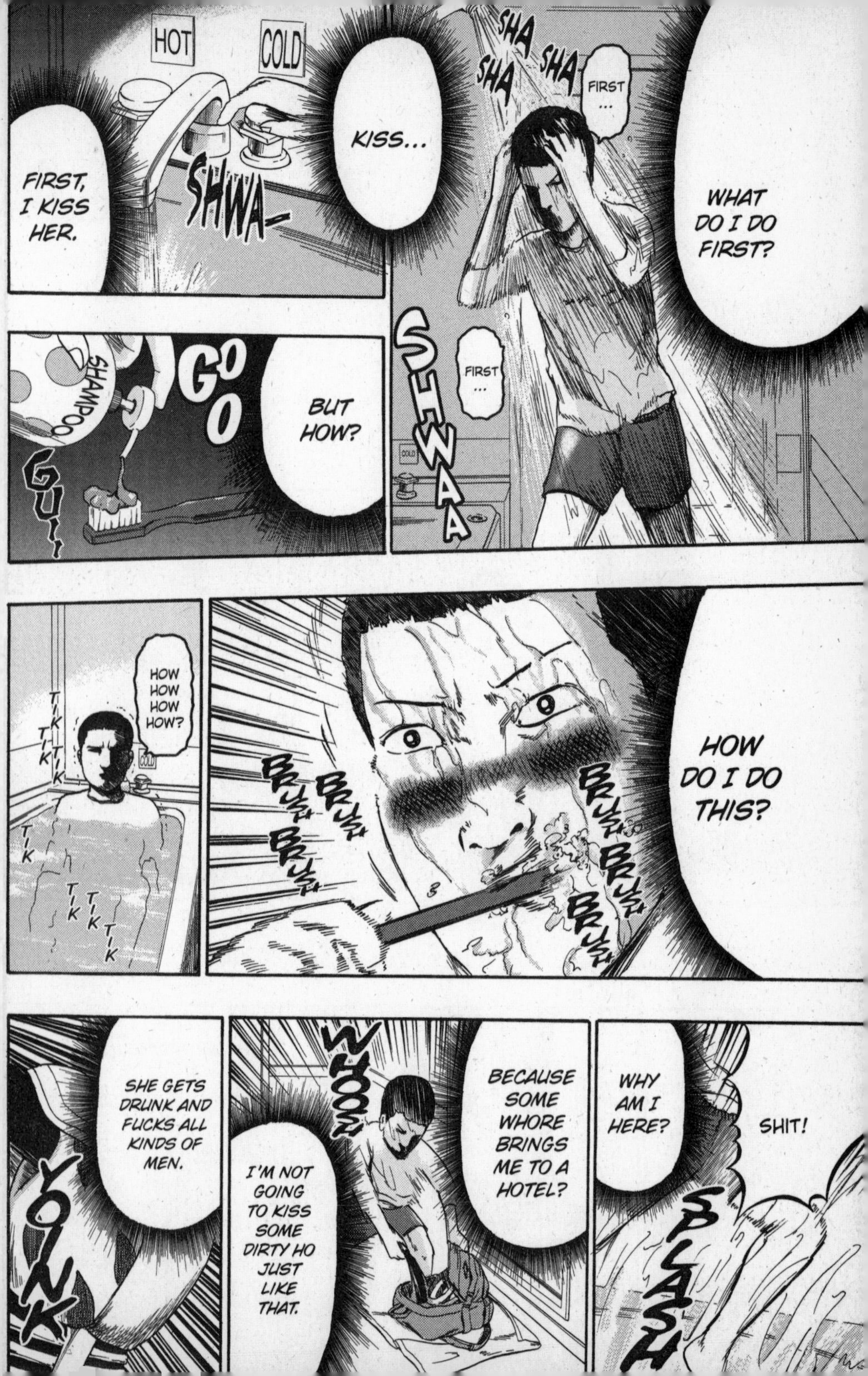
WHAT DO I DO FIRST?
SHA SHA SHA
FIRST ...
FIRST ...
SHWAA
KISS...
HOT
COLD
SHWA-
FIRST, I KISS HER.
BUT HOW?
GOGO
SHAMPOO
GUI
HOW DO I DO THIS?
BRUSH BRUSH BRUSH
BRUSH BRUSH BRUSH
HOW HOW HOW HOW?
COLD
TIK TIK TIK TIK TIK TIK TIK TIK TIK
SHIT!
SPLASH
WHY AM I HERE?
BECAUSE SOME WHORE BRINGS ME TO A HOTEL?
WHOOSH
I'M NOT GOING TO KISS SOME DIRTY HO JUST LIKE THAT.
SHE GETS DRUNK AND FUCKS ALL KINDS OF MEN.
YOINK

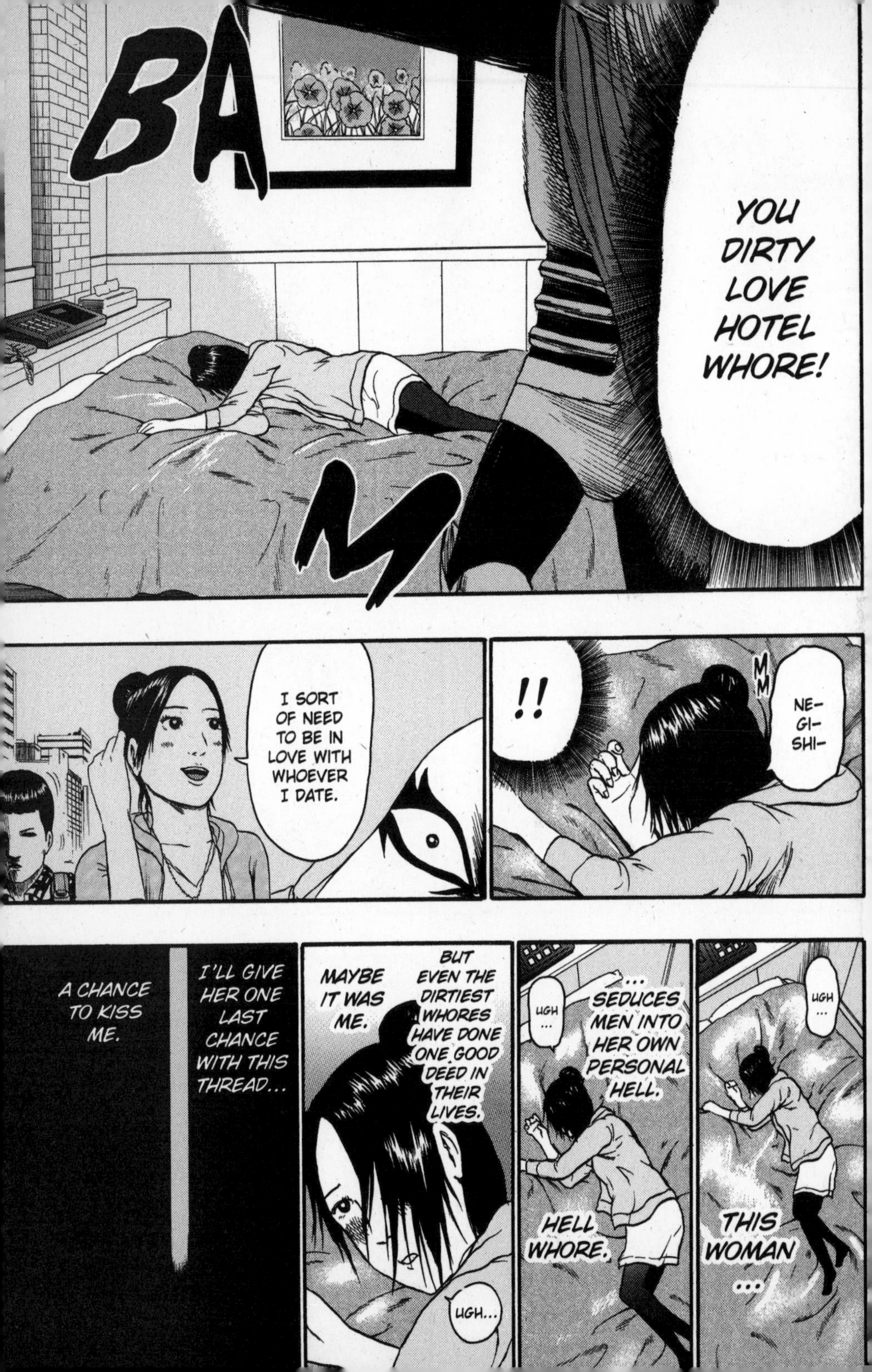
BA
M
YOU DIRTY LOVE HOTEL WHORE!
MM
NE-GI-SHI-
!!
I SORT OF NEED TO BE IN LOVE WITH WHOEVER I DATE.
UGH ...
THIS WOMAN ...
... SEDUCES MEN INTO HER OWN PERSONAL HELL.
UGH ...
HELL WHORE.
BUT EVEN THE DIRTIEST WHORES HAVE DONE ONE GOOD DEED IN THEIR LIVES.
MAYBE IT WAS ME.
UGH...
I'LL GIVE HER ONE LAST CHANCE WITH THIS THREAD...
A CHANCE TO KISS ME.

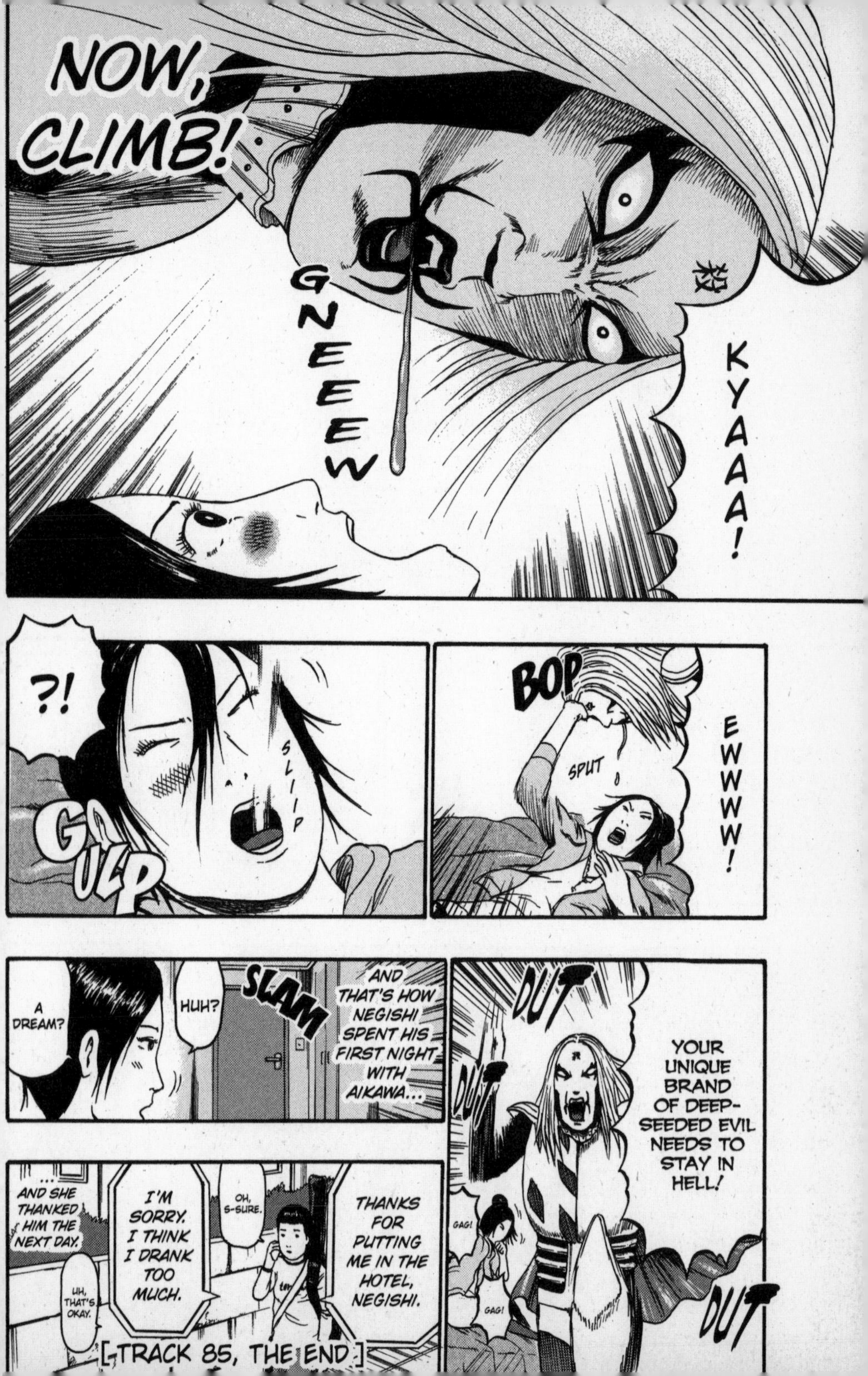
KYAAAA!
NOW, CLIMB!
GNEEEEW
BOP
EWWWWW!
SPUT
?!
SLIIIP
GULP
DUT
YOUR UNIQUE BRAND OF DEEP-SEEDED EVIL NEEDS TO STAY IN HELL!
DUT
GAG!
GAG!
DUT
AND THAT'S HOW NEGISHI SPENT HIS FIRST NIGHT WITH AIKAWA...
SLAM
HUH?
A DREAM?
THANKS FOR PUTTING ME IN THE HOTEL, NEGISHI.
OH, S-SURE.
I'M SORRY. I THINK I DRANK TOO MUCH.
UH, THAT'S OKAY.
...AND SHE THANKED HIM THE NEXT DAY.
[TRACK 85, THE END]

DMC LEXICON
🐱 KYUSHU BOY

Males who have been born and raised in
Kyushu. Obviously, everyone's different, but
stereotypically speaking, a Kyushu boy is
someone who is "just a friend but acts like a
boyfriend," or who "counts to ten before taking
you to a love hotel."

Usage: "Are you or aren't you a Kyushu boy?"
"I'm sorry. I am a Kyushu boy, but I can't date you because I'm gay!"

デトロイト・メタル・シティ
Detroit Metal City

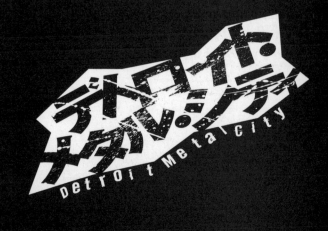

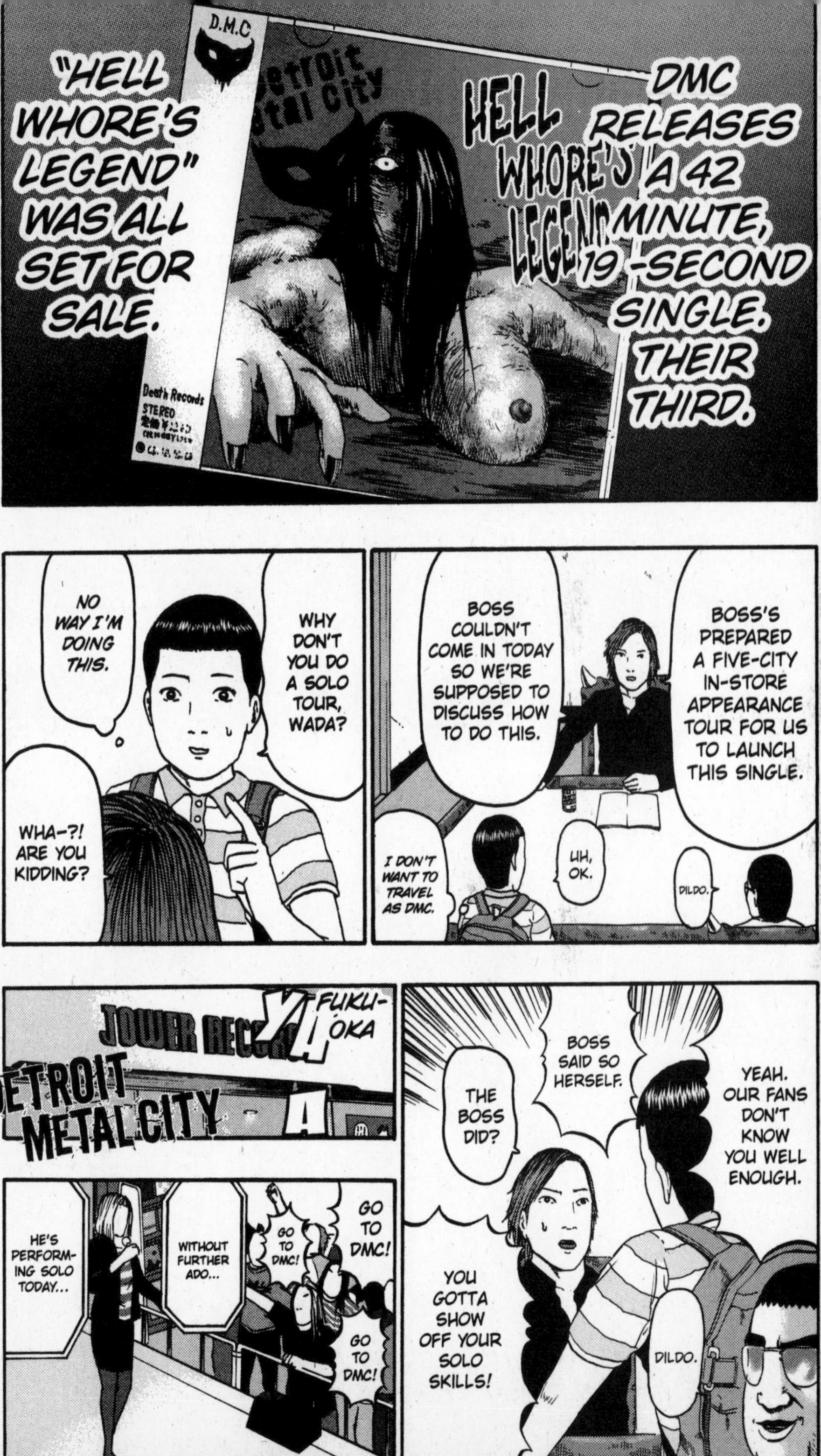
DMC RELEASES A 42 MINUTE, 19-SECOND SINGLE. THEIR THIRD.
HELL WHORE'S LEGEND
D.M.C
Death Records
STEREO
"HELL WHORE'S LEGEND" WAS ALL SET FOR SALE.
BOSS'S PREPARED A FIVE-CITY IN-STORE APPEARANCE TOUR FOR US TO LAUNCH THIS SINGLE.
BOSS COULDN'T COME IN TODAY SO WE'RE SUPPOSED TO DISCUSS HOW TO DO THIS.
DILDO.
UH, OK.
I DON'T WANT TO TRAVEL AS DMC.
WHY DON'T YOU DO A SOLO TOUR, WADA?
NO WAY I'M DOING THIS.
WHA-?! ARE YOU KIDDING?
YEAH. OUR FANS DON'T KNOW YOU WELL ENOUGH.
BOSS SAID SO HERSELF.
THE BOSS DID?
YOU GOTTA SHOW OFF YOUR SOLO SKILLS!
DILDO.
FUKU-OKA
DETROIT METAL CITY
GO TO DMC!
GO TO DMC!
WITHOUT FURTHER ADO...
HE'S PERFORMING SOLO TODAY...
GO TO DMC!

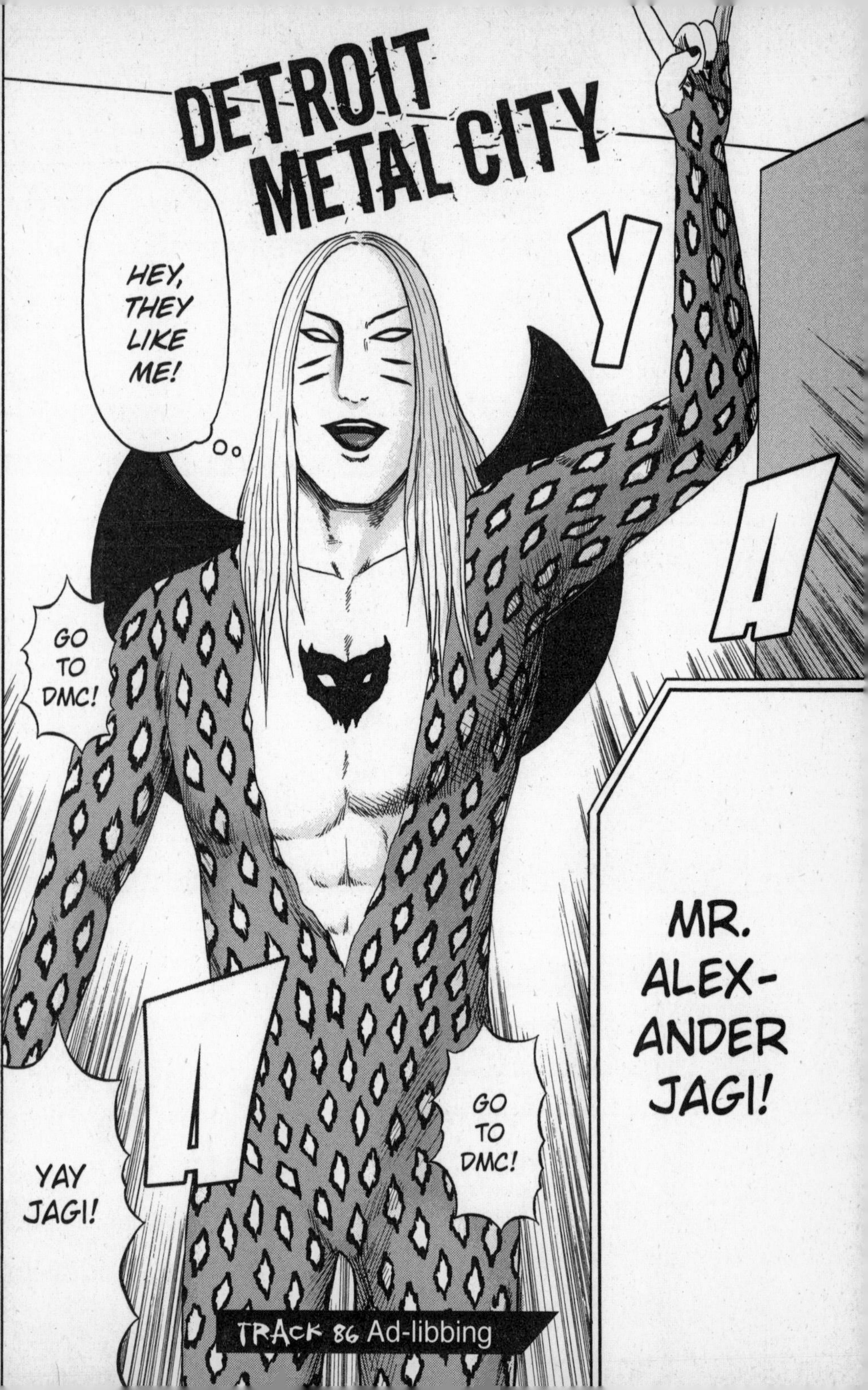
DETROIT METAL CITY
Y
HEY, THEY LIKE ME!
A
MR. ALEX-ANDER JAGI!
GO TO DMC!
A
GO TO DMC!
YAY JAGI!

TRACK 86 Ad-libbing

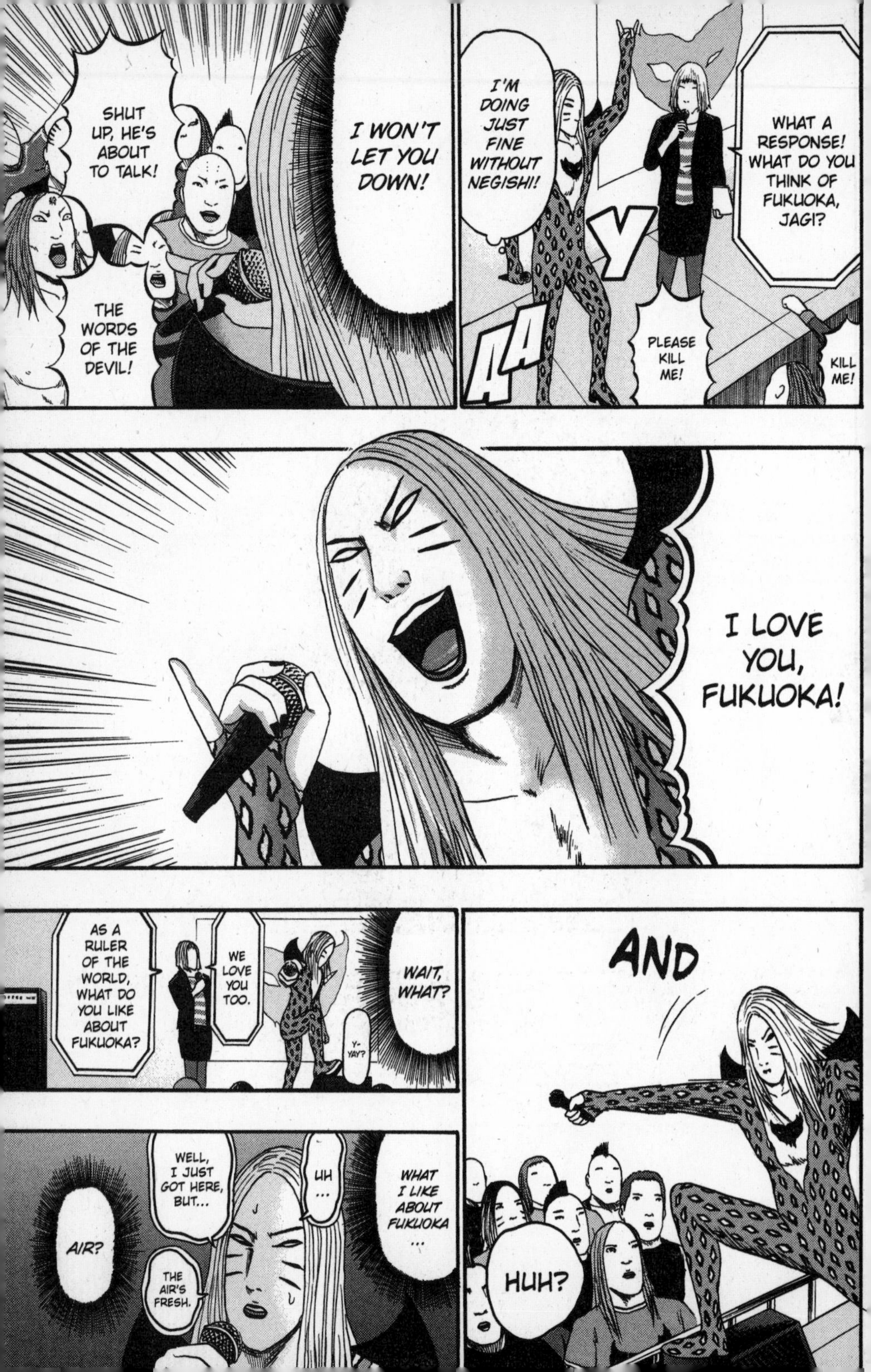
WHAT A RESPONSE! WHAT DO YOU THINK OF FUKUOKA, JAGI?
I'M DOING JUST FINE WITHOUT NEGISHI!
YAA
PLEASE KILL ME!
KILL ME!
I WON'T LET YOU DOWN!
SHUT UP, HE'S ABOUT TO TALK!
THE WORDS OF THE DEVIL!
I LOVE YOU, FUKUOKA!
AND
HUH?
WAIT, WHAT?
Y-YAY?
WE LOVE YOU TOO.
AS A RULER OF THE WORLD, WHAT DO YOU LIKE ABOUT FUKUOKA?
WHAT I LIKE ABOUT FUKUOKA ...
UH ...
WELL, I JUST GOT HERE, BUT...
AIR?
THE AIR'S FRESH.

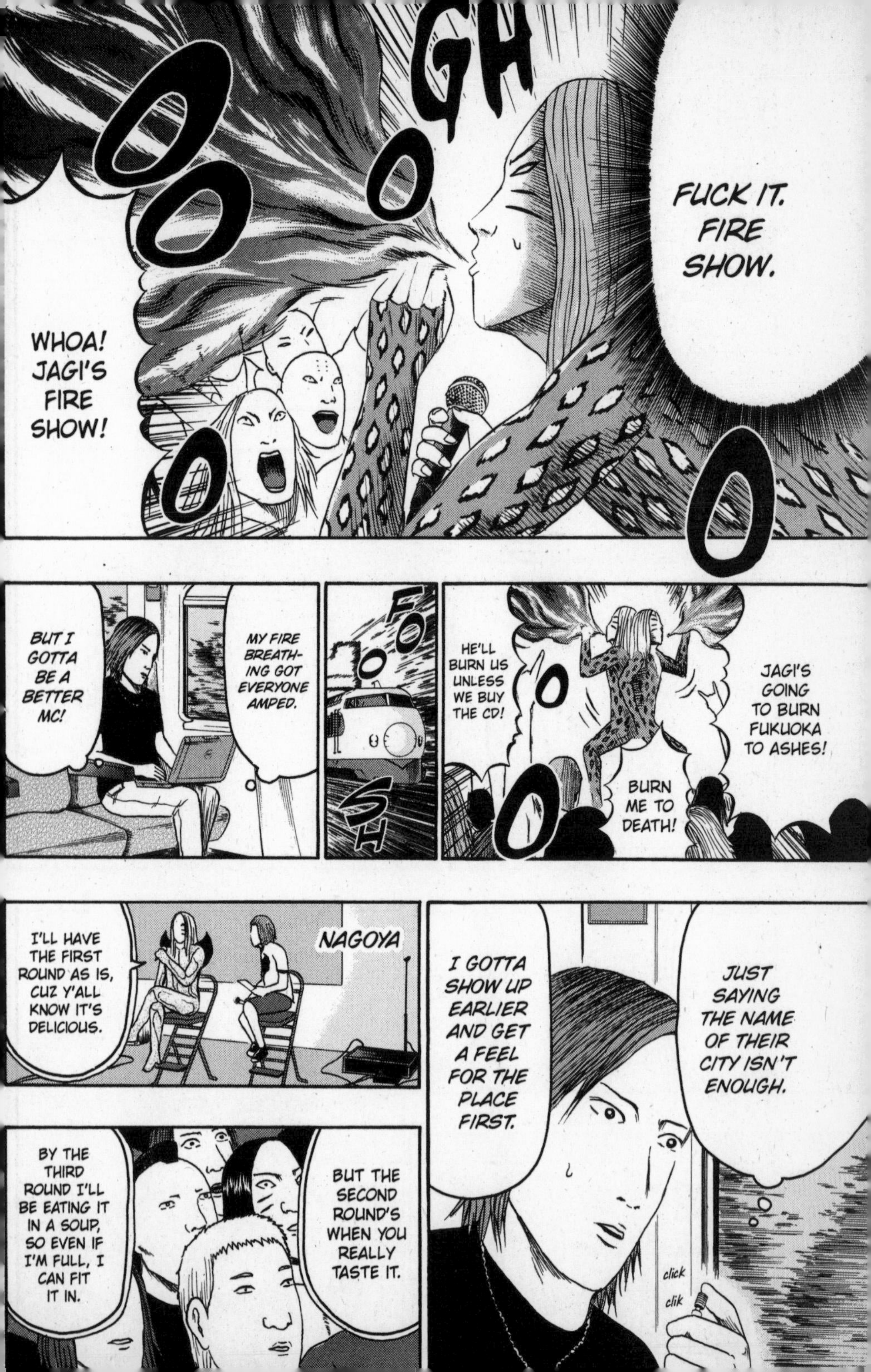
FUCK IT. FIRE SHOW.
OOOOGH
O
WHOA! JAGI'S FIRE SHOW!
JAGI'S GOING TO BURN FUKUOKA TO ASHES!
HE'LL BURN US UNLESS WE BUY THE CD!
OOO
BURN ME TO DEATH!
FOOOSH
MY FIRE BREATH-ING GOT EVERYONE AMPED.
BUT I GOTTA BE A BETTER MC!
JUST SAYING THE NAME OF THEIR CITY ISN'T ENOUGH.
I GOTTA SHOW UP EARLIER AND GET A FEEL FOR THE PLACE FIRST.
click
clik
NAGOYA
I'LL HAVE THE FIRST ROUND AS IS, CUZ Y'ALL KNOW IT'S DELICIOUS.
BUT THE SECOND ROUND'S WHEN YOU REALLY TASTE IT.
BY THE THIRD ROUND I'LL BE EATING IT IN A SOUP, SO EVEN IF I'M FULL, I CAN FIT IT IN.

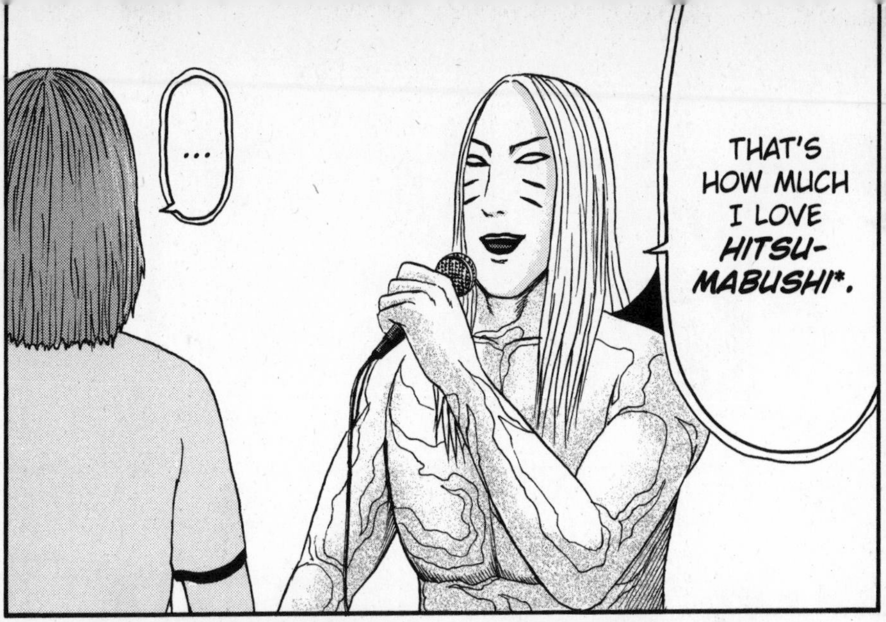
THAT'S HOW MUCH I LOVE HITSU-MABUSHI*.
...

*HITSUMABUSHI = A FAMOUS NAGOYA DISH OF BROILED EEL OVER RICE.

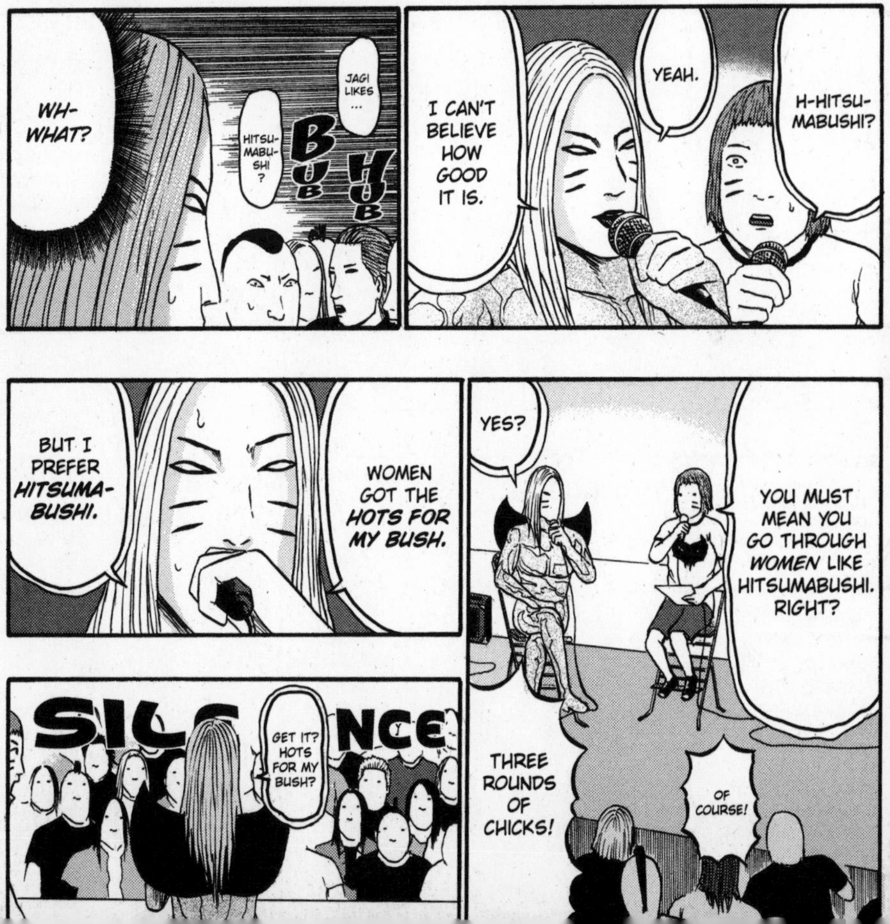
H-HITSU-MABUSHI?
YEAH.
I CAN'T BELIEVE HOW GOOD IT IS.
JAGI LIKES ...
HITSU-MABU-SHI ?
HUB BUB
WH-WHAT?
YOU MUST MEAN YOU GO THROUGH WOMEN LIKE HITSUMABUSHI. RIGHT?
YES?
THREE ROUNDS OF CHICKS!
OF COURSE!
WOMEN GOT THE HOTS FOR MY BUSH.
BUT I PREFER HITSUMA-BUSHI.
SILENCE
GET IT? HOTS FOR MY BUSH?

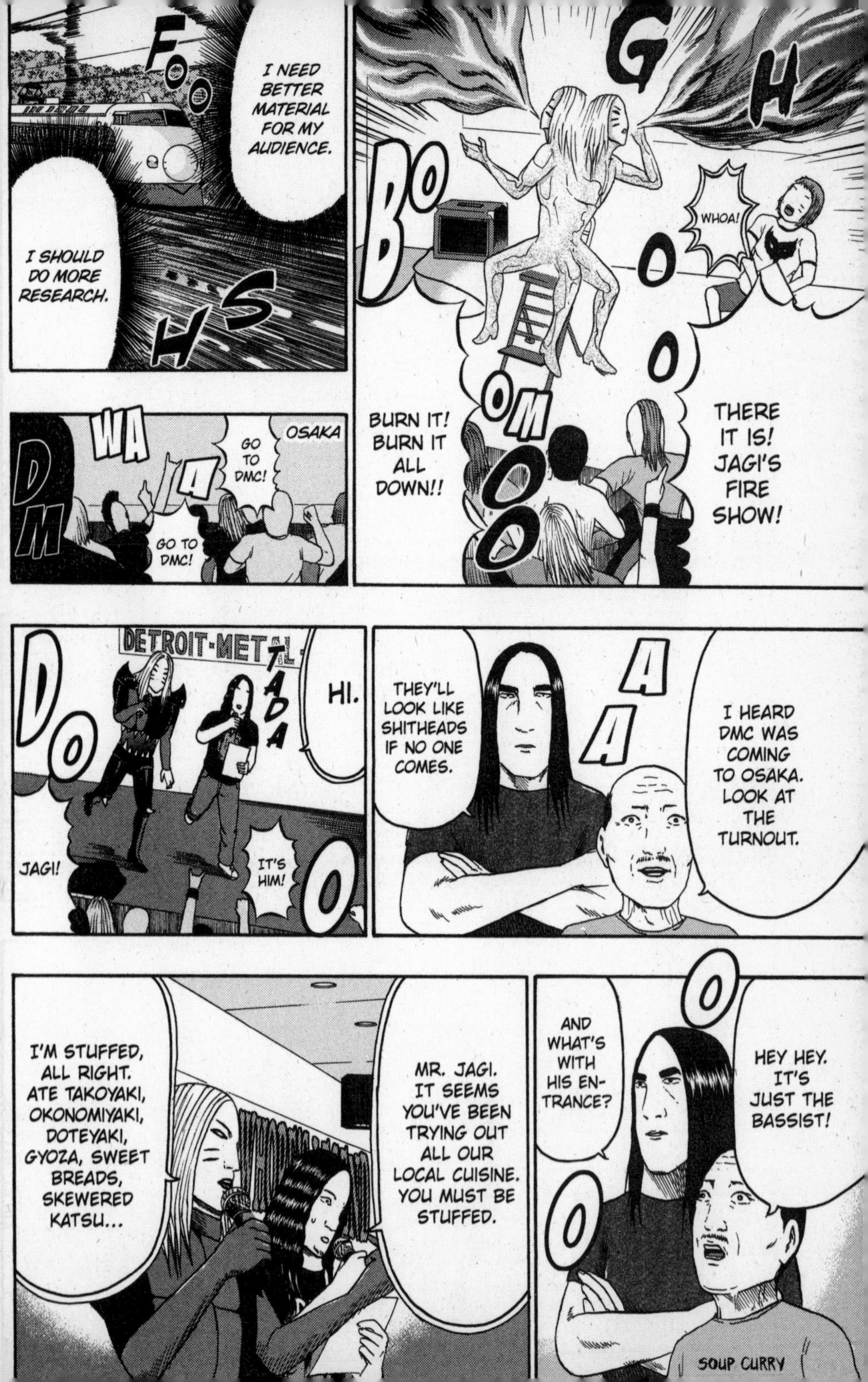

G
H
BO
WHOA!
THERE IT IS! JAGI'S FIRE SHOW!
OOOOOM
BURN IT! BURN IT ALL DOWN!!
FOO
I NEED BETTER MATERIAL FOR MY AUDIENCE.
I SHOULD DO MORE RESEARCH.
SH
OSAKA
GO TO DMC!
WA
A
GO TO DMC!
DM
I HEARD DMC WAS COMING TO OSAKA. LOOK AT THE TURNOUT.
AAA
THEY'LL LOOK LIKE SHITHEADS IF NO ONE COMES.
HI.
DETROIT-METAL
TADA
DO
O
IT'S HIM!
JAGI!
HEY HEY. IT'S JUST THE BASSIST!
OOO
AND WHAT'S WITH HIS EN-TRANCE?
SOUP CURRY
MR. JAGI. IT SEEMS YOU'VE BEEN TRYING OUT ALL OUR LOCAL CUISINE. YOU MUST BE STUFFED.
I'M STUFFED, ALL RIGHT. ATE TAKOYAKI, OKONOMIYAKI, DOTEYAKI, GYOZA, SWEET BREADS, SKEWERED KATSU...

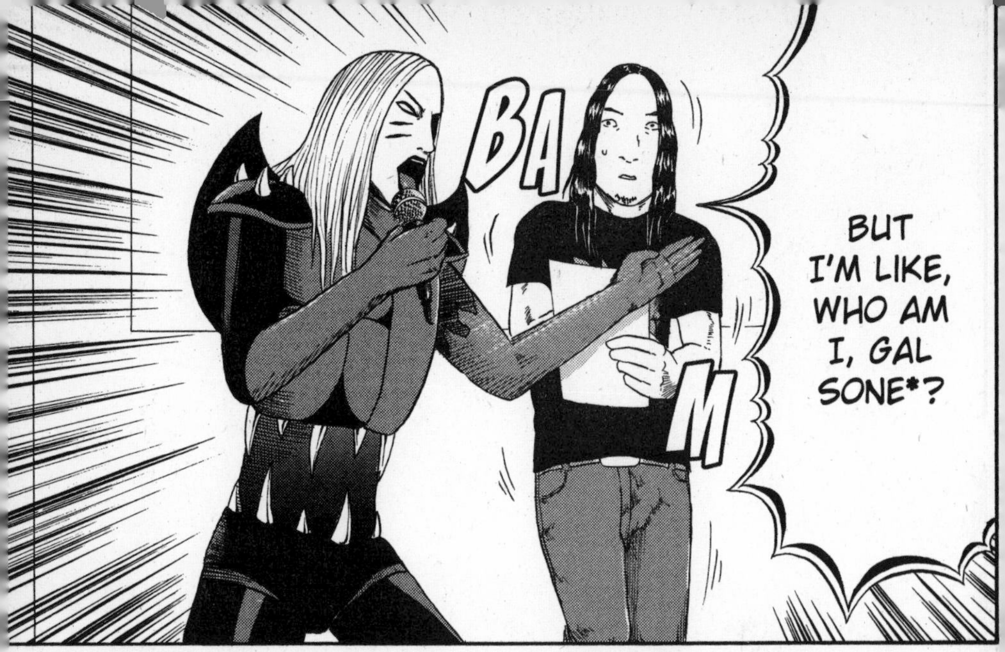
BAM
BUT I'M LIKE, WHO AM I, GAL SONE*?

*GAL SONE = FAMOUS OSAKA-BASED FOOD CRITIC/CELEBRITY.

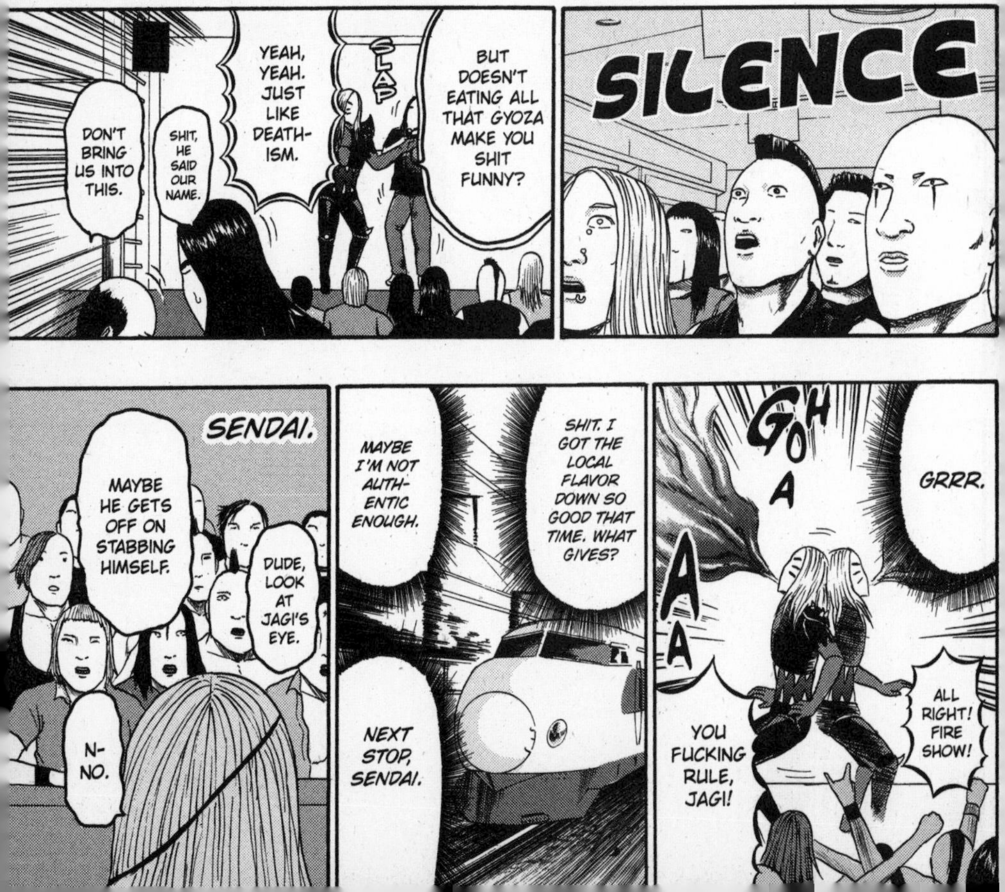
SILENCE
BUT DOESN'T EATING ALL THAT GYOZA MAKE YOU SHIT FUNNY?
SLAP
YEAH, YEAH. JUST LIKE DEATH-ISM.
SHIT, HE SAID OUR NAME.
DON'T BRING US INTO THIS.
GOHA
AA
GRRR.
ALL RIGHT! FIRE SHOW!
YOU FUCKING RULE, JAGI!
SHIT. I GOT THE LOCAL FLAVOR DOWN SO GOOD THAT TIME. WHAT GIVES?
MAYBE I'M NOT AUTH-ENTIC ENOUGH.
NEXT STOP, SENDAI.
SENDAI.
DUDE, LOOK AT JAGI'S EYE.
MAYBE HE GETS OFF ON STABBING HIMSELF.
N-NO.

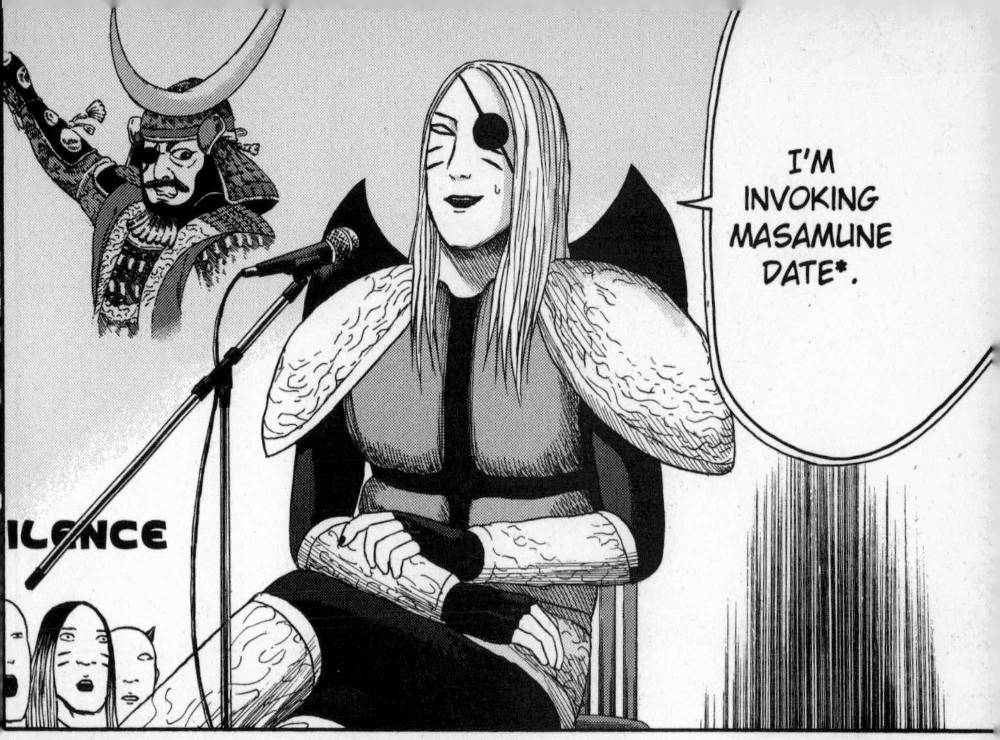
I'M INVOKING MASAMUNE DATE*.
ILENCE

* MASAMUNE DATE = A LEGENDARY SHOGUN FROM SENDAI.

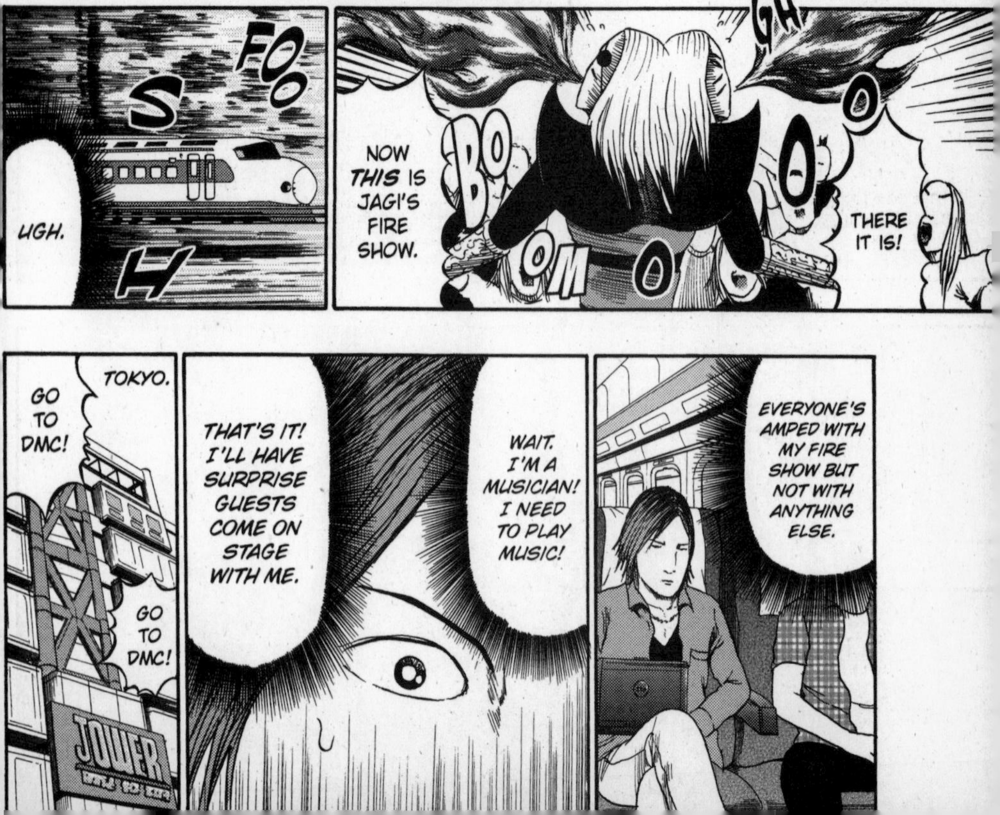
GH
THERE IT IS!
BOOOOM
NOW THIS IS JAGI'S FIRE SHOW.
FOOSH
UGH.
EVERYONE'S AMPED WITH MY FIRE SHOW BUT NOT WITH ANYTHING ELSE.
WAIT. I'M A MUSICIAN! I NEED TO PLAY MUSIC!
THAT'S IT! I'LL HAVE SURPRISE GUESTS COME ON STAGE WITH ME.
TOKYO.
GO TO DMC!
GO TO DMC!
TOWER

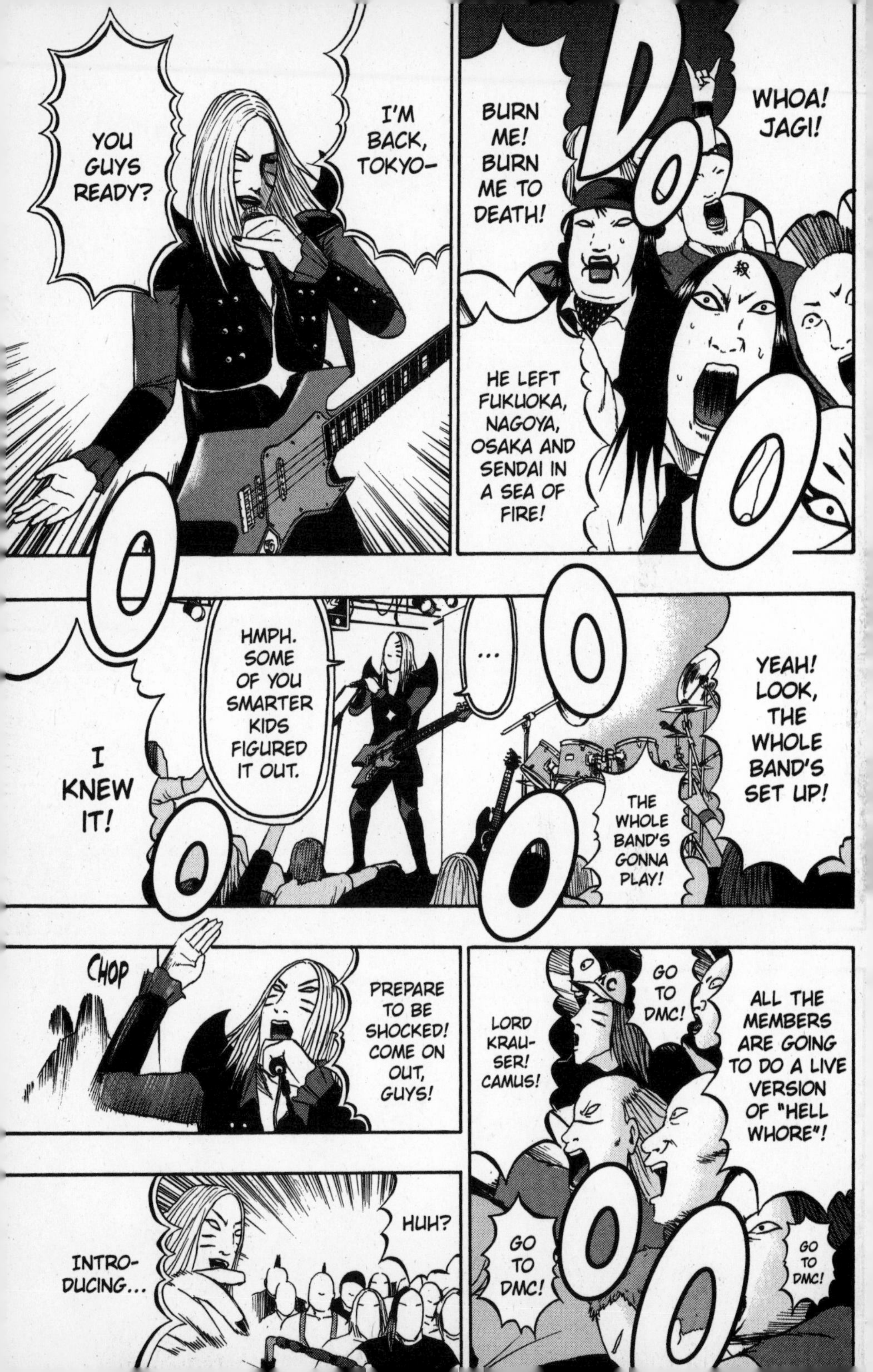
WHOA! JAGI!
BURN ME! BURN ME TO DEATH!
HE LEFT FUKUOKA, NAGOYA, OSAKA AND SENDAI IN A SEA OF FIRE!
I'M BACK, TOKYO-
YOU GUYS READY?
YEAH! LOOK, THE WHOLE BAND'S SET UP!
THE WHOLE BAND'S GONNA PLAY!
...
HMPH. SOME OF YOU SMARTER KIDS FIGURED IT OUT.
I KNEW IT!
ALL THE MEMBERS ARE GOING TO DO A LIVE VERSION OF "HELL WHORE"!
GO TO DMC!
LORD KRAUSER! CAMUS!
GO TO DMC!
GO TO DMC!
PREPARE TO BE SHOCKED! COME ON OUT, GUYS!
CHOP
HUH?
INTRODUCING...

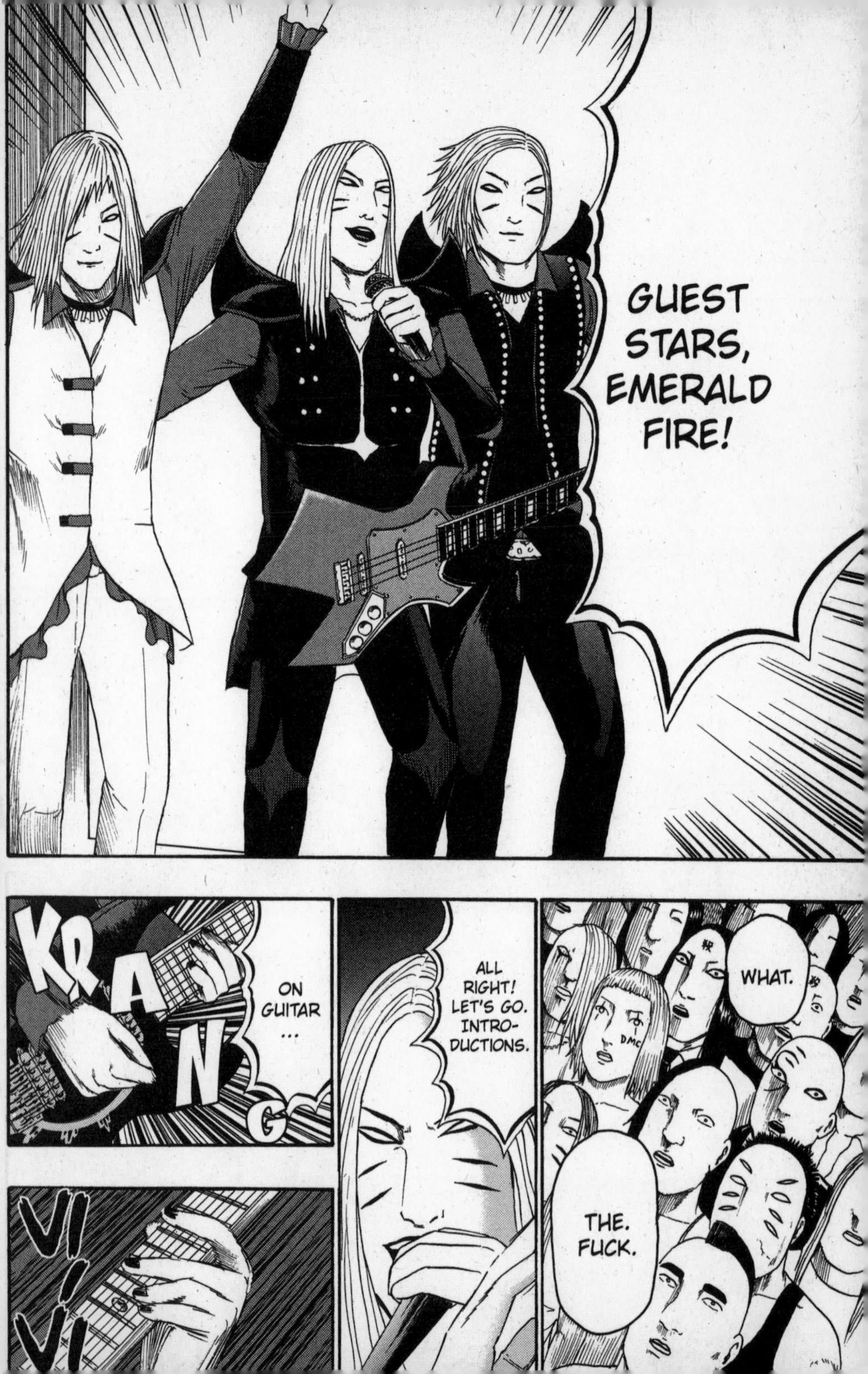
GUEST STARS, EMERALD FIRE!
WHAT.
THE. FUCK.
ALL RIGHT! LET'S GO. INTRO-DUCTIONS.
ON GUITAR ...
KRANG
VI VI VI

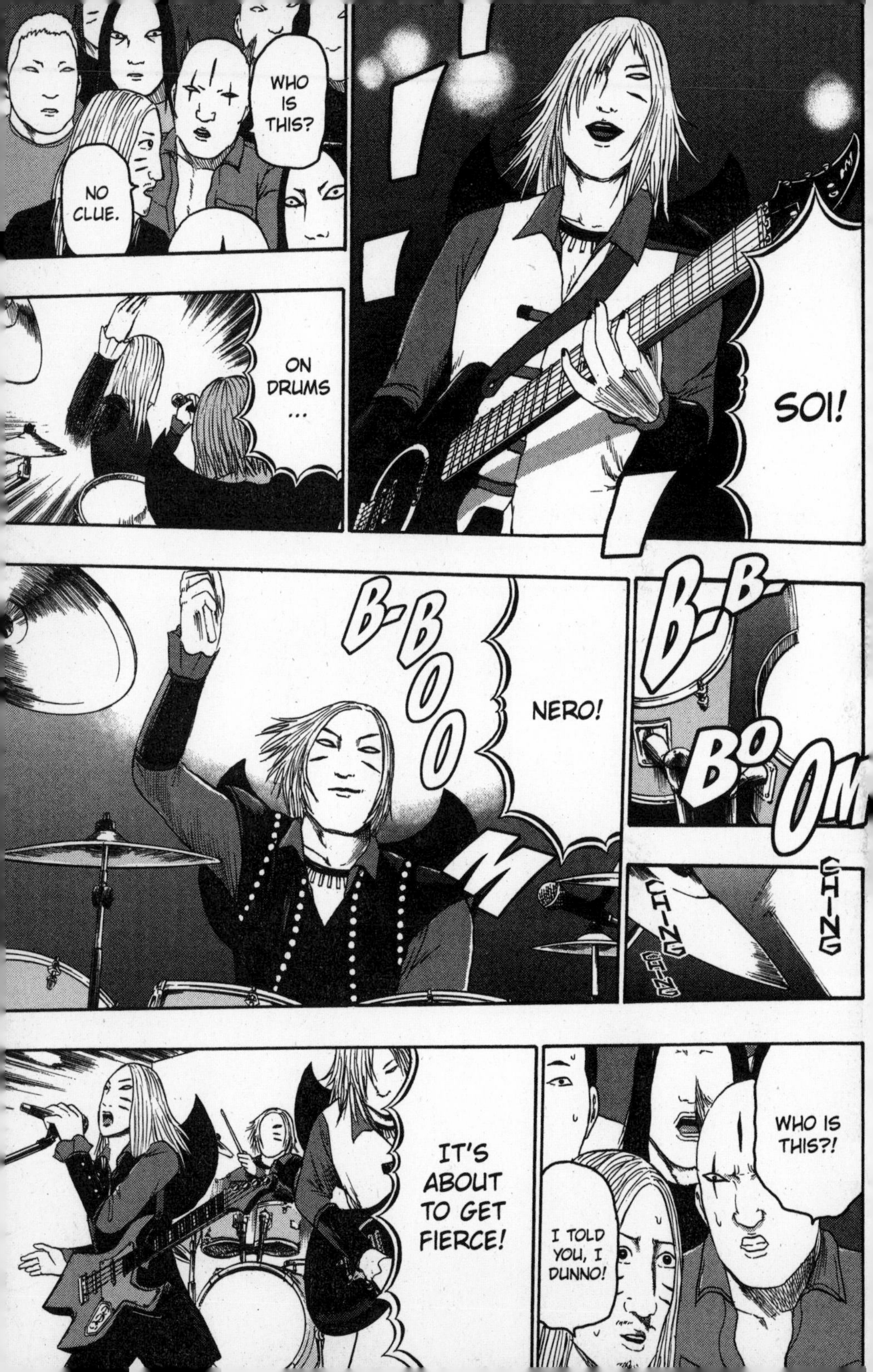

SOI!
WHO IS THIS?
NO CLUE.
ON DRUMS ...
B-B-BOOM
CHING
CHING
CHING
B-BOOOM
NERO!
WHO IS THIS?!
I TOLD YOU, I DUNNO!
IT'S ABOUT TO GET FIERCE!

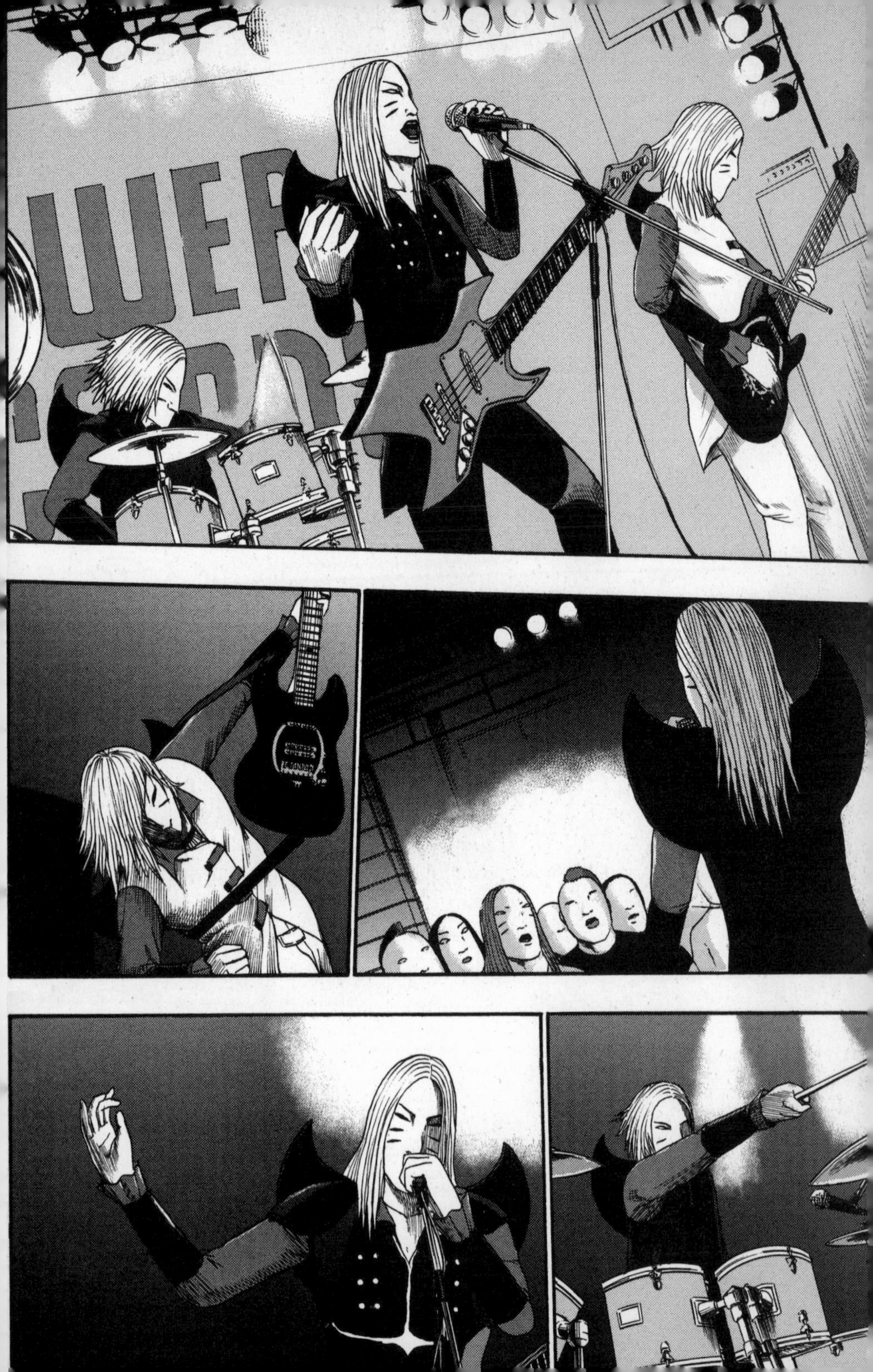

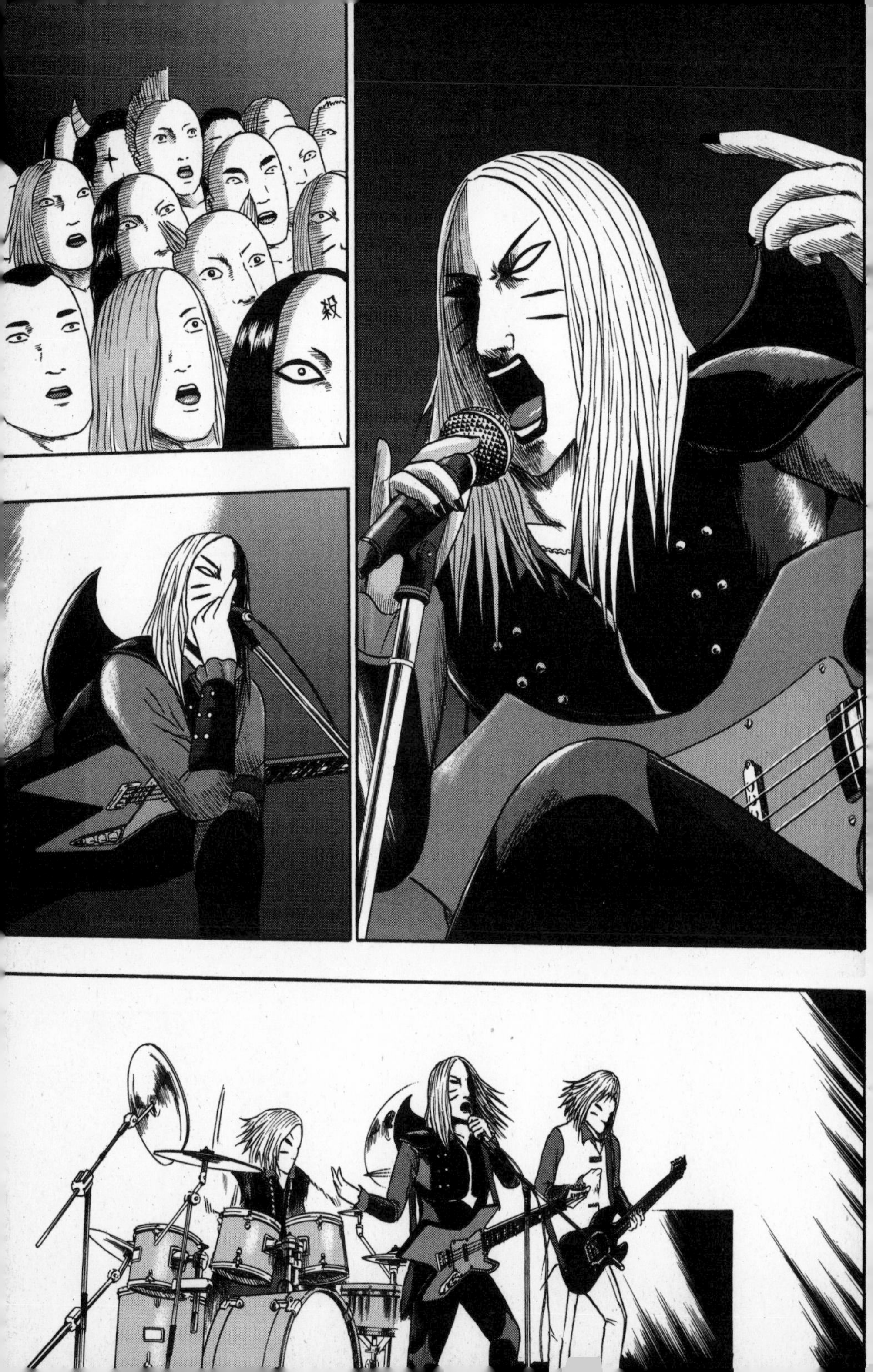
殺

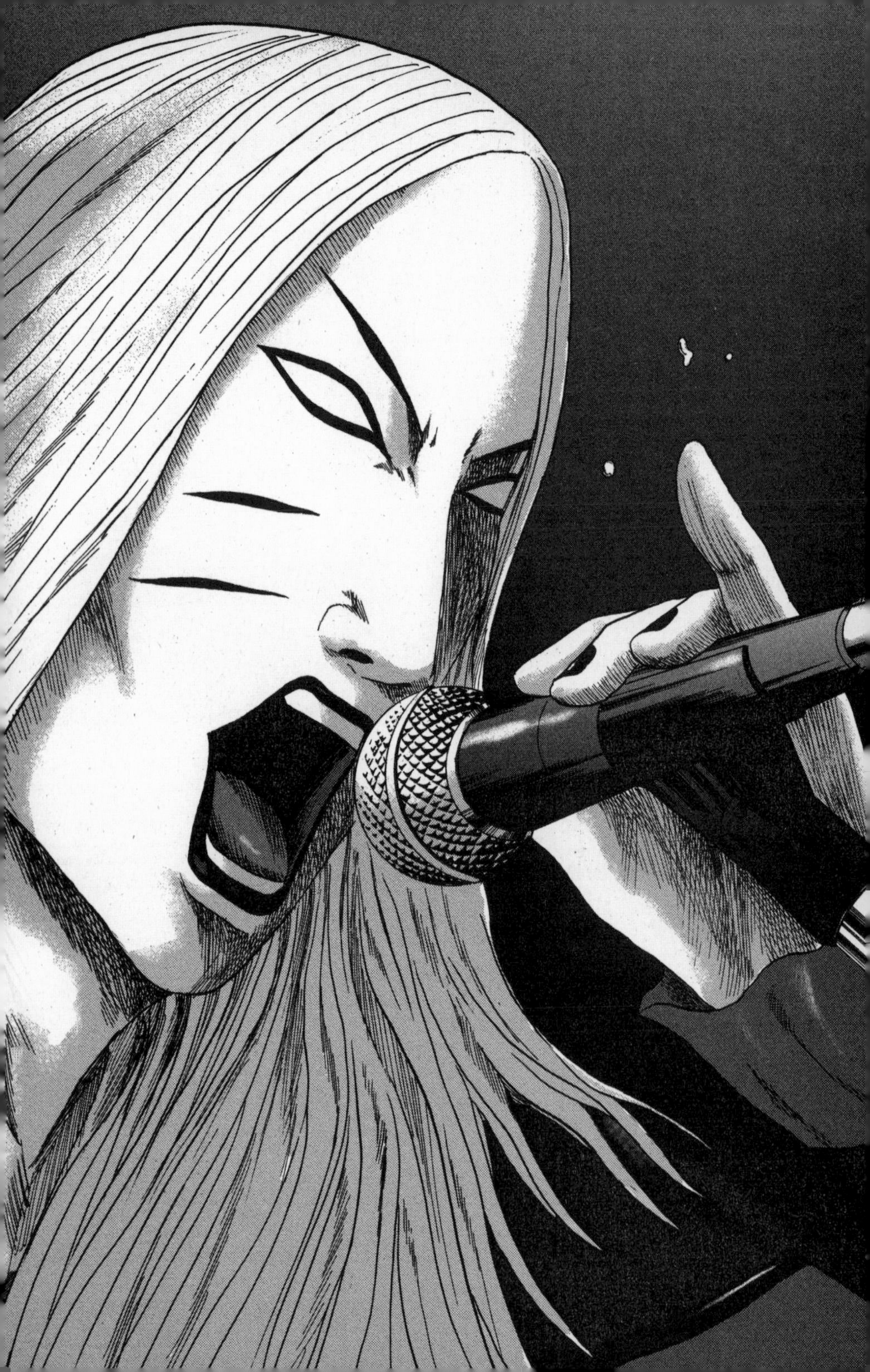

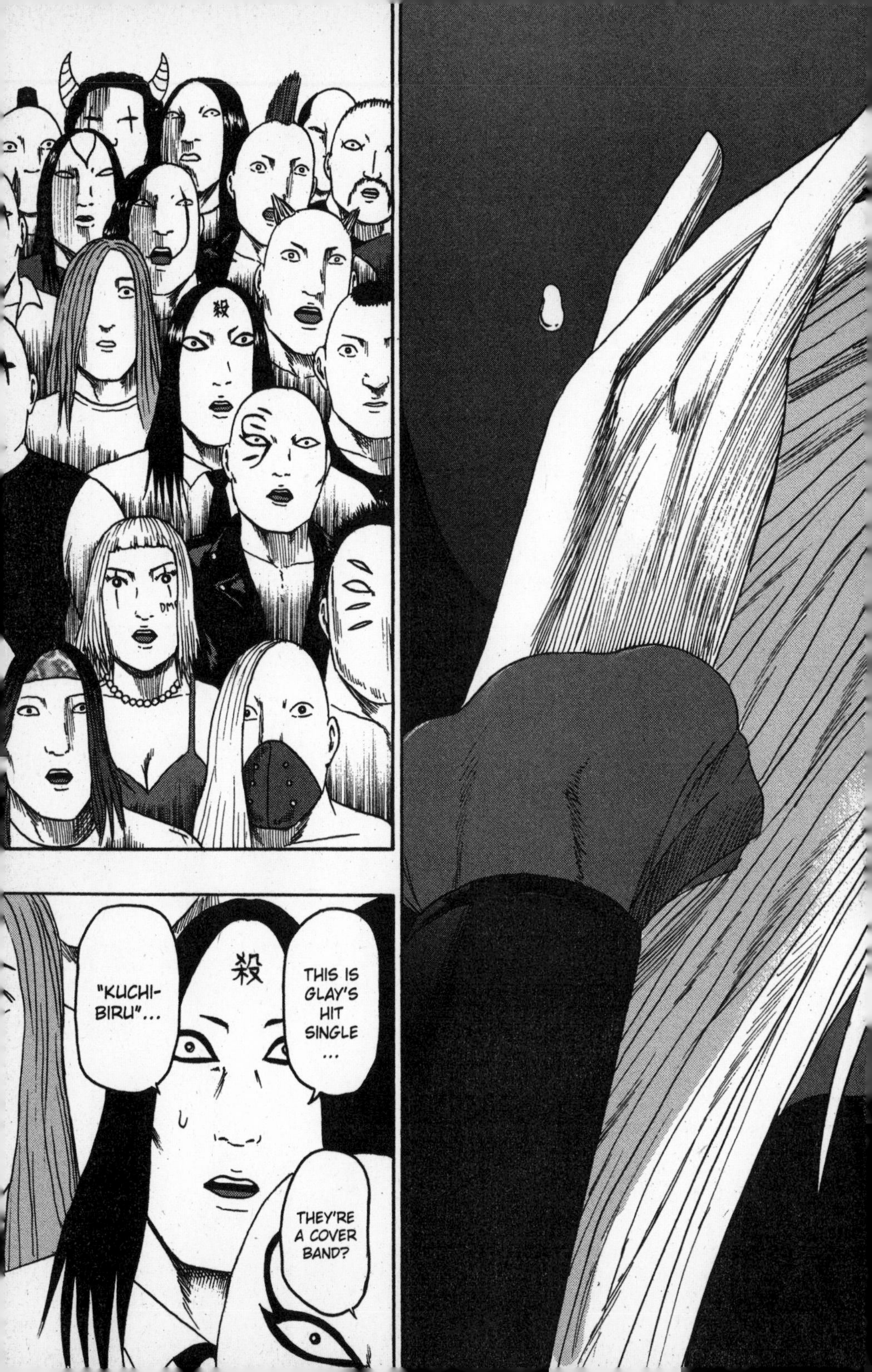
THIS IS GLAY'S HIT SINGLE ...
"KUCHI-BIRU"...
THEY'RE A COVER BAND?

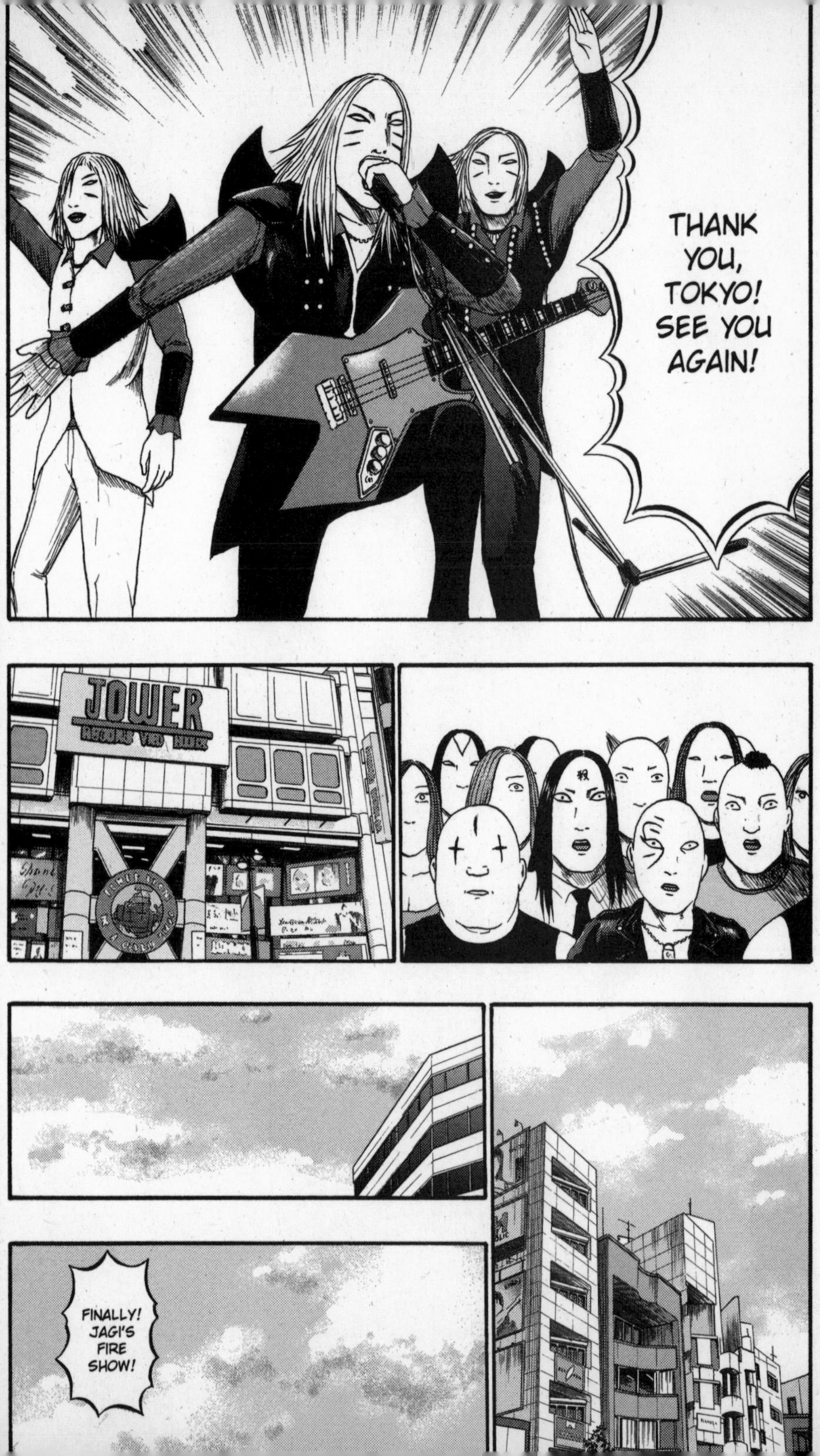
THANK YOU, TOKYO! SEE YOU AGAIN!
JOWER
FINALLY! JAGI'S FIRE SHOW!

デトロイト・メタル・シティ

Detroit Metal City

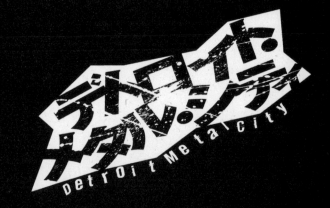

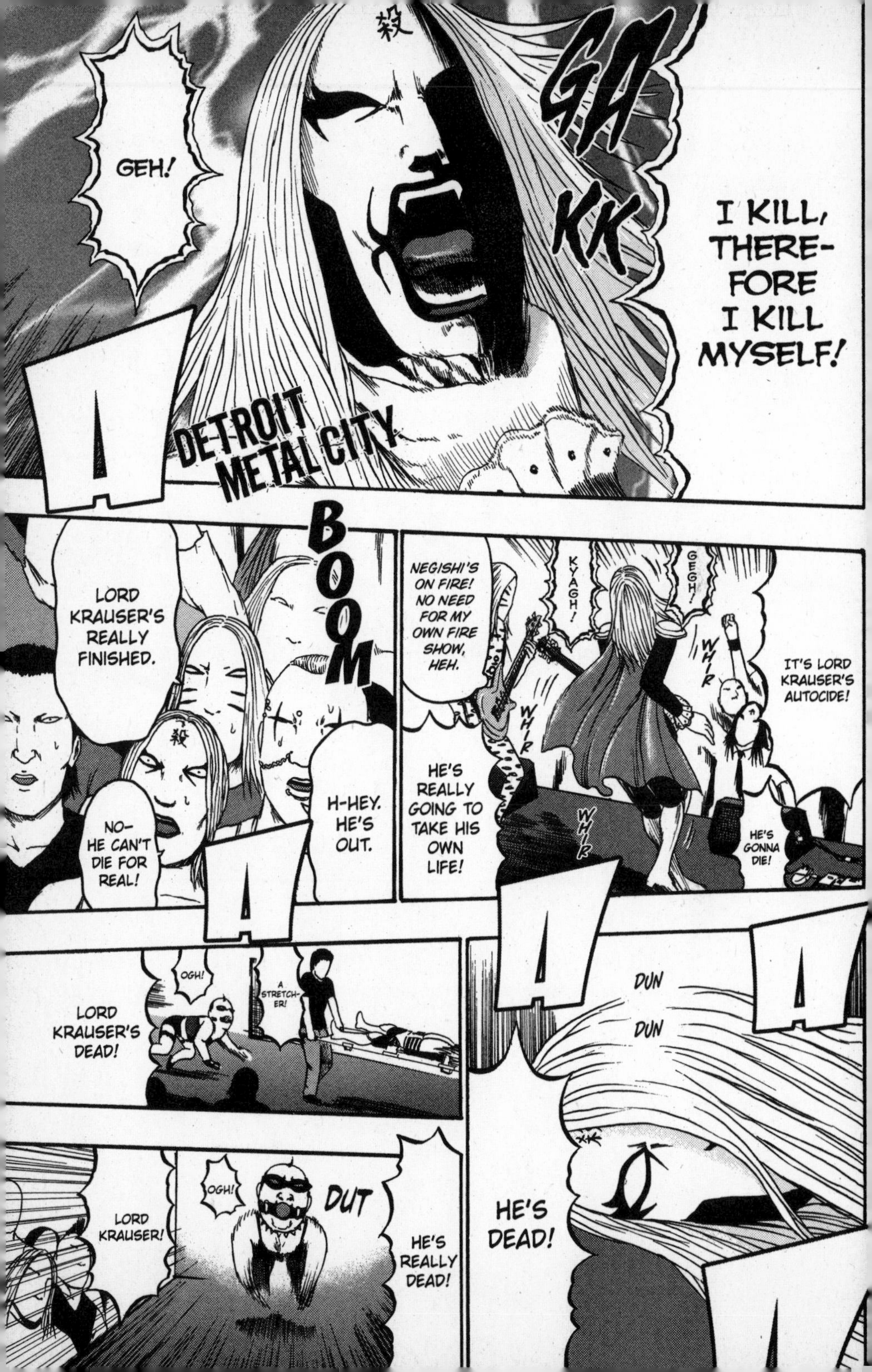
I KILL, THEREFORE I KILL MYSELF!
GAKK
GEH!
DETROIT METAL CITY
A
IT'S LORD KRAUSER'S AUTOCIDE!
GEGH!
WHIR
KYAGH!
NEGISHI'S ON FIRE! NO NEED FOR MY OWN FIRE SHOW, HEH.
HE'S GONNA DIE!
WHIR
HE'S REALLY GOING TO TAKE HIS OWN LIFE!
WHIR
BOOM
LORD KRAUSER'S REALLY FINISHED.
H-HEY. HE'S OUT.
NO- HE CAN'T DIE FOR REAL!
A
A
A
DUN
DUN
HE'S DEAD!
A STRETCHER!
OGH!
LORD KRAUSER'S DEAD!
HE'S REALLY DEAD!
DUT
OGH!
LORD KRAUSER!

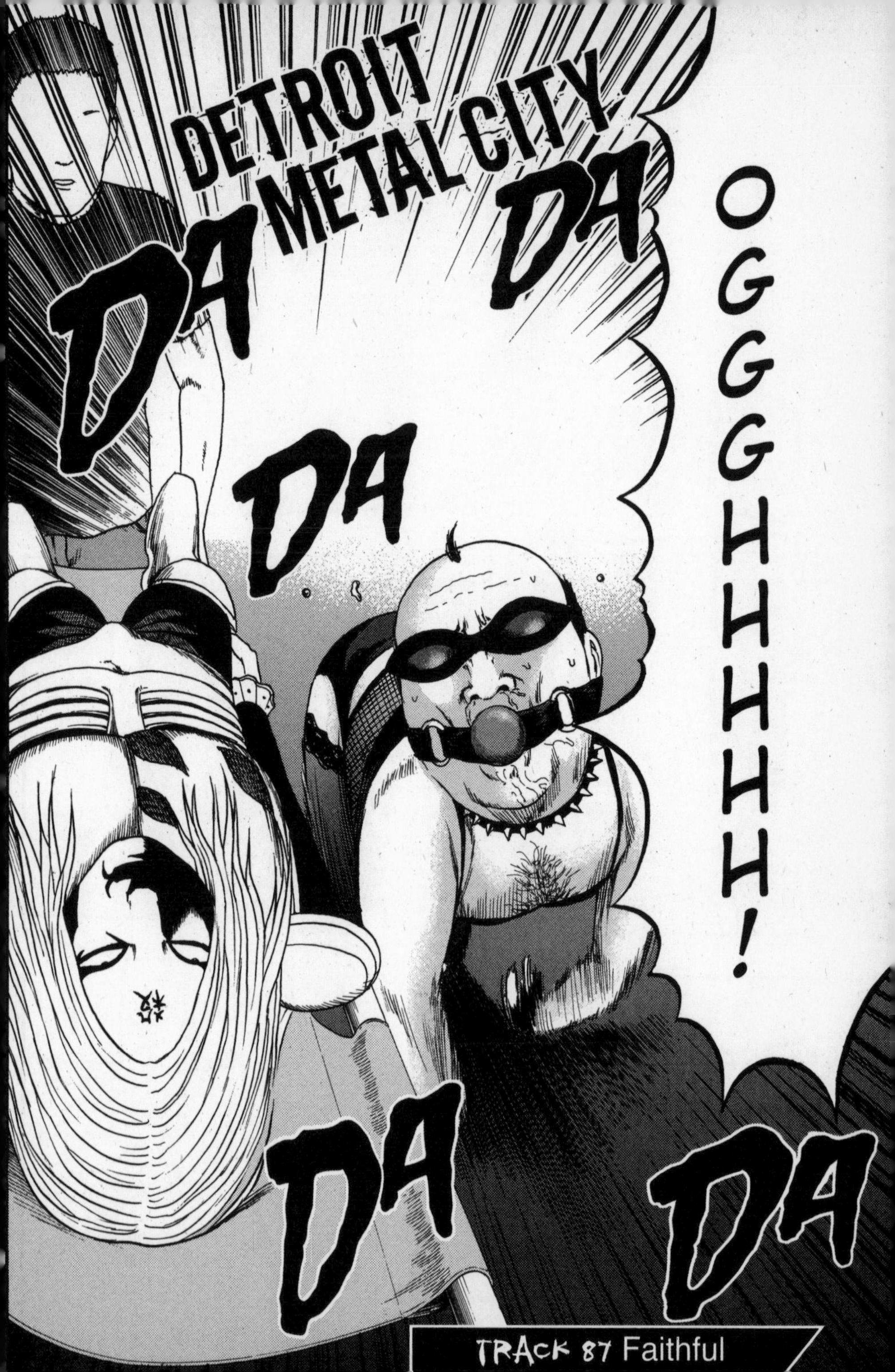
DETROIT METAL CITY
OGGGHHHHH!
DA
DA
DA
DA
DA
DA

TRACK 87 Faithful

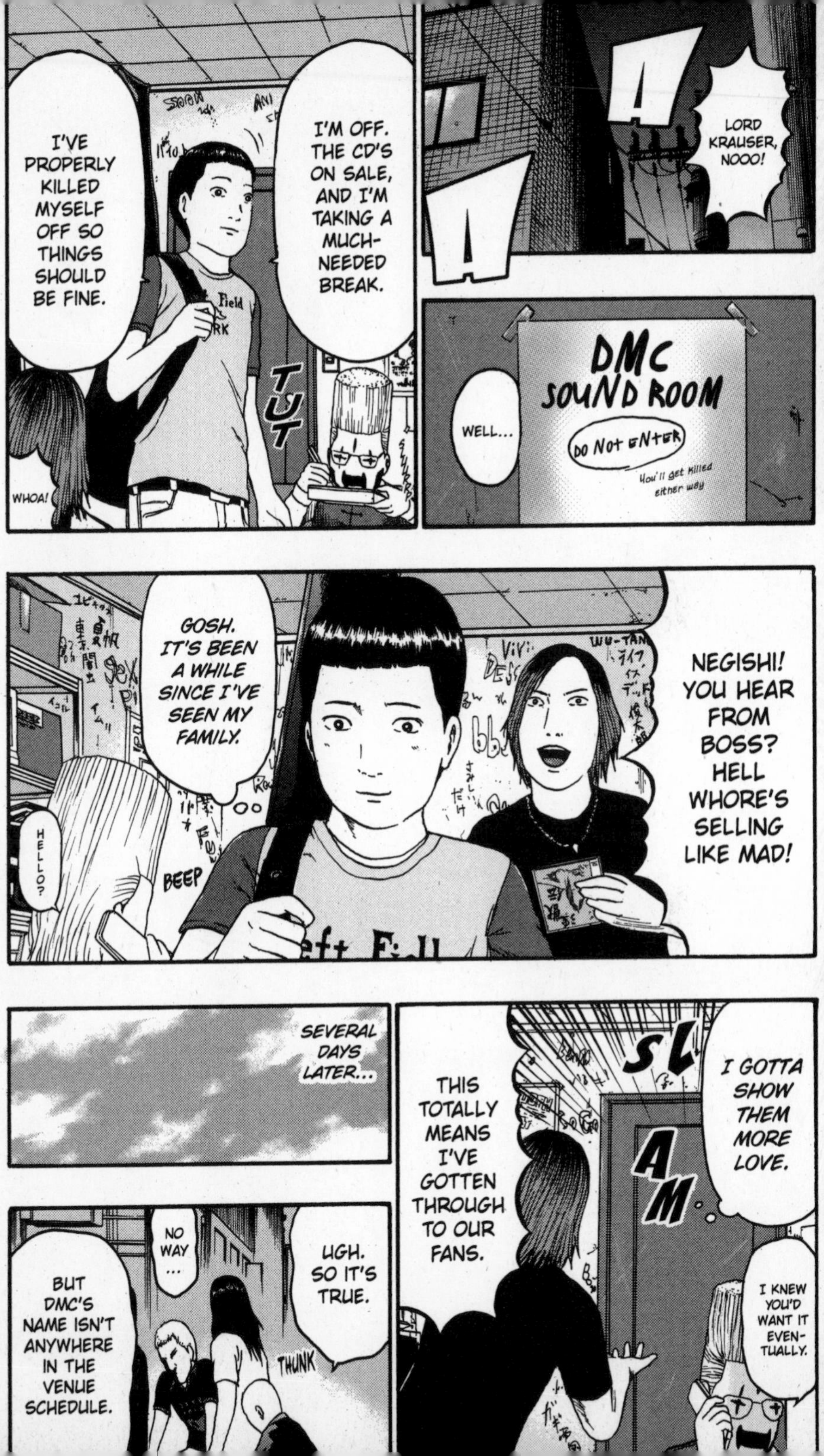
AA
LORD KRAUSER, NOOO!
DMC SOUND ROOM
DO NOT ENTER
You'll get killed either way
WELL...
I'M OFF. THE CD'S ON SALE, AND I'M TAKING A MUCH-NEEDED BREAK.
I'VE PROPERLY KILLED MYSELF OFF SO THINGS SHOULD BE FINE.
TUT
WHOA!
NEGISHI! YOU HEAR FROM BOSS? HELL WHORE'S SELLING LIKE MAD!
GOSH. IT'S BEEN A WHILE SINCE I'VE SEEN MY FAMILY.
HELLO?
BEEP
SLAM
I GOTTA SHOW THEM MORE LOVE.
THIS TOTALLY MEANS I'VE GOTTEN THROUGH TO OUR FANS.
I KNEW YOU'D WANT IT EVENTUALLY.
SEVERAL DAYS LATER...
UGH. SO IT'S TRUE.
NO WAY...
BUT DMC'S NAME ISN'T ANYWHERE IN THE VENUE SCHEDULE.
THUNK

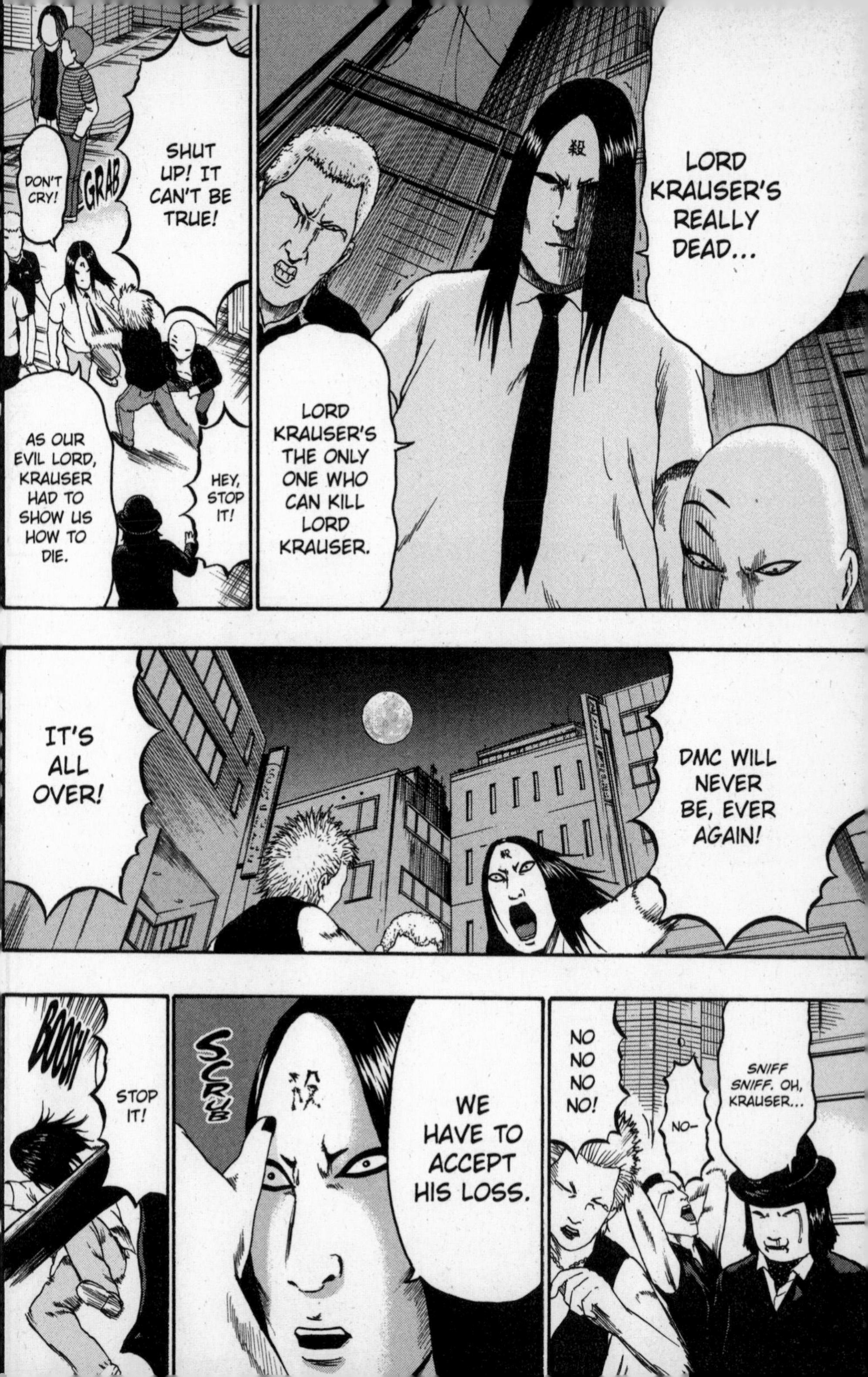
LORD KRAUSER'S REALLY DEAD...
LORD KRAUSER'S THE ONLY ONE WHO CAN KILL LORD KRAUSER.
SHUT UP! IT CAN'T BE TRUE!
GRAB
DON'T CRY!
HEY, STOP IT!
AS OUR EVIL LORD, KRAUSER HAD TO SHOW US HOW TO DIE.
DMC WILL NEVER BE, EVER AGAIN!
IT'S ALL OVER!
SNIFF SNIFF. OH, KRAUSER...
NO-
NO NO NO NO!
WE HAVE TO ACCEPT HIS LOSS.
SCRUB
BOOSH
STOP IT!

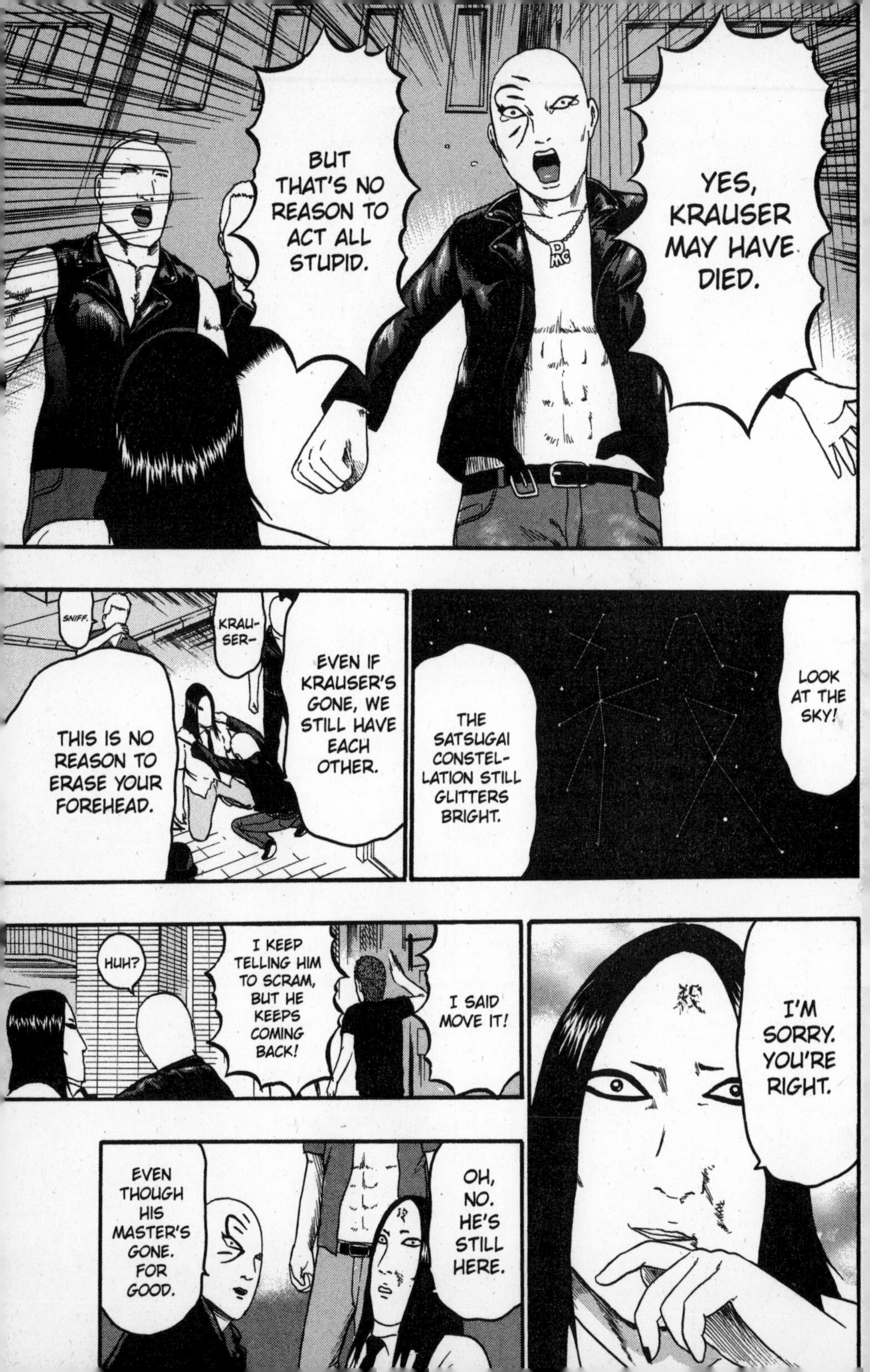
YES, KRAUSER MAY HAVE DIED.
BUT THAT'S NO REASON TO ACT ALL STUPID.
LOOK AT THE SKY!
THE SATSUGAI CONSTEL-LATION STILL GLITTERS BRIGHT.
EVEN IF KRAUSER'S GONE, WE STILL HAVE EACH OTHER.
KRAU-SER-
THIS IS NO REASON TO ERASE YOUR FOREHEAD.
SNIFF.
I'M SORRY. YOU'RE RIGHT.
I SAID MOVE IT!
I KEEP TELLING HIM TO SCRAM, BUT HE KEEPS COMING BACK!
HUH?
OH, NO. HE'S STILL HERE.
EVEN THOUGH HIS MASTER'S GONE. FOR GOOD.

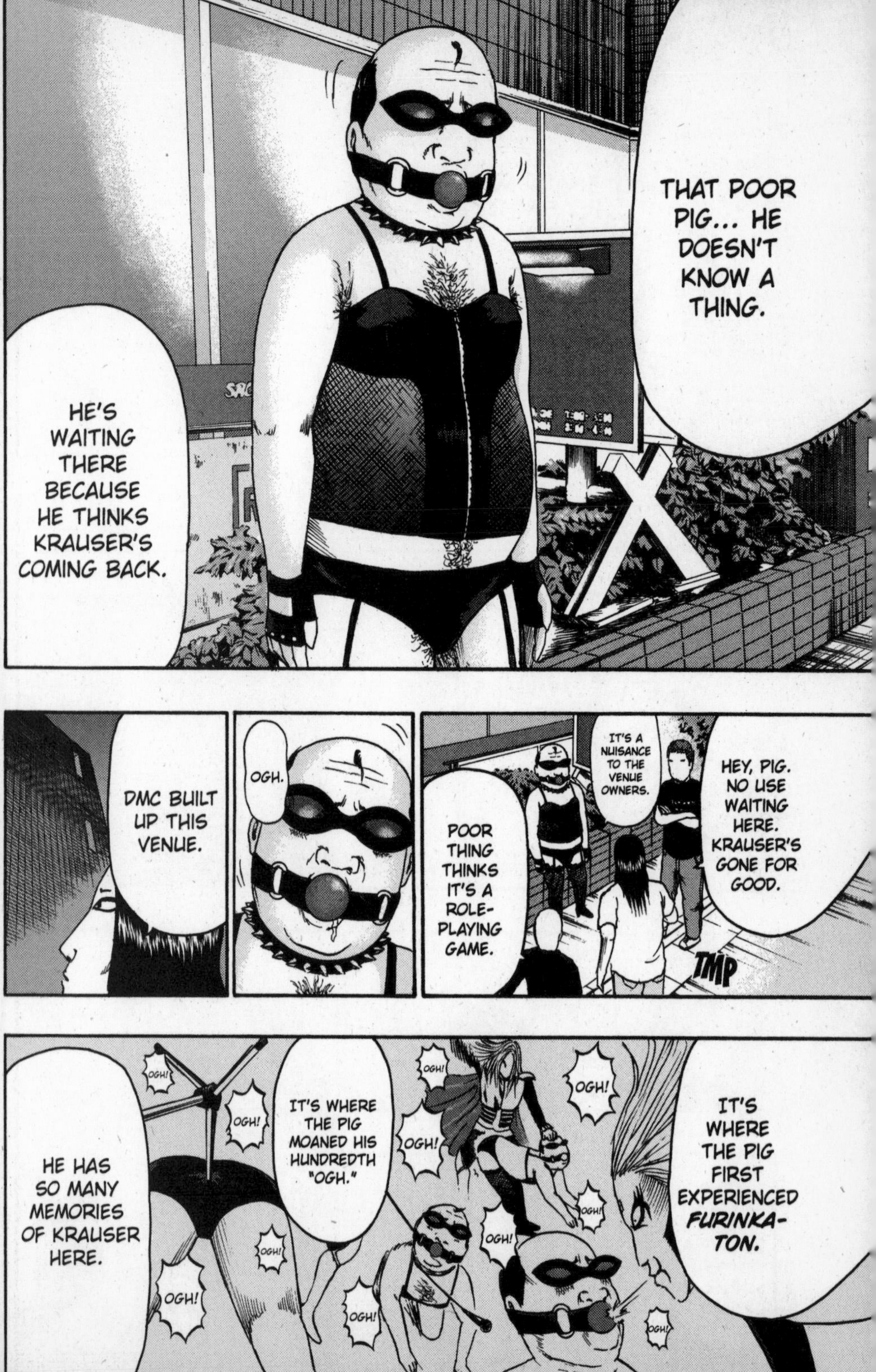
THAT POOR PIG... HE DOESN'T KNOW A THING.
HE'S WAITING THERE BECAUSE HE THINKS KRAUSER'S COMING BACK.
HEY, PIG. NO USE WAITING HERE. KRAUSER'S GONE FOR GOOD.
IT'S A NUISANCE TO THE VENUE OWNERS.
POOR THING THINKS IT'S A ROLE-PLAYING GAME.
TMP
OGH.
DMC BUILT UP THIS VENUE.
IT'S WHERE THE PIG FIRST EXPERIENCED *FURINKA-TON.*
OGH!
OGH!
OGH!
IT'S WHERE THE PIG MOANED HIS HUNDREDTH "OGH."
OGH!
OGH!
OGH!
HE HAS SO MANY MEMORIES OF KRAUSER HERE.
OGH!
OGH!
OGH!
OGH!
OGH!

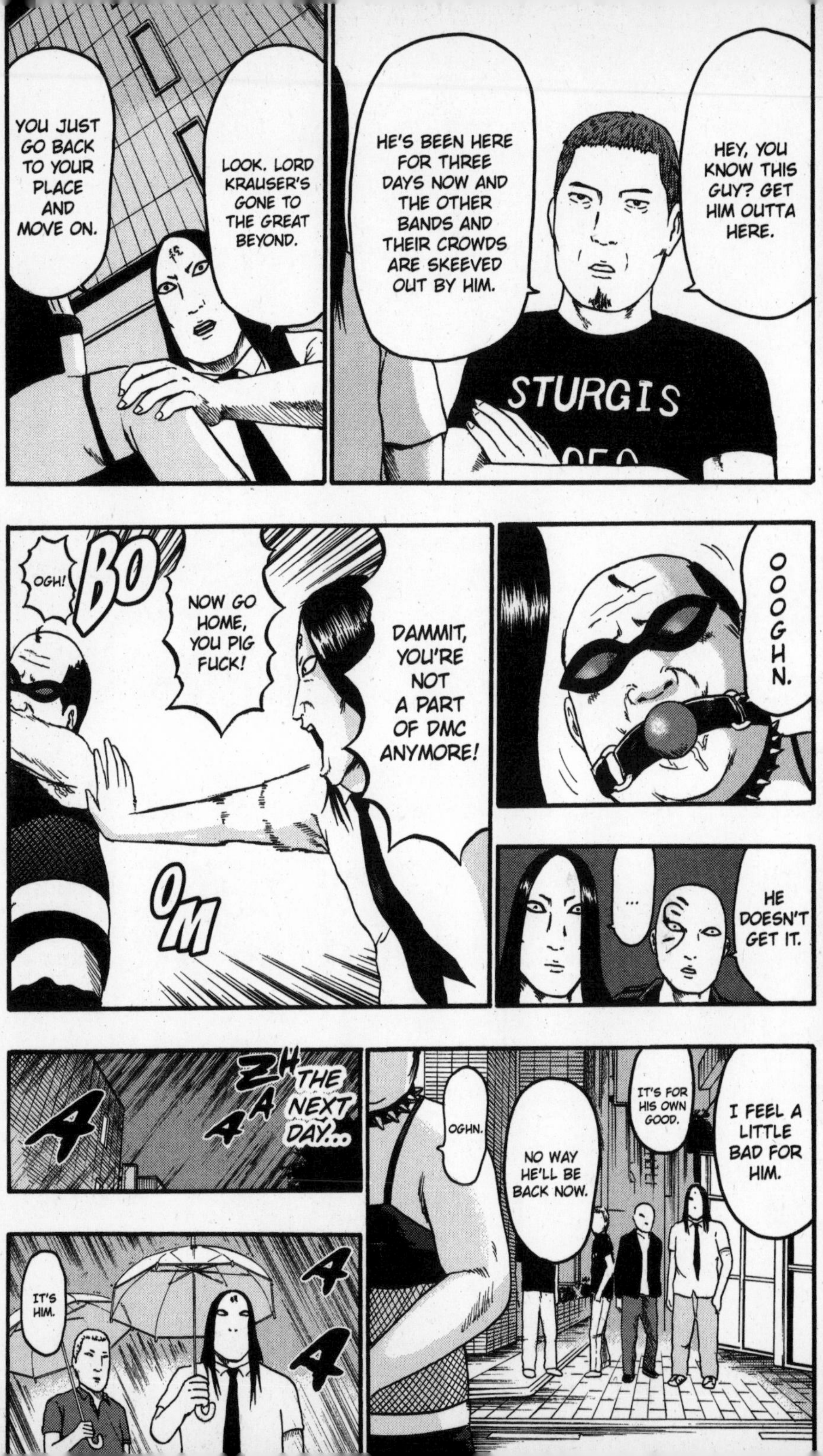
HEY, YOU KNOW THIS GUY? GET HIM OUTTA HERE.
HE'S BEEN HERE FOR THREE DAYS NOW AND THE OTHER BANDS AND THEIR CROWDS ARE SKEEVED OUT BY HIM.
STURGIS
LOOK. LORD KRAUSER'S GONE TO THE GREAT BEYOND.
YOU JUST GO BACK TO YOUR PLACE AND MOVE ON.
OOOGHN.
HE DOESN'T GET IT.
...
DAMMIT, YOU'RE NOT A PART OF DMC ANYMORE!
NOW GO HOME, YOU PIG FUCK!
BO
OGH!
OM
I FEEL A LITTLE BAD FOR HIM.
IT'S FOR HIS OWN GOOD.
NO WAY HE'LL BE BACK NOW.
OGHN.
THE NEXT DAY...
ZHAAA
IT'S HIM.

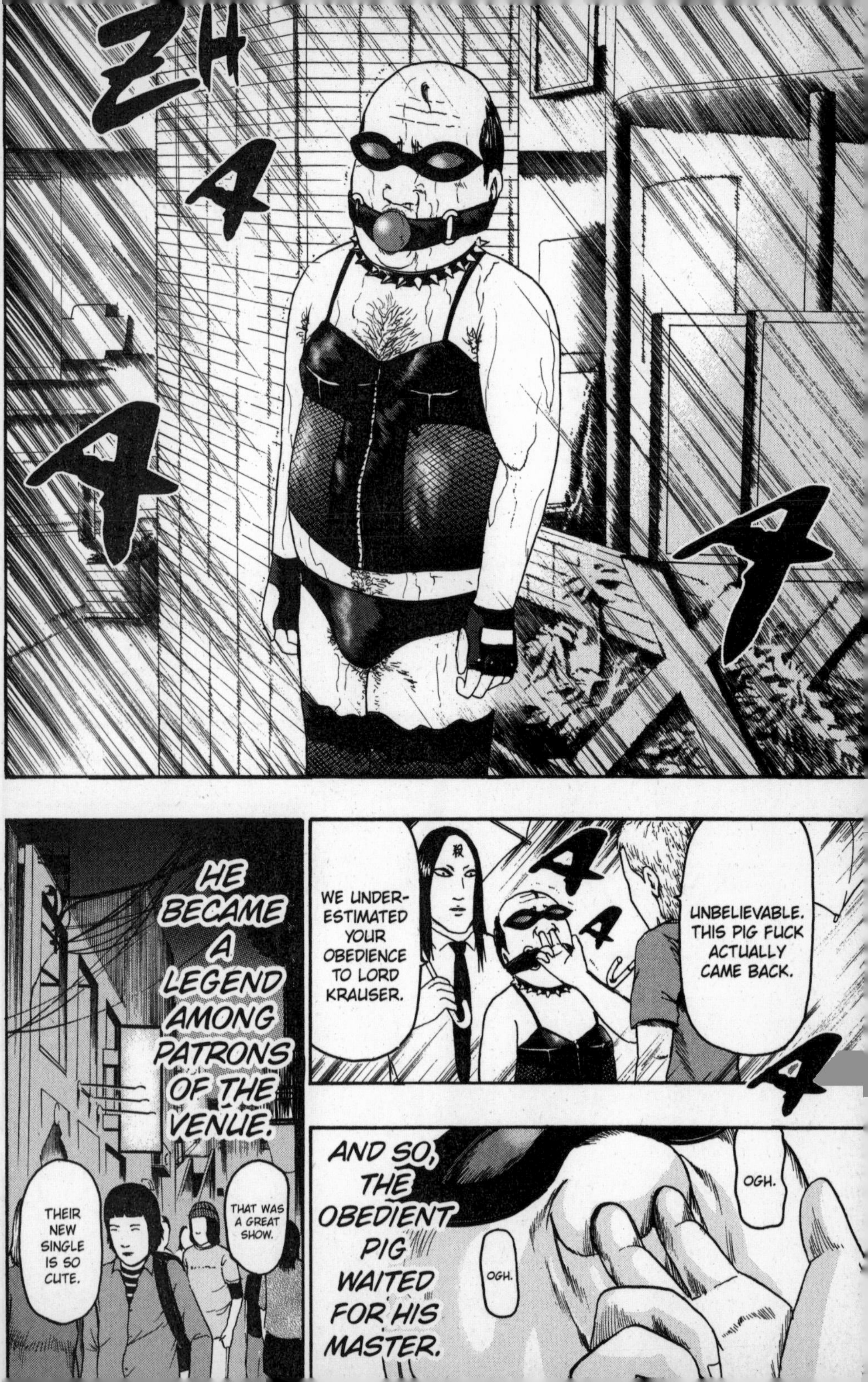
ZH
UNBELIEVABLE. THIS PIG FUCK ACTUALLY CAME BACK.
WE UNDER-ESTIMATED YOUR OBEDIENCE TO LORD KRAUSER.
AND SO, THE OBEDIENT PIG WAITED FOR HIS MASTER.
OGH.
OGH.
HE BECAME A LEGEND AMONG PATRONS OF THE VENUE.
THAT WAS A GREAT SHOW.
THEIR NEW SINGLE IS SO CUTE.

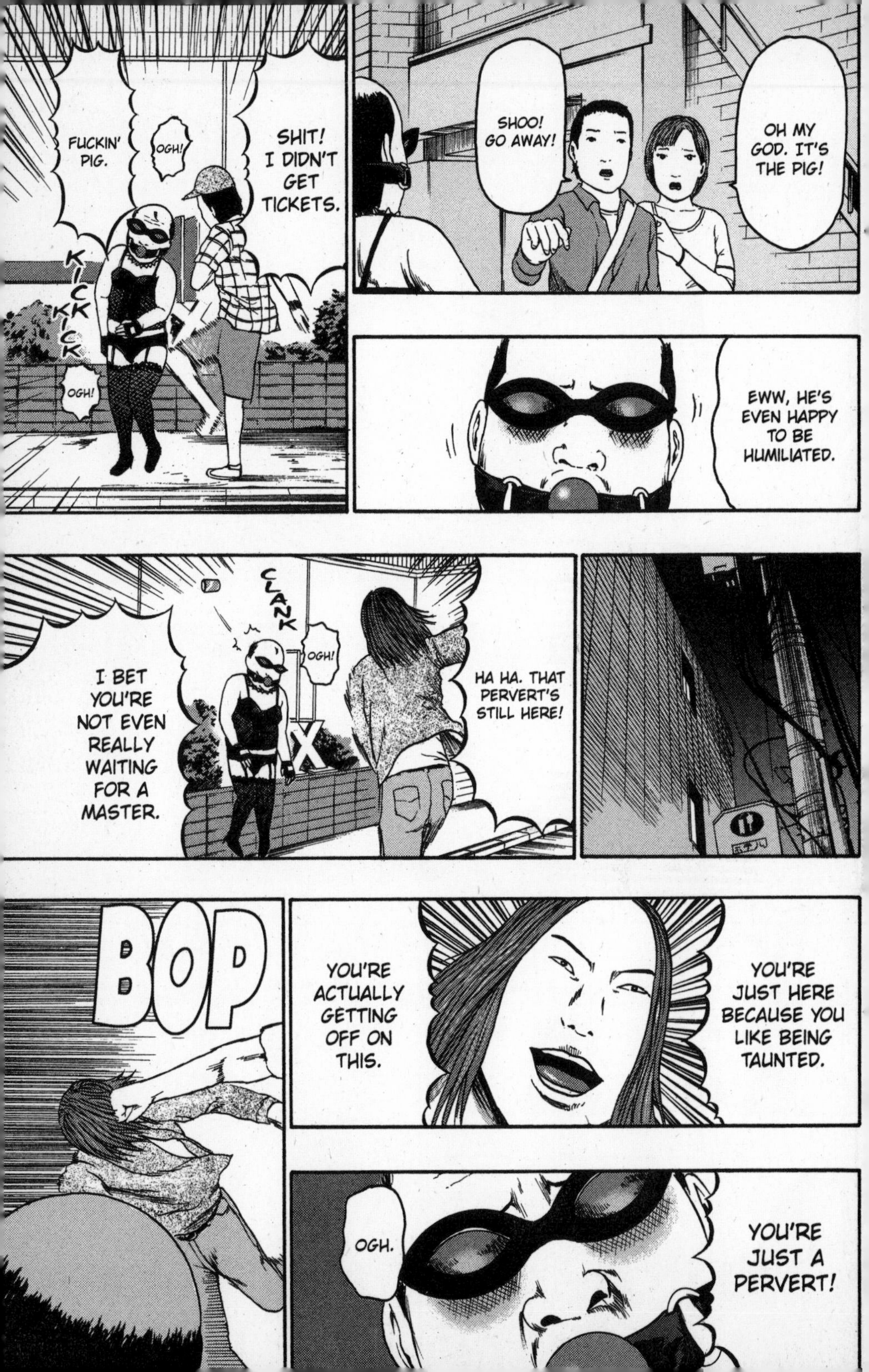
OH MY GOD. IT'S THE PIG!
SHOO! GO AWAY!
EWW, HE'S EVEN HAPPY TO BE HUMILIATED.
SHIT! I DIDN'T GET TICKETS.
OGH!
FUCKIN' PIG.
KICK
KICK
OGH!
HA HA. THAT PERVERT'S STILL HERE!
OGH!
CLANK
I BET YOU'RE NOT EVEN REALLY WAITING FOR A MASTER.
YOU'RE JUST HERE BECAUSE YOU LIKE BEING TAUNTED.
YOU'RE ACTUALLY GETTING OFF ON THIS.
YOU'RE JUST A PERVERT!
OGH.
BOP

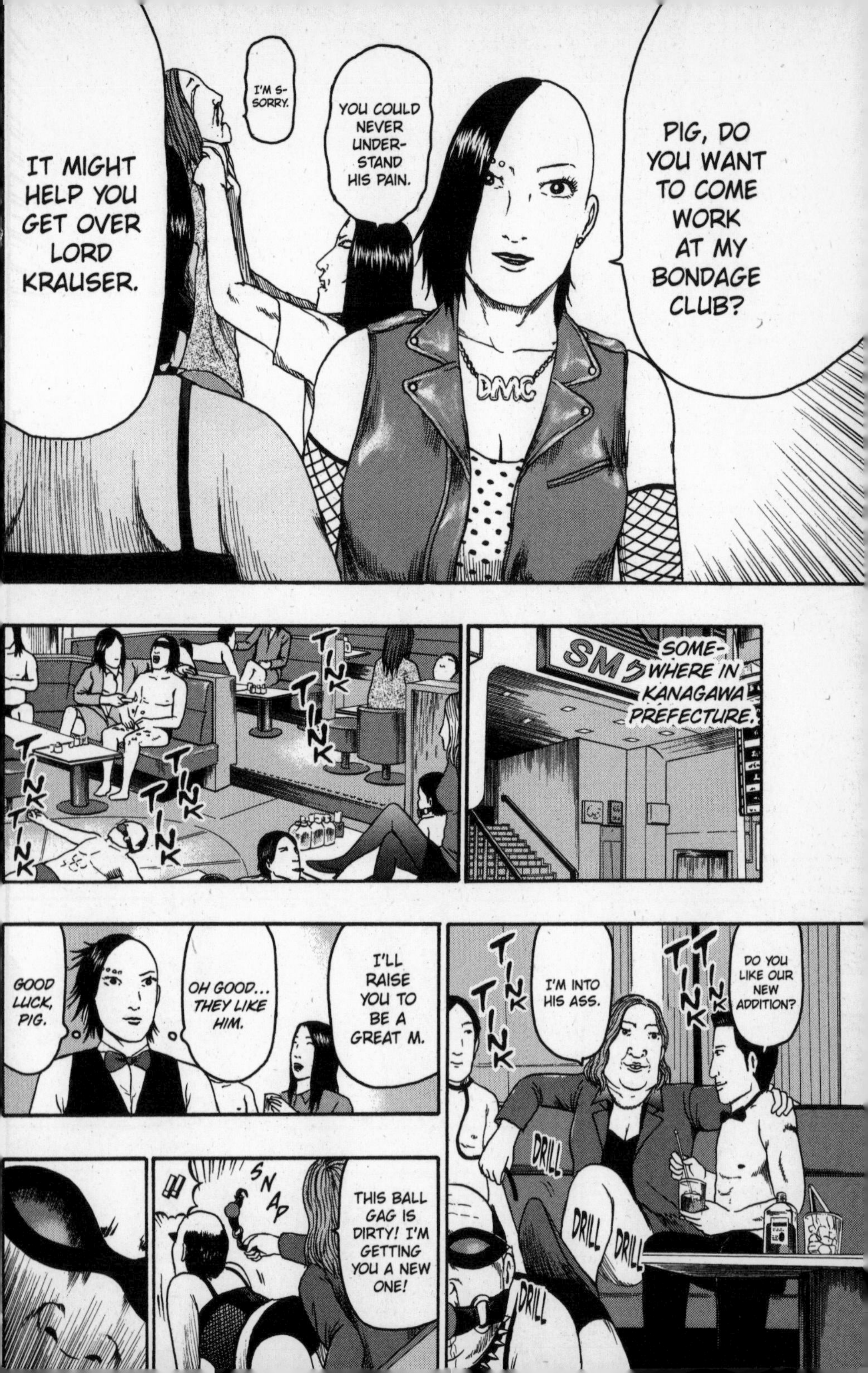
PIG, DO YOU WANT TO COME WORK AT MY BONDAGE CLUB?
DMC
YOU COULD NEVER UNDER-STAND HIS PAIN.
I'M S-SORRY.
IT MIGHT HELP YOU GET OVER LORD KRAUSER.
SM
SOME-WHERE IN KANAGAWA PREFECTURE.
TINK TINK
TINK TINK
TINK TINK
DO YOU LIKE OUR NEW ADDITION?
TINK TINK
I'M INTO HIS ASS.
TINK TINK
DRILL
DRILL DRILL
DRILL
I'LL RAISE YOU TO BE A GREAT M.
OH GOOD... THEY LIKE HIM.
GOOD LUCK, PIG.
THIS BALL GAG IS DIRTY! I'M GETTING YOU A NEW ONE!
SNAP
!!

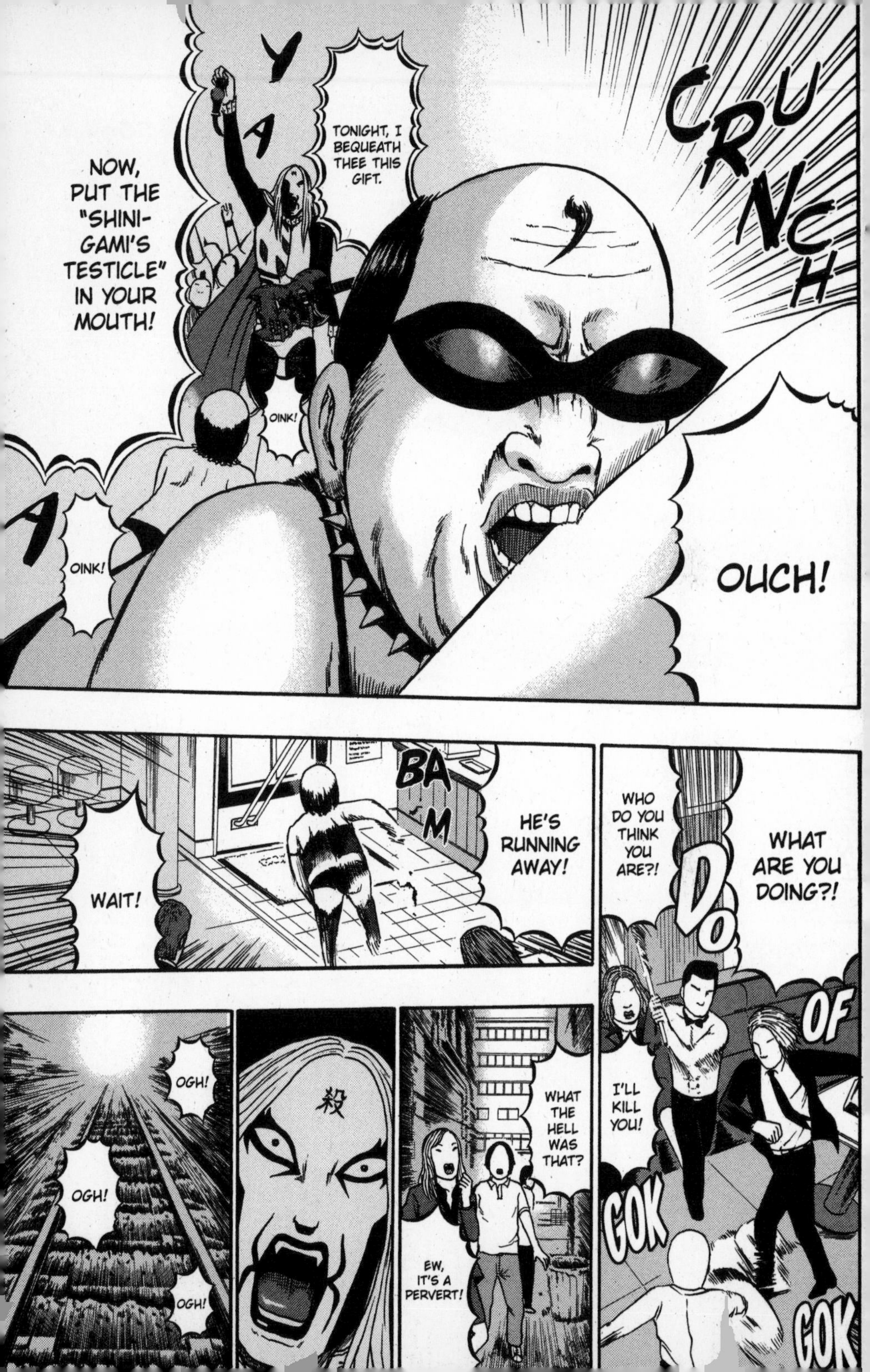
CRUNCH
OUCH!
TONIGHT, I BEQUEATH THEE THIS GIFT.
YAA
NOW, PUT THE "SHINIGAMI'S TESTICLE" IN YOUR MOUTH!
OINK!
OINK!
WHAT ARE YOU DOING?!
WHO DO YOU THINK YOU ARE?!
DO
OF
I'LL KILL YOU!
GOK
GOK
HE'S RUNNING AWAY!
BAM
WAIT!
WHAT THE HELL WAS THAT?
EW, IT'S A PERVERT!
殺
OGH!
OGH!
OGH!

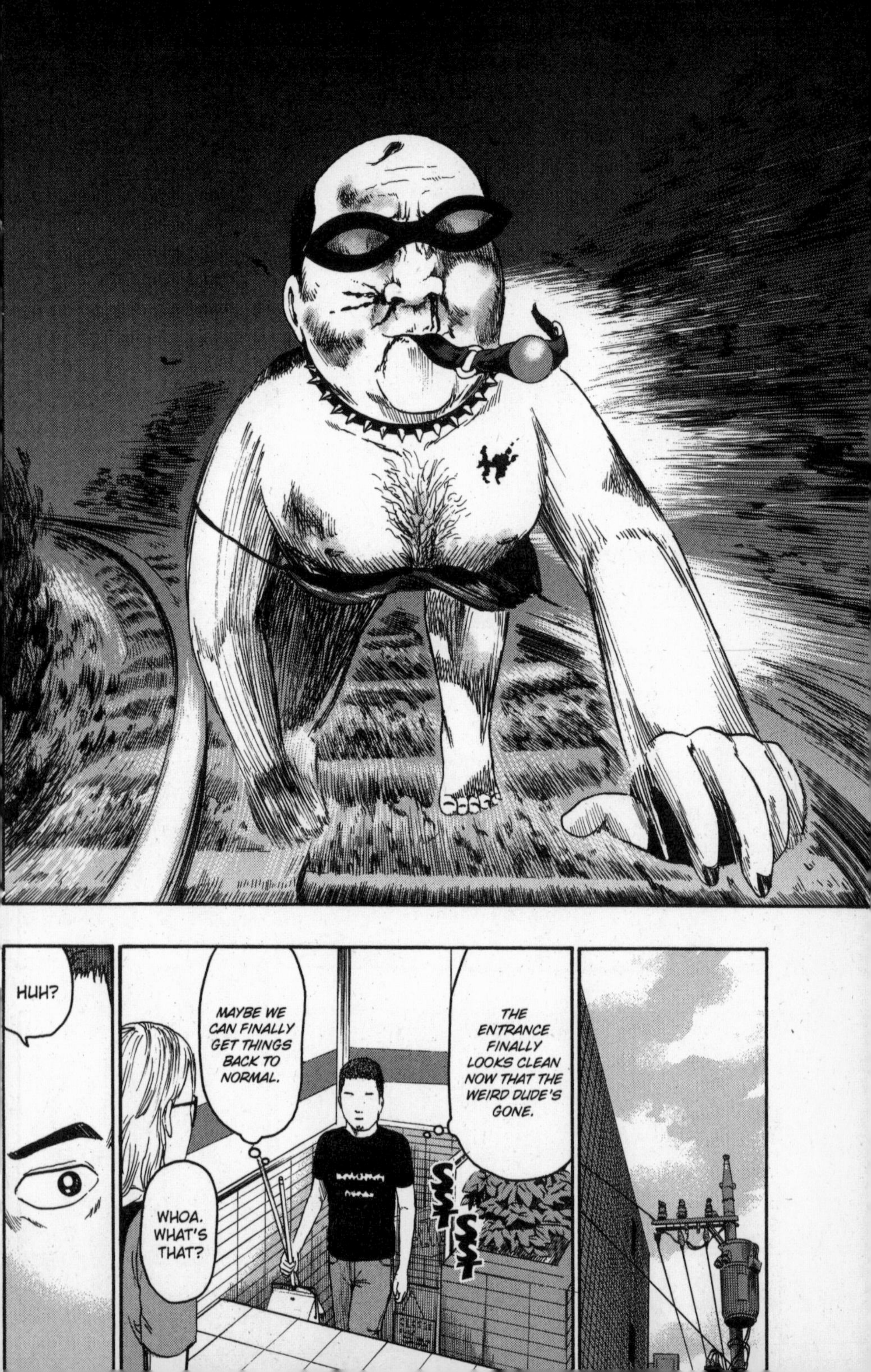
THE ENTRANCE FINALLY LOOKS CLEAN NOW THAT THE WEIRD DUDE'S GONE.
MAYBE WE CAN FINALLY GET THINGS BACK TO NORMAL.
SST
SST
SST
WHOA. WHAT'S THAT?
HUH?

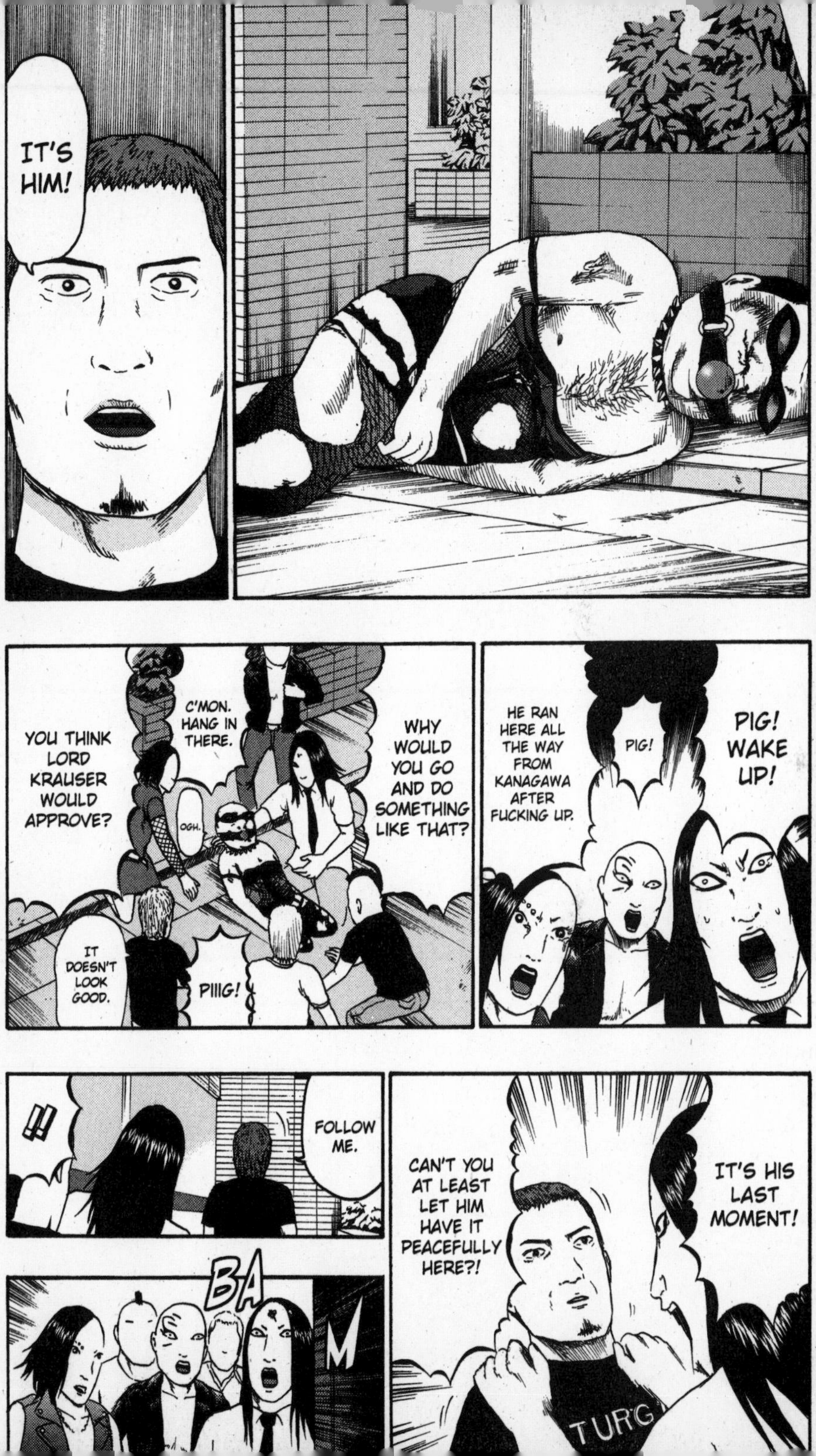
IT'S HIM!
PIG! WAKE UP!
PIG!
HE RAN HERE ALL THE WAY FROM KANAGAWA AFTER FUCKING UP.
WHY WOULD YOU GO AND DO SOMETHING LIKE THAT?
C'MON. HANG IN THERE.
YOU THINK LORD KRAUSER WOULD APPROVE?
OGH.
PIIIG!
IT DOESN'T LOOK GOOD.
IT'S HIS LAST MOMENT!
CAN'T YOU AT LEAST LET HIM HAVE IT PEACEFULLY HERE?!
TURG
FOLLOW ME.
!!
BAM

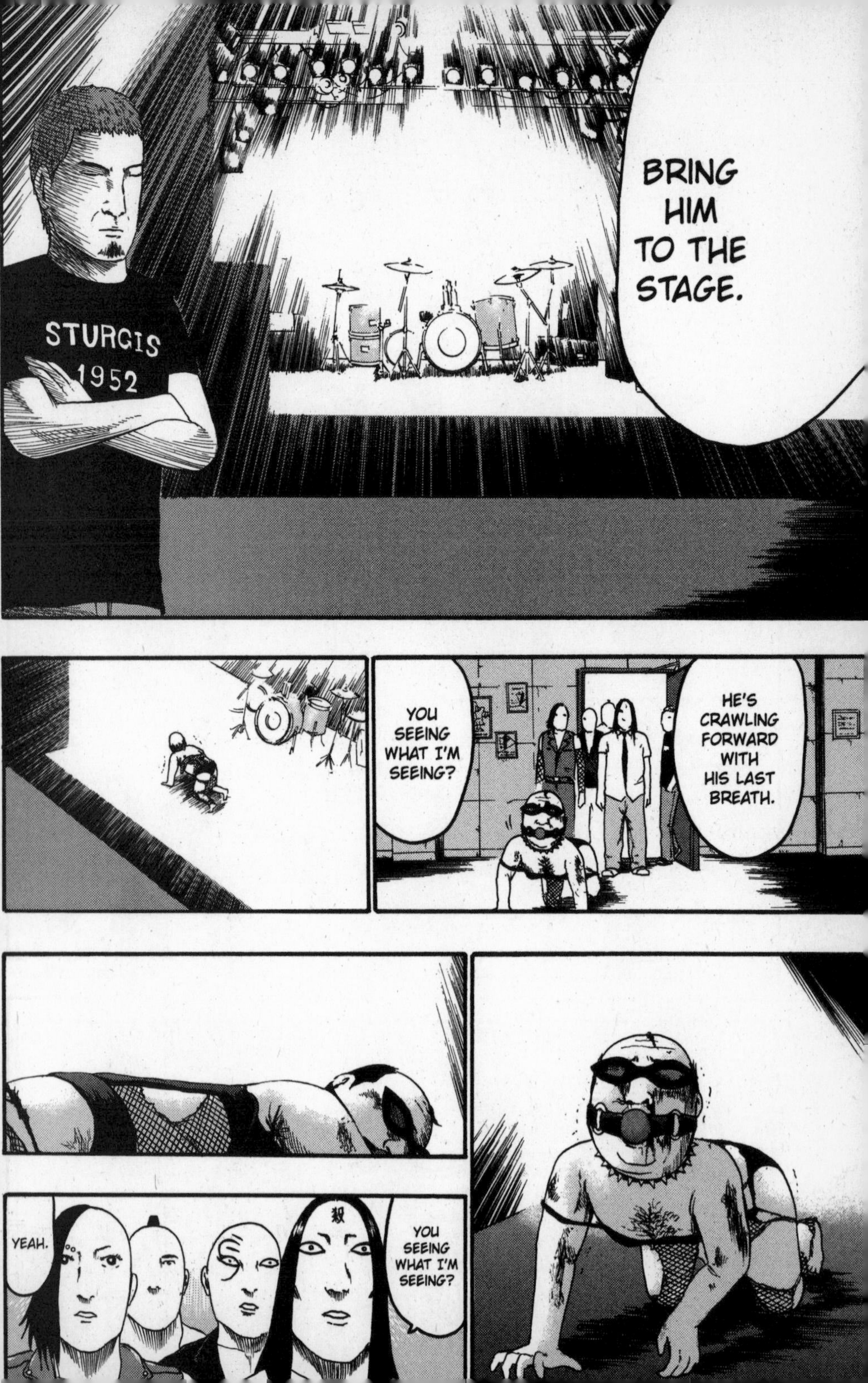
BRING HIM TO THE STAGE.
STURGIS 1952
HE'S CRAWLING FORWARD WITH HIS LAST BREATH.
YOU SEEING WHAT I'M SEEING?
YOU SEEING WHAT I'M SEEING?
YEAH.

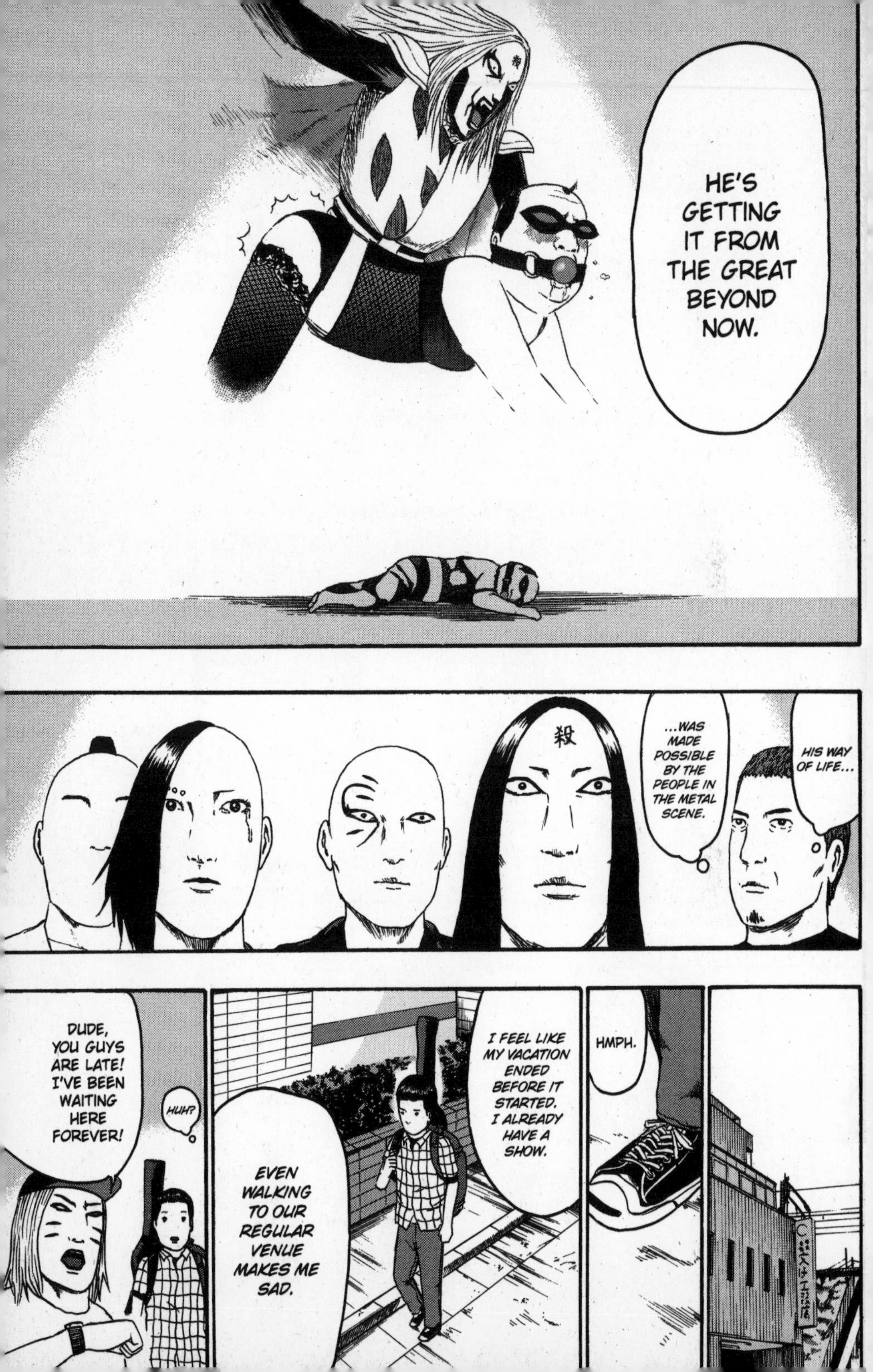
HE'S GETTING IT FROM THE GREAT BEYOND NOW.
HIS WAY OF LIFE...
...WAS MADE POSSIBLE BY THE PEOPLE IN THE METAL SCENE.
HMPH.
I FEEL LIKE MY VACATION ENDED BEFORE IT STARTED. I ALREADY HAVE A SHOW.
EVEN WALKING TO OUR REGULAR VENUE MAKES ME SAD.
DUDE, YOU GUYS ARE LATE! I'VE BEEN WAITING HERE FOREVER!
HUH?

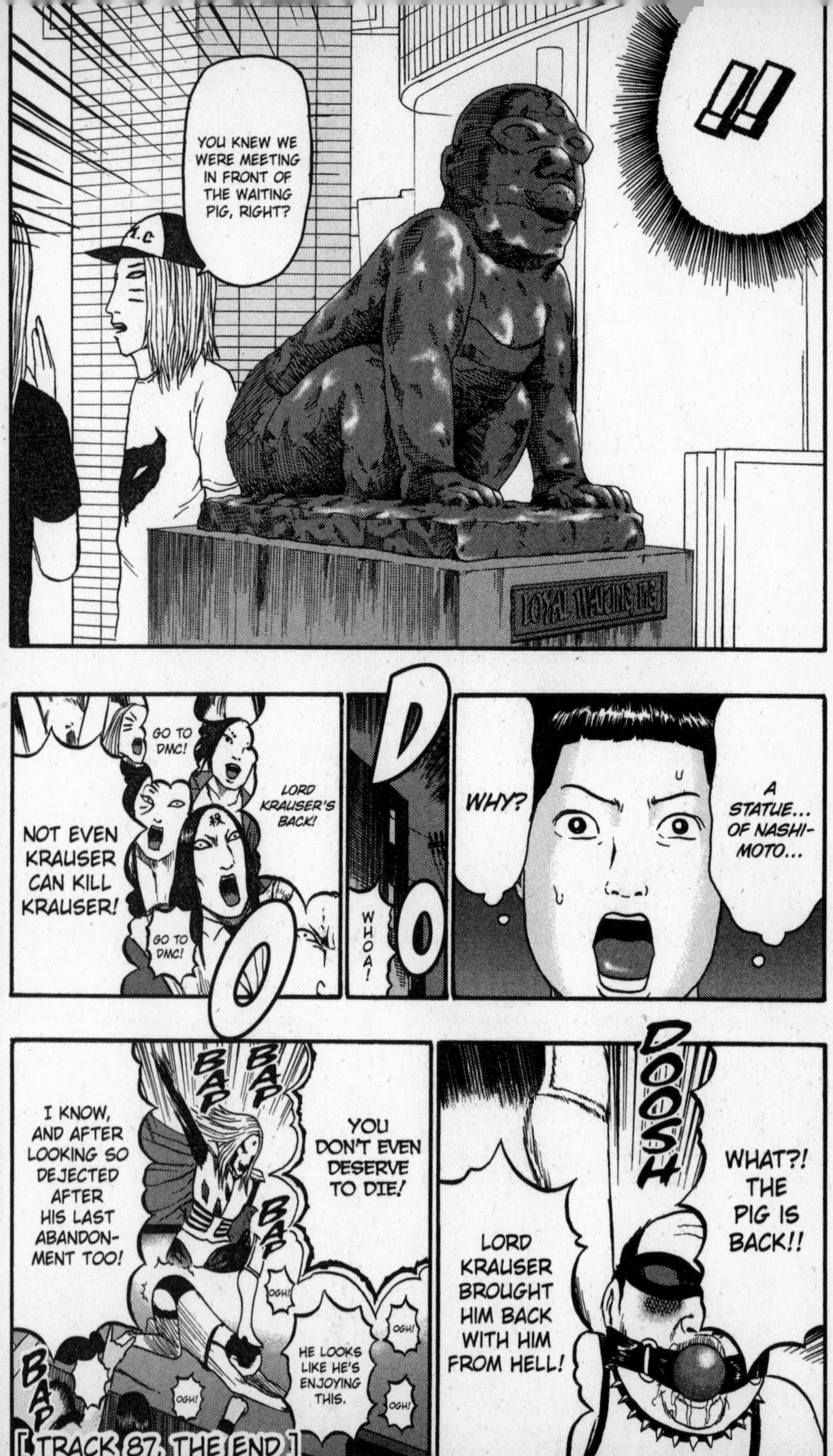
!!
YOU KNEW WE WERE MEETING IN FRONT OF THE WAITING PIG, RIGHT?
A STATUE... OF NASHIMOTO...
WHY?
D
WHOA!
O
O
LORD KRAUSER'S BACK!
GO TO DMC!
NOT EVEN KRAUSER CAN KILL KRAUSER!
GO TO DMC!
DOOSH
WHAT?! THE PIG IS BACK!!
LORD KRAUSER BROUGHT HIM BACK WITH HIM FROM HELL!
BAP BAP
YOU DON'T EVEN DESERVE TO DIE!
I KNOW, AND AFTER LOOKING SO DEJECTED AFTER HIS LAST ABANDONMENT TOO!
BAP
OGH!
OGH!
HE LOOKS LIKE HE'S ENJOYING THIS.
OGH!
OGH!
BAP
[TRACK 87, THE END]

DMC LEXICON

🐾 LOYAL WAITING PIG

Inspired by the tale of a fabled pig who waited
obediently for his master to return, a group of people
erected a statue in its honor. Today it is known best
as a meeting point. There were rumors of a Hollywood
adaptation of the story starring Richard Gere as
Nashimoto, called "Nashi: The Abandoned Pig," but it's
likely to be about an obedient gerbil.

Usage: Opponents of the Loyal Waiting Pig statue's erection
have made their voices heard!

デトロイト・メタル・シティ
Detroit Metal City

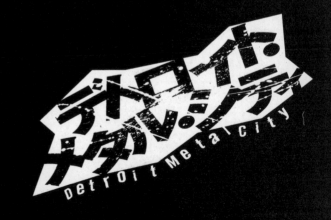

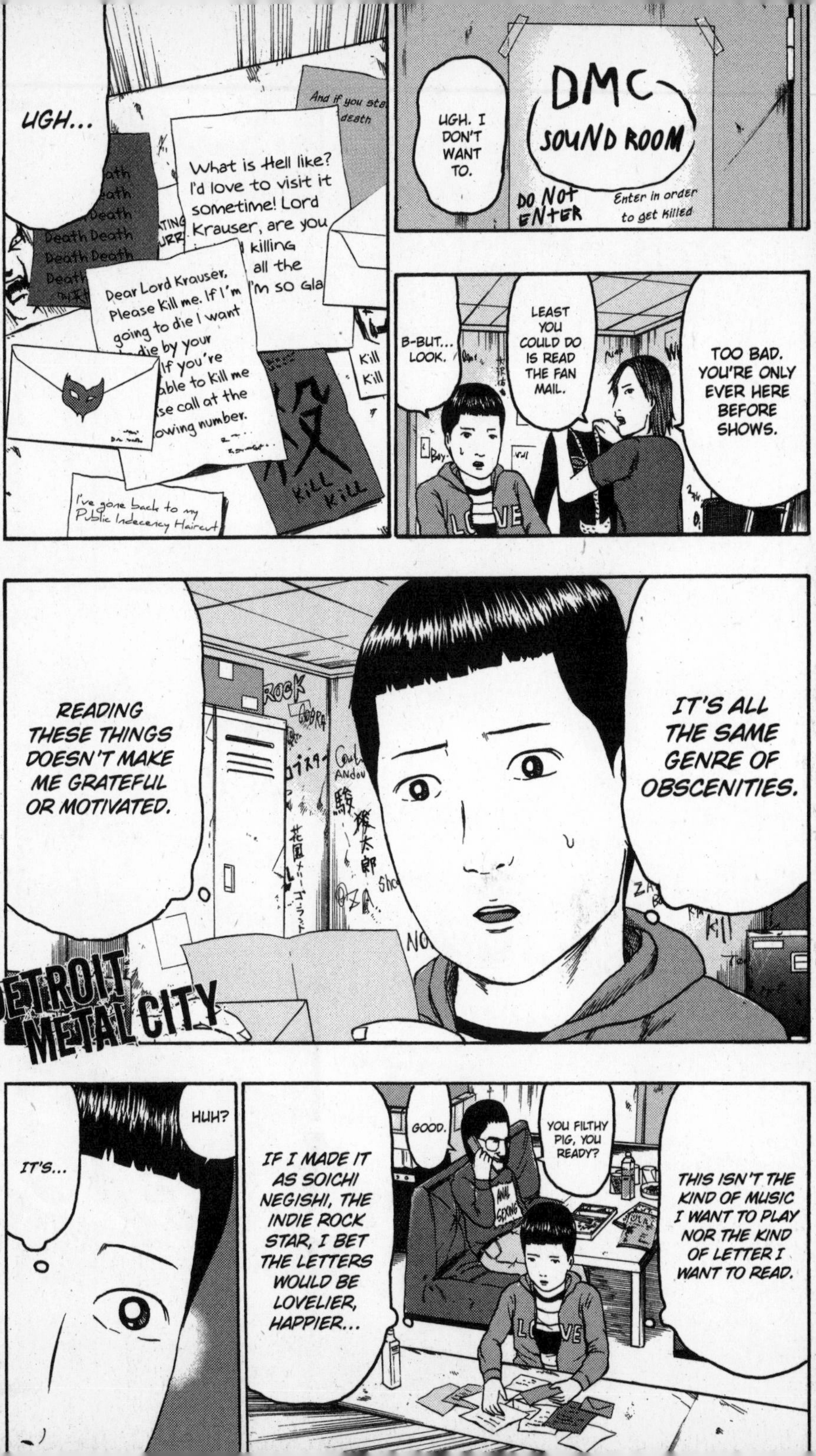
DMC
SOUND ROOM
DO NOT ENTER
Enter in order to get killed
UGH. I DON'T WANT TO.
TOO BAD. YOU'RE ONLY EVER HERE BEFORE SHOWS.
LEAST YOU COULD DO IS READ THE FAN MAIL.
B-BUT... LOOK.
UGH...
What is Hell like? I'd love to visit it sometime! Lord Krauser, are you
Dear Lord Krauser, Please kill me. If I'm going to die I want
I've gone back to my Public Indecency Haircut
KILL KILL
IT'S ALL THE SAME GENRE OF OBSCENITIES.
READING THESE THINGS DOESN'T MAKE ME GRATEFUL OR MOTIVATED.
DETROIT METAL CITY
THIS ISN'T THE KIND OF MUSIC I WANT TO PLAY NOR THE KIND OF LETTER I WANT TO READ.
YOU FILTHY PIG, YOU READY?
GOOD.
IF I MADE IT AS SOICHI NEGISHI, THE INDIE ROCK STAR, I BET THE LETTERS WOULD BE LOVELIER, HAPPIER...
HUH?
IT'S...

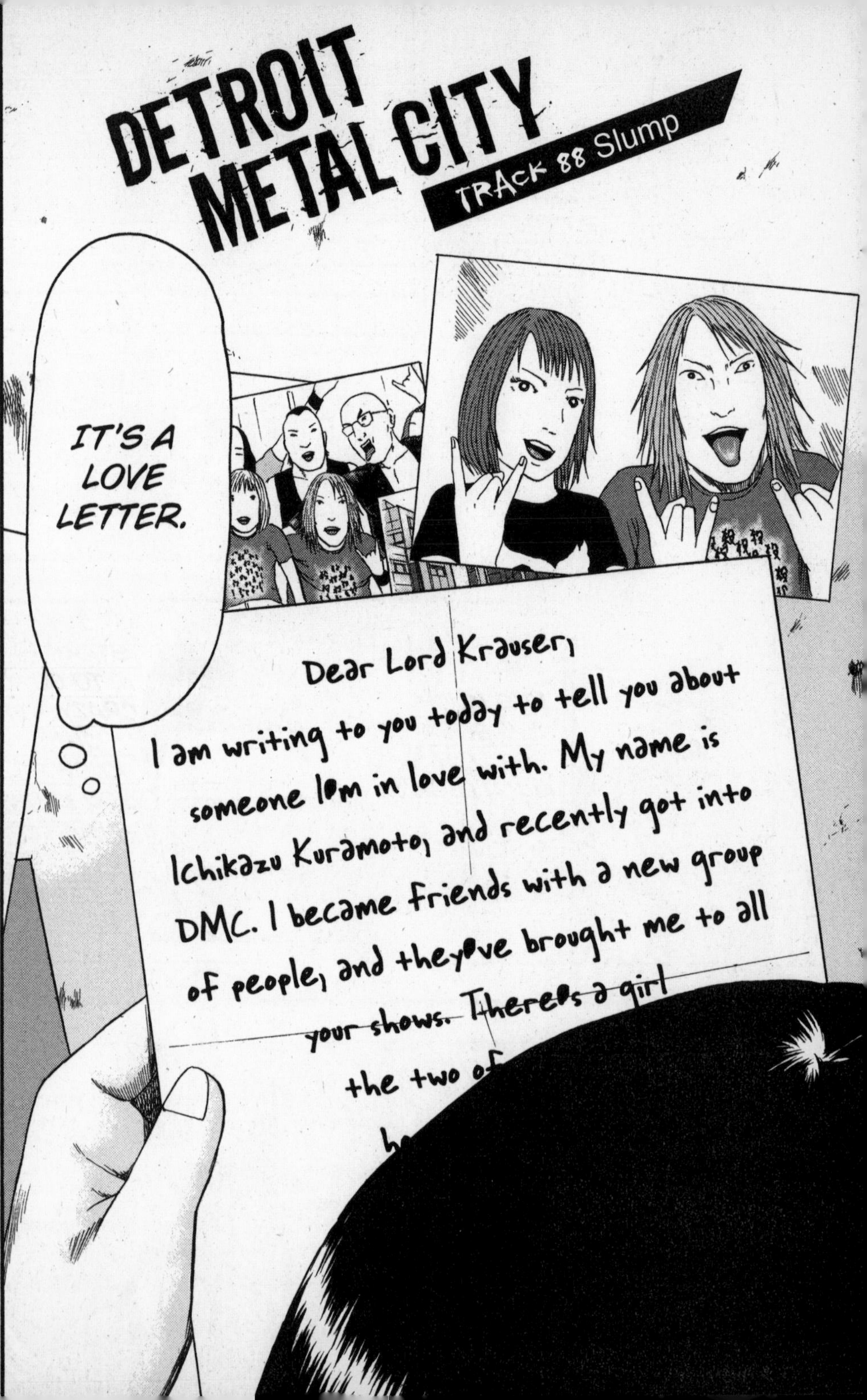
DETROIT METAL CITY
TRACK 88 Slump
IT'S A LOVE LETTER.
Dear Lord Krauser,
I am writing to you today to tell you about
someone I'm in love with. My name is
Ichikazu Kuramoto, and recently got into
DMC. I became friends with a new group
of people, and they've brought me to all
your shows. There's a girl
the two

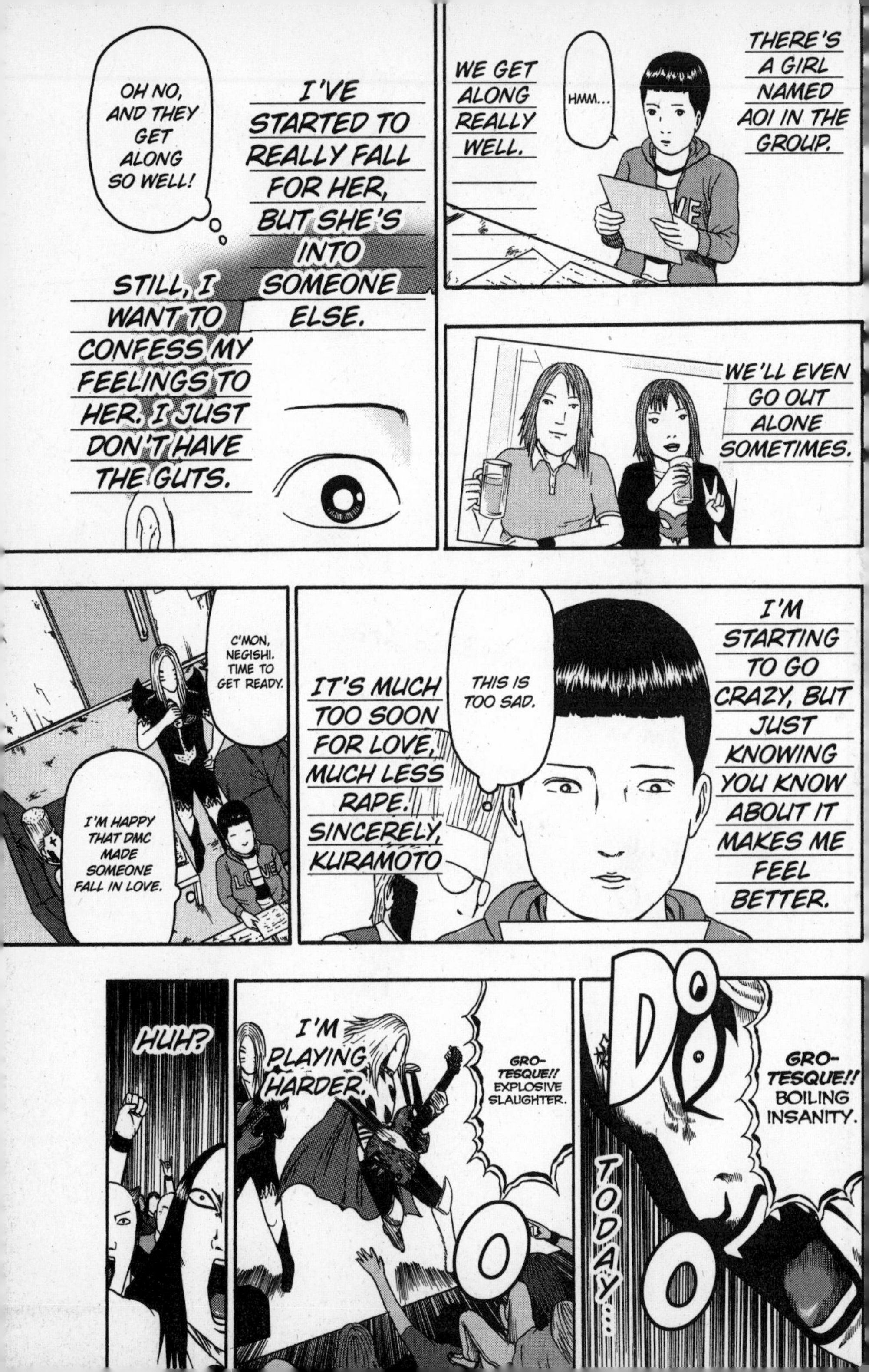
THERE'S A GIRL NAMED AOI IN THE GROUP.
HMM...
WE GET ALONG REALLY WELL.
WE'LL EVEN GO OUT ALONE SOMETIMES.
I'VE STARTED TO REALLY FALL FOR HER, BUT SHE'S INTO SOMEONE ELSE.
OH NO, AND THEY GET ALONG SO WELL!
STILL, I WANT TO CONFESS MY FEELINGS TO HER. I JUST DON'T HAVE THE GUTS.
I'M STARTING TO GO CRAZY, BUT JUST KNOWING YOU KNOW ABOUT IT MAKES ME FEEL BETTER.
THIS IS TOO SAD.
IT'S MUCH TOO SOON FOR LOVE, MUCH LESS RAPE. SINCERELY, KURAMOTO
C'MON, NEGISHI. TIME TO GET READY.
I'M HAPPY THAT DMC MADE SOMEONE FALL IN LOVE.
DO
GRO-TESQUE!! BOILING INSANITY.
TODAY...
O
I'M PLAYING HARDER.
GRO-TESQUE!! EXPLOSIVE SLAUGHTER.
O
HUH?

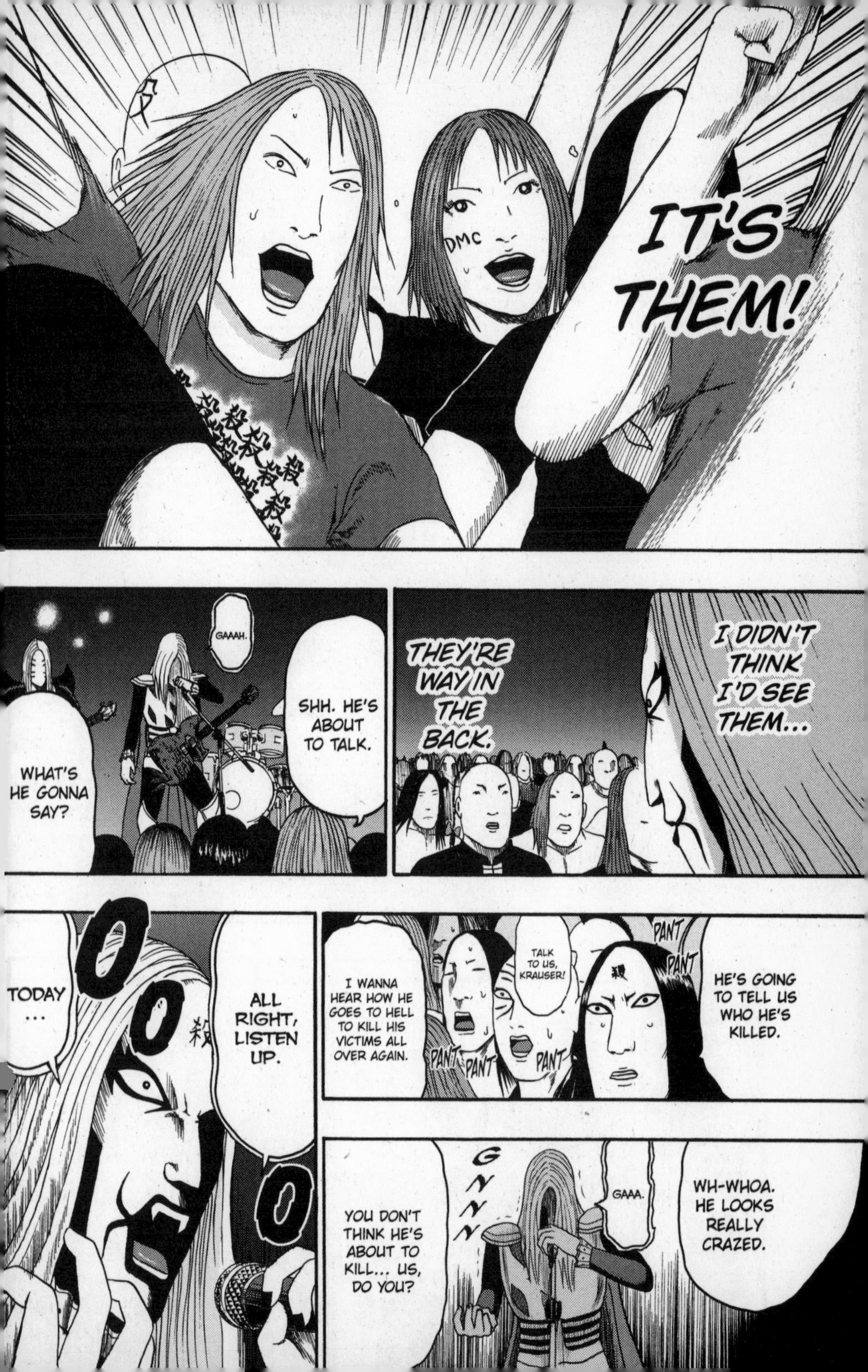

IT'S THEM!
I DIDN'T THINK I'D SEE THEM...
THEY'RE WAY IN THE BACK.
GAAAH.
SHH. HE'S ABOUT TO TALK.
WHAT'S HE GONNA SAY?
HE'S GOING TO TELL US WHO HE'S KILLED.
PANT PANT
TALK TO US, KRAUSER!
I WANNA HEAR HOW HE GOES TO HELL TO KILL HIS VICTIMS ALL OVER AGAIN.
PANT PANT PANT
WH-WHOA. HE LOOKS REALLY CRAZED.
GAAA.
GNNN
YOU DON'T THINK HE'S ABOUT TO KILL... US, DO YOU?
ALL RIGHT, LISTEN UP.
TODAY ...

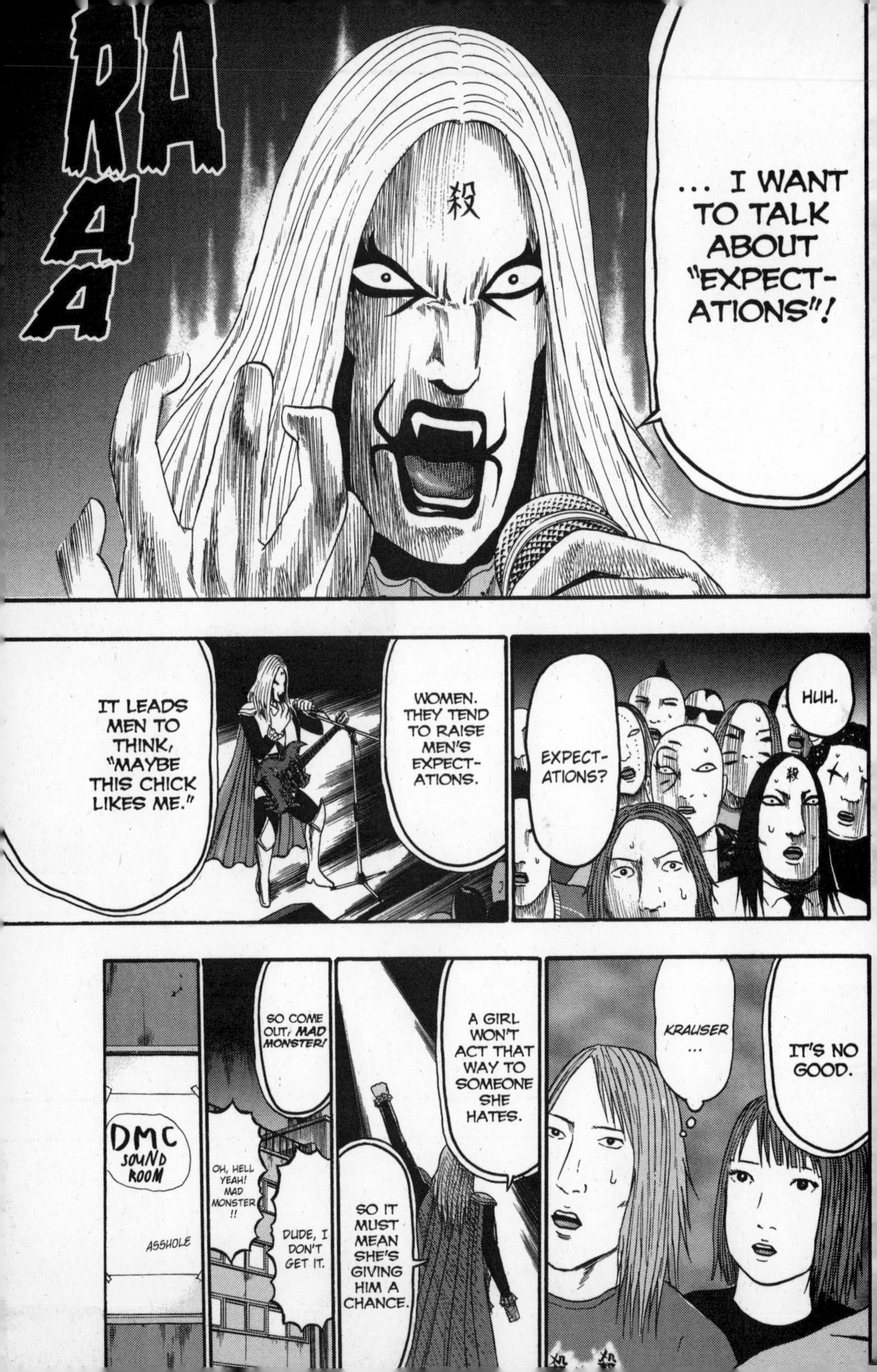
... I WANT TO TALK ABOUT "EXPECT-ATIONS"!
RAAA
HUH.
EXPECT-ATIONS?
WOMEN. THEY TEND TO RAISE MEN'S EXPECT-ATIONS.
IT LEADS MEN TO THINK, "MAYBE THIS CHICK LIKES ME."
IT'S NO GOOD.
KRAUSER ...
A GIRL WON'T ACT THAT WAY TO SOMEONE SHE HATES.
SO IT MUST MEAN SHE'S GIVING HIM A CHANCE.
SO COME OUT, MAD MONSTER!
OH, HELL YEAH! MAD MONSTER!!
DUDE, I DON'T GET IT.
DMC SOUND ROOM
ASSHOLE

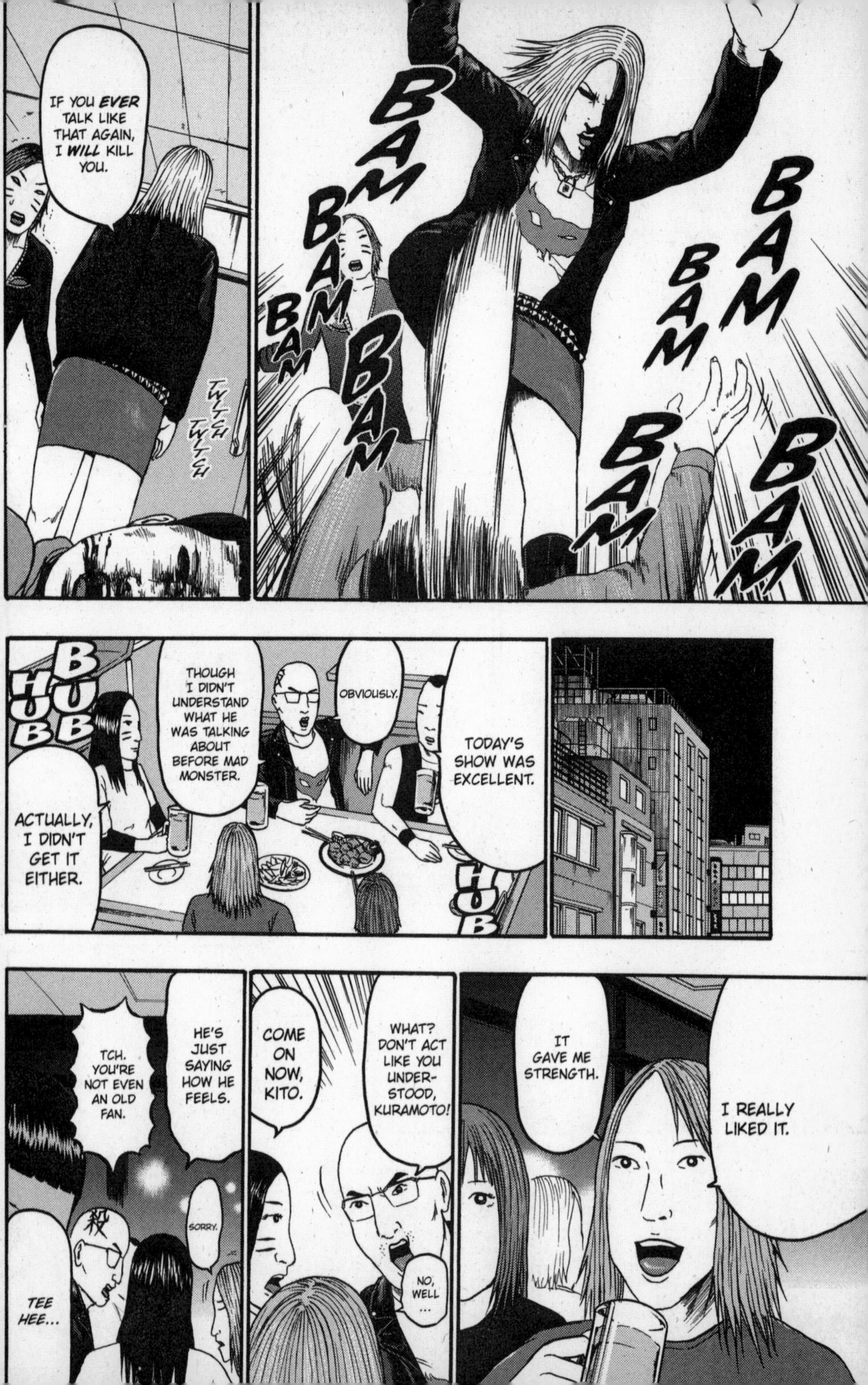
BAM
BAM
BAM
BAM
BAM
BAM
BAM
BAM
BAM
BAM
IF YOU *EVER* TALK LIKE THAT AGAIN, I *WILL* KILL YOU.
TWITCH TWITCH
HUBBUB
TODAY'S SHOW WAS EXCELLENT.
OBVIOUSLY.
THOUGH I DIDN'T UNDERSTAND WHAT HE WAS TALKING ABOUT BEFORE MAD MONSTER.
ACTUALLY, I DIDN'T GET IT EITHER.
HUBBUB
I REALLY LIKED IT.
IT GAVE ME STRENGTH.
WHAT? DON'T ACT LIKE YOU UNDER-STOOD, KURAMOTO!
COME ON NOW, KITO.
NO, WELL ...
HE'S JUST SAYING HOW HE FEELS.
TCH. YOU'RE NOT EVEN AN OLD FAN.
SORRY.
TEE HEE...

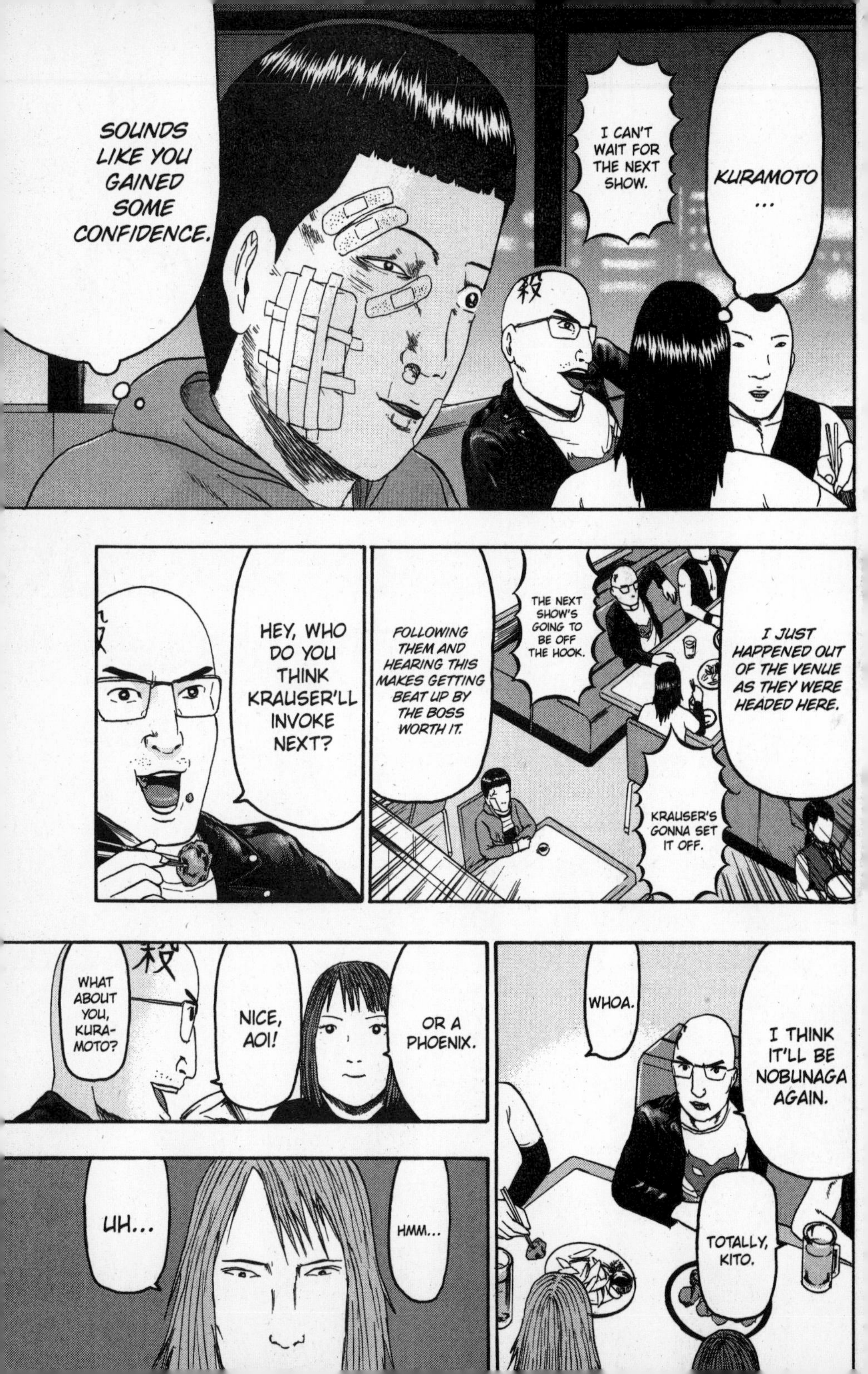
KURAMOTO ...
I CAN'T WAIT FOR THE NEXT SHOW.
SOUNDS LIKE YOU GAINED SOME CONFIDENCE.
I JUST HAPPENED OUT OF THE VENUE AS THEY WERE HEADED HERE.
THE NEXT SHOW'S GOING TO BE OFF THE HOOK.
KRAUSER'S GONNA SET IT OFF.
FOLLOWING THEM AND HEARING THIS MAKES GETTING BEAT UP BY THE BOSS WORTH IT.
HEY, WHO DO YOU THINK KRAUSER'LL INVOKE NEXT?
I THINK IT'LL BE NOBUNAGA AGAIN.
WHOA.
TOTALLY, KITO.
OR A PHOENIX.
NICE, AOI!
WHAT ABOUT YOU, KURA-MOTO?
HMM...
UH...

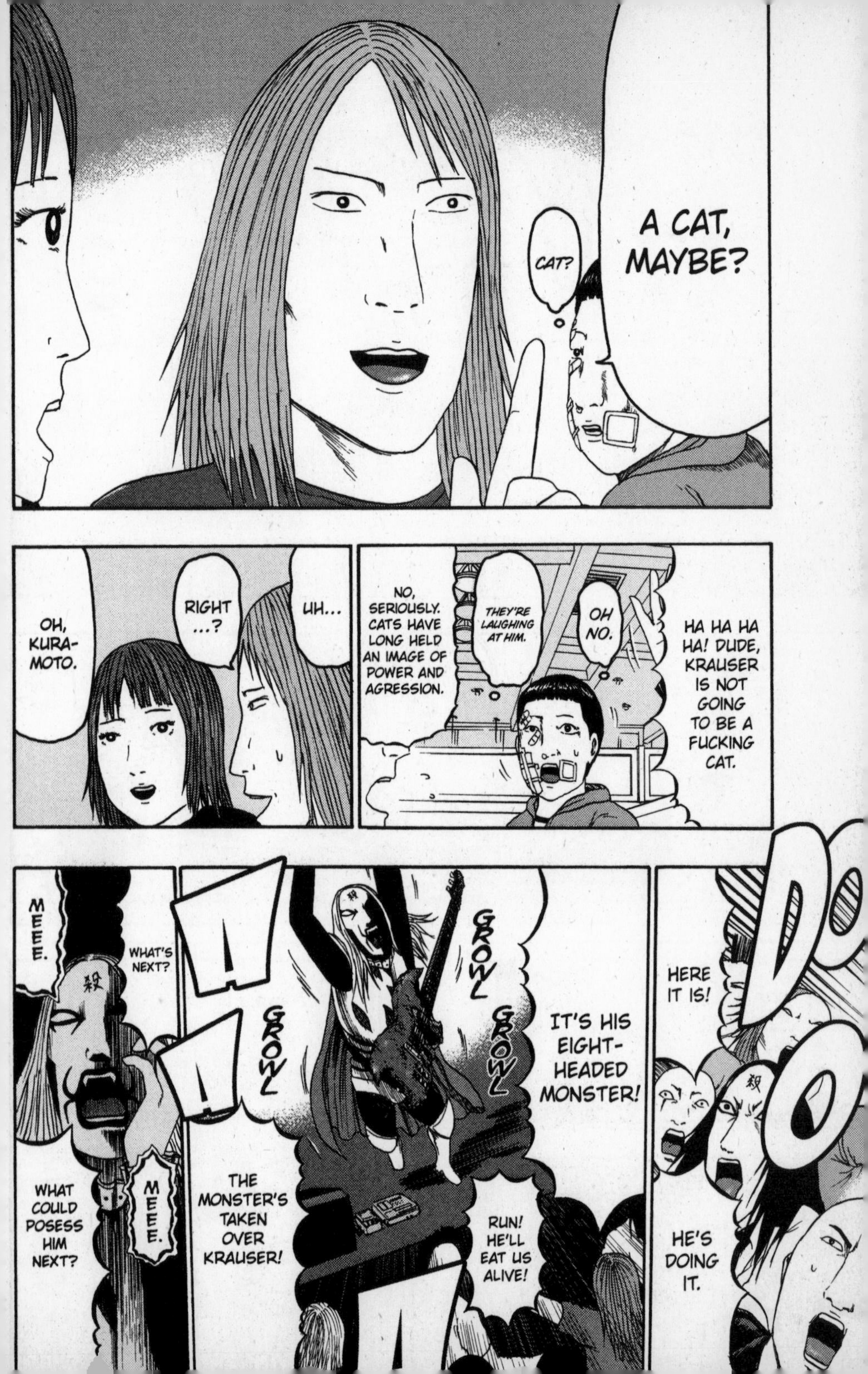
A CAT, MAYBE?
CAT?
HA HA HA HA! DUDE, KRAUSER IS NOT GOING TO BE A FUCKING CAT.
OH NO.
THEY'RE LAUGHING AT HIM.
NO, SERIOUSLY. CATS HAVE LONG HELD AN IMAGE OF POWER AND AGRESSION.
UH...
RIGHT ...?
OH, KURA-MOTO.
DO
HERE IT IS!
HE'S DOING IT.
GROWL
GROWL
GROWL
IT'S HIS EIGHT-HEADED MONSTER!
RUN! HE'LL EAT US ALIVE!
THE MONSTER'S TAKEN OVER KRAUSER!
MEEE.
WHAT'S NEXT?
MEEE.
WHAT COULD POSESS HIM NEXT?

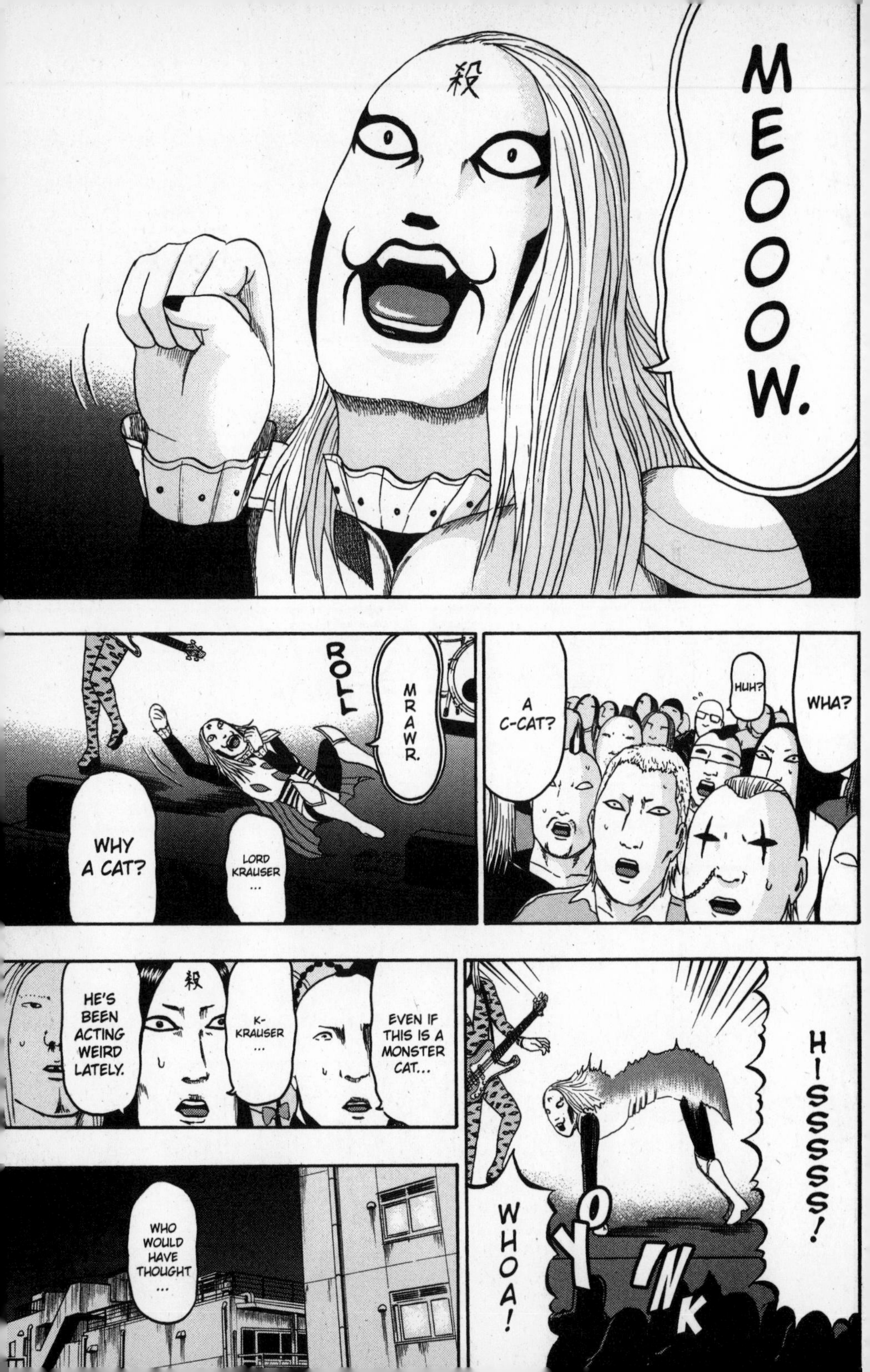
殺
MEOOOW.
WHA?
HUH?
A C-CAT?
ROLL
MRAWR.
LORD KRAUSER ...
WHY A CAT?
HISSSS!
YOWINK
WHOA!
EVEN IF THIS IS A MONSTER CAT...
K-KRAUSER ...
殺
HE'S BEEN ACTING WEIRD LATELY.
WHO WOULD HAVE THOUGHT ...

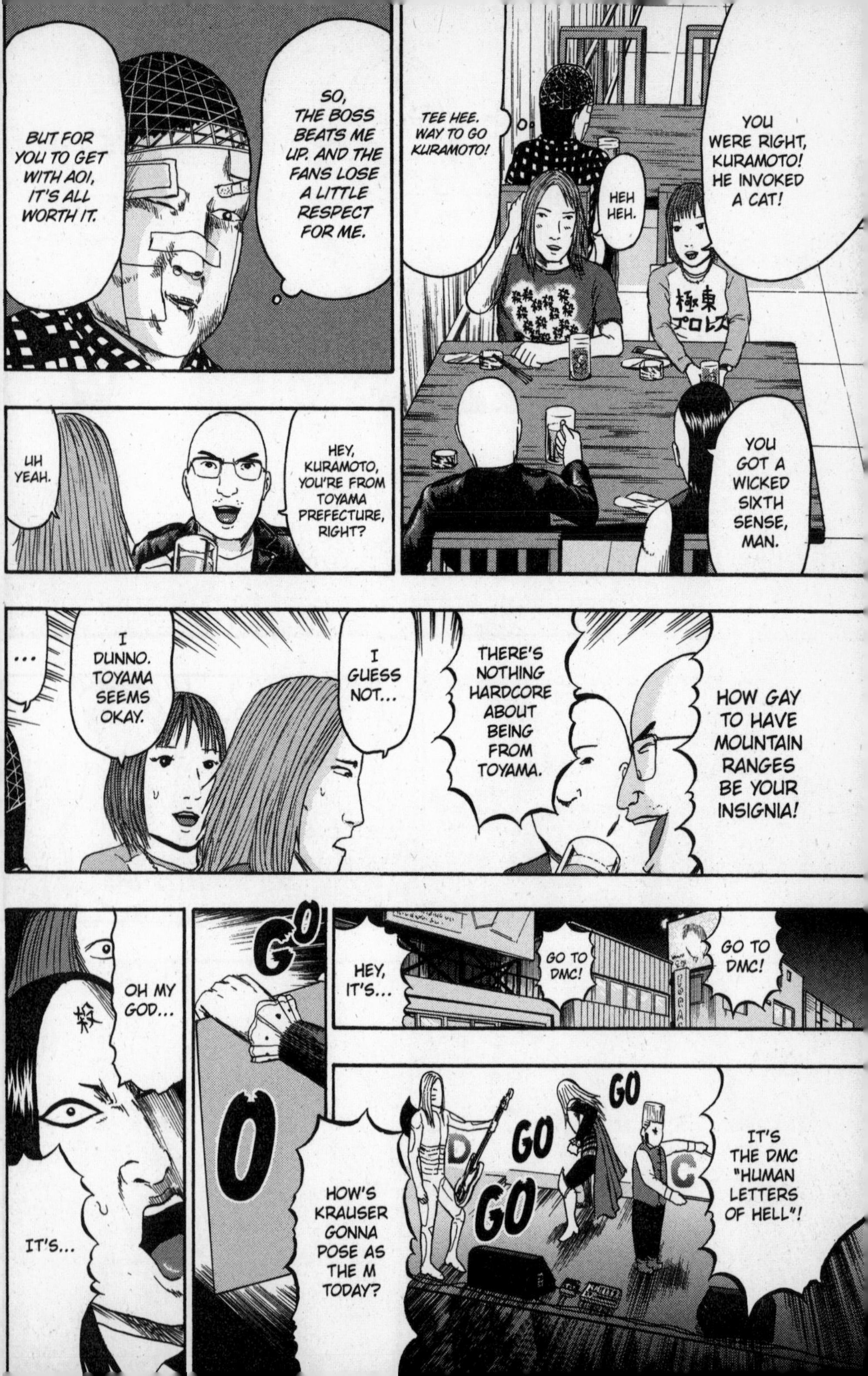
YOU WERE RIGHT, KURAMOTO! HE INVOKED A CAT!
HEH HEH.
TEE HEE. WAY TO GO KURAMOTO!
YOU GOT A WICKED SIXTH SENSE, MAN.
SO, THE BOSS BEATS ME UP. AND THE FANS LOSE A LITTLE RESPECT FOR ME.
BUT FOR YOU TO GET WITH AOI, IT'S ALL WORTH IT.
HEY, KURAMOTO, YOU'RE FROM TOYAMA PREFECTURE, RIGHT?
UH YEAH.
HOW GAY TO HAVE MOUNTAIN RANGES BE YOUR INSIGNIA!
THERE'S NOTHING HARDCORE ABOUT BEING FROM TOYAMA.
I GUESS NOT...
I DUNNO. TOYAMA SEEMS OKAY.
...
GO TO DMC!
GO TO DMC!
HEY, IT'S...
IT'S THE DMC "HUMAN LETTERS OF HELL"!
GO
GO
GO
GO
D
C
HOW'S KRAUSER GONNA POSE AS THE M TODAY?
GO
O
OH MY GOD...
IT'S...

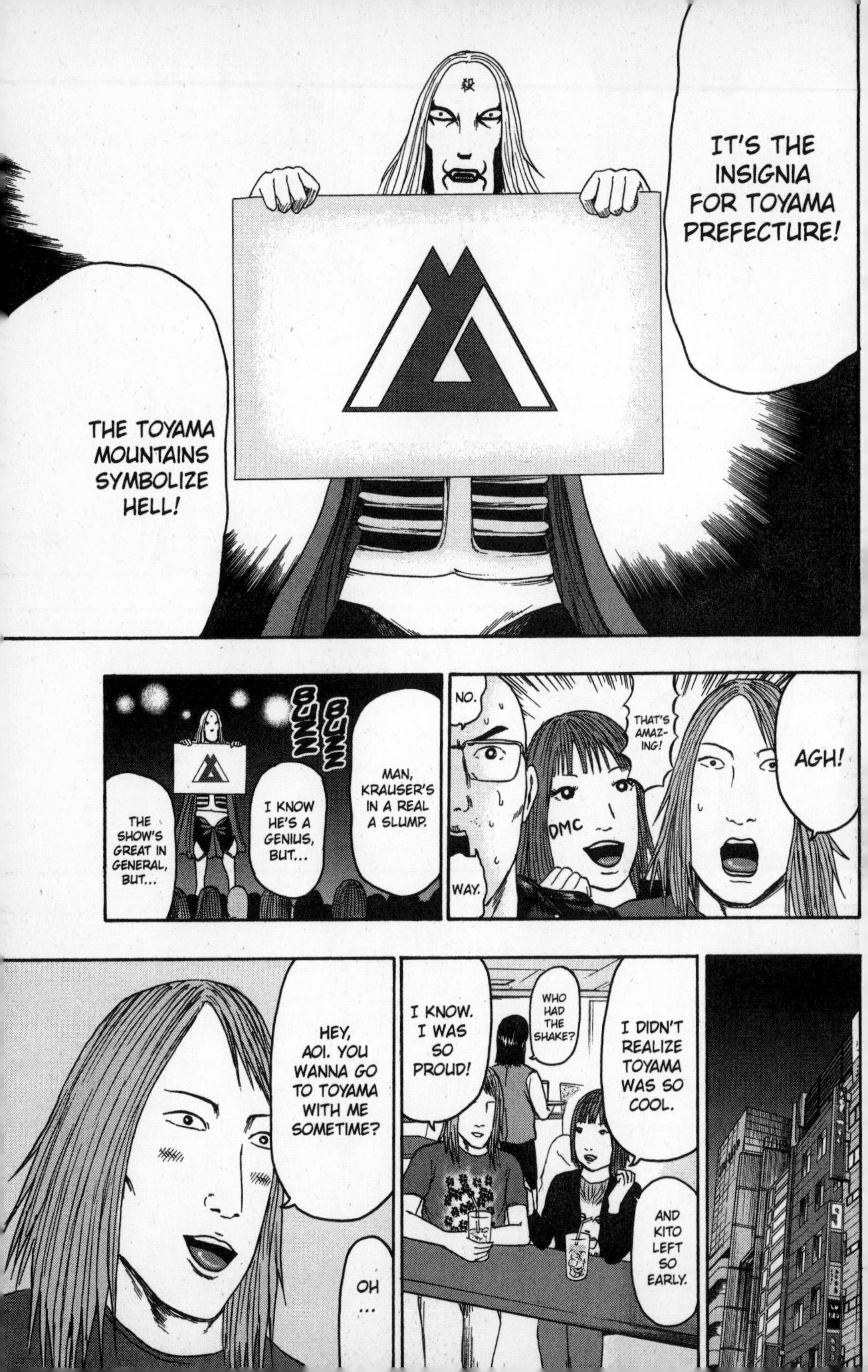
IT'S THE INSIGNIA FOR TOYAMA PREFECTURE!
THE TOYAMA MOUNTAINS SYMBOLIZE HELL!
AGH!
THAT'S AMAZ-ING!
DMC
NO. WAY.
BUZZ BUZZ
MAN, KRAUSER'S IN A REAL A SLUMP.
I KNOW HE'S A GENIUS, BUT...
THE SHOW'S GREAT IN GENERAL, BUT...
I DIDN'T REALIZE TOYAMA WAS SO COOL.
WHO HAD THE SHAKE?
I KNOW. I WAS SO PROUD!
AND KITO LEFT SO EARLY.
HEY, AOI. YOU WANNA GO TO TOYAMA WITH ME SOMETIME?
OH ...

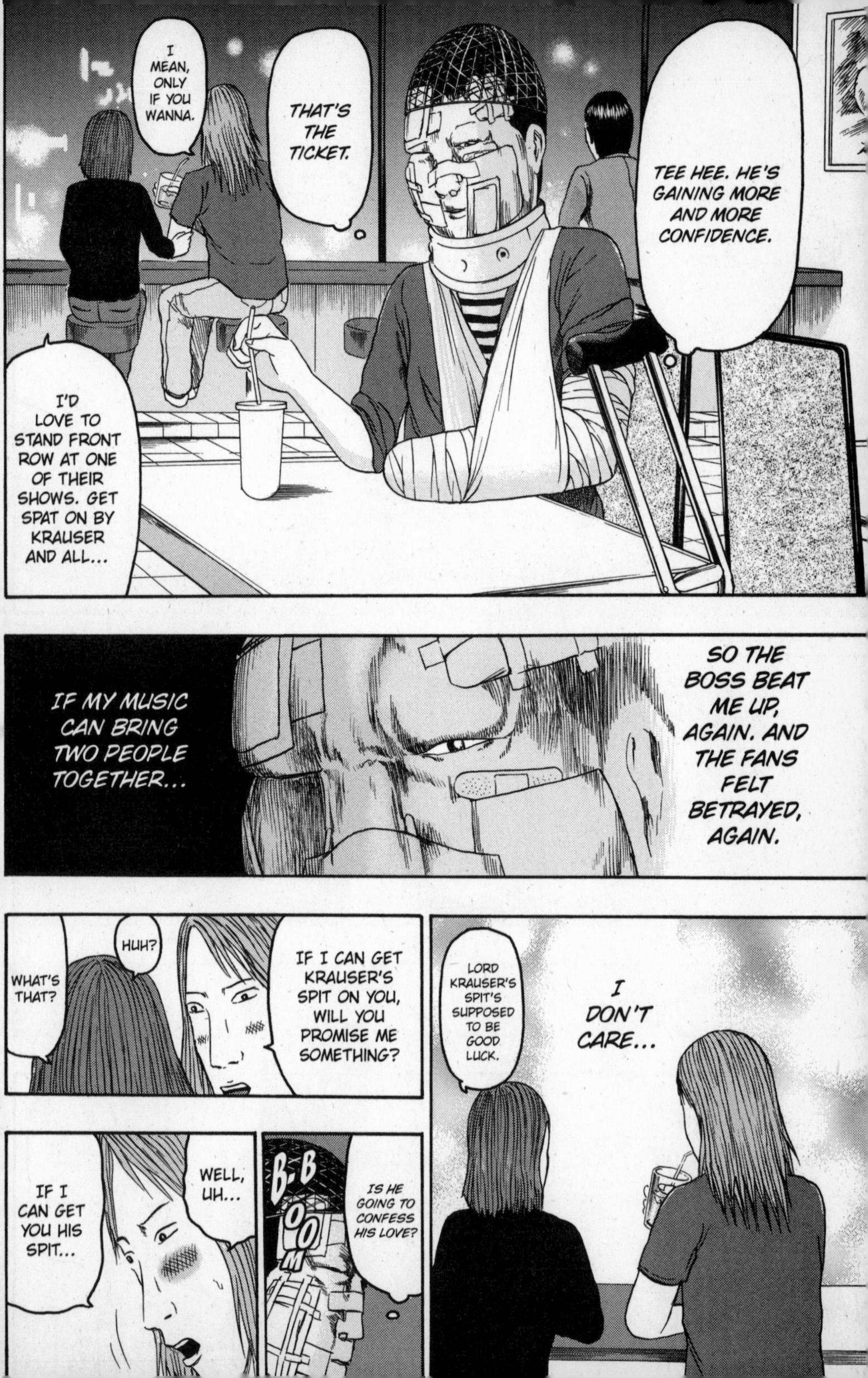
TEE HEE. HE'S GAINING MORE AND MORE CONFIDENCE.
THAT'S THE TICKET.
I MEAN, ONLY IF YOU WANNA.
I'D LOVE TO STAND FRONT ROW AT ONE OF THEIR SHOWS. GET SPAT ON BY KRAUSER AND ALL...
SO THE BOSS BEAT ME UP, AGAIN. AND THE FANS FELT BETRAYED, AGAIN.
IF MY MUSIC CAN BRING TWO PEOPLE TOGETHER...
I DON'T CARE...
LORD KRAUSER'S SPIT'S SUPPOSED TO BE GOOD LUCK.
IF I CAN GET KRAUSER'S SPIT ON YOU, WILL YOU PROMISE ME SOMETHING?
HUH?
WHAT'S THAT?
IS HE GOING TO CONFESS HIS LOVE?
B-BOOOM
WELL, UH...
IF I CAN GET YOU HIS SPIT...

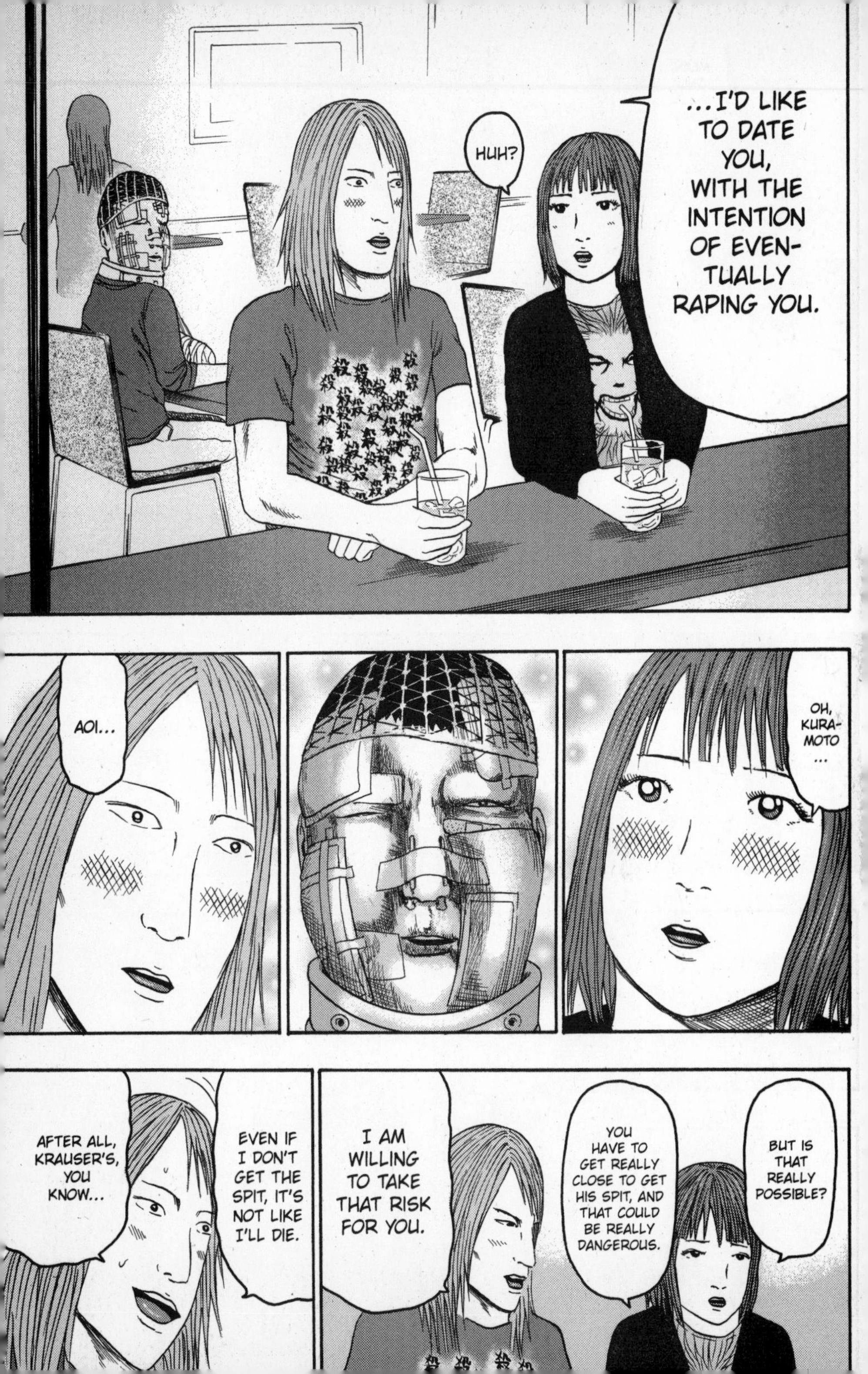
...I'D LIKE TO DATE YOU, WITH THE INTENTION OF EVEN-TUALLY RAPING YOU.
HUH?
OH, KURA-MOTO ...
AOI...
BUT IS THAT REALLY POSSIBLE?
YOU HAVE TO GET REALLY CLOSE TO GET HIS SPIT, AND THAT COULD BE REALLY DANGEROUS.
I AM WILLING TO TAKE THAT RISK FOR YOU.
EVEN IF I DON'T GET THE SPIT, IT'S NOT LIKE I'LL DIE.
AFTER ALL, KRAUSER'S, YOU KNOW...

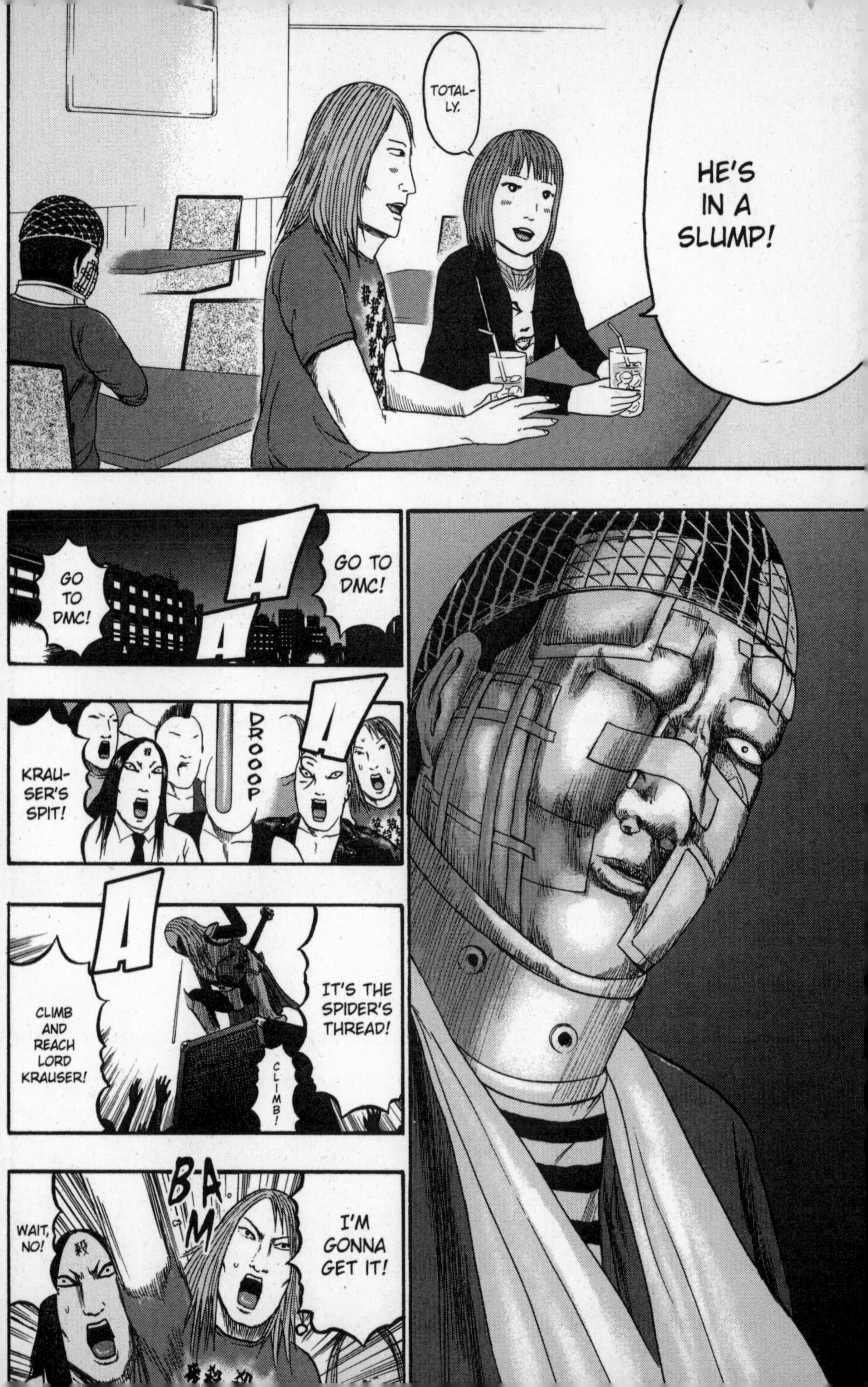
HE'S IN A SLUMP!
TOTAL-LY.
GO TO DMC!
A
A
GO TO DMC!
A
DROOOP
KRAU-SER'S SPIT!
IT'S THE SPIDER'S THREAD!
CLIMB!
A
CLIMB AND REACH LORD KRAUSER!
I'M GONNA GET IT!
BAM
WAIT, NO!

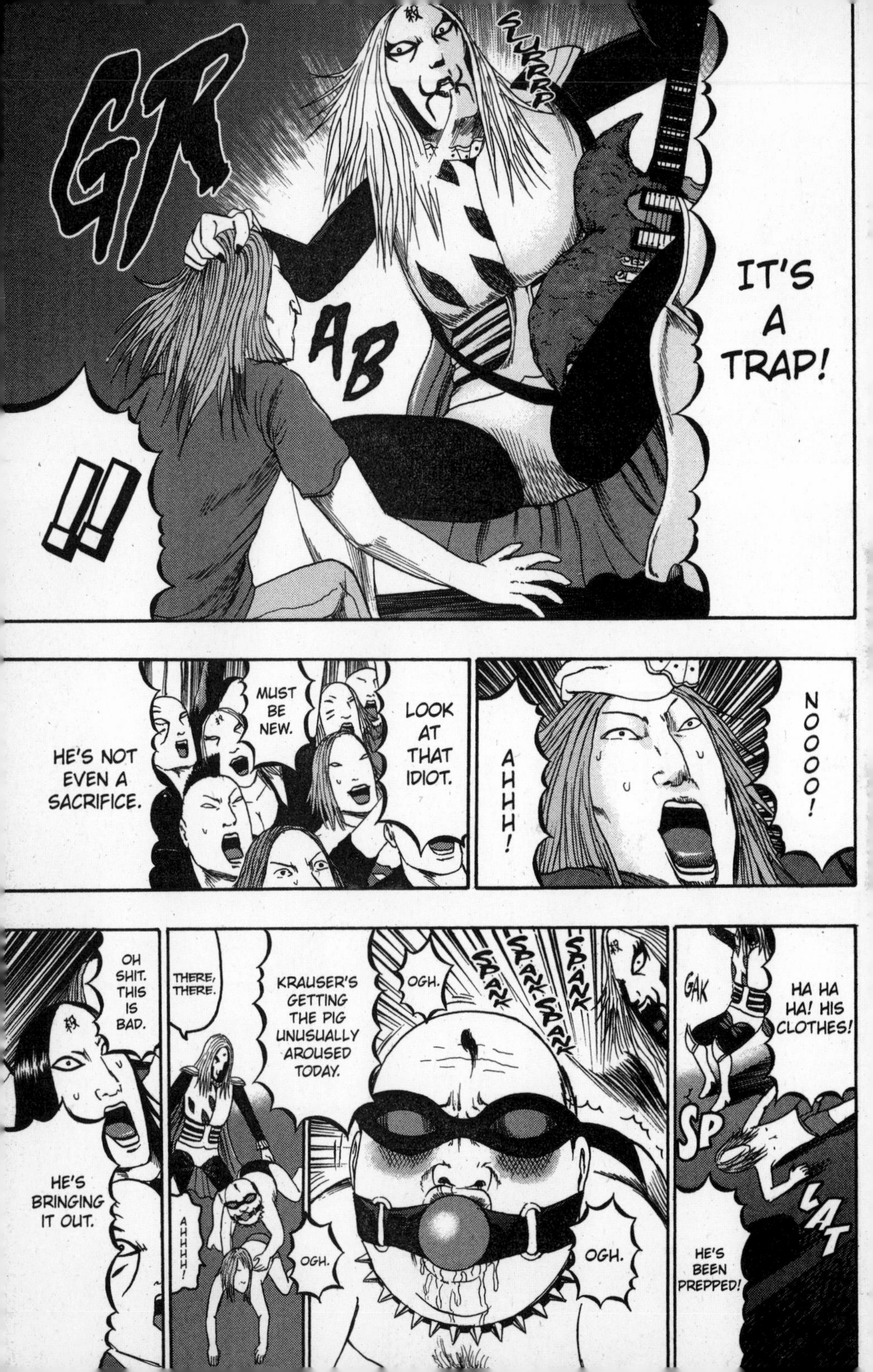
SLURRRP
IT'S A TRAP!
GR
AB
!!
NOOOO!
AHHH!
LOOK AT THAT IDIOT.
MUST BE NEW.
HE'S NOT EVEN A SACRIFICE.
HA HA HA! HIS CLOTHES!
GAK
SPLAT
HE'S BEEN PREPPED!
SPANK SPANK SPANK SPANK
OGH.
OGH.
OGH.
THERE, THERE.
KRAUSER'S GETTING THE PIG UNUSUALLY AROUSED TODAY.
AHHHH!
OH SHIT. THIS IS BAD.
HE'S BRINGING IT OUT.

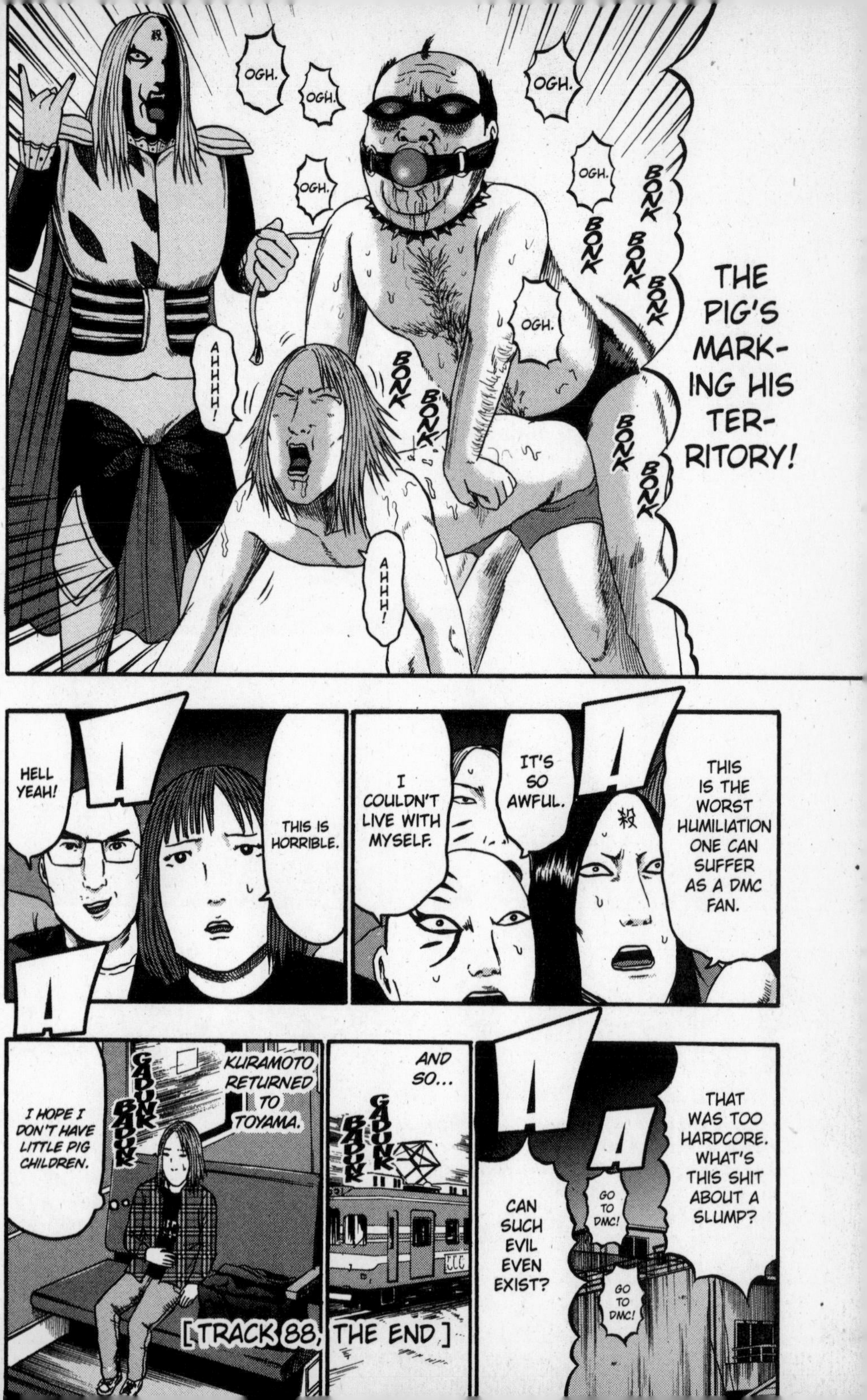
THE PIG'S MARKING HIS TERRITORY!
OGH.
BONK BONK BONK
BONK BONK
OGH.
OGH.
OGH.
OGH.
OGH.
OGH.
BONK BONK
AHHHH!
AHHHH!
THIS IS THE WORST HUMILIATION ONE CAN SUFFER AS A DMC FAN.
IT'S SO AWFUL.
I COULDN'T LIVE WITH MYSELF.
THIS IS HORRIBLE.
HELL YEAH!
THAT WAS TOO HARDCORE. WHAT'S THIS SHIT ABOUT A SLUMP?
GO TO DMC!
CAN SUCH EVIL EVEN EXIST?
GO TO DMC!
AND SO...
GADUNK BADUNK
KURAMOTO RETURNED TO TOYAMA.
GADUNK BADUNK
I HOPE I DON'T HAVE LITTLE PIG CHILDREN.
[TRACK 88, THE END]

DMC LEXICON

 ## CAT

Feline species from the mammal kingdom. According to
sources we trust, odds are good that the nationally
revered cartoon character "Doraemon" is modeled
after a cat. The publisher of this manga (in Japan),
and the publisher of Doraemon (in Japan) are both
owned by the same company. Do you still doubt our
information?

Usage: The cat's being a total pussy. (Laughter)

デトロイト・メタル・シティ
Detroit Metal City

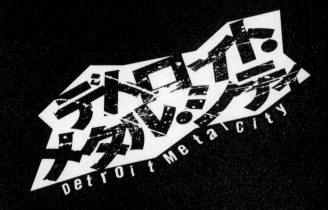

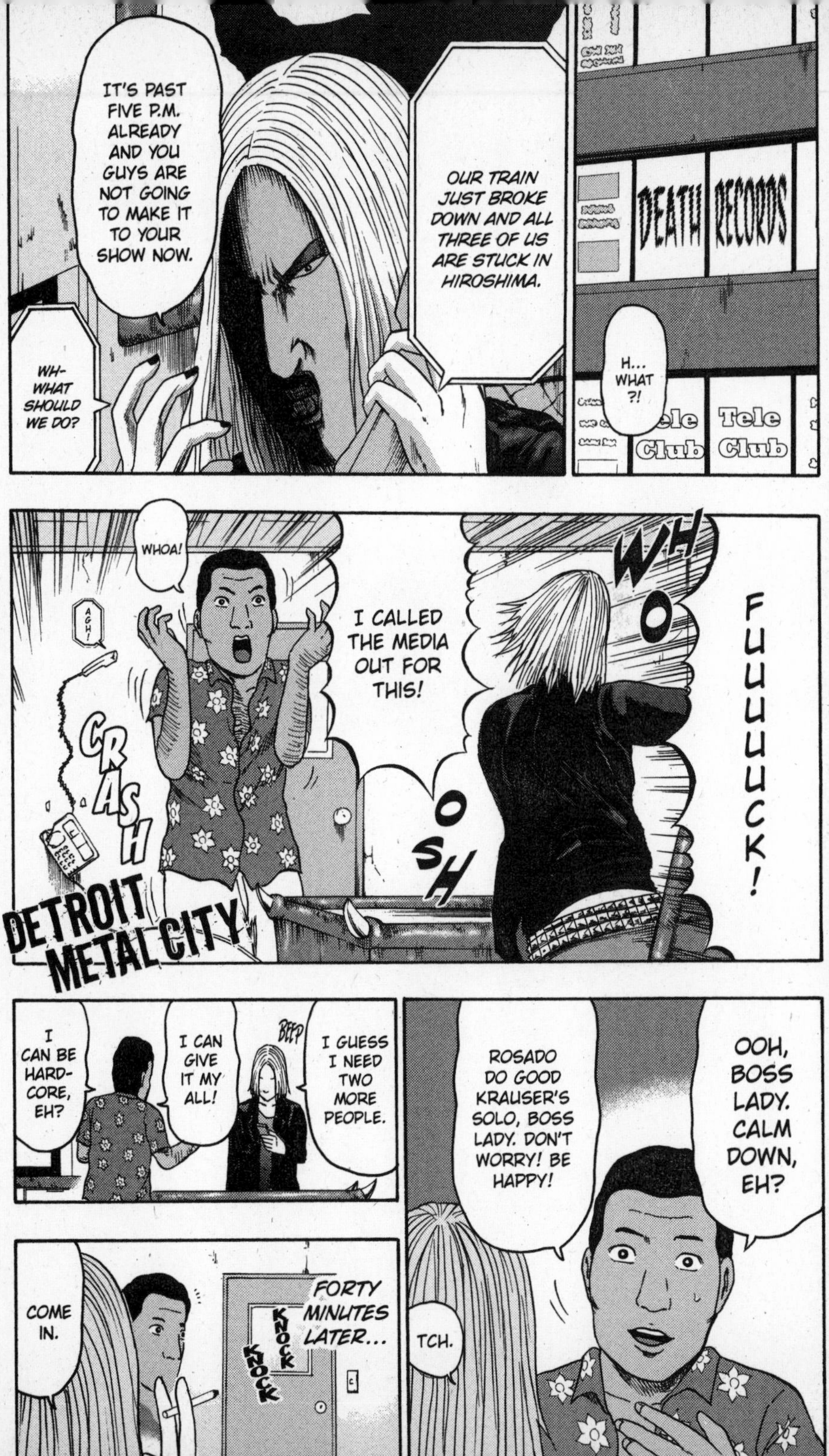
DEATH RECORDS
Tele Club
Tele Club
H... WHAT ?!
OUR TRAIN JUST BROKE DOWN AND ALL THREE OF US ARE STUCK IN HIROSHIMA.
IT'S PAST FIVE P.M. ALREADY AND YOU GUYS ARE NOT GOING TO MAKE IT TO YOUR SHOW NOW.
WH- WHAT SHOULD WE DO?
FUUUUUCK!
WHOOSH
I CALLED THE MEDIA OUT FOR THIS!
WHOA!
AGH!
CRASH
DETROIT METAL CITY
OOH, BOSS LADY. CALM DOWN, EH?
ROSADO DO GOOD KRAUSER'S SOLO, BOSS LADY. DON'T WORRY! BE HAPPY!
TCH.
I GUESS I NEED TWO MORE PEOPLE.
BEEP
I CAN GIVE IT MY ALL!
I CAN BE HARDCORE, EH?
FORTY MINUTES LATER...
KNOCK
KNOCK
COME IN.

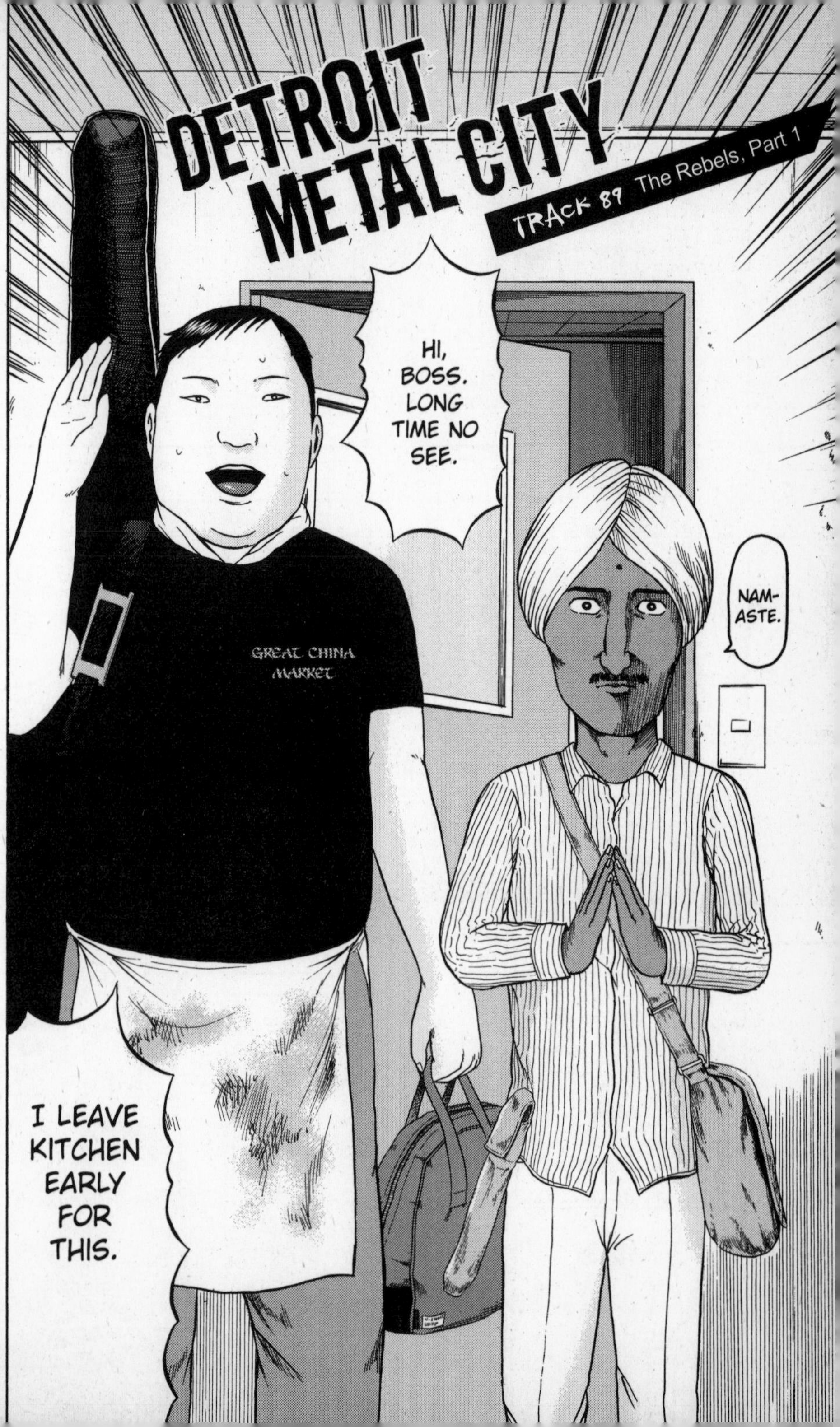
DETROIT METAL CITY
TRACK 89 The Rebels, Part 1
HI, BOSS. LONG TIME NO SEE.
NAM-ASTE.
GREAT CHINA MARKET
I LEAVE KITCHEN EARLY FOR THIS.

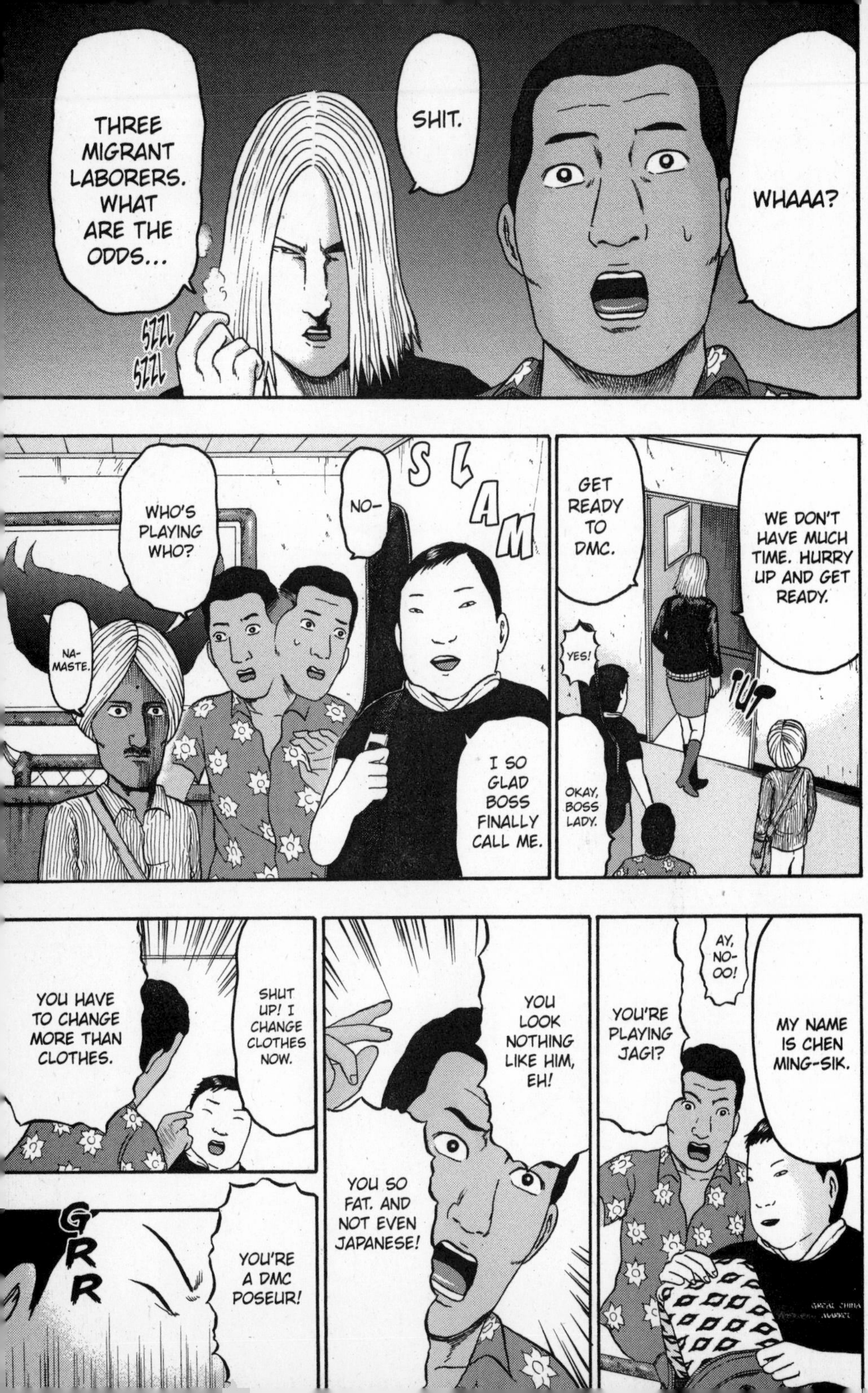
WHAAA?
SHIT.
THREE MIGRANT LABORERS. WHAT ARE THE ODDS...
SZZL SZZL
WE DON'T HAVE MUCH TIME. HURRY UP AND GET READY.
GET READY TO DMC.
YES!
TUT
OKAY, BOSS LADY.
SLAM
NO-
WHO'S PLAYING WHO?
I SO GLAD BOSS FINALLY CALL ME.
NAMASTE.
MY NAME IS CHEN MING-SIK.
AY, NO-OO!
YOU'RE PLAYING JAGI?
GREAT CHINA MARKET
YOU LOOK NOTHING LIKE HIM, EH!
YOU SO FAT. AND NOT EVEN JAPANESE!
SHUT UP! I CHANGE CLOTHES NOW.
YOU HAVE TO CHANGE MORE THAN CLOTHES.
YOU'RE A DMC POSEUR!
GRR

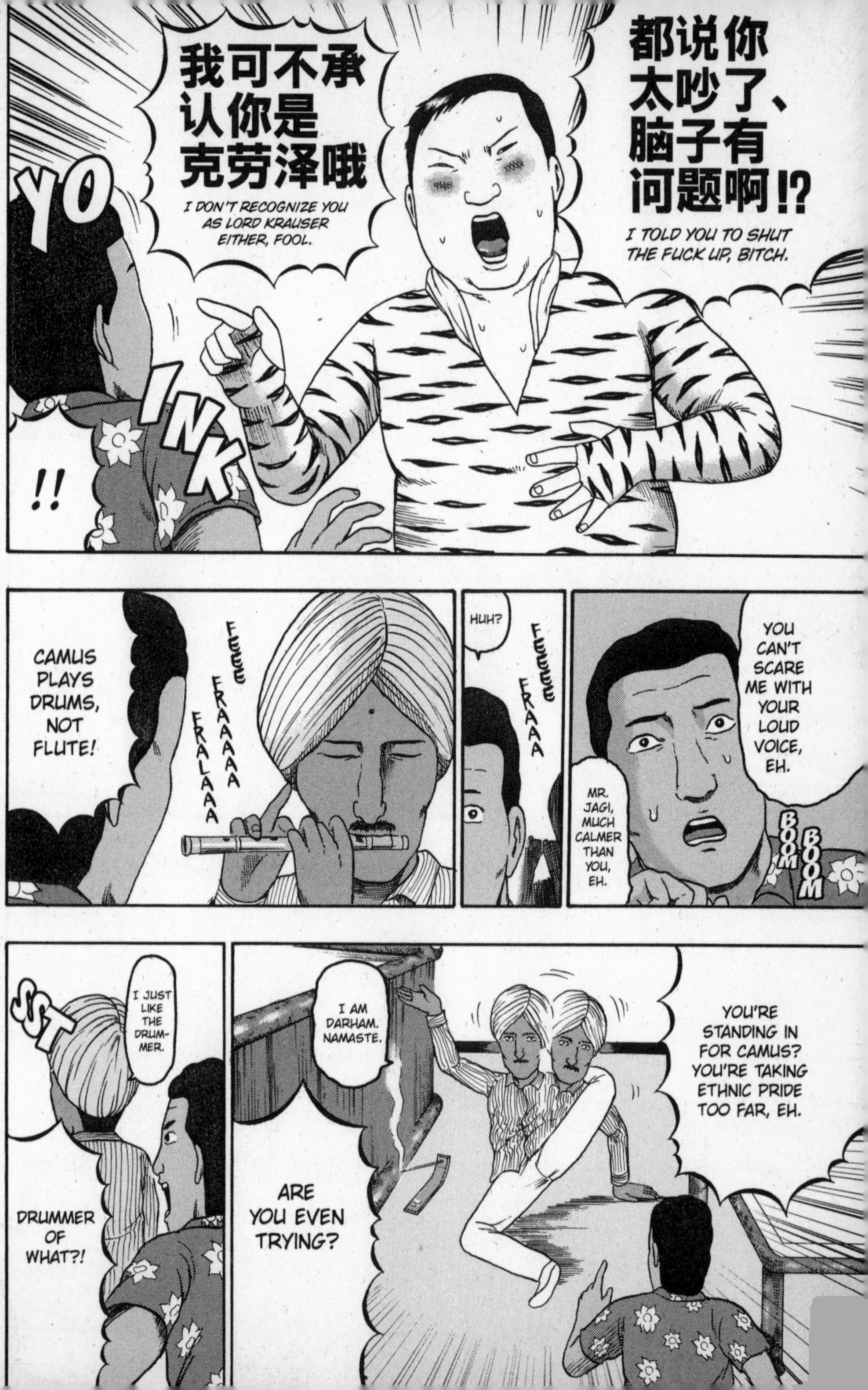
都说你太吵了、脑子有问题啊!?
I TOLD YOU TO SHUT THE FUCK UP, BITCH.
我可不承认你是克劳泽哦
I DON'T RECOGNIZE YOU AS LORD KRAUSER EITHER, FOOL.
YO
INK
!!
YOU CAN'T SCARE ME WITH YOUR LOUD VOICE, EH.
BOOM BOOM
MR. JAGI, MUCH CALMER THAN YOU, EH.
FEEEE FRAAA
HUH?
FEEE FRAAAAA FRALAAA
CAMUS PLAYS DRUMS, NOT FLUTE!
YOU'RE STANDING IN FOR CAMUS? YOU'RE TAKING ETHNIC PRIDE TOO FAR, EH.
I AM DARHAM. NAMASTE.
ARE YOU EVEN TRYING?
I JUST LIKE THE DRUMMER.
SST
DRUMMER OF WHAT?!

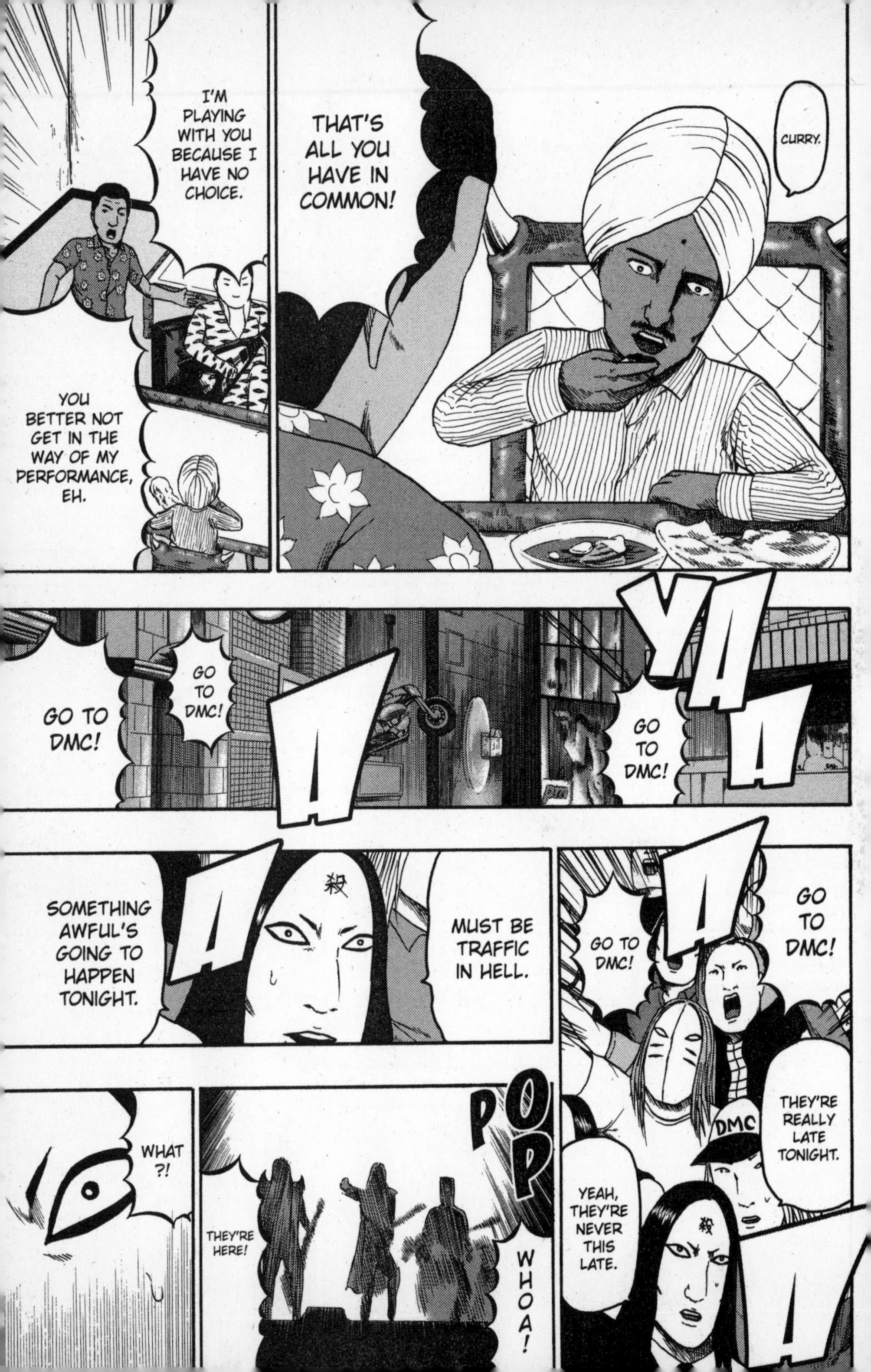
CURRY.
THAT'S ALL YOU HAVE IN COMMON!
I'M PLAYING WITH YOU BECAUSE I HAVE NO CHOICE.
YOU BETTER NOT GET IN THE WAY OF MY PERFORMANCE, EH.
YAAA
GO TO DMC!
GO TO DMC!
GO TO DMC!
A
GO TO DMC!
A
GO TO DMC!
THEY'RE REALLY LATE TONIGHT.
DMC
YEAH, THEY'RE NEVER THIS LATE.
A
MUST BE TRAFFIC IN HELL.
SOMETHING AWFUL'S GOING TO HAPPEN TONIGHT.
A
POP
WHOA!
THEY'RE HERE!
WHAT ?!

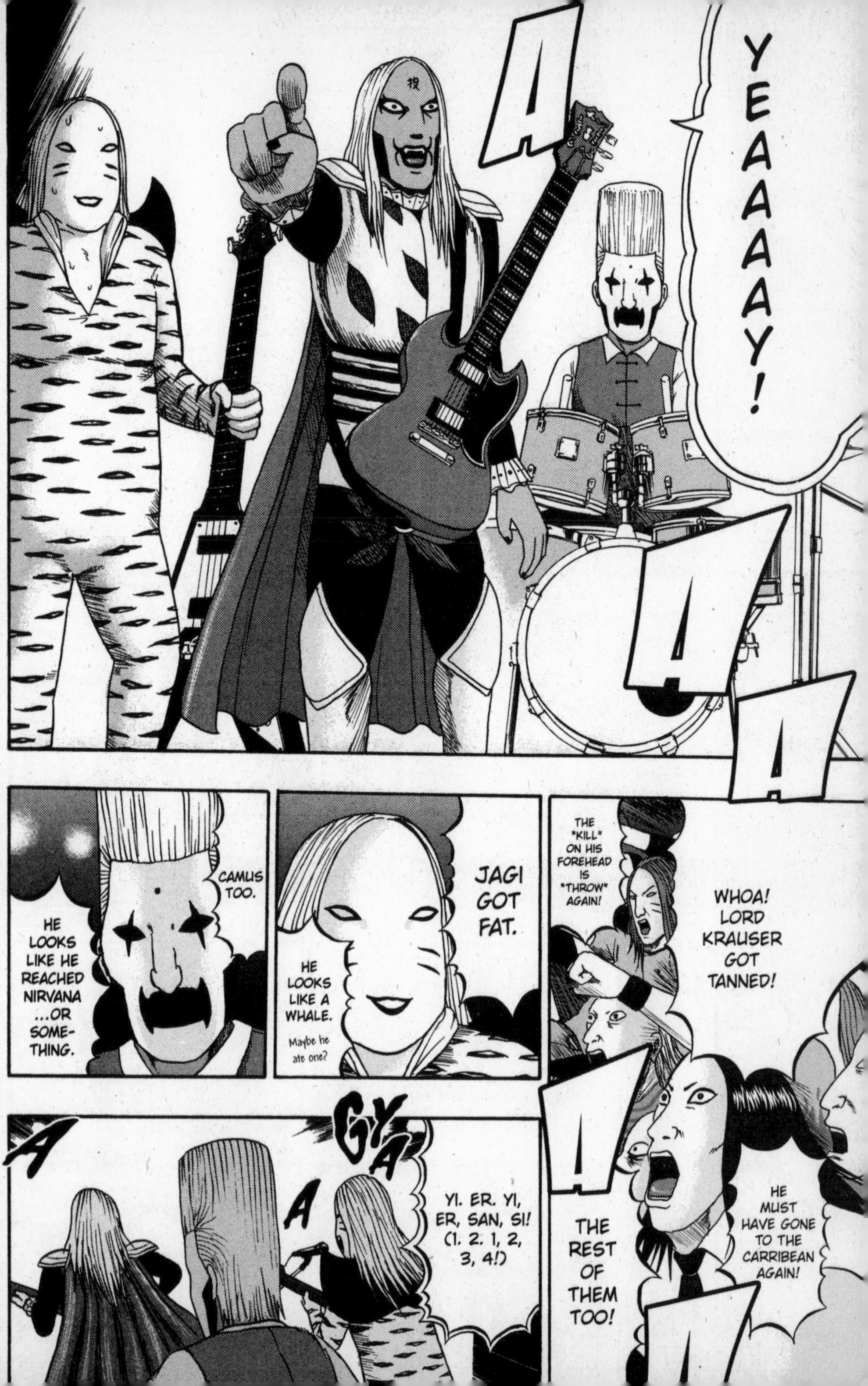
YEAAAAY!
A
A
A
A
THE "KILL" ON HIS FOREHEAD IS "THROW" AGAIN!
WHOA! LORD KRAUSER GOT TANNED!
JAGI GOT FAT.
HE LOOKS LIKE A WHALE.
Maybe he ate one?
CAMUS TOO.
HE LOOKS LIKE HE REACHED NIRVANA ...OR SOMETHING.
A
HE MUST HAVE GONE TO THE CARRIBEAN AGAIN!
THE REST OF THEM TOO!
GYA
A
A
YI. ER. YI, ER, SAN, SI! (1. 2. 1, 2, 3, 4!)

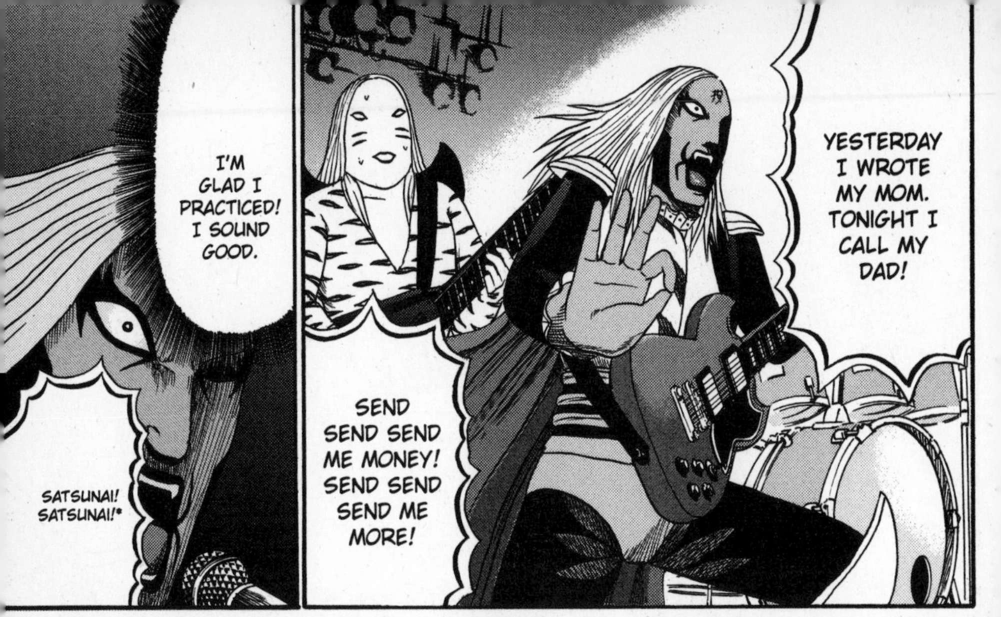
YESTERDAY I WROTE MY MOM. TONIGHT I CALL MY DAD!
SEND SEND SEND ME MONEY! SEND SEND SEND ME MORE!
I'M GLAD I PRACTICED! I SOUND GOOD.
SATSUNAI! SATSUNAI!*

*SATSUNAI = JAPANESE FOR "I'M BROKE."

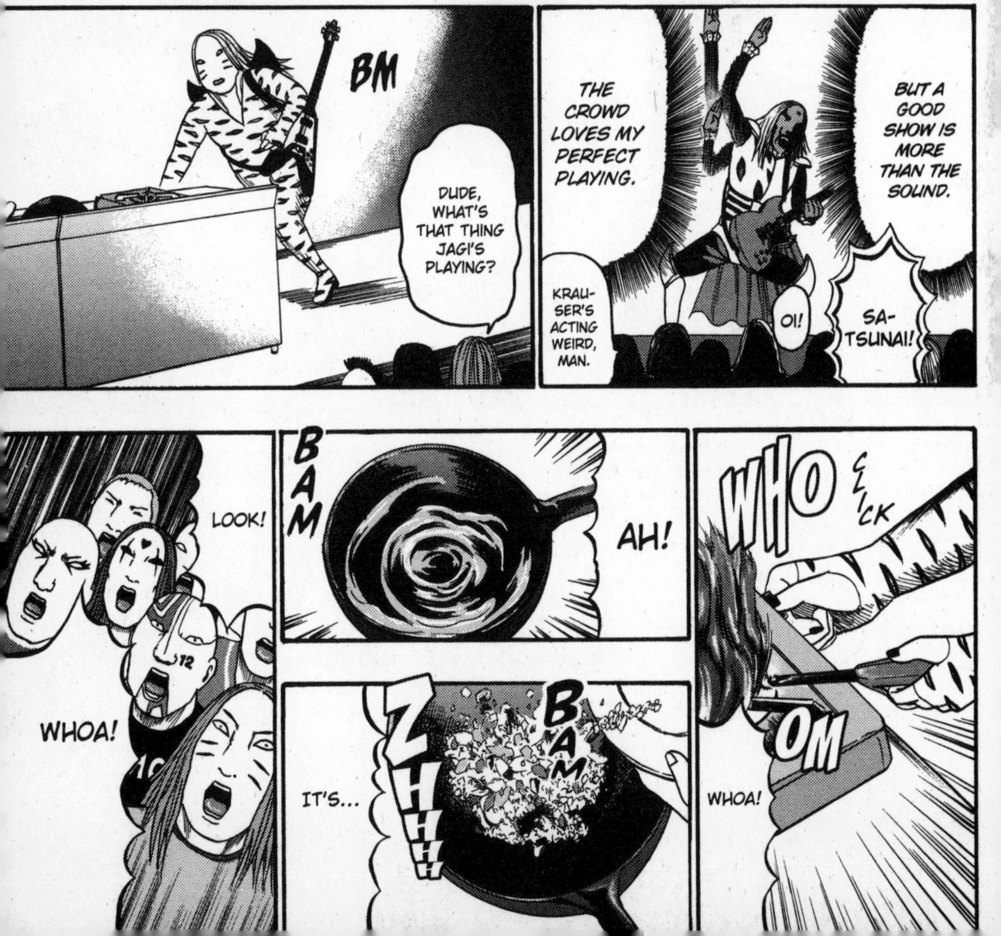
BUT A GOOD SHOW IS MORE THAN THE SOUND.
THE CROWD LOVES MY PERFECT PLAYING.
SA-TSUNAI!
OI!
KRAU-SER'S ACTING WEIRD, MAN.
BM
DUDE, WHAT'S THAT THING JAGI'S PLAYING?
WHO
CLICK
OM
WHOA!
BAM
AH!
BAM
ZHHHH
IT'S...
LOOK!
WHOA!

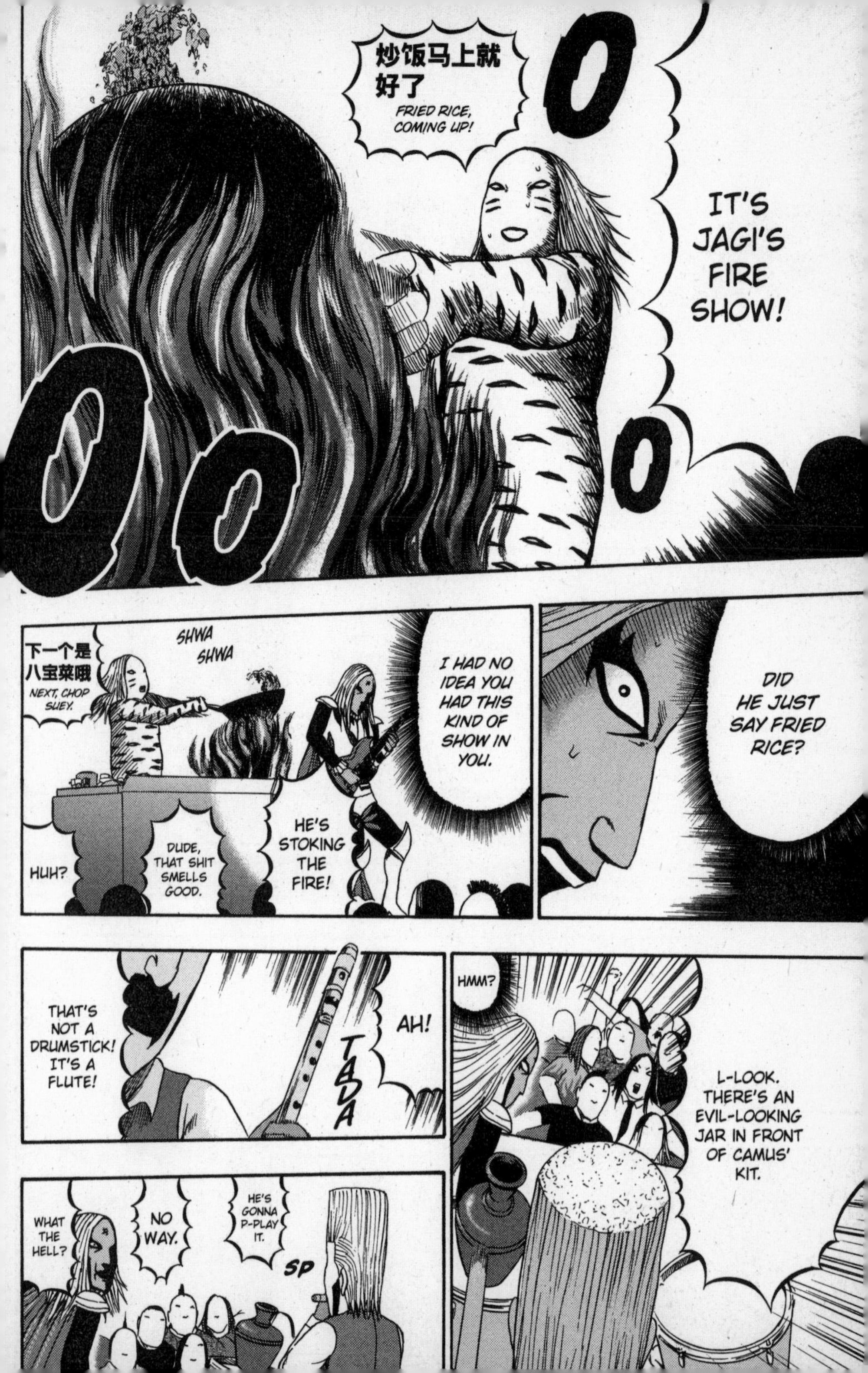

IT'S JAGI'S FIRE SHOW!
炒饭马上就好了
FRIED RICE, COMING UP!
DID HE JUST SAY FRIED RICE?
I HAD NO IDEA YOU HAD THIS KIND OF SHOW IN YOU.
SHWA SHWA
下一个是八宝菜哦
NEXT, CHOP SUEY.
HE'S STOKING THE FIRE!
DUDE, THAT SHIT SMELLS GOOD.
HUH?
HMM?
L-LOOK. THERE'S AN EVIL-LOOKING JAR IN FRONT OF CAMUS' KIT.
AH!
TADA
THAT'S NOT A DRUMSTICK! IT'S A FLUTE!
HE'S GONNA P-PLAY IT.
NO WAY.
WHAT THE HELL?
SP

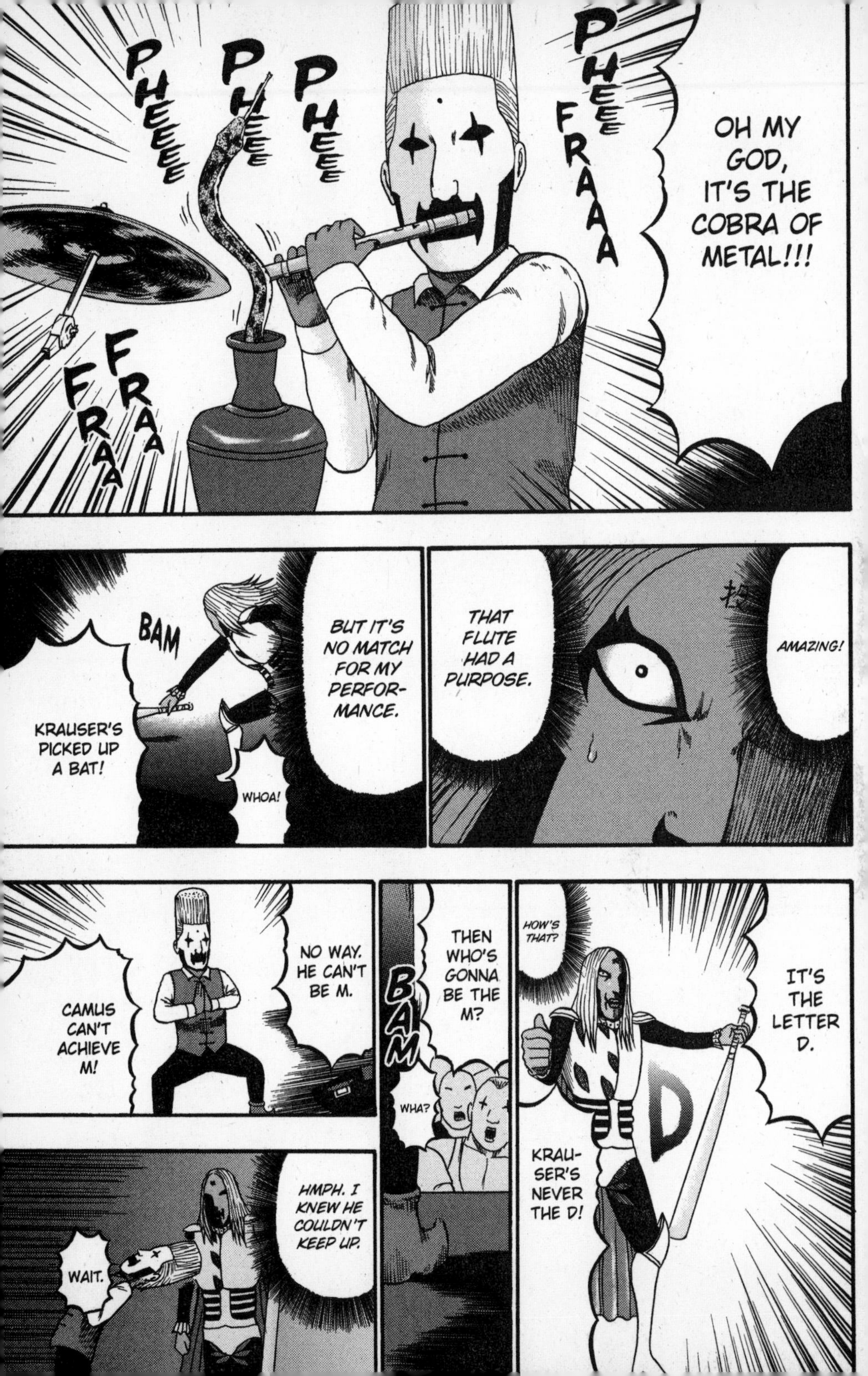
OH MY GOD, IT'S THE COBRA OF METAL!!!
PHEEE
FRAAAA
PHEEE
PHEEE
PHEEEE
FRAA
FRAA
AMAZING!
THAT FLUTE HAD A PURPOSE.
BUT IT'S NO MATCH FOR MY PERFORMANCE.
BAM
KRAUSER'S PICKED UP A BAT!
WHOA!
HOW'S THAT?
IT'S THE LETTER D.
KRAUSER'S NEVER THE D!
THEN WHO'S GONNA BE THE M?
BAM
WHA?
NO WAY. HE CAN'T BE M.
CAMUS CAN'T ACHIEVE M!
HMPH. I KNEW HE COULDN'T KEEP UP.
WAIT.

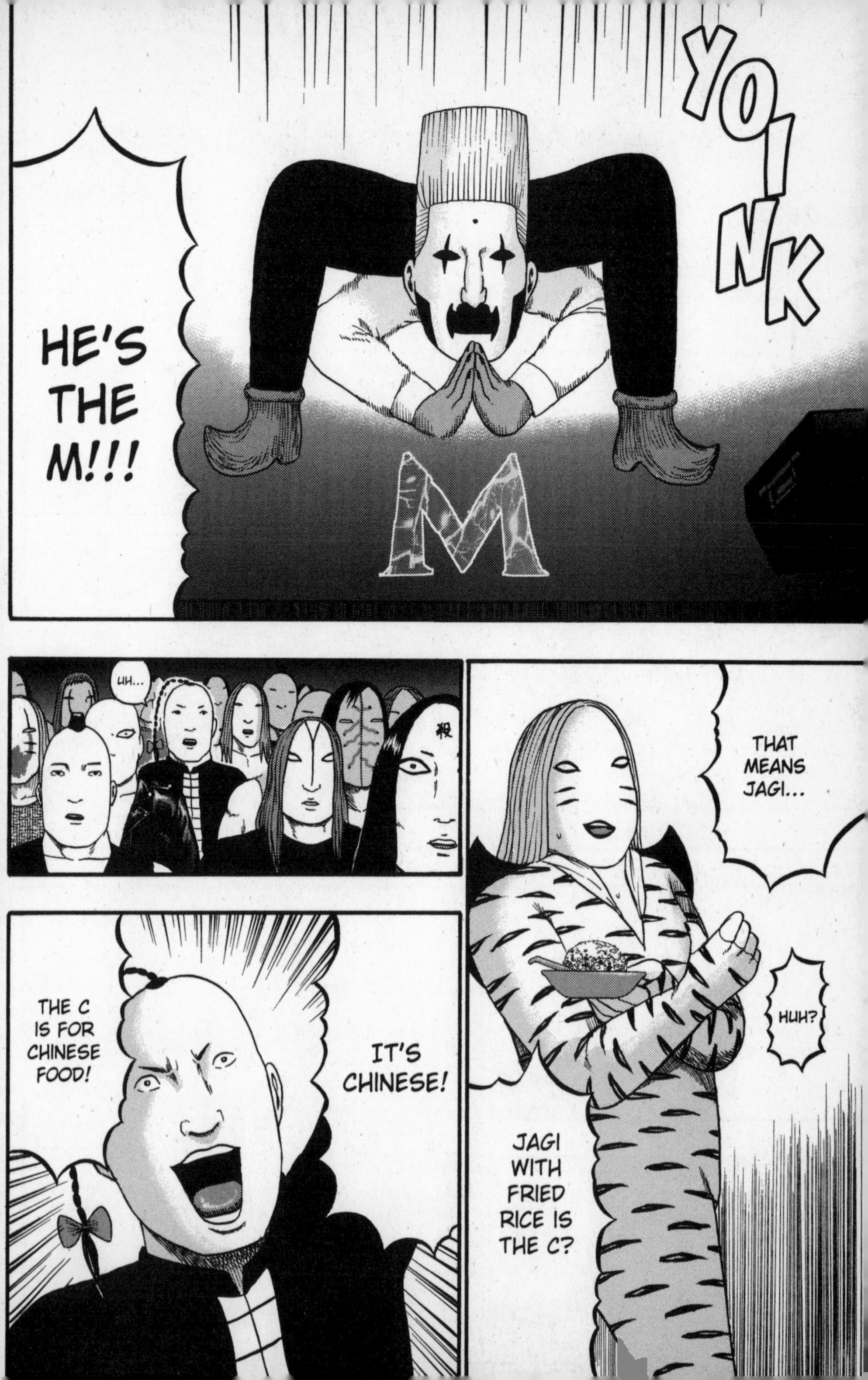
YOINK
HE'S THE M!!!
THAT MEANS JAGI...
HUH?
JAGI WITH FRIED RICE IS THE C?
UH...
IT'S CHINESE!
THE C IS FOR CHINESE FOOD!

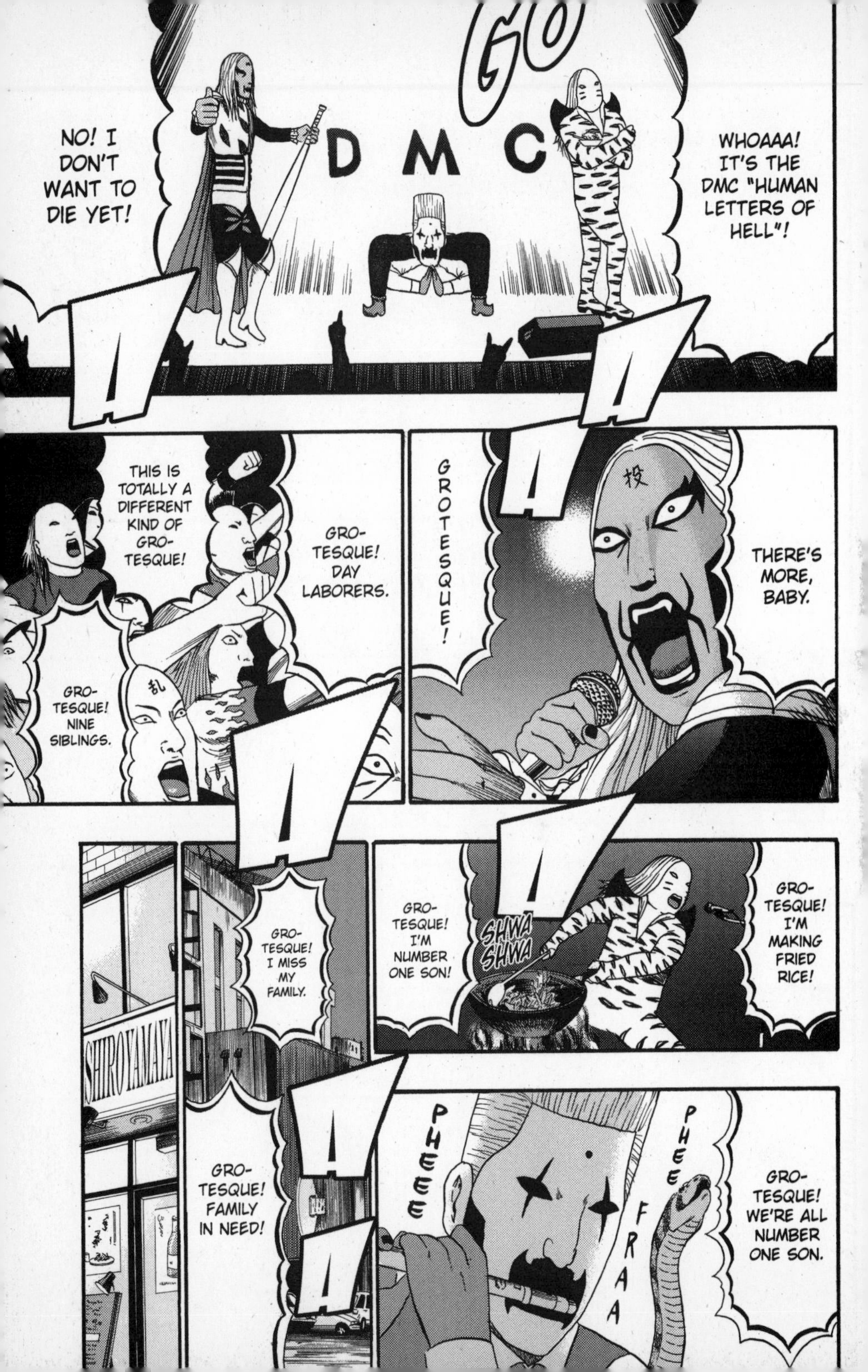
GO
WHOAAA! IT'S THE DMC "HUMAN LETTERS OF HELL"!
D M C
NO! I DON'T WANT TO DIE YET!
A
A
A
THERE'S MORE, BABY.
GROTESQUE!
GRO-TESQUE! DAY LABORERS.
THIS IS TOTALLY A DIFFERENT KIND OF GRO-TESQUE!
GRO-TESQUE! NINE SIBLINGS.
A
GRO-TESQUE! I'M MAKING FRIED RICE!
A
SHWA SHWA
GRO-TESQUE! I'M NUMBER ONE SON!
GRO-TESQUE! I MISS MY FAMILY.
GRO-TESQUE! WE'RE ALL NUMBER ONE SON.
PHEE
FRAA
PHEEE
GRO-TESQUE! FAMILY IN NEED!
A
A
SHIROYAMAYA

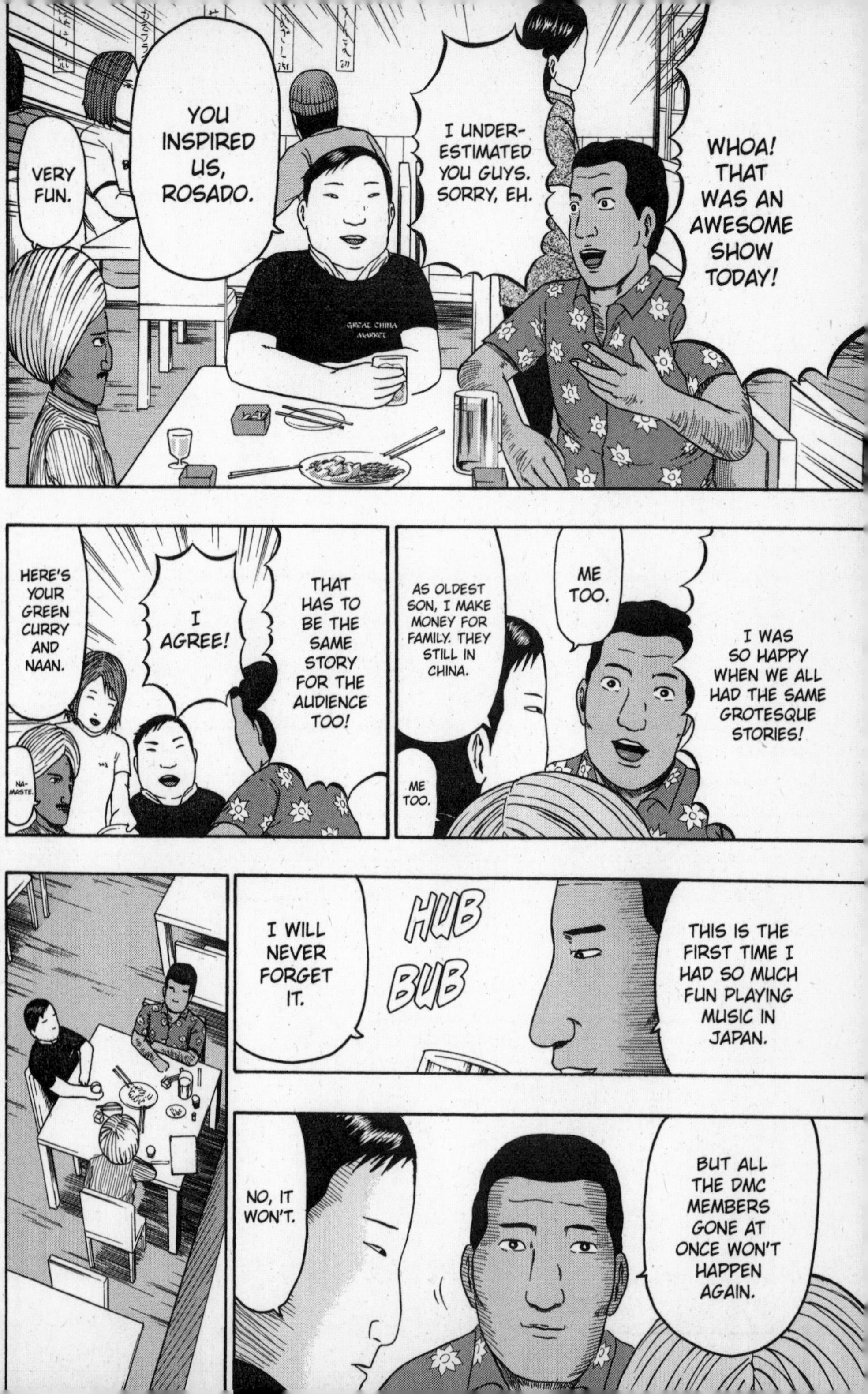
WHOA! THAT WAS AN AWESOME SHOW TODAY!
I UNDER-ESTIMATED YOU GUYS. SORRY, EH.
YOU INSPIRED US, ROSADO.
VERY FUN.
GREAT CHINA MARKET
I WAS SO HAPPY WHEN WE ALL HAD THE SAME GROTESQUE STORIES!
ME TOO.
AS OLDEST SON, I MAKE MONEY FOR FAMILY. THEY STILL IN CHINA.
ME TOO.
THAT HAS TO BE THE SAME STORY FOR THE AUDIENCE TOO!
I AGREE!
HERE'S YOUR GREEN CURRY AND NAAN.
NAMASTE.
THIS IS THE FIRST TIME I HAD SO MUCH FUN PLAYING MUSIC IN JAPAN.
HUB BUB
I WILL NEVER FORGET IT.
BUT ALL THE DMC MEMBERS GONE AT ONCE WON'T HAPPEN AGAIN.
NO, IT WON'T.

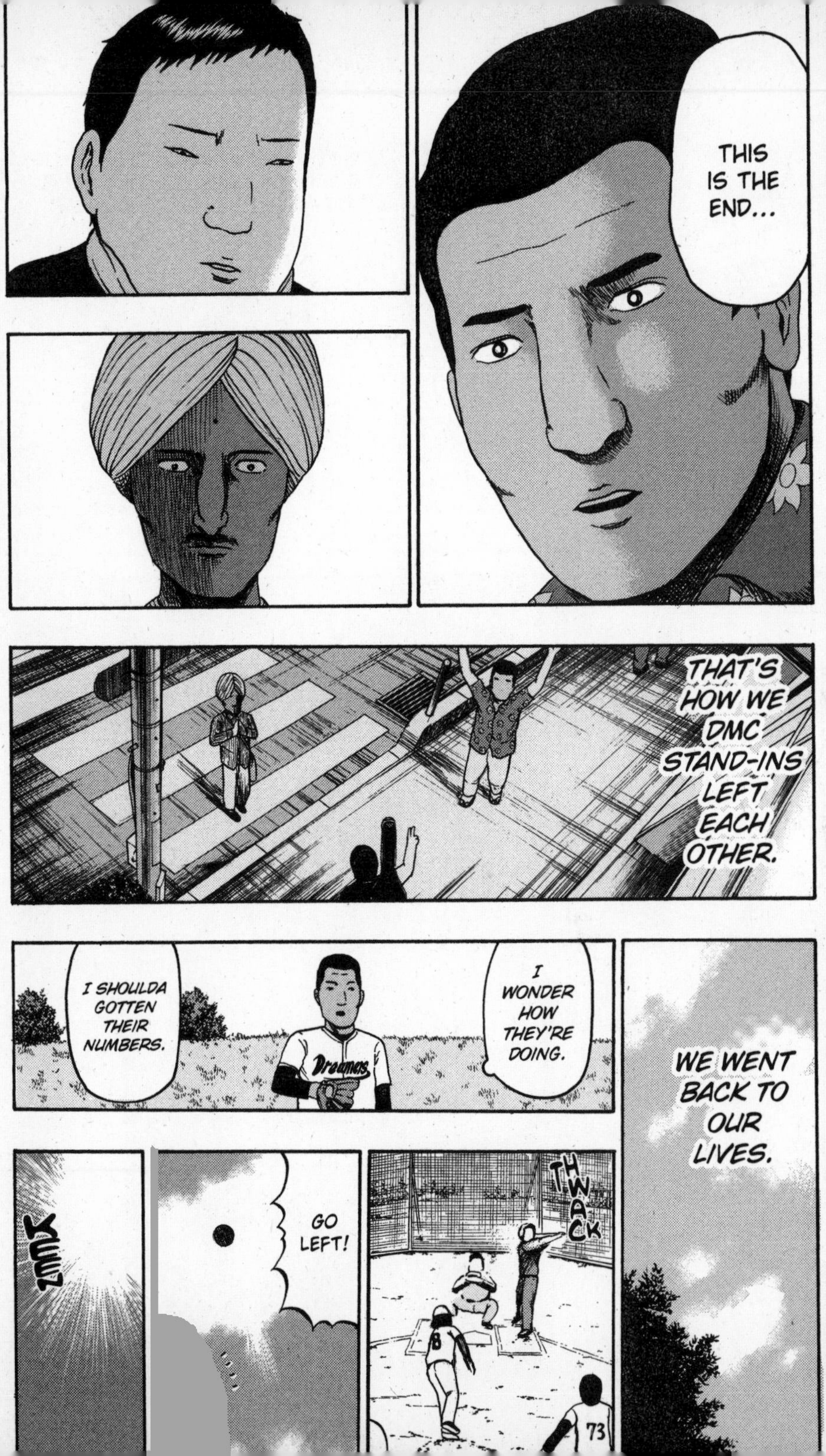
THIS IS THE END...
THAT'S HOW WE DMC STAND-INS LEFT EACH OTHER.
WE WENT BACK TO OUR LIVES.
I WONDER HOW THEY'RE DOING.
I SHOULDA GOTTEN THEIR NUMBERS.
THWACK
GO LEFT!

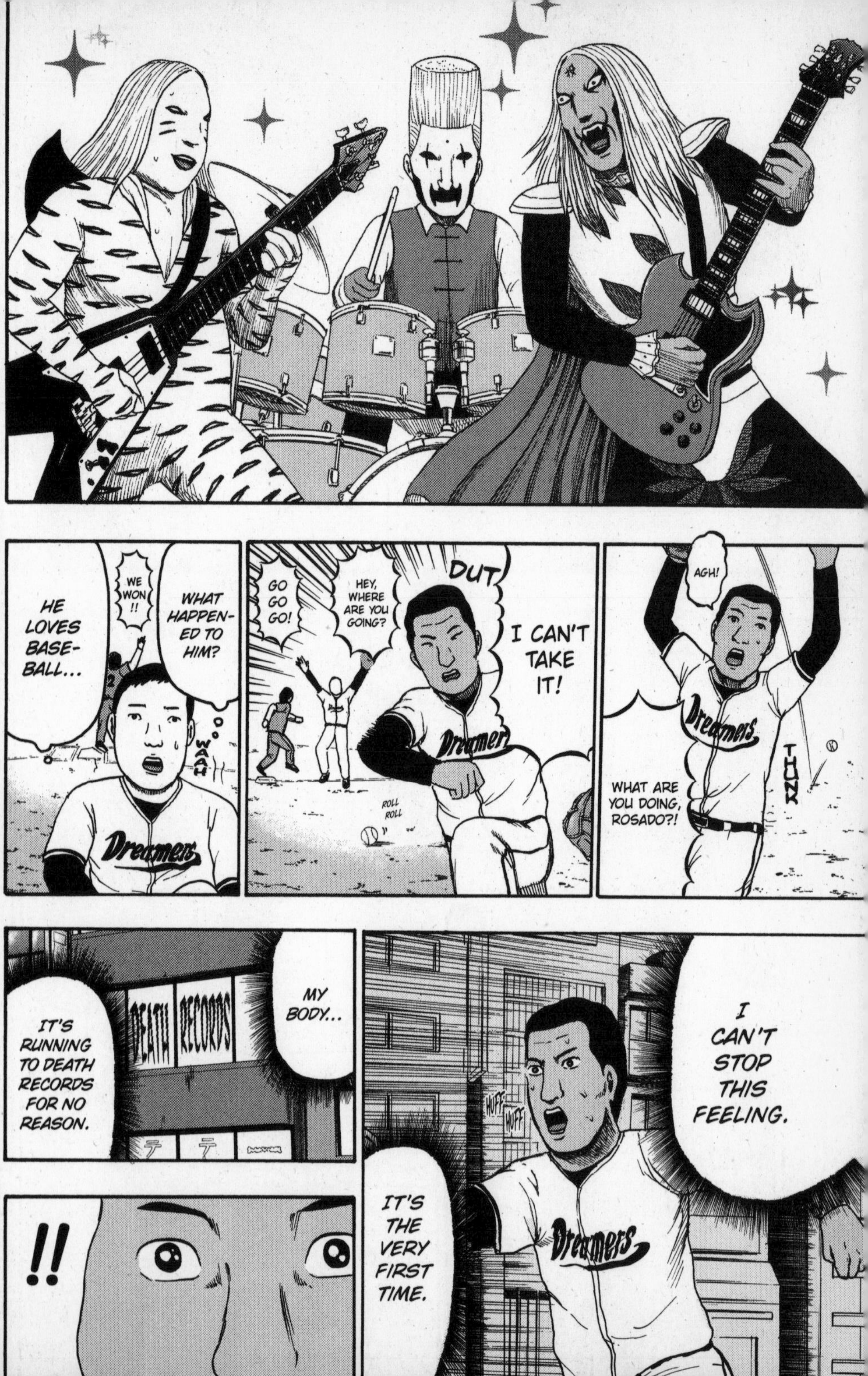
AGH!
WHAT ARE YOU DOING, ROSADO?!
THUNK
DUT
HEY, WHERE ARE YOU GOING?
I CAN'T TAKE IT!
GO GO GO!
ROLL ROLL
WHAT HAPPEN-ED TO HIM?
WE WON!!
HE LOVES BASE-BALL...
WAAH
I CAN'T STOP THIS FEELING.
HUFF HUFF
IT'S THE VERY FIRST TIME.
MY BODY...
DEATH RECORDS
IT'S RUNNING TO DEATH RECORDS FOR NO REASON.
!!

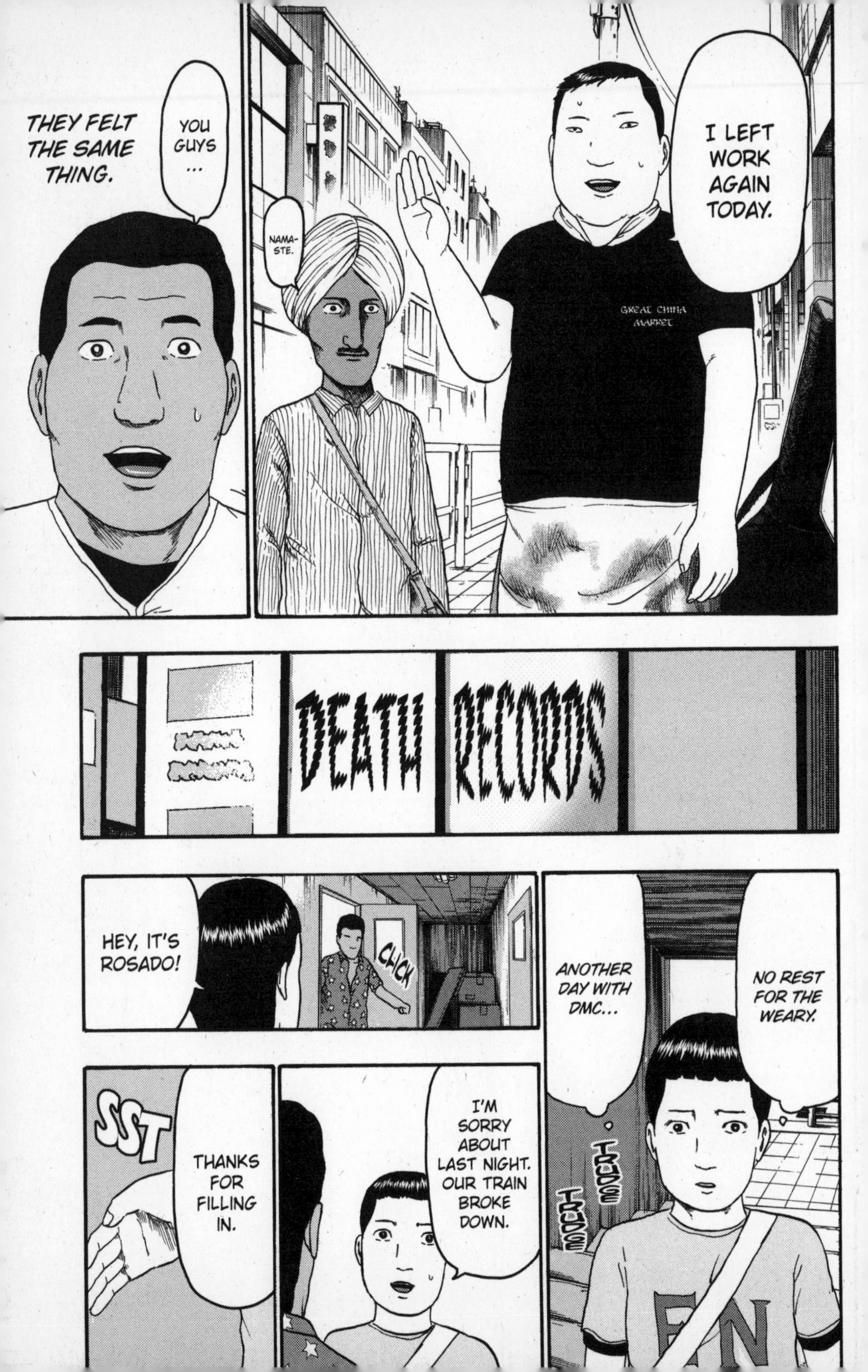
I LEFT WORK AGAIN TODAY.
NAMA-STE.
GREAT CHINA MARKET
YOU GUYS ...
THEY FELT THE SAME THING.
DEATH RECORDS
NO REST FOR THE WEARY.
ANOTHER DAY WITH DMC...
TRUDGE
TRUDGE
HEY, IT'S ROSADO!
CLICK
I'M SORRY ABOUT LAST NIGHT. OUR TRAIN BROKE DOWN.
SST
THANKS FOR FILLING IN.

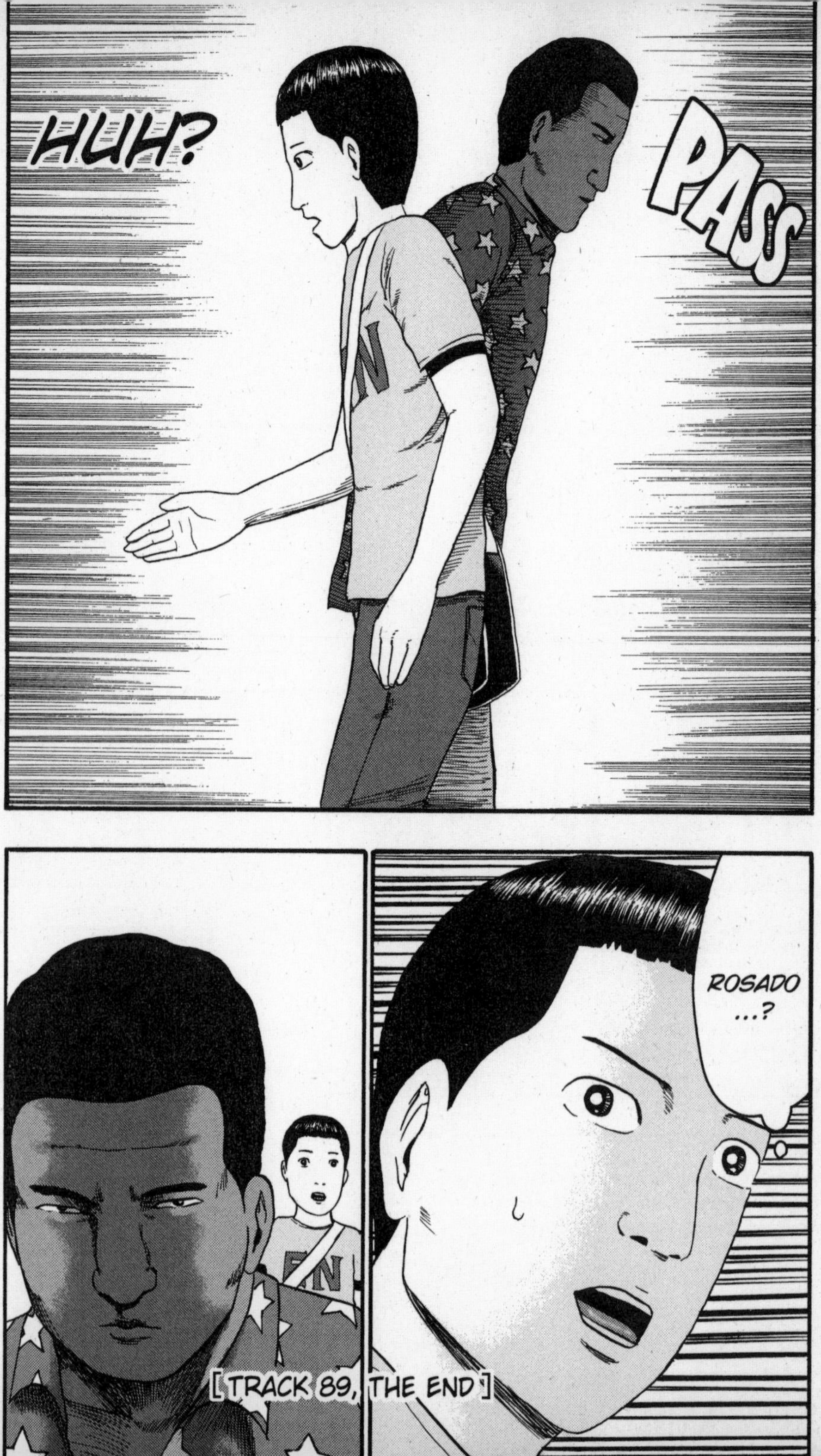
PASS
HUH?
ROSADO ...?
[TRACK 89, THE END]

DMC LEXICON

🐾 FRIED RICE

Just like beginning guitarists get stuck on playing F chords, the first riff many bassists master is fried rice. Those who are serious about becoming pro, though, should be able to do "Chop Suey," "General Tso's Chicken" and "Chow Mein" with their eyes closed.

Usage: The best fried rice is from Nagatanien! Delish!
(*Note: This was not a paid advertisement)

デトロイト・メタル・シティ

Detroit Metal City

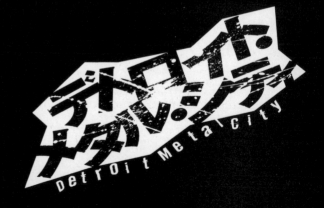

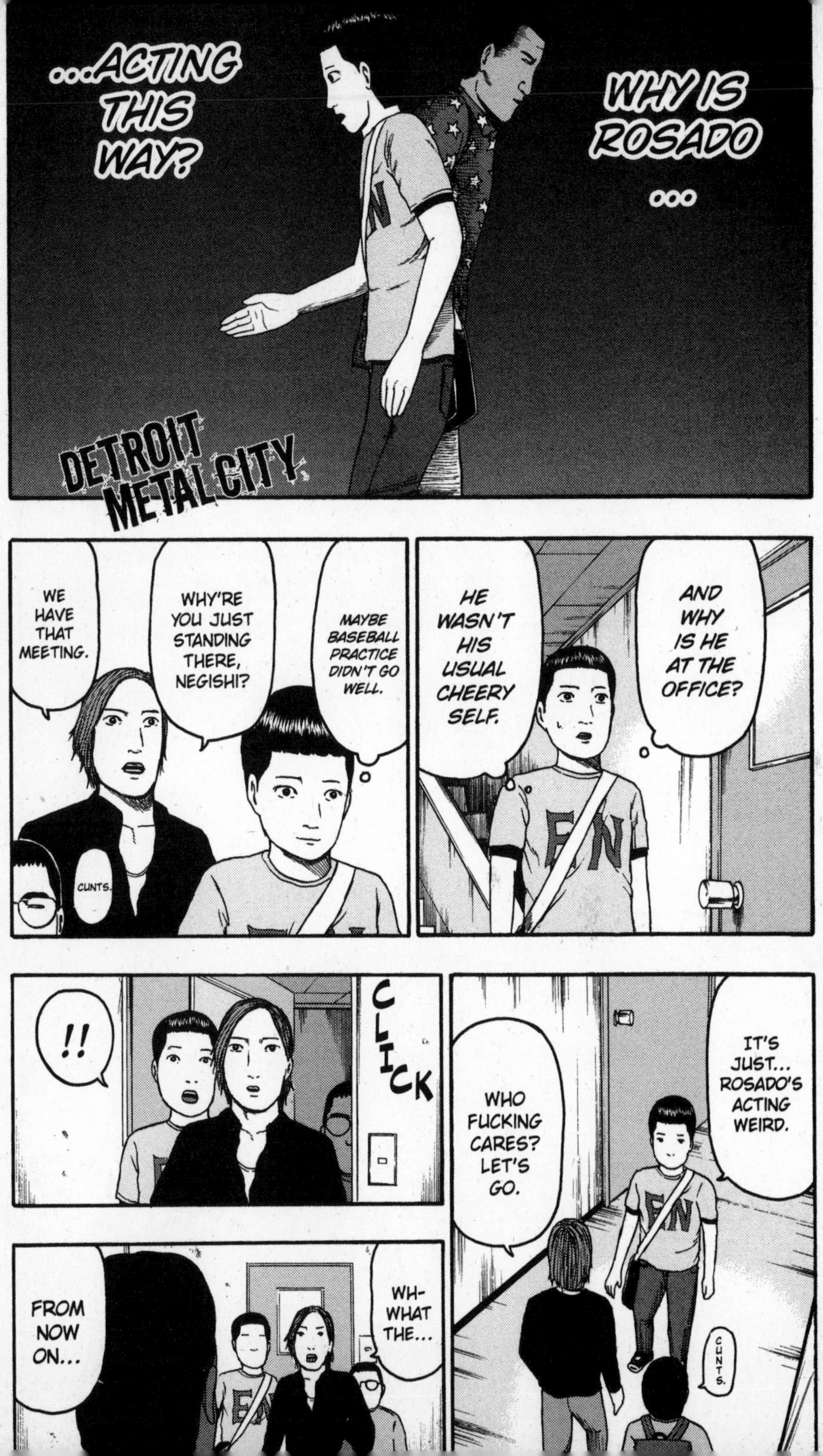
WHY IS ROSADO ...
...ACTING THIS WAY?
DETROIT METAL CITY
AND WHY IS HE AT THE OFFICE?
HE WASN'T HIS USUAL CHEERY SELF.
MAYBE BASEBALL PRACTICE DIDN'T GO WELL.
WHY'RE YOU JUST STANDING THERE, NEGISHI?
WE HAVE THAT MEETING.
CUNTS.
IT'S JUST... ROSADO'S ACTING WEIRD.
WHO FUCKING CARES? LET'S GO.
CUNTS.
CLICK
!!
WH-WHAT THE...
FROM NOW ON...

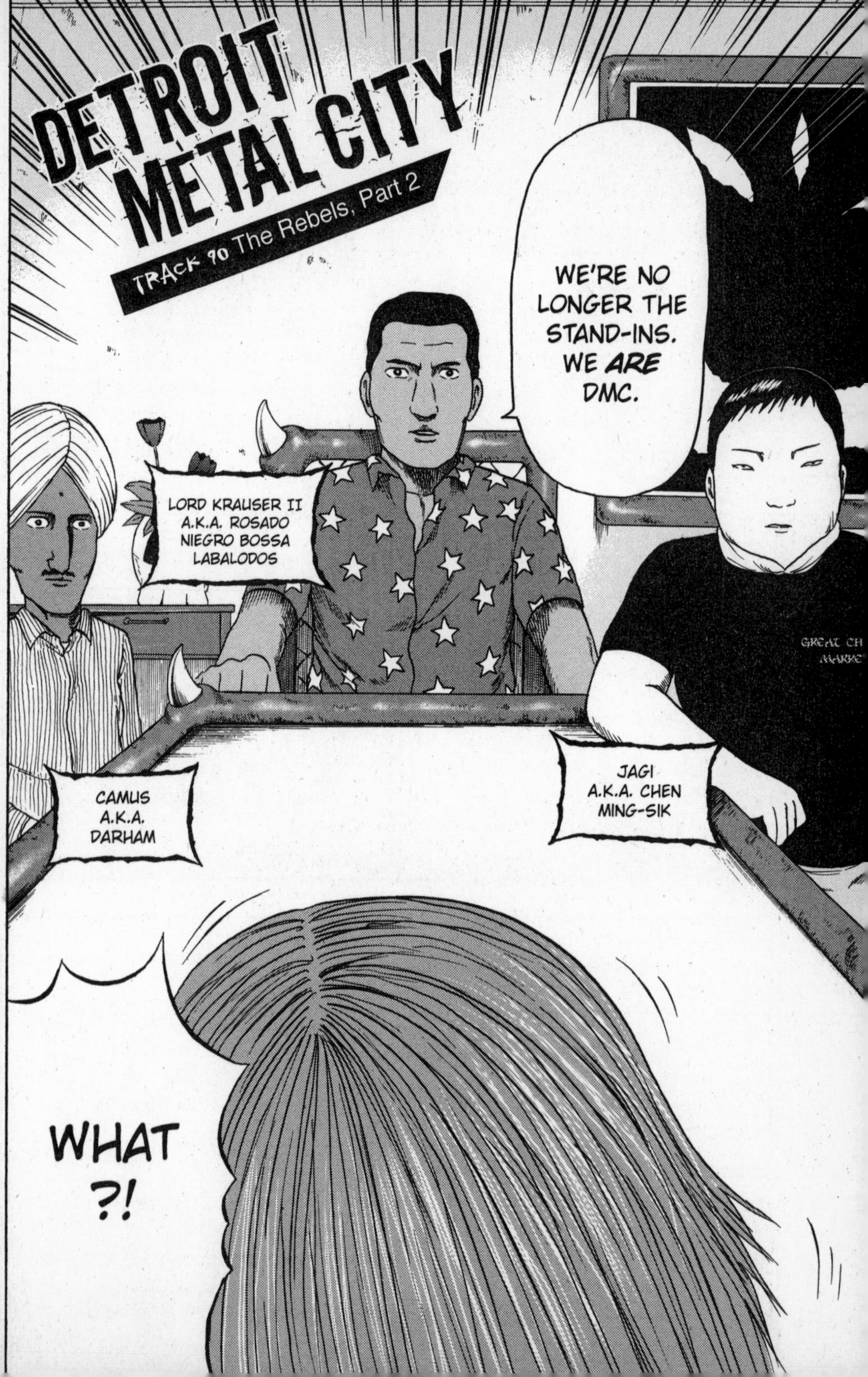
DETROIT METAL CITY
TRACK 90 The Rebels, Part 2
WE'RE NO LONGER THE STAND-INS. WE ARE DMC.
LORD KRAUSER II A.K.A. ROSADO NIEGRO BOSSA LABALODOS
JAGI A.K.A. CHEN MING-SIK
CAMUS A.K.A. DARHAM
WHAT ?!

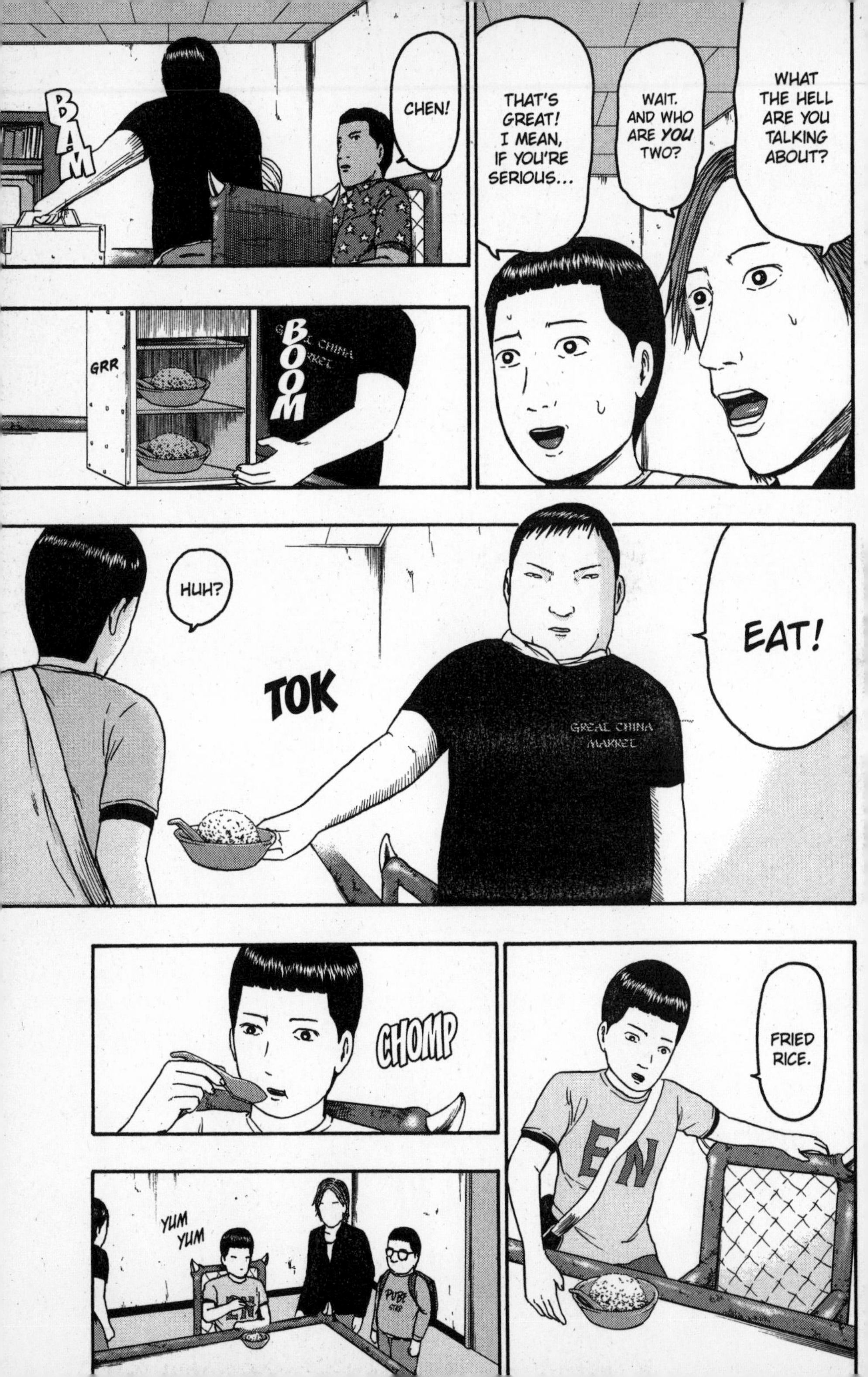
WHAT THE HELL ARE YOU TALKING ABOUT?
WAIT. AND WHO ARE *YOU* TWO?
THAT'S GREAT! I MEAN, IF YOU'RE SERIOUS...
CHEN!
BAM
GRR
BOOM
EAT!
TOK
HUH?
FRIED RICE.
CHOMP
YUM YUM

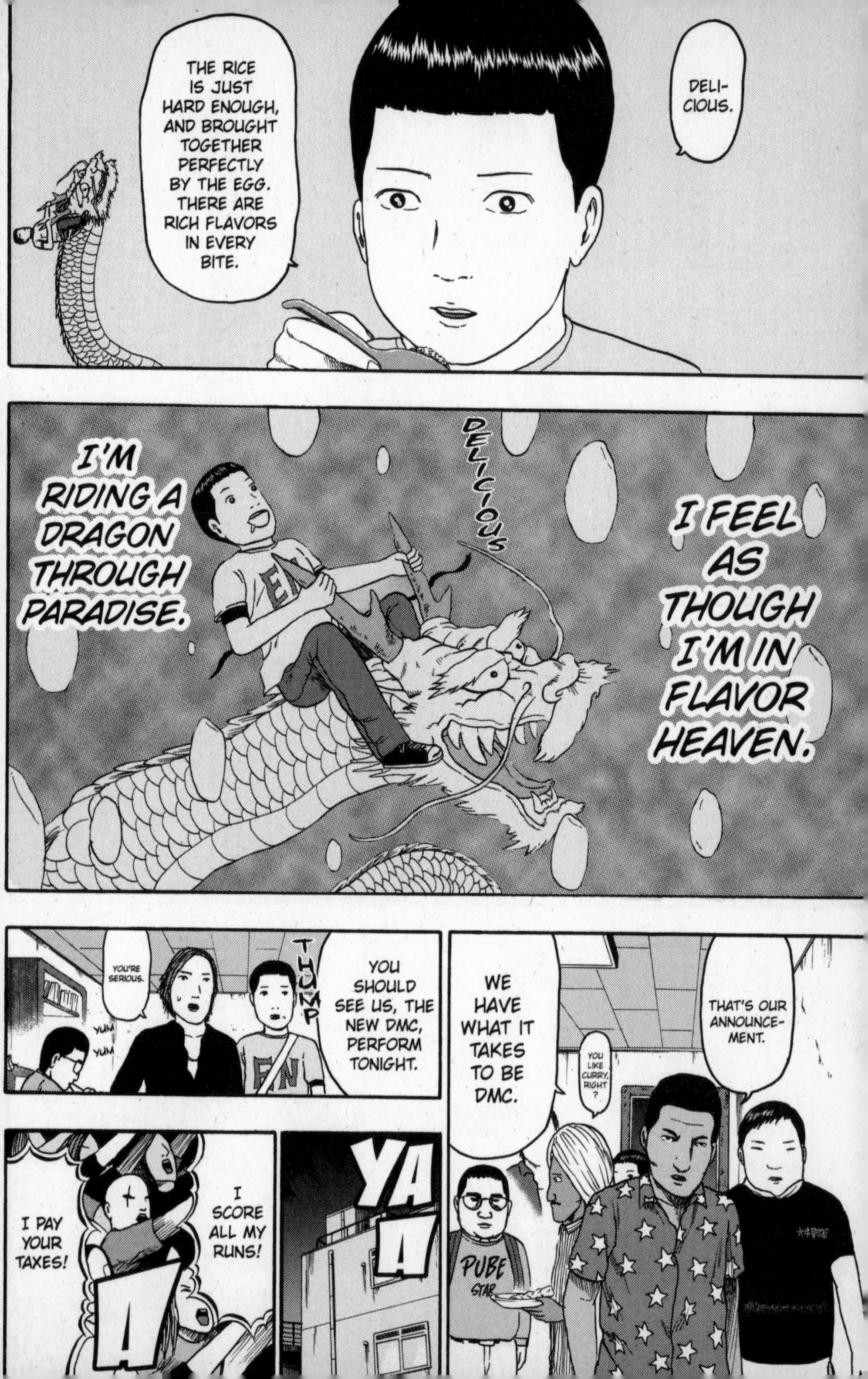
DELI-CIOUS.
THE RICE IS JUST HARD ENOUGH, AND BROUGHT TOGETHER PERFECTLY BY THE EGG. THERE ARE RICH FLAVORS IN EVERY BITE.
I FEEL AS THOUGH I'M IN FLAVOR HEAVEN.
DELICIOUS
I'M RIDING A DRAGON THROUGH PARADISE.
THAT'S OUR ANNOUNCE-MENT.
YOU LIKE CURRY, RIGHT?
WE HAVE WHAT IT TAKES TO BE DMC.
PUBE STAR
YOU SHOULD SEE US, THE NEW DMC, PERFORM TONIGHT.
THUMP
YOU'RE SERIOUS.
YUM YUM
YA
A
I SCORE ALL MY RUNS!
I PAY YOUR TAXES!
A

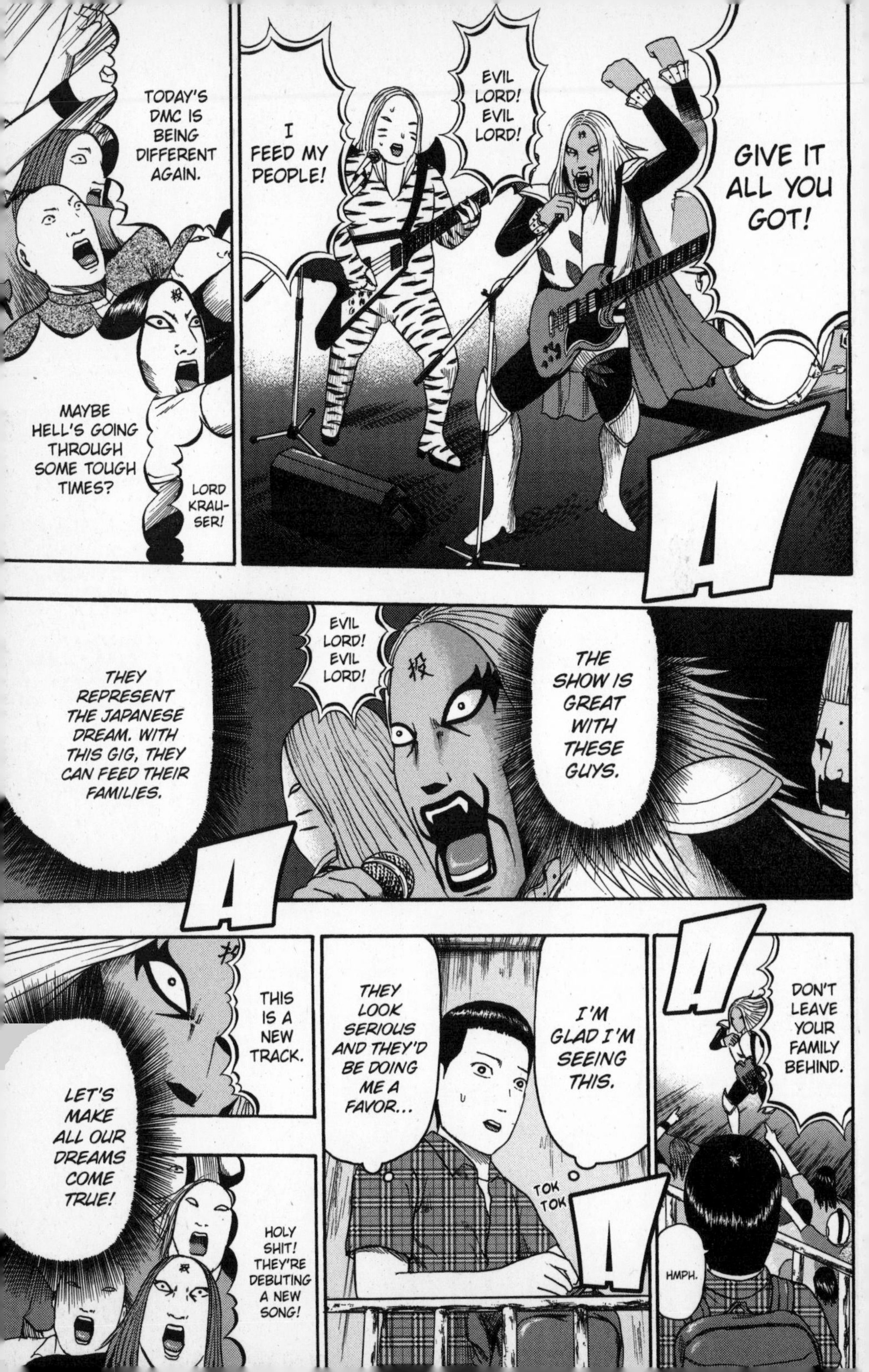
GIVE IT ALL YOU GOT!
EVIL LORD! EVIL LORD!
I FEED MY PEOPLE!
A
TODAY'S DMC IS BEING DIFFERENT AGAIN.
MAYBE HELL'S GOING THROUGH SOME TOUGH TIMES?
LORD KRAU-SER!
THE SHOW IS GREAT WITH THESE GUYS.
EVIL LORD! EVIL LORD!
THEY REPRESENT THE JAPANESE DREAM. WITH THIS GIG, THEY CAN FEED THEIR FAMILIES.
A
A
DON'T LEAVE YOUR FAMILY BEHIND.
HMPH.
I'M GLAD I'M SEEING THIS.
THEY LOOK SERIOUS AND THEY'D BE DOING ME A FAVOR...
TOK TOK
A
THIS IS A NEW TRACK.
LET'S MAKE ALL OUR DREAMS COME TRUE!
HOLY SHIT! THEY'RE DEBUTING A NEW SONG!

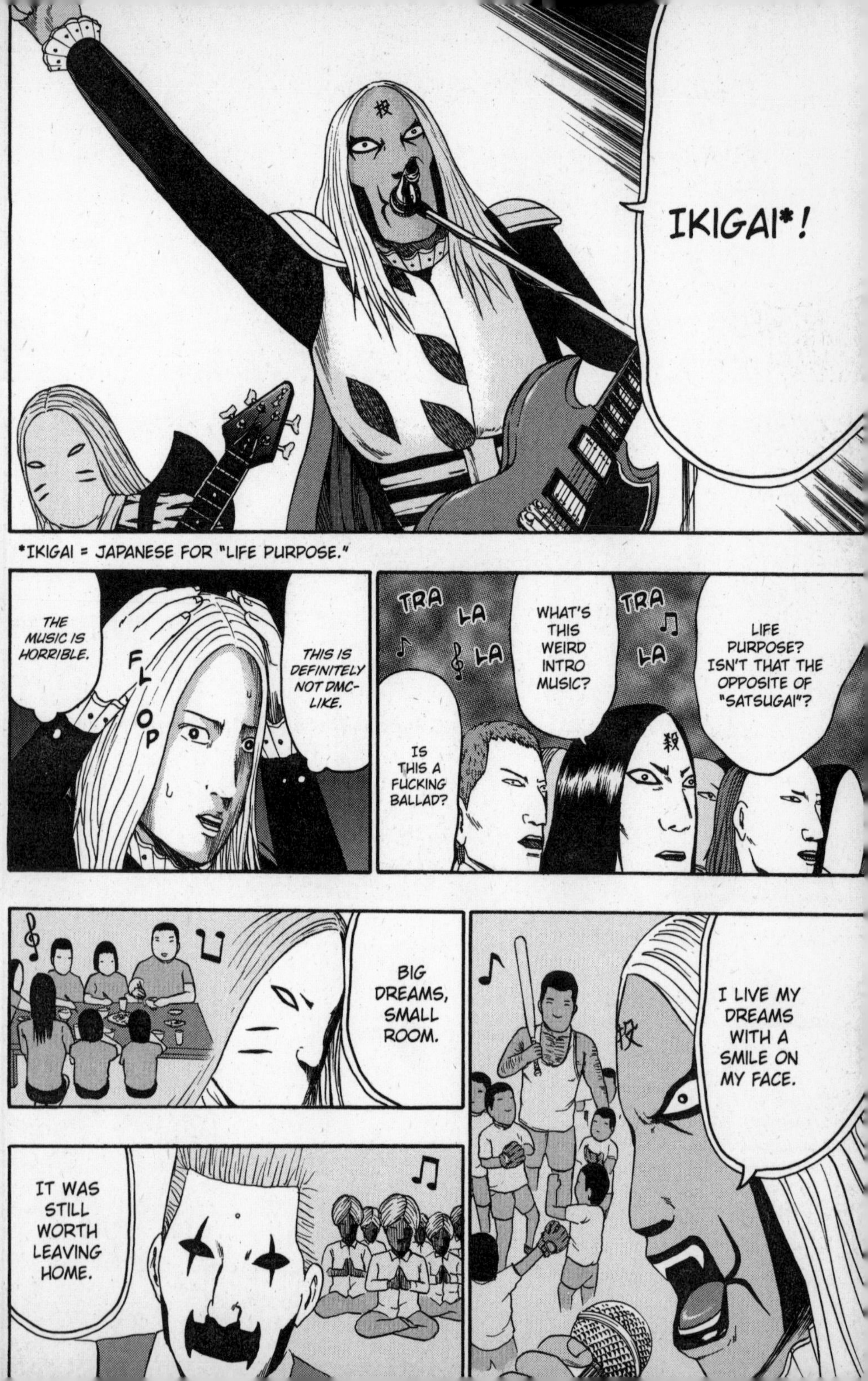
IKIGAI*!
*IKIGAI = JAPANESE FOR "LIFE PURPOSE."
LIFE PURPOSE? ISN'T THAT THE OPPOSITE OF "SATSUGAI"?
TRA LA
WHAT'S THIS WEIRD INTRO MUSIC?
TRA LA LA
IS THIS A FUCKING BALLAD?
THIS IS DEFINITELY NOT DMC-LIKE.
FLOP
THE MUSIC IS HORRIBLE.
I LIVE MY DREAMS WITH A SMILE ON MY FACE.
BIG DREAMS, SMALL ROOM.
IT WAS STILL WORTH LEAVING HOME.

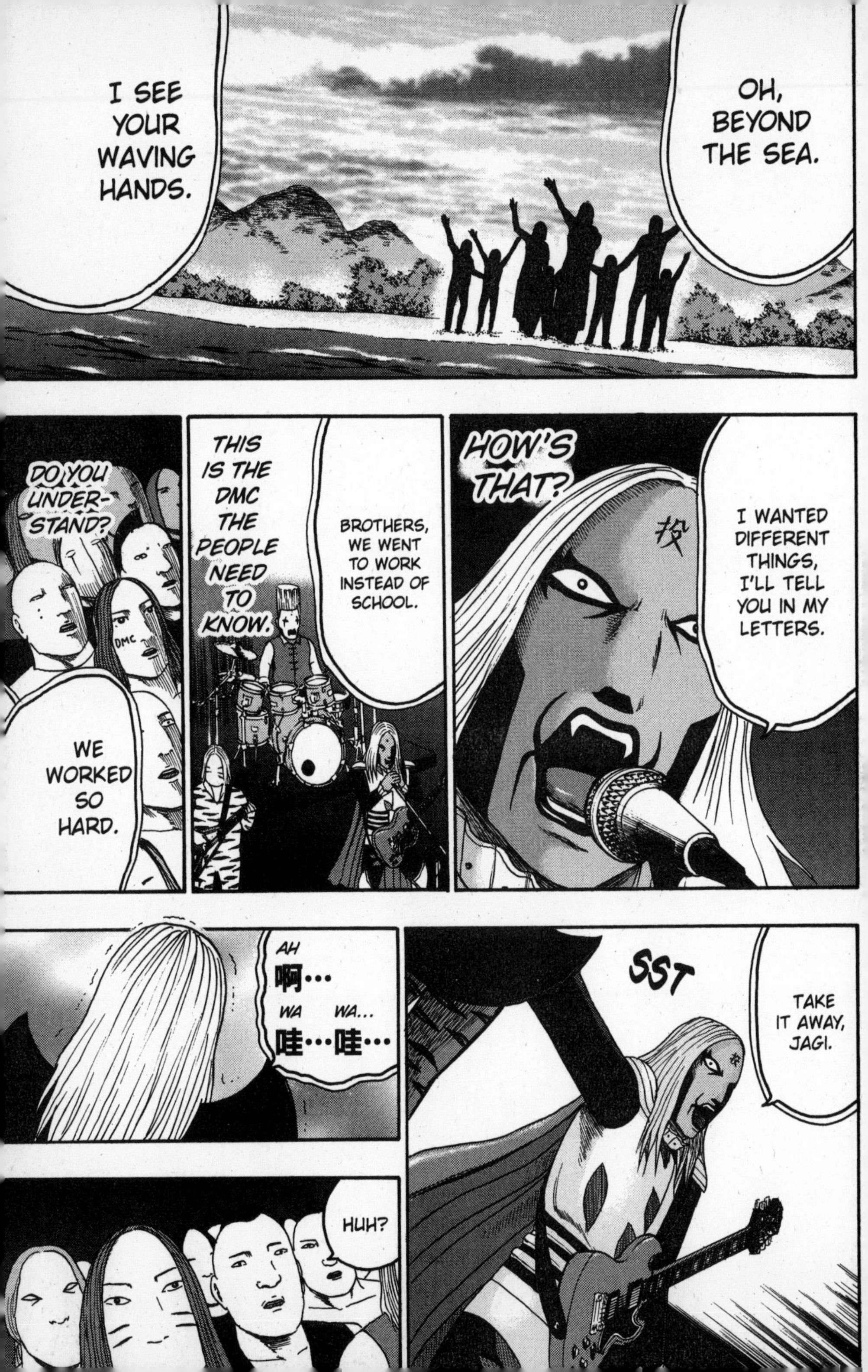
OH, BEYOND THE SEA.
I SEE YOUR WAVING HANDS.
I WANTED DIFFERENT THINGS, I'LL TELL YOU IN MY LETTERS.
HOW'S THAT?
BROTHERS, WE WENT TO WORK INSTEAD OF SCHOOL.
THIS IS THE DMC THE PEOPLE NEED TO KNOW.
DO YOU UNDER-STAND?
DMC
WE WORKED SO HARD.
TAKE IT AWAY, JAGI.
SST
AH 啊…
WA 哇… WA… 哇…
HUH?

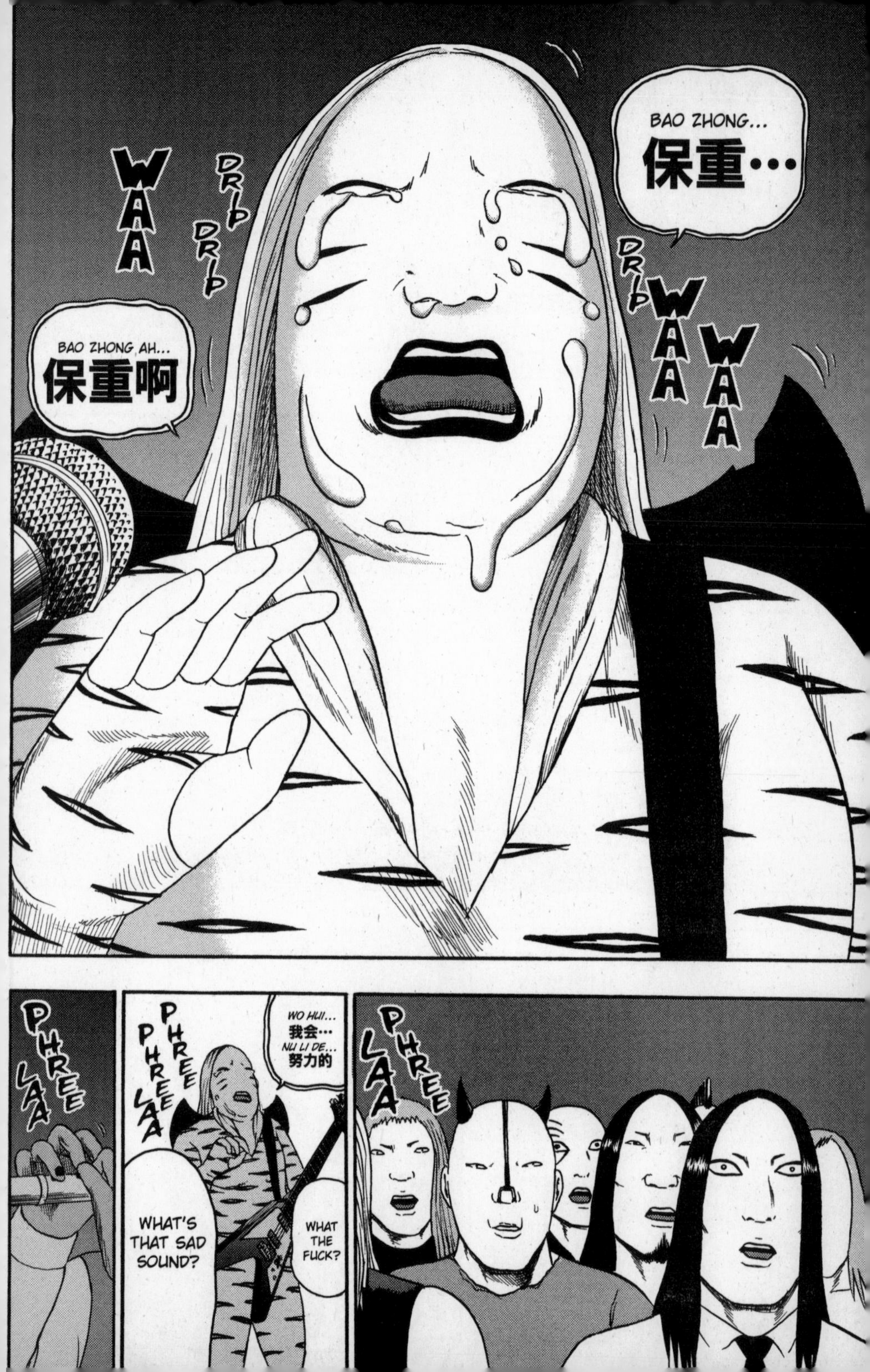
BAO ZHONG...
保重…
DRIP
WAAA
WAAA
WAAA
DRIP DRIP
BAO ZHONG AH...
保重啊
PHREE LAA
WO HUI...
我会…
NU LI DE...
努力的
PHREE PHREE LAA
WHAT THE FUCK?
WHAT'S THAT SAD SOUND?
PHREE LAA

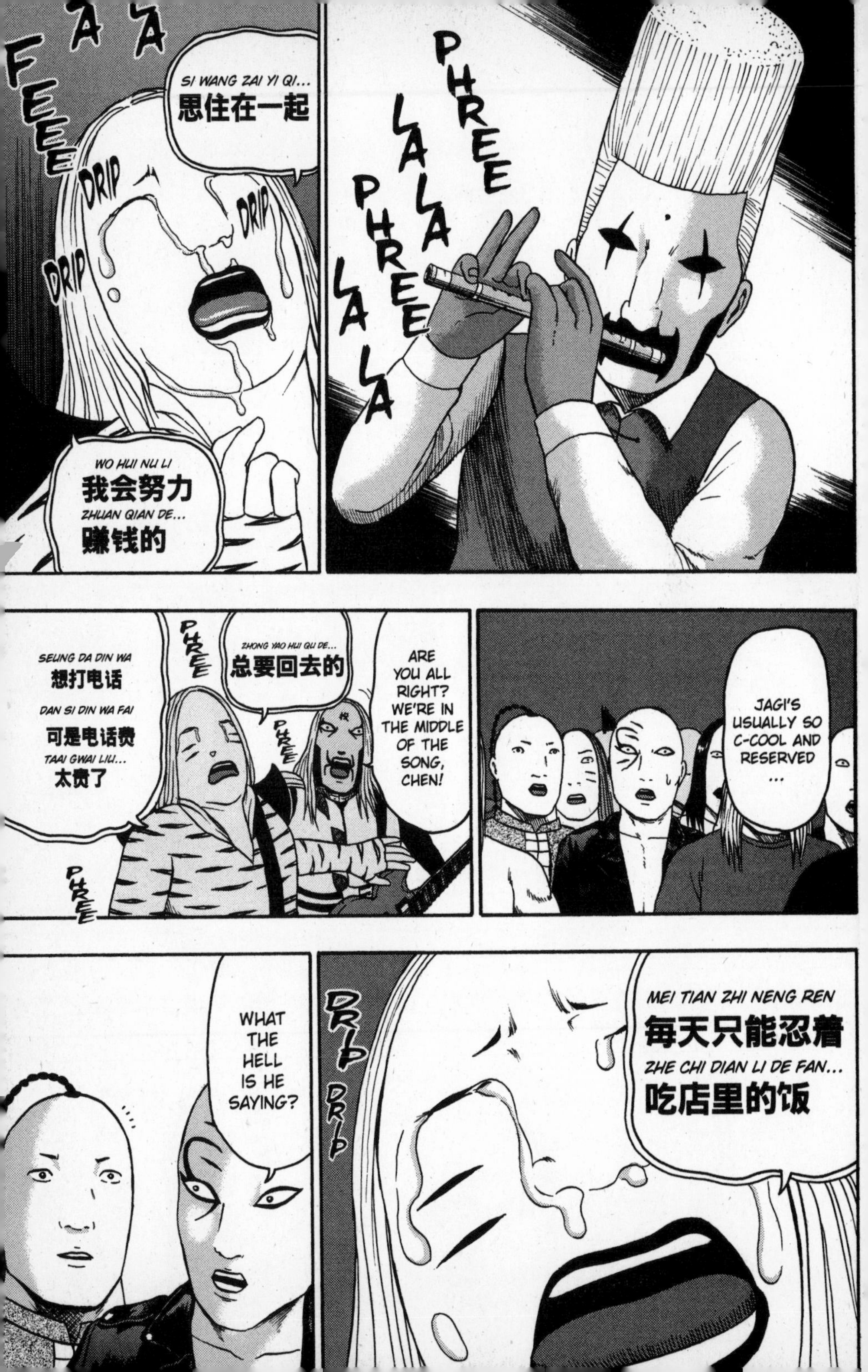
PHREE
LALA
PHREE
LALA
FEEE
AA
SI WANG ZAI YI QI... 思住在一起
DRIP
DRIP
DRIP
WO HUI NU LI 我会努力 ZHUAN QIAN DE... 赚钱的
JAGI'S USUALLY SO C-COOL AND RESERVED ...
ARE YOU ALL RIGHT? WE'RE IN THE MIDDLE OF THE SONG, CHEN!
ZHONG YAO HUI QU DE... 总要回去的
PHREE
PHREE
SEUNG DA DIN WA 想打电话 DAN SI DIN WA FAI 可是电话费 TAAI GWAI LIU... 太贵了
PHREE
MEI TIAN ZHI NENG REN 每天只能忍着 ZHE CHI DIAN LI DE FAN... 吃店里的饭
DRIP
DRIP
WHAT THE HELL IS HE SAYING?

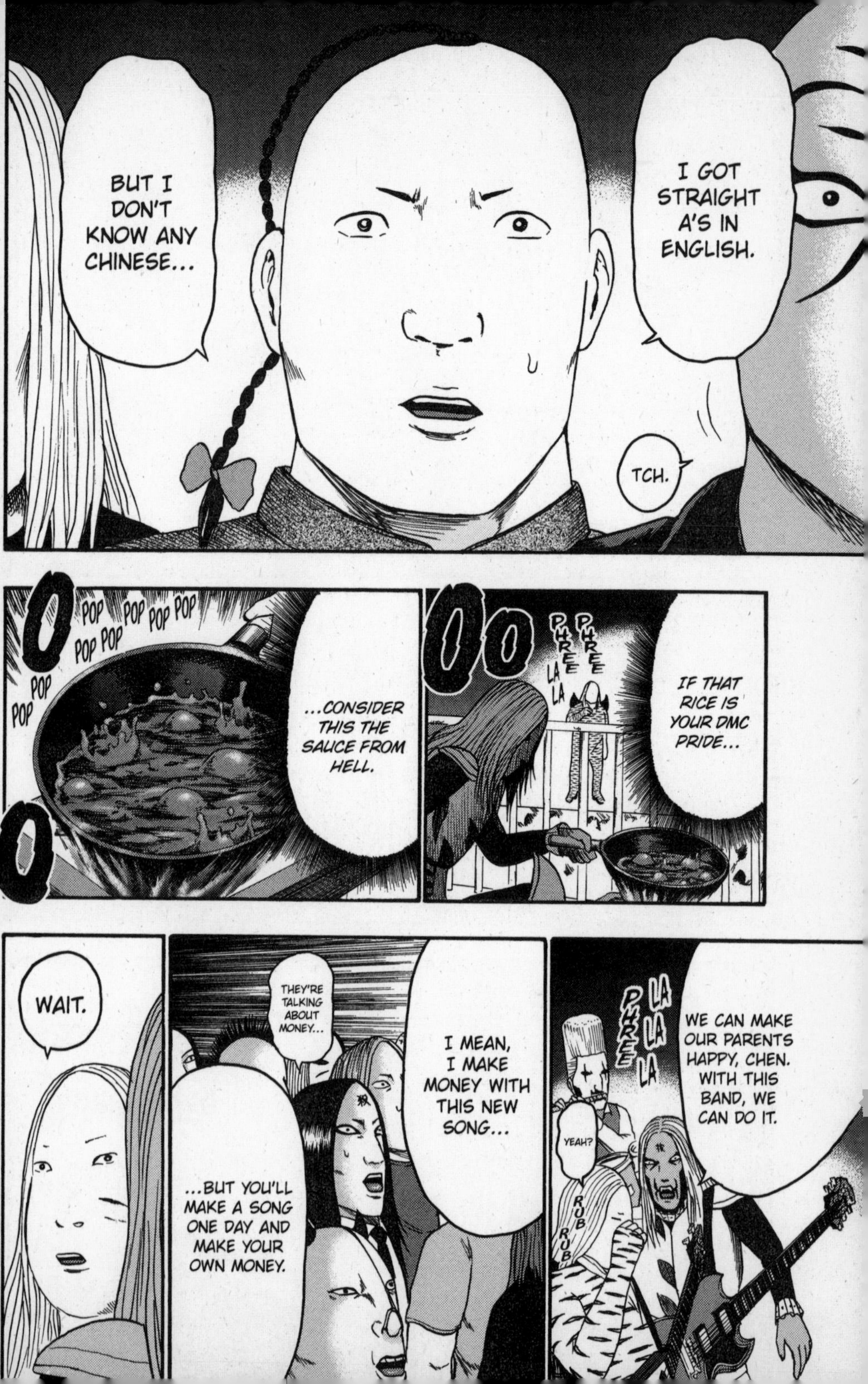
I GOT STRAIGHT A'S IN ENGLISH.
BUT I DON'T KNOW ANY CHINESE...
TCH.
PHREE PHREE
LA LA
OO
IF THAT RICE IS YOUR DMC PRIDE...
...CONSIDER THIS THE SAUCE FROM HELL.
POP POP POP POP POP POP
POP POP
O
O
PHREE
LA LA LA
WE CAN MAKE OUR PARENTS HAPPY, CHEN. WITH THIS BAND, WE CAN DO IT.
YEAH?
RUB RUB
I MEAN, I MAKE MONEY WITH THIS NEW SONG...
THEY'RE TALKING ABOUT MONEY...
...BUT YOU'LL MAKE A SONG ONE DAY AND MAKE YOUR OWN MONEY.
WAIT.

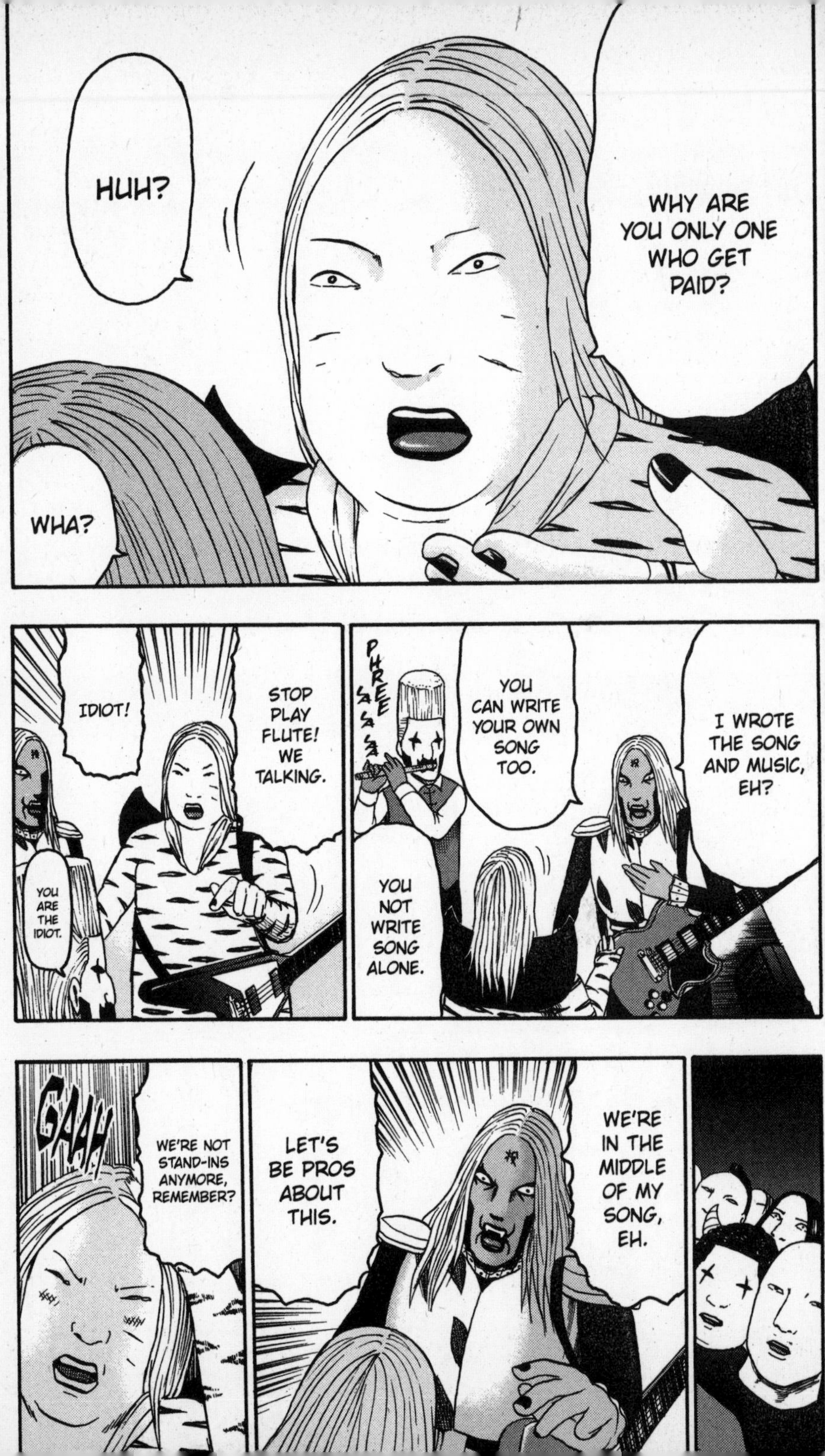
WHY ARE YOU ONLY ONE WHO GET PAID?
HUH?
WHA?
I WROTE THE SONG AND MUSIC, EH?
YOU CAN WRITE YOUR OWN SONG TOO.
PHREE
SA SA SA
YOU NOT WRITE SONG ALONE.
STOP PLAY FLUTE! WE TALKING.
IDIOT!
YOU ARE THE IDIOT.
WE'RE IN THE MIDDLE OF MY SONG, EH.
LET'S BE PROS ABOUT THIS.
WE'RE NOT STAND-INS ANYMORE, REMEMBER?
GAAH

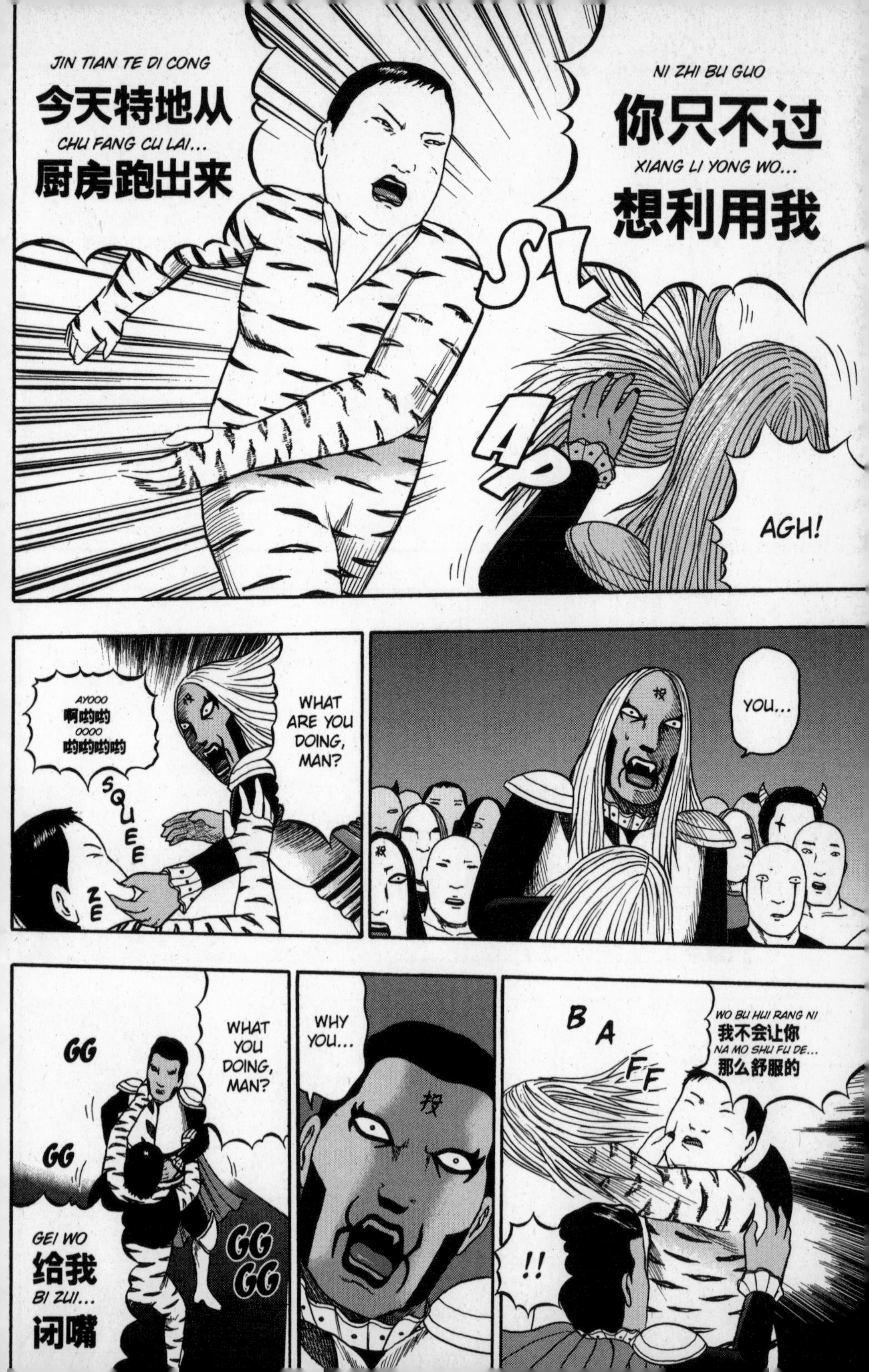
NI ZHI BU GUO 你只不过 XIANG LI YONG WO... 想利用我
JIN TIAN TE DI CONG 今天特地从 CHU FANG CU LAI... 厨房跑出来
SL
AP
AGH!
YOU...
WHAT ARE YOU DOING, MAN?
AYOOO 啊哟哟 OOOO 哟哟哟哟
SQUEEE
ZE
BAFF
WO BU HUI RANG NI 我不会让你 NA MO SHU FU DE... 那么舒服的
!!
WHY YOU...
GG GG
WHAT YOU DOING, MAN?
GG
GG
GEI WO 给我 BI ZUI... 闭嘴

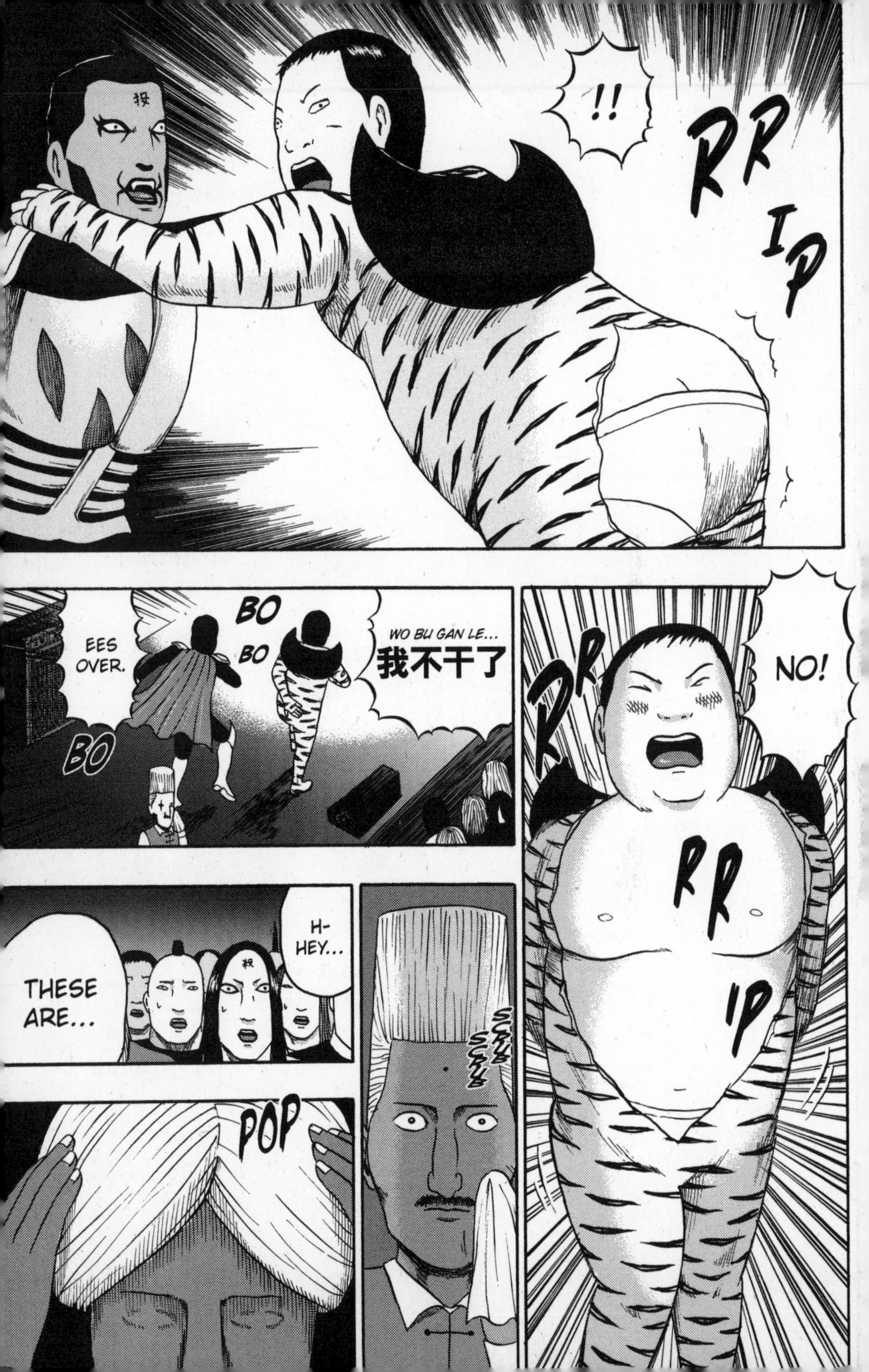
!!
RRIP
NO!
RRR
RRIP
WO BU GAN LE...
我不干了
BO
BO
EES OVER.
BO
SCRUB SCRUB
H- HEY...
THESE ARE...
POP

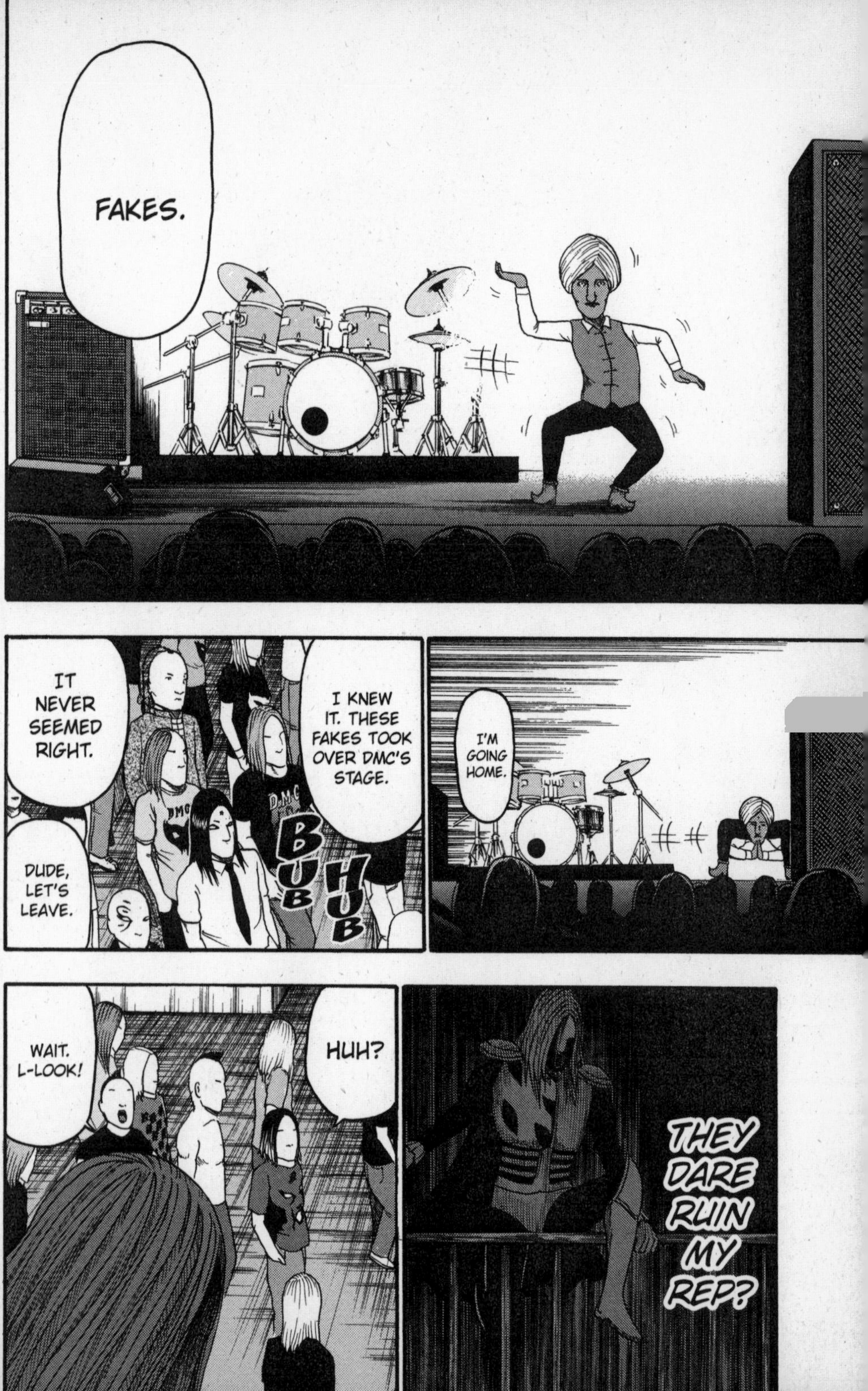
FAKES.
I'M GOING HOME.
I KNEW IT. THESE FAKES TOOK OVER DMC'S STAGE.
IT NEVER SEEMED RIGHT.
HUB
BUB
DUDE, LET'S LEAVE.
THEY DARE RUIN MY REP?
HUH?
WAIT. L-LOOK!

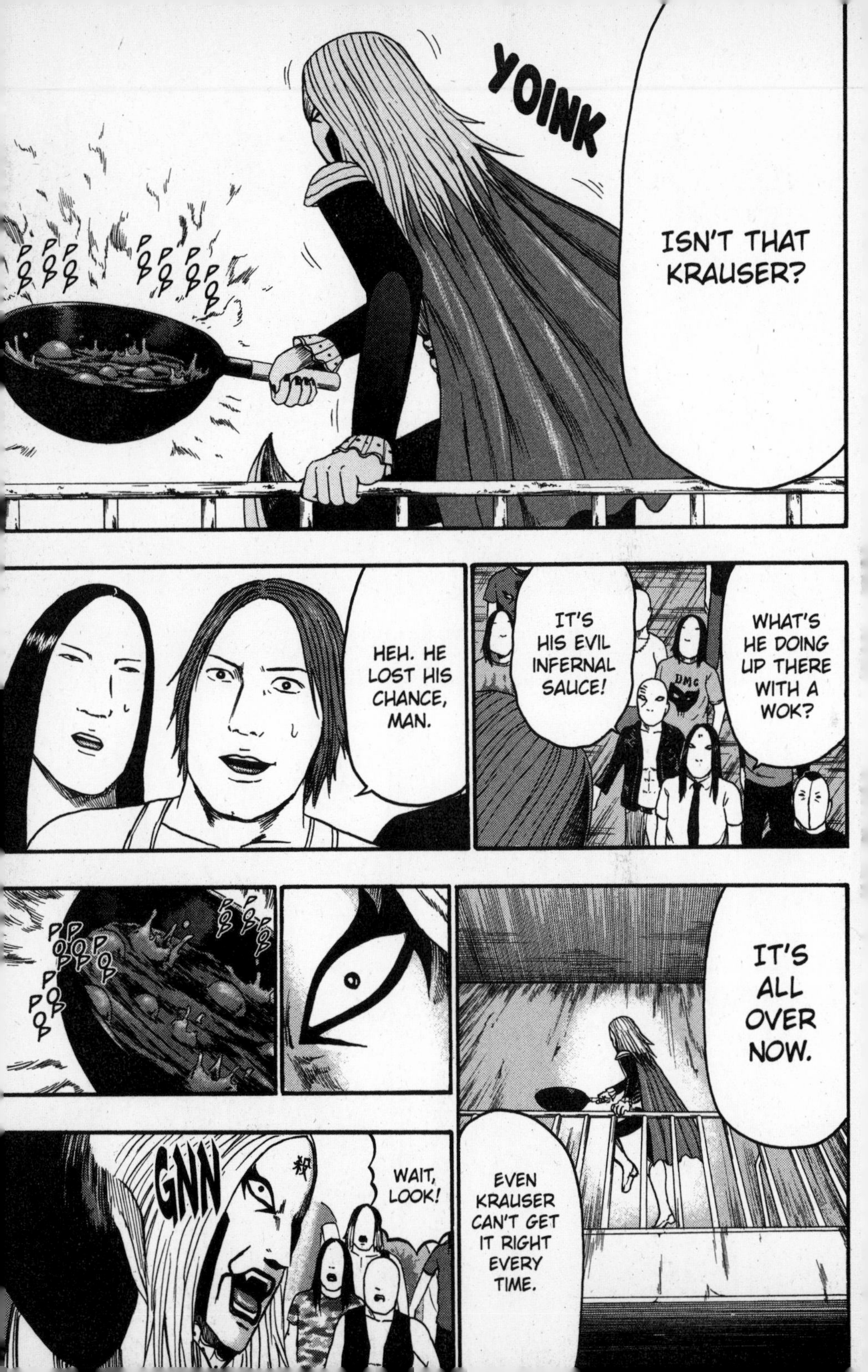
YOINK
ISN'T THAT KRAUSER?
WHAT'S HE DOING UP THERE WITH A WOK?
IT'S HIS EVIL INFERNAL SAUCE!
HEH. HE LOST HIS CHANCE, MAN.
IT'S ALL OVER NOW.
EVEN KRAUSER CAN'T GET IT RIGHT EVERY TIME.
GNN
WAIT, LOOK!

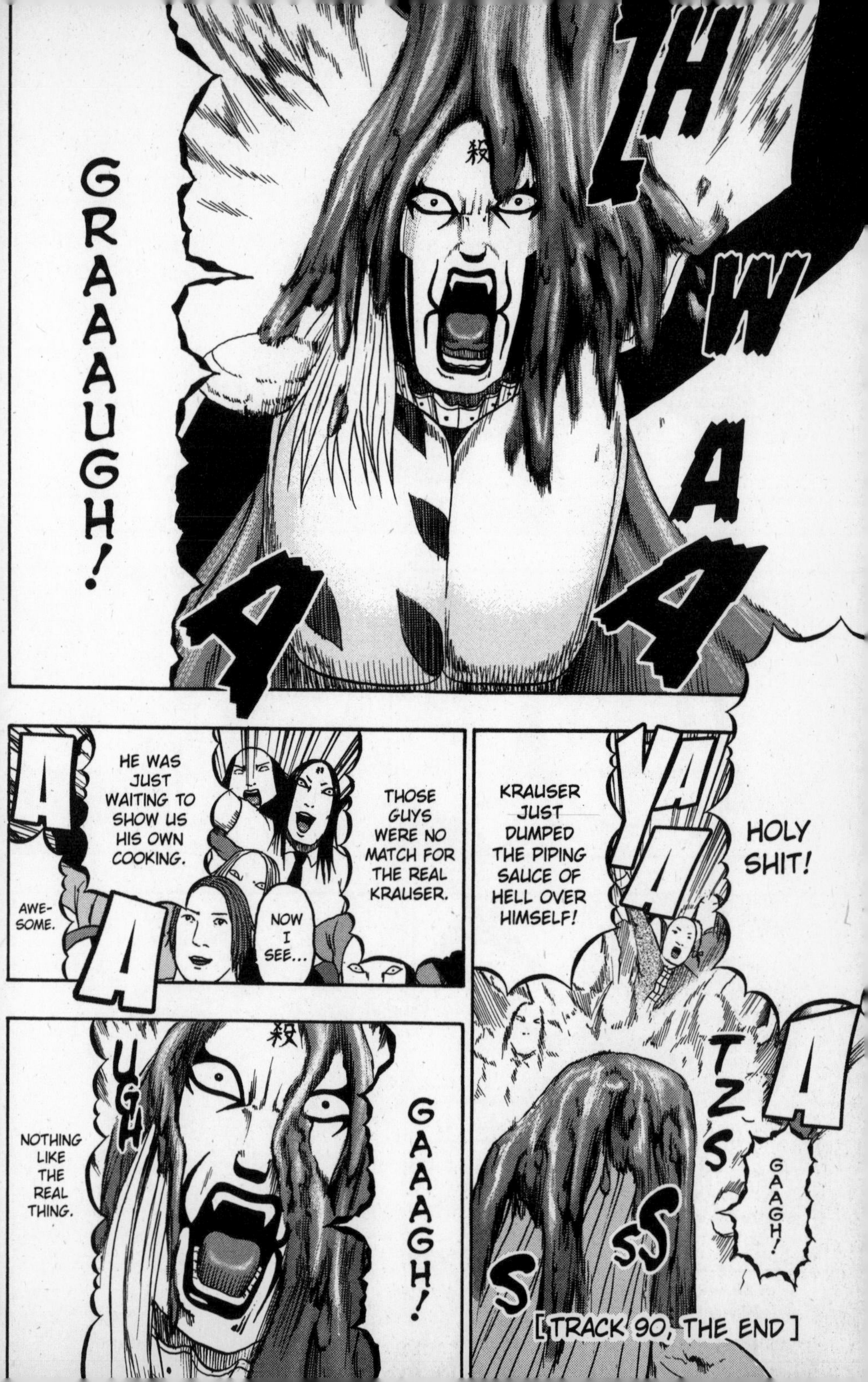
GRAAAAUGH!
HOLY SHIT!
KRAUSER JUST DUMPED THE PIPING SAUCE OF HELL OVER HIMSELF!
THOSE GUYS WERE NO MATCH FOR THE REAL KRAUSER.
HE WAS JUST WAITING TO SHOW US HIS OWN COOKING.
NOW I SEE...
AWE-SOME.
GAAGH!
TZSSSS
GAAAAGH!
UGH
NOTHING LIKE THE REAL THING.
[TRACK 90, THE END]

DMC LEXICON

🎭 SAUCE

A liquid mixture thickened with starch. It's usually sticky and takes a while to cool down. It's common for death metal performers to depend on too much of it. But if you're serious about going pro, you should know how to make "stew" and "gravy" with your eyes closed.

Usage: I'm having the Nagatanien rice with sauce for dinner tonight!
(Note: This was not a paid advertisement.)

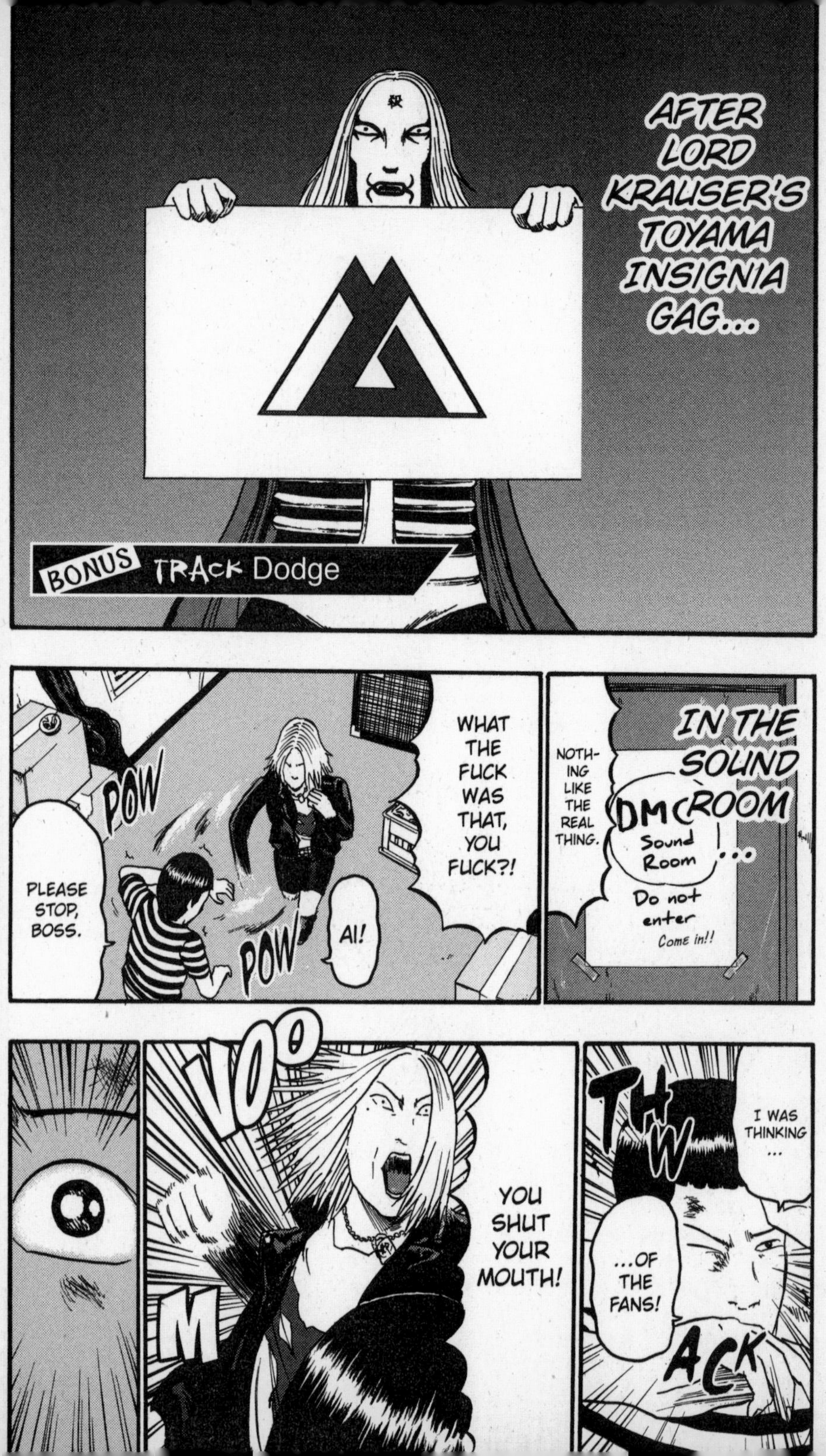
AFTER LORD KRAUSER'S TOYAMA INSIGNIA GAG...
BONUS TRACK Dodge
IN THE SOUND ROOM...
DMC Sound Room
Do not enter
Come in!!
NOTHING LIKE THE REAL THING.
WHAT THE FUCK WAS THAT, YOU FUCK?!
AI!
POW
POW
PLEASE STOP, BOSS.
I WAS THINKING...
THW
...OF THE FANS!
ACK
VOO
M
YOU SHUT YOUR MOUTH!

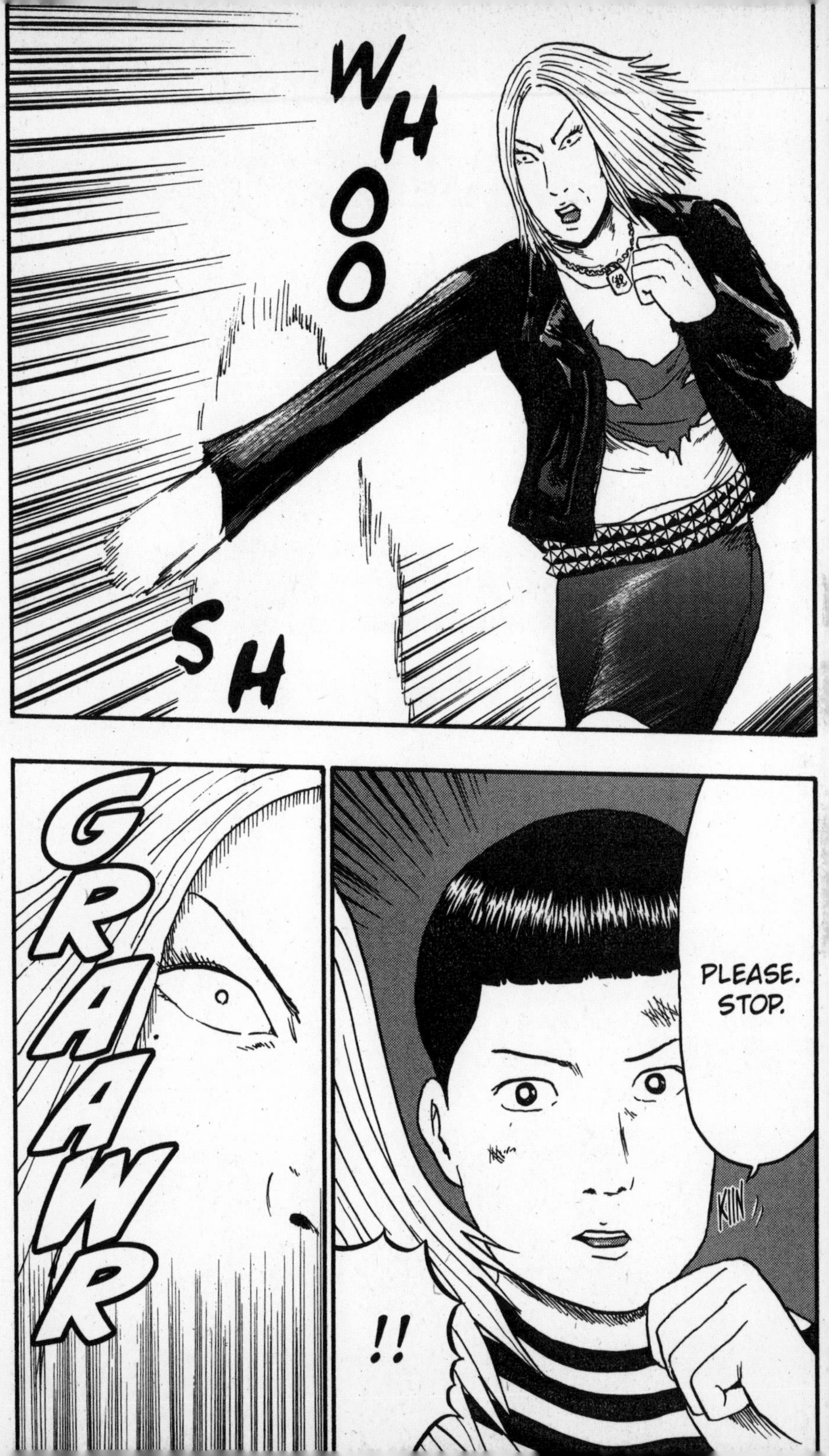
WHOOOSH
PLEASE. STOP.
KIIN
!!
GRAAWR

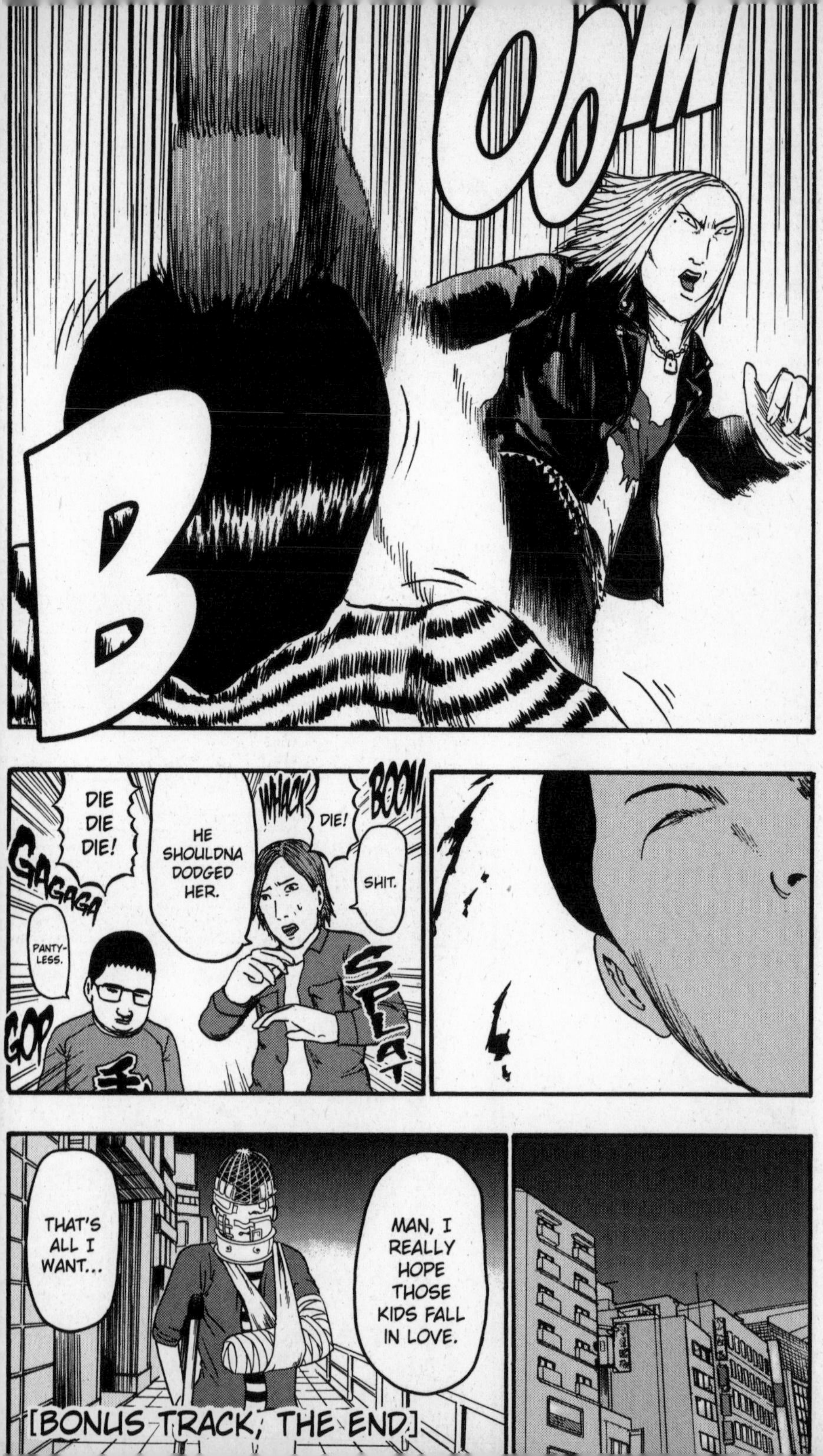
OOM
B
BOOM
DIE!
SHIT.
WHACK
HE SHOULDNA DODGED HER.
DIE DIE DIE!
GAGAGA
PANTY-LESS.
SPLAT
GOP
MAN, I REALLY HOPE THOSE KIDS FALL IN LOVE.
THAT'S ALL I WANT...
[BONUS TRACK, THE END]

Detroit Metal City

VOLUME 8

STORY AND ART BY KIMINORI WAKASUGI
VIZ SIGNATURE EDITION

ENGLISH ADAPTATION Annus Itchii
TOUCH-UP ART & LETTERING John Hunt
DESIGN Courtney Utt, Sam Elzway
EDITOR Mike Montesa

Detroit Metal City by Kiminori Wakasugi
© Kiminori Wakasugi 2009
All rights reserved
First published in Japan in 2009 by HAKUSENSHA, Inc., Tokyo.
English language translation rights arranged with HAKUSENSHA, Inc., Tokyo.

HOWEVER
USED BY PERMISSION OF JASRAC
LICENSE NO. 1004671-001

HAKONE HACHIRINO HANJIROU
Used By Permission of Nagara Ongaku Shuppan. All Rights Reserved.

Printed in the U.S.A.

Published by VIZ Media, LLC
P.O. Box 77010
San Francisco, CA 94107

10 9 8 7 6 5 4 3 2 1
First printing, March 2011

VIZ SIGNATURE
{ www.vizsignature.com }

VIZ media
{ www.viz.com }

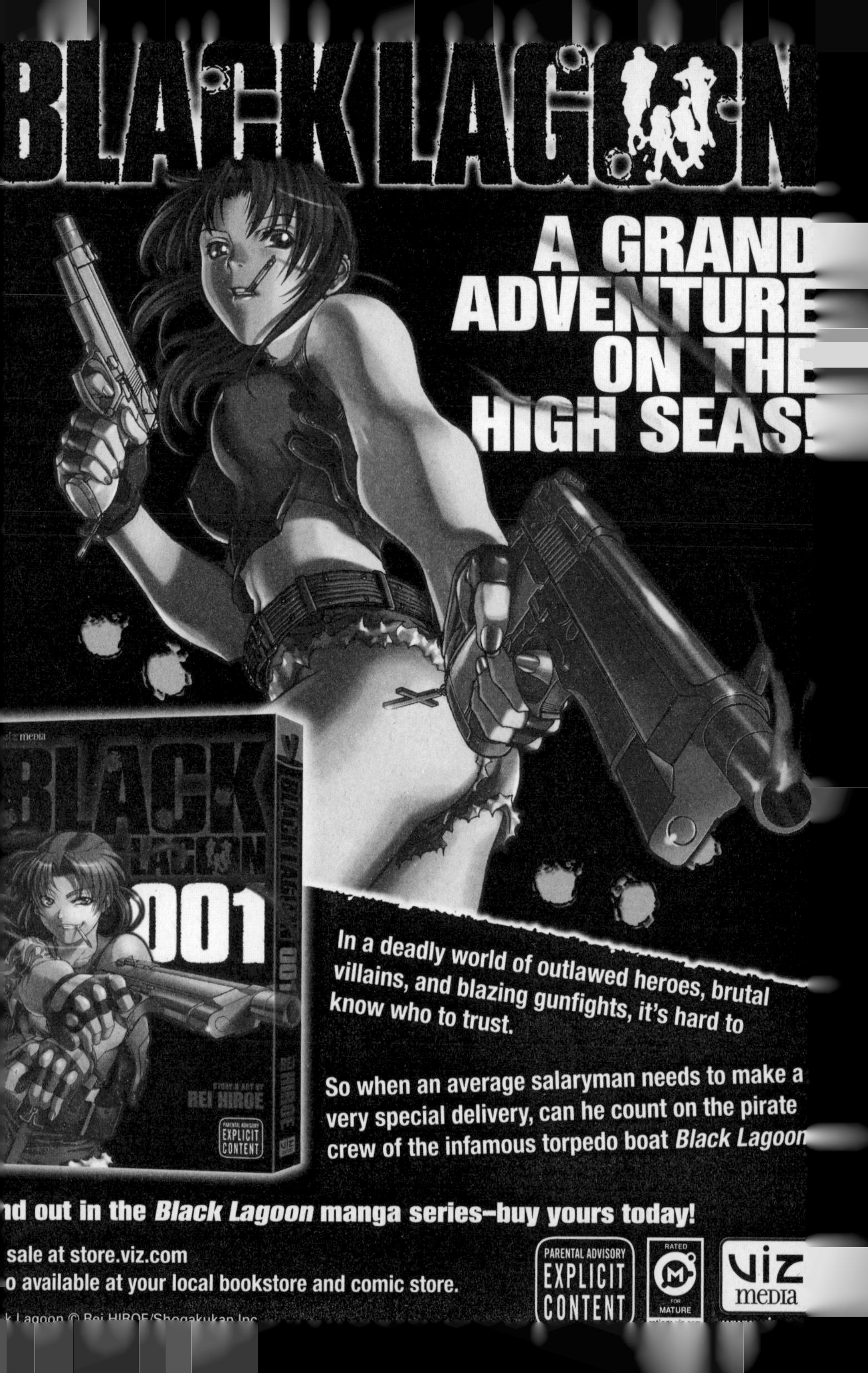
BLACK LAGOON
A GRAND ADVENTURE ON THE HIGH SEAS!
viz media
BLACK LAGOON
001
BLACK LAGOON 001
STORY & ART BY
REI HIROE
PARENTAL ADVISORY
EXPLICIT CONTENT
In a deadly world of outlawed heroes, brutal villains, and blazing gunfights, it's hard to know who to trust.
So when an average salaryman needs to make a very special delivery, can he count on the pirate crew of the infamous torpedo boat *Black Lagoon*
nd out in the *Black Lagoon* manga series–buy yours today!
sale at store.viz.com
o available at your local bookstore and comic store.
PARENTAL ADVISORY
EXPLICIT CONTENT
RATED
M
FOR
MATURE
viz media
k Lagoon © Rei HIROE/Shogakukan Inc.

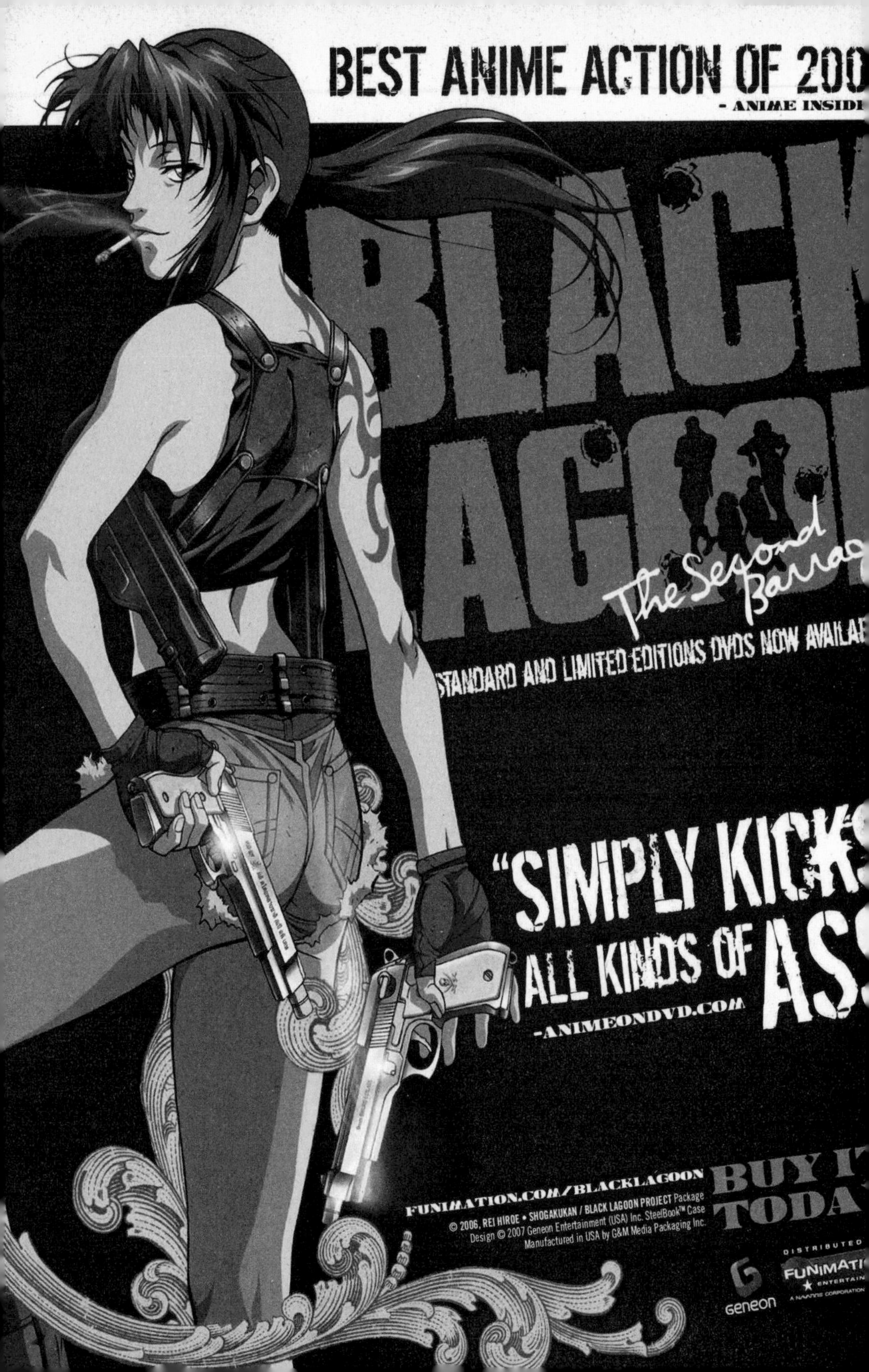

BEST ANIME ACTION OF 200
- ANIME INSID
BLACK LAGOO
The Second Barra
STANDARD AND LIMITED EDITIONS DVDS NOW AVAILA
"SIMPLY KICKS ALL KINDS OF AS
-ANIMEONDVD.COM
FUNIMATION.COM/BLACKLAGOON
© 2006, REI HIROE • SHOGAKUKAN / BLACK LAGOON PROJECT Package Design © 2007 Geneon Entertainment (USA) Inc. SteelBook™ Case Manufactured in USA by G&M Media Packaging Inc.
BUY I TODA
Geneon
DISTRIBUTED
FUNIMATI

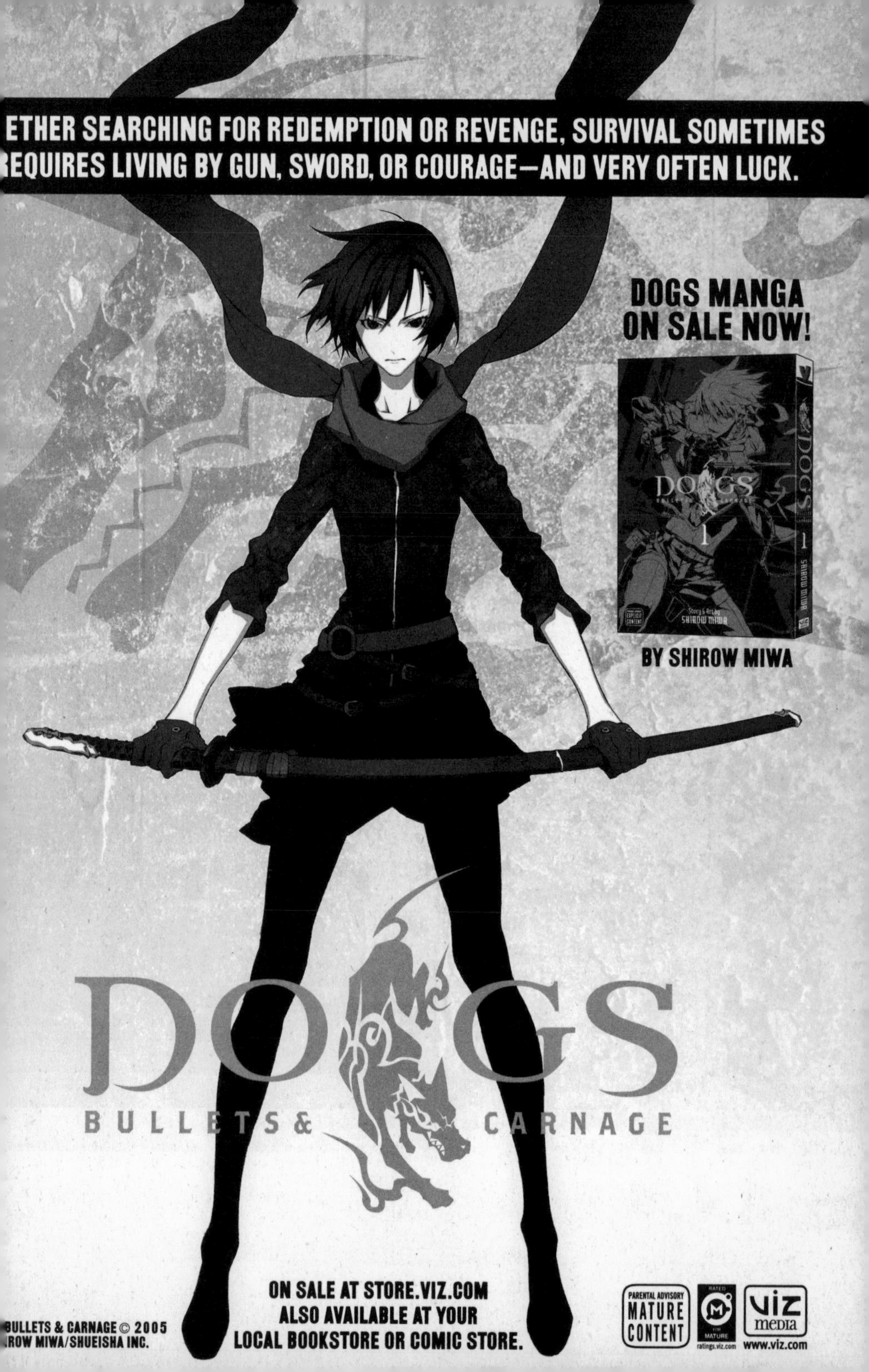
ETHER SEARCHING FOR REDEMPTION OR REVENGE, SURVIVAL SOMETIMES
EQUIRES LIVING BY GUN, SWORD, OR COURAGE—AND VERY OFTEN LUCK.
DOGS MANGA
ON SALE NOW!
DOGS
1
Story & Art by
SHIROW MIWA
BY SHIROW MIWA
DOGS
BULLETS & CARNAGE
ON SALE AT STORE.VIZ.COM
ALSO AVAILABLE AT YOUR
LOCAL BOOKSTORE OR COMIC STORE.
BULLETS & CARNAGE © 2005
ROW MIWA/SHUEISHA INC.
PARENTAL ADVISORY
MATURE
CONTENT
RATED
M
FOR
MATURE
ratings.viz.com
viz
media
www.viz.com

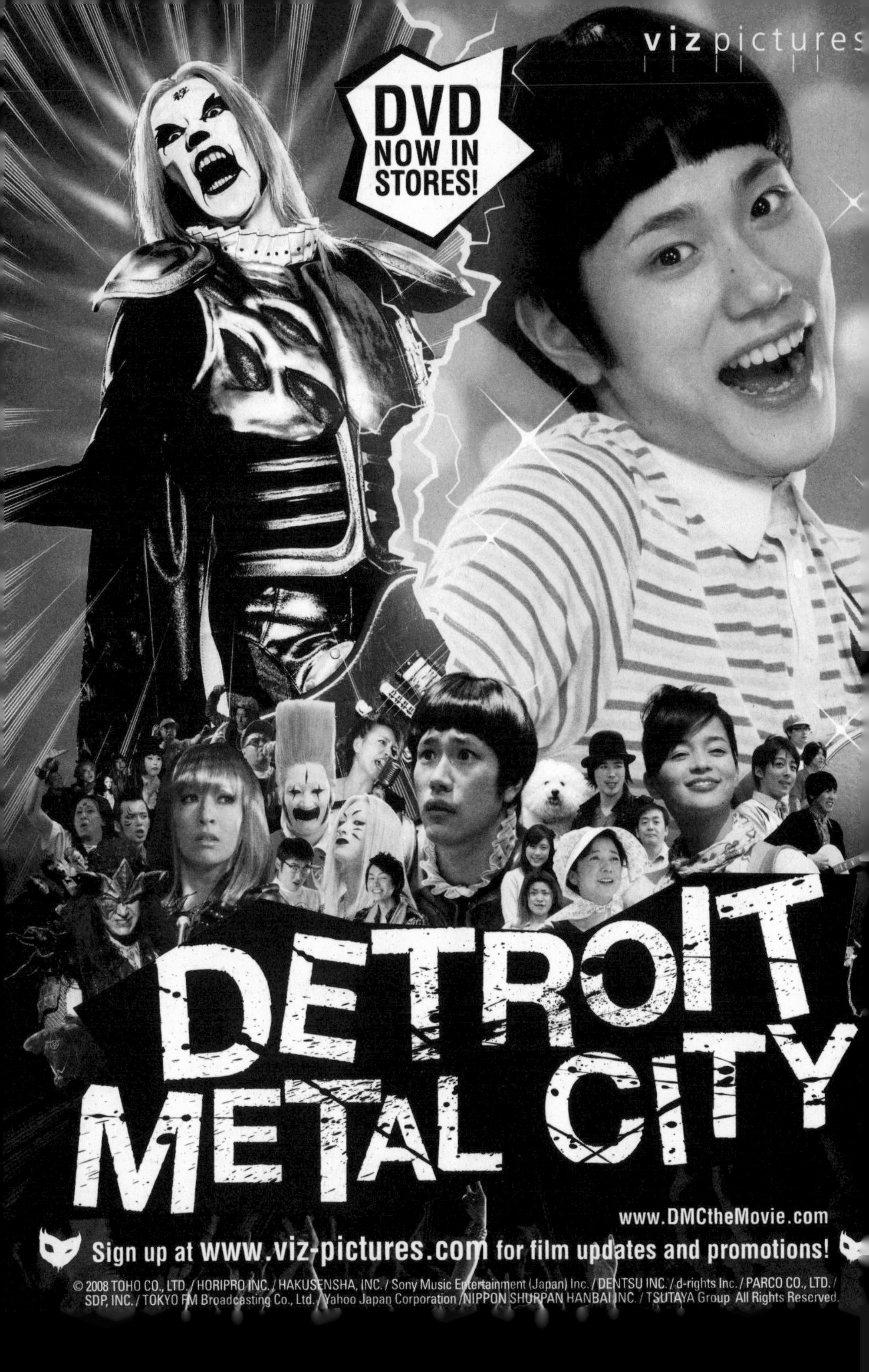

viz pictures
DVD NOW IN STORES!
DETROIT METAL CITY
www.DMCtheMovie.com
Sign up at www.viz-pictures.com for film updates and promotions!
© 2008 TOHO CO., LTD. / HORIPRO INC. / HAKUSENSHA, INC. / Sony Music Entertainment (Japan) Inc. / DENTSU INC. / d-rights Inc. / PARCO CO., LTD. / SDP, INC. / TOKYO FM Broadcasting Co., Ltd. / Yahoo Japan Corporation / NIPPON SHUPPAN HANBAI INC. / TSUTAYA Group All Rights Reserved.